The Abused and the Abuser

Severe abuse often occurs in settings where the grouping, whether based around a family or a community organisation or institution, outwardly appears to be very respectable. The nature of attachment dynamics allied with threat, discrediting, the manipulation of the victim's dissociative defences, long-term conditioning and the endless invoking of shame mean that sexual, physical and emotional abuse may, in some instances, be essentially unending. Even when separation from the long-term abuser is attempted, it may initially be extremely difficult to achieve, and there are some individuals who never achieve this parting. Even when the abuser is dead, the intrapsychic nature of the enduring attachment experienced by their victim remains complicated and difficult to resolve.

This book includes multiple perspectives from highly experienced clinicians, researchers and writers on the nature of the relationship between the abused and their abuser(s). No less than five of this international grouping of authors have been president of the International Society for the Study of Trauma and Dissociation, the world's oldest international trauma society. This book, which opens with a highly original clinical paper on 'weaponized sex' by Richard Kluft, one of the foremost pioneers of the modern dissociative disorders field, concludes with a gripping historical perspective written by Jeffrey Masson as he reengages with issues that first brought him to worldwide prominence in the 1980s. Between these two pieces, the contributors, all highly acclaimed for their clinical, theoretical or research work, present original, cutting edge work on this complex subject.

The chapters in this book were originally published as a double special issue of the *Journal of Trauma & Dissociation.*

Warwick Middleton was the primary author of the first published series on patients with dissociative identity disorder to appear in the Australian scientific literature. For over 20 years, he has been the Foundation Director of the Trauma and Dissociation Unit, Belmont Hospital, Australia. He is a pioneer researcher in the area of ongoing incest during adulthood; he chairs the Cannan Institute, Australia; and is a past president of the International Society for the Study of Trauma and Dissociation.

Adah Sachs is an attachment-based psychoanalytic psychotherapist. Her main theoretical contribution is outlining several subcategories of disorganised attachment, and linking those with childhood abuse and with trauma-based mental disorders. She is an NHS consultant and heads the Psychotherapy Service for Redbridge Borough, London, UK.

Martin J. Dorahy is Director of the clinical psychology programme at the University of Canterbury, New Zealand, and current immediate past-president (2018) of the International Society for the Study of Trauma and Dissociation. His published work has primarily explored cognitive and emotional underpinnings of dissociation and dissociative disorders, with a particular focus on shame. His clinical work is focused on the adult outcomes of abuse and neglect.

The Abused and the Abuser

Victim–Perpetrator Dynamics

Edited by
Warwick Middleton, Adah Sachs and Martin J. Dorahy

Routledge
Taylor & Francis Group
LONDON AND NEW YORK

First published 2018
by Routledge
2 Park Square, Milton Park, Abingdon, Oxon, OX14 4RN, UK

and by Routledge
711 Third Avenue, New York, NY 10017, USA

Routledge is an imprint of the Taylor & Francis Group, an informa business

British Library Cataloguing in Publication Data
A catalogue record for this book is available from the British Library

ISBN13: 978-0-8153-8011-5

Typeset in MinionPro
by diacriTech, Chennai

Publisher's Note
The publisher accepts responsibility for any inconsistencies that may have arisen during the conversion of this book from journal articles to book chapters, namely the possible inclusion of journal terminology.

Disclaimer
Every effort has been made to contact copyright holders for their permission to reprint material in this book. The publishers would be grateful to hear from any copyright holder who is not here acknowledged and will undertake to rectify any errors or omissions in future editions of this book.

Contents

Citation Information

The chapters in this book were originally published in the *Journal of Trauma & Dissociation*, volume 18, issue 3 (May–June 2017). When citing this material, please use the original page numbering for each article, as follows:

Chapter 1

Weaponized sex: Defensive pseudo-erotic aggression in the service of safety
Richard P. Kluft
Journal of Trauma & Dissociation, volume 18, issue 3 (May–June 2017) pp. 259–283

Chapter 2

Extreme adaptations in extreme and chronic circumstances: The application of "weaponized sex" to those exposed to ongoing incestuous abuse
Warwick Middleton
Journal of Trauma & Dissociation, volume 18, issue 3 (May–June 2017) pp. 284–303

Chapter 3

Conflicts between motivational systems related to attachment trauma: Key to understanding the intra-family relationship between abused children and their abusers
Giovanni Liotti
Journal of Trauma & Dissociation, volume 18, issue 3 (May–June 2017) pp. 304–318

Chapter 4

Through the lens of attachment relationship: Stable DID, active DID and other trauma-based mental disorders
Adah Sachs
Journal of Trauma & Dissociation, volume 18, issue 3 (May–June 2017) pp. 319–339

Chapter 5
Dying for love: An attachment problem with some perpetrator introjects
Valerie Sinason
Journal of Trauma & Dissociation, volume 18, issue 3 (May–June 2017) pp. 340–355

Chapter 6
Predicting a dissociative disorder from type of childhood maltreatment and abuser–abused relational tie
Christa Krüger and Lizelle Fletcher
Journal of Trauma & Dissociation, volume 18, issue 3 (May–June 2017) pp. 356–372

Chapter 7
Victim–perpetrator dynamics through the lens of betrayal trauma theory
Kerry L. Gagnon, Michelle Seulki Lee, and Anne P. DePrince
Journal of Trauma & Dissociation, volume 18, issue 3 (May–June 2017) pp. 373–382

Chapter 8
Shame as a compromise for humiliation and rage in the internal representation of abuse by loved ones: Processes, motivations, and the role of dissociation
Martin J. Dorahy
Journal of Trauma & Dissociation, volume 18, issue 3 (May–June 2017) pp. 383–396

Chapter 9
Knowing and not knowing: A frequent human arrangement
Sylvia Solinski
Journal of Trauma & Dissociation, volume 18, issue 3 (May–June 2017) pp. 397–408

Chapter 10
Mother–child incest, psychosis, and the dynamics of relatedness
Joan Haliburn
Journal of Trauma & Dissociation, volume 18, issue 3 (May–June 2017) pp. 409–426

Chapter 11
Dissociation in families experiencing intimate partner violence
Alison Miller
Journal of Trauma & Dissociation, volume 18, issue 3 (May–June 2017) pp. 427–440

Chapter 12

Organized abuse in adulthood: Survivor and professional perspectives
Michael Salter
Journal of Trauma & Dissociation, volume 18, issue 3 (May–June 2017) pp. 441–453

Chapter 13

Treatment strategies for programming and ritual abuse
Colin Ross
Journal of Trauma & Dissociation, volume 18, issue 3 (May–June 2017) pp. 454–464

Chapter 14

Issues in consultation for treatments with distressed activated abuser/protector self-states in dissociative identity disorder
Richard A. Chefetz
Journal of Trauma & Dissociation, volume 18, issue 3 (May–June 2017) pp. 465–475

End note

A personal perspective: The response to child abuse then and now
Jeffrey Masson
Journal of Trauma & Dissociation, volume 18, issue 3 (May–June 2017) pp. 476–482

Notes on Contributors

Richard A. Chefetz is a psychiatrist in private practice. He was President of the International Society for the Study of Trauma and Dissociation (2002–2003), USA, and is a Distinguished Visiting Lecturer at the William Alanson White Institute of Psychiatry, Psychoanalysis, and Psychology, USA.

Anne P. DePrince is Professor and Chair in the Psychology Department at the University of Denver, USA. Her research focuses on how individual characteristics as well as interpersonal, community and spatial contexts relate to violence/abuse exposure as well as clinical symptoms and interventions.

Martin J. Dorahy is Director of the clinical psychology programme at the University of Canterbury, New Zealand, and current immediate past-president (2018) of the International Society for the Study of Trauma and Dissociation. His published work has primarily explored cognitive and emotional underpinnings of dissociation and dissociative disorders, with a particular focus on shame. His clinical work is focused on the adult outcomes of abuse and neglect.

Lizelle Fletcher is a Senior Lecturer at the University of Pretoria, South Africa.

Kerry L. Gagnon is a PhD candidate and Graduate Research Assistant at the Department of Child Clinical Psychology at the University of Denver, USA.

Joan Haliburn is a Clinical Senior Lecturer of Psychiatry at the University of Sydney, Australia. She is a child, adolescent, family and adult psychiatrist, Fellow of the Royal Australia & New Zealand College of Psychiatrists and trained in the Conversational Model of psychodynamic psychotherapy.

Richard P. Kluft is a Clinical Professor of Psychiatry at Temple University School of Medicine, USA. He has extensive experience in treating victims of sexual exploitation by psychotherapists, and has served as an expert witness in several malpractice cases involving boundary violations. His contributions to the diagnosis and treatment of dissociative disorders and his research on how to enhance the safety of hypnosis and hypnosis training are considered landmarks in these fields.

Christa Krüger is a Professor of Psychiatry at the University of Pretoria, South Africa.

Michelle Seulki Lee is a Graduate Teaching and Research Assistant at the University of Denver, USA.

Giovanni Liotti is an independent researcher concerned with attachment theory. He teaches at the APC School of Psychotherapy, Italy.

Jeffrey Masson is a writer, best known for his conclusions about Sigmund Freud and psychoanalysis.

Warwick Middleton was the primary author of the first published series on patients with dissociative identity disorder to appear in the Australian scientific literature. For over 20 years, he has been the Foundation Director of the Trauma and Dissociation Unit, Belmont Hospital, Australia. He is a pioneer researcher in the area of ongoing incest during adulthood; he chairs the Cannan Institute, Australia; and is a past president of the International Society for the Study of Trauma and Dissociation.

Alison Miller is a psychologist in private practice. She worked for many years in child and youth mental health services, and has come to specialise in working with survivors of ritual abuse and mind control.

Colin Ross is the founder and President of the Colin A. Ross Institute for Psychological Trauma, USA. He is an internationally renowned clinician, researcher, author and lecturer in the field of dissociation and trauma-related disorders.

Adah Sachs is an attachment-based psychoanalytic psychotherapist. Her main theoretical contribution is outlining several subcategories of disorganised attachment, and linking those with childhood abuse and with trauma-based mental disorders. She is an NHS consultant and heads the Psychotherapy Service for Redbridge Borough, London, UK.

Michael Salter is Senior Lecturer in Criminology at Western Sydney University, Australia. His research is focused on violence against women, child abuse, primary prevention and complex forms of victimisation including organised abuse and technologically facilitated abuse.

Valerie Sinason is an adult psychoanalyst, and adult and child psychotherapist, specialising in disability, trauma and abuse. She is registered with the BPC, ACP and UKCP and is also an SCID-D National Assessor. She established the Clinic for Dissociative Studies in 1998.

Sylvia Solinski is a psychiatrist at the Malvern Psychotherapy Centre, Australia. Her expertise is in anxiety, obsessive-compulsive disorder (OCD), sexual abuse, trauma, grief and loss, mood disorders and post-traumatic stress disorder.

Introduction – The abused and the abuser: Victim–perpetrator dynamics

Warwick Middleton, Adah Sachs and Martin J. Dorahy

From the beginning, humanity has been riddled with brutality. Slavery, human sacrifice, burning "witches," publically punishing women for disobeying their husbands, religious massacres, legitimized torture, grotesque public executions, and what we would now call inhumane treatment of children (e.g., caning) were not only common, but sanctioned as central activities in the sociocultural foundation of most societies. Fear was embedded in law, morality, and culture. What we now look at as the relationship between abused and abuser was at one time simply the relationship between adults and children (DeMause, 1998), slaves and their owners, men and women, a perpetrator and his victim, and a prisoner and his jailer (Şar, Middleton, & Dorahy, 2014). Over the years, our views and values have changed (Pinker, 2011). In today's Western culture, such actions and interactions are largely illegal, or their morality is strongly questioned, even though they occur with not uncommon frequency. Where brutal interactions do occur, they are thought to be the cause of *trauma*: a potentially irreparable injury to the person's psyche, and a potential cause of mental disorders.

Modern Western culture holds human rights as a central value, which applies to *everyone*. A person of any age, gender, race, religion, or nation should be safe from degrading or violent treatment. We should all be free to make personal choices. Our bodies must be respected. Children have to be safe from harm. While these expectations are still very far from being reached, they do mark our values and laws. This in itself brings us closer to them than we have ever been before. It is a great achievement. A disturbing side effect of this achievement, however, is that where offences against human rights (e.g., child abuse, human trafficking, torture) continue to occur, they are characterized by greater organization and concealment.

Dickensian children could be hurt openly, as they were deemed someone's property (and referred to as "it"). Generally, today's children are better off; but where they are hurt, such behavior is hidden. Silence from perpetrators, witnesses, and victims create and perpetuate the hidden nature of abuse and human rights violations. The perpetrators of acts which are now both illegal and shameful do their best to keep their actions a secret. Witnesses are reluctant to get "involved" and demonstrate an unwillingness to register fully the perpetration of abuse and act on it. The victims themselves often feel too powerless, too shamed by their weakness, and too contaminated with the evil done to them to come out from the shadows. And very often, they also feel deeply connected to their abusers.

The perpetrators, their victims, and the reluctant witnesses form together a complex and highly emotive relationship, bound in secrets and silence. These are not strangers, but people often who know each other well and play central roles in each other lives. Disentangling their relationship from the harm which is done through it is as painful as the harm itself, and very hard to reach. Shedding light on this complicated and charged relationship is the task that we have asked the contributors to this book, to engage with.

As the chapters for this book were being written two unfolding enterprises in particular, were under way in the world that had the potential to shed light on the nature of the abused–abuser relationship, particularly where the abuser was aligned with a powerful, hierarchical institution, which provided both the opportunity to access victims, as well as protection from reporting and prosecution. The first of these was the Australian Royal Commission into Institutional Responses to Child Sexual Abuse, for which Letters Patent were issued on January 11, 2013, and which as of December 15, 2017, when it concluded, had held 8,013 private sessions with abuse survivors, had conducted 57 public hearings over 444 hearing days (involving a total of 1,302 witnesses), and had made 2,575 referrals to authorities (including police) (Royal Commission into Institutional Responses to Child Sexual Abuse, 2017). The second enterprise was the Independent Inquiry into Child Sexual Abuse announced by the British government on July 7, 2014, in the wake of the Jimmy Savile scandal and persistent reports of other historical child sexual abuse perpetrated by British parliamentarians and associated establishment figures. The evidence gathered, as well as the different fortunes of these two initiatives, provide much to inform perspectives on the relationships between the abuser and the abused. They, in their processes and findings, serve as an evolving backdrop for the subject matter covered here.

Chapters in this book address the abused and the abuser from empirical (Gagnon, Lee, & DePrince; Krüger & Fletcher), therapeutic (Ross), and theoretical (Dorahy; Liotti; Sachs; Sinason; Solinski) angles, drawing on neuroscientific, cognitive, affective, attachment, relational, psychodynamic, betrayal trauma, and animal models, among others. Abused and abuser dynamics are examined primarily in child–adult relationships, with some attention also given to adult dyads (Miller). Topics still lingering on the fringe of the trauma literature, or those largely absent, such as mother–son incest (Haliburn), organized abuse (Salter), supervisory challenges in managing dissociative abuser dynamics (Chefetz), ongoing incestuous abuse (Middleton), and sexual enactment in the therapy context as a form of safety (Kluft), are addressed. Reflections of a lived experience of professional ostracization associated with espousing the reality and effect of abuse are also shared (Masson). The uniqueness of bringing together such a collection of papers on the abused and the abuser in this book is reflected in the content initially being published as the first ever Special Double Issue of the *Journal of Trauma and Dissociation (JTD)*. For this book edition, one additional paper (Middleton) has been added, which incorporates an historical perspective on how the field of psychoanalysis previously engaged with that grouping of dissociative and traumatized individuals subsumed by the diagnostic entity known as "hysteria."

Cover up dynamics and the dynamics of openness

In September 1897, 41-year-old Sigmund Freud, in a letter to Wilhelm Fliess, who is considered by many to represent the closest male friendship of his life, famously renounced his "seduction theory" and thus positioned the about-to-be-born field of psychoanalysis solidly in the province of Oedipal fantasy, an early and not unwelcome revision as judged by several of Freud's peers (Masson, 1984). The particular irony of Freud sharing his perspective about what he claimed were inaccurate recollections of childhood sexual abuse is that he was sharing them with a man who appeared to be an abuser. In the writings of his son Robert and daughter-in-law Elenore, Wilhelm Fliess is portrayed as having "ambulatory psychosis": "The child of such a parent becomes the object of substantially defused aggression (maltreated and beaten almost to within an inch of his life), and of a perverse sexuality that hardly knows an incest barrier (is seduced in the most bizarre ways by the parent and, at his instigation, by others) ..." (Fliess, 1956, p. xvii). Elenore describes her father-in-law as a man "who however charming to patients and acquaintances was a tyrant at home. His children were second-class citizens, from diet to schooling" (as quoted by Sulloway, 1992, p. 191).

It is clear that right from the time that Freud announced his original theory regarding a sexual abuse etiology for hysteria in 1896, that the abused and the abuser have been inexorably entwined. Like many abuse victims, it took most of his life for Robert Fliess to even briefly draw attention to the fact that despite the outer trappings of professional respectability, his father was highly abusive. The fact that Freud and many of his fellow early analysts were sexually abused as children did not stop mainstream psychoanalysis from de-emphasizing the reality of childhood sexual abuse (Middleton, chapter 15, this volume). Robert Fliess hinted strongly of an awareness that many of his fellow psychoanalysts had been sexually abused as children.

> If originally I had held the hope that my findings would be subjected to competent examination, I have gradually become aware that this expectation has on several counts been unjustifiably naïve. For one thing, from what I have heard and read, few analysts master Freud's method to the degree that would enable them to confirm my findings. Since this holds true for their teachers as well, the average analyst thus remains ignorant of his own psychotic parent, should he have one, and hence is not equipped for patients who confront him with fragments that are replicas of his own history – fragments that should, were he properly 'trained' no longer be traumatic but actually still are (1973, p. 204).

Cogently Fliess went on to reflect,

> One is quite generally reminded of the almost daily reports in newspapers where someone, after having committed a crime so bizarre that it fairly shouts out the psychosis, faces an outraged judge without showing the slightest feeling of guilt (Fliess, 1973, p. 214).

Years earlier Fliess astutely had observed,

> It appears as though the child takes over all of the feelings of guilt over incest that the parent should have had, but being psychotic, did not. I have never had the slightest indication that the exploiter felt guilty, but merely that he was afraid of being found out (Fliess, 1956, p. xvii).

Many extreme abusers live among us hiding in plain sight, frequently not publicly identified in their lifetime, despite abusing multiple victims over decades. This points to the existence of powerful long-term dynamics, which cause the victims to remain silent. Common reasons for such silence are that victims have been threatened about the consequences of telling, that they have been convinced that they will not be believed, that they have already experienced poor outcomes from attempts to report ongoing abuse, that the shame occasioned by accommodating sexual assaults makes them extremely avoidant about speaking of what was done to them, or that some or all of the details of the abuse self-protectively got buried behind a dissociative amnestic barrier, frequently associated with an alternative personality state. Of course some victims are essentially captives or slaves and have little or no opportunity to tell anyone who is likely to help, and no one with sufficient power to protect them.

In his early theorizing, Freud gave particular importance to the "pleasure principle" – the notion that the central guiding characteristic of human functioning was the seeking of pleasure and the avoidance of unpleasure. Repeatedly putting oneself in traumatic situations or repetitively reliving trauma contradicted the central tenet of the "pleasure principle," leading Freud, who had witnessed the carnage of World War I envelop humanity, to seek an understanding of the compulsion to repeat trauma that went *beyond the pleasure principle* (1920), leading him to philosophical speculations about a "death instinct," which he theorized, when externalized, becomes the source of aggression. In evolutionary terms, however, where the principle of "survival of the fittest" has such centrality, a "death instinct" for the human species proved hard to rationally integrate (Breger, 2000). Yet what continues to challenge social thinking, and is wrestled with in one way or another in many papers in this special issue, is the compulsion to repeat trauma and/or remain subject to victimization.

Ferenczi in 1932/1984, engaging with the complexity of the dynamic involving the abused and the abuser, introduced the concept of introjection of, or identification with the aggressor (Masson, 1984), and over the years there have been multiple attempts to better understand the dynamics of repetition compulsion, the cycles of domestic violence, the nature of trans-generational trauma, and the dynamics between captor and captive, including the delineation of the "Stockholm Syndrome." The latter does not require an actual hostage, but encompasses strong emotional ties that develop when one side intermittently harasses, threatens, beats, abuses, or intimidates the other (Dutton & Painter, 1981). Variations on this dynamic are associated with incest scenarios, cults, concentration camps, prisoner of war camps, the conditioning of child soldiers or those perpetrating modern-day slavery – indeed with any enduring relationship where an abuser exerts physical/psychological control. Increasingly into the mix there has been a focus on the actions (or lack thereof) of witnesses or those indirectly aware of the abuser's actions and the abused's victimization. The bystander effect (anticipating others will respond) and a raft of other rationalizations designed to neutralize threats to the world being safe, just and fair, support and promote inaction.

Recent history has seen an important (if insufficient) openness of society to recognizing multiple forms of trauma, as well as progression of human rights and the related issues of gender, sexual, racial, and religious/ethnic equality. The world has patchily become more democratic and an emphasis on human rights more prominent. The manner in which the relationship between abusers and their victims maintains silence and acquiescence is the central reason for many grievous crimes never being reported. And even where they are reported, the victim's attachment to their perpetrator is such that police and child protection authorities are frequently stymied in their actions. Indeed they may rationalize nonintervention on the basis that such victims are uncooperative, somehow active participants, or of such low value, as to not merit active assistance – in effect a powerless underclass.

As a backdrop to a volume concerned with victim–perpetrator dynamics, it is useful to reflect on a world that has repeatedly found new ways to dismiss credible information about trauma and abuse, while society's established institutions have on many occasions provided another shelter for abusers to access the vulnerable and collaborate with other abusers, while being shielded by processes that protect the institution and thus facilitate victims becoming expendable. Social media allows the possibility for like-minded perpetrators to coalesce and expand, creating more victims. The Australian Royal Commission arguably represents mankind's most comprehensive attempt to date, to look very closely at the network of society's institutions involved in the sexual abuse of children and the protection of abusers. The Australian findings are of direct relevance to all comparable societies. The next step will be for a society to similarly look closely at what happens to children in that other "institution," the extended family.

There are a great many examples from the last 120 years that followed on from Freud's renunciation of his own so-called "seduction theory," which chart a progression in our understanding of trauma. Unfortunately, repeated regressions are also very common. A few selected examples are illustrative.

Bleuler's construct of "schizophrenia" as laid out in his classic 1911/1950 text effectively subsumed multiple personality disorder (MPD) (dissociative identity disorder [DID]) as well as hysterical psychosis. By the 1970s, the use of the diagnosis "schizophrenia," along with its presumed biological/genetic etiology, marginalized any focus on trauma as an etiological factor in the causation of mental illness (Middleton, Dorahy, & Moskowitz, 2008; Ross, 2004). Early studies that demonstrated the widespread nature of intrafamilial child abuse had little impact. For example, in a study of 295 female middle-class hospital patients, Landis (1940) found that 23.7% had been sexually abused before puberty, 12.5% by a family member. The Kinsey report (Kinsey, Pomeroy, Martin, & Gebhard,

1953) included a finding that of the 4,441 white middle-class females examined, 24% had been sexually abused before puberty, 5.5% by a family member, and 1% by a father/stepfather.

When Leontine Young (1964) published *Wednesday's Children: A Study of Child Neglect and Abuse*, she describes her research beginning "almost by accident" when she read case records in the public child welfare department of a small Midwestern city and "discovered this nightmare world within a world" (p. 4). Yet despite widespread press reports including accounts of 662 cases of severe child abuse published from January through December 1962 in US newspapers that involved incest and other forms of child abuse, such reports failed to ignite much scientific study, despite the fact that 178 of the children died as a result of their injuries. Although the "battered child syndrome" (Kempe, Silverman, Droegemuller, & Silver, 1962) entered the literature in 1962, the profound psychological effects of trauma were something repeatedly avoided. The publication of *Diagnostic and Statistical Manual of Mental Disorders, Second Edition (DSM-II)* coincided with the 1968 Tet offensive in Vietnam. It replaced "gross stress reaction" with "(transient) adjustment disorder of adult life." There was one reference to combat – as "fear associated with military combat and manifested by trembling, running, and hiding" (*DSM-II*, p. 49). This was categorized as equivalent to an "unwanted pregnancy."

When Bowers and coauthors (Bowers, Brecher-Marer, Newton, Piotrowski, Spyer, Taylor, & Watkins, 1971) wrote about the therapy of MPD, there was little reason to believe that a dissociative disorders field would form or that their paper would be other than another orphan.

Holroyd and Brodsky in 1977 opened another window into the complexity of victim–perpetrator dynamics when they reported on a sample of 1,000 psychologists. Of the 70% who completed the survey, 12.1% of male psychologists and 2.6% of female psychologists acknowledged having had erotic contact with at least one opposite-sex patient. The same year saw the publication of Rush's feminist analysis, "The Freudian Cover-up," no less than 80 years after Freud retreated from the field of researching child sexual abuse. Seven years later Jeffrey Masson, armed with access to key correspondence from Freud to his then friend, Fliess, extended the examination of the relevant evidence as to why Freud abandoned his seduction theory when he published, *The Assault on Truth: Freud's Suppression of the Seduction Theory* (see Masson this book).

DSM-III was published in 1980 and it included as entities with diagnostic criteria, borderline personality disorder, multiple personality disorder (MPD) (which was renamed dissociative identity disorder [DID] in the *DSM-IV*), and post-traumatic stress disorder. A fledgling coalition of those aligned with the psychological processes of traumatized veterans and researchers who incorporated a feminist perspective was in evidence. Important books and papers soon came out on issues related to the sexual mistreatment of children and its impact, including within the sacrosanct confines of the family (e.g., Herman, 1981; Russell, 1986; Yates, 1982). But again these largely failed at the time to ignite widespread scientific interest in abuser–abused dynamics.

The year associated with the introduction of the United Nations Convention on the Rights of the Child, 1989, saw the publication of the first comprehensive texts on the diagnosis and treatment of MPD (Putnam, 1989; Ross, 1989). By this time, a brewing challenge was evident for the dissociative disorders field. There was a renewed focus on therapeutic boundaries, the nature of human memory and influences on it. The trauma field found itself having to scientifically address with urgency the challenges of what became known as the (false) recovered memory debate. An organization (the False Memory Syndrome Foundation) came into existence claiming that no one "forgets" major trauma and alleging that large numbers of practitioners were practicing a form of therapy that created false memories of abuse that had never in fact occurred. At one level, it assumed that therapists were capable of wielding enormous psychological power – manipulating the minds of patients to convince them that major sexual traumas had occurred in their childhood. But it became apparent that where individuals initially recovered memories of past sexual traumas, therapy was not the usual precipitant and the degree to which memories can be truly completely created appears to have been inflated (Brewin & Andrews, 2016). Those whose trauma involved betrayal seemed more likely than others to experience amnesia for their childhood trauma (Freyd, 1996; Middleton, De Marni Cromer, & Freyd, 2005). Elliott and Briere (1995) reported that a history of "complete" memory loss was most common among victims of child sexual abuse (20%), while a substantially higher proportion of such victims had significant amnesia for particular details of their traumas. This indicated, as did later research, that ongoing child sexual abuse required a profound adaptation on the part of the victim in respect to living with their abuse.

The year 1992 marked the publication of Judith Herman's classic integrative text, *Trauma and Recovery* (1992a) as well as her initial description of *Complex PTSD* (Herman, 1992b). The same year saw the first major book dealing with the US Catholic Church child abuse scandal (Berry, 1992). The Catholic Church became a focal example of the role institutions can play in the widespread sexual abuse of children, a role that is the antithesis of their reasons for existing, but now uncovered, has much to teach on how institutions and the abusers' standing within them can be incorporated into the abuser–victim dynamics.

Speaking directly to dynamics involving the abused, the abuser and those that bear witness or have knowledge of what has occurred or is occurring, 300,000 Belgian citizens in 1996 marched in protest at perceived cover-ups by police and compromised politicians concerning the serial killer and pedophile Marc Dutroux and his accomplices. In 2000, there was the initiation of a Royal Commission into sexual abuse of children by members of the Irish Catholic clergy. Two years later, the Archdiocese of Boston was the focus of worldwide attention as it became apparent that in excess of 10% of its priests had been involved in the sexual abuse of children (Sullivan, 2002; France, 2004).

In 2008, the case of Josef Fritzl attracted global attention. He had imprisoned his daughter Elisabeth in an underground cellar for 24 years while treating her as a sexual slave who bore him seven children. This brought with it an unprecedented press focus on cases of ongoing sexual abuse during adulthood from around the globe (Middleton, 2014). The fact that this form of extreme and enduring abuse (which frequently has a trans-generational dimension) could have been reported on in a piecemeal manner for a century and a half before the first scientific investigation into populations of such victims is illustrative of the ineffectiveness of child protection agencies and police in substantiating such abuse, even when there have been repeated notifications, as well perhaps as caution from a trauma field still assimilating the lessons of the Satanic Ritual Abuse controversy and the so-called "memory wars." It also speaks of the effectiveness of perpetrators (themselves seemingly frequently the victims of similar abuse) in maintaining high levels of control of their victims. Such victims usually had not been permitted to develop enough selfhood to establish ownership of their own bodies or to feel other than fused with their primary abuser (Middleton, 2013). Thus, further complexity is added to the abused–abuser dynamics.

In 2011, "Operation Rescue" was publicly revealed, involving an international police operation that destroyed the largest pedophile-oriented network in world history, one that had in excess of 70,000 members (Casciani, 2011). The following year there was global exposure of the (mainly) child sex abuses perpetrated by prominent TV personality, charity supporter, and friend of Prince Charles, Jimmy Savile, who had amassed some 500 victims over a period that extended beyond 50 years (Middleton, 2015).

Where the abuser enjoys the status and protection of established and powerful institutions, not only is there the opportunity to join with similarly oriented abusers who have much the same access to victims by dint of their roles, there is an institutional allegiance that is invoked to keep victims and their families quiet, as well as keeping any investigations of abuse "in house" and away from the public's gaze. Victims are repeatedly sacrificed to protect the reputation and assets of the institution.

Not until he became the Archbishop of Sydney in 2001 was there ever a suggestion that Australia's most senior Catholic clergyman Cardinal George Pell might, himself have abused children. In 2002, he stood aside for some months while a church-appointed commission investigated allegations which, in the end, a retired Victorian supreme court judge found not to be proven. Pell played a leading role in severely limiting any compensation victims of Church-related sexual abuse might receive from the Church (Marr, 2014). Pell, the third most senior Catholic clergyman in the world, created history when he appeared in the Melbourne Magistrate's Court on July 28, 2017, in respect to charges that he personally sexually abused children. Victoria's Deputy Police Commissioner confirmed there were multiple charges and multiple complainants. In the free world, a cardinal has never been charged with criminal offences before.

In 1973, Father Gerald Ridsdale and Father George Pell had been both located in a parish within the city of Ballarat (Victoria), living together in the parish house of St Alipius in Ballarat East. As detectives interviewed more of his victims, Ridsdale, one of Australia's most notorious pedophiles, who had originally been sentenced in 1993 was brought back to court in 1994 and in 2006 and in 2013 to be sentenced again. Pell and Risdale lived merely meters away from a ring of pedophiles who operated out of St Alipius as teachers. They included Edward Dowlan, Robert Charles Best, Gerald Fitzgerald, and Stephen Francis Farrell. As of 2015, the Catholic Church had spent in excess of $1.5 million in legal fees on Best, despite many of his victims suiciding and despite him, along with Risdale, being identified as among the very worst of Australia's pedophiles. In 2015, the Christian Brothers said they would welcome Best back into their ranks upon his release from prison (Mannix & Donelly, 2017). In the years following Ridsdale's reign of terror at St Alipius, his accusers were silenced or dismissed. Instead, church authorities moved Ridsdale around to other parishes, including Elsternwick in 1980 and Horsham in 1986 (Marr, 2014; Morris-Marr, 2015). Many have commented that it seemed a little incomprehensible for Cardinal Pell to have been living in the middle of a community of pedophiles and to have remained completely unaware of what was going around him. Pell, via a video link to a Rome hotel, would explain to Australia's royal commission in respect to Fr Risdale's abuse in Ballarat, "It was a sad story and of not much interest to me." He sat on a church committee that transferred Father Gerard Ridsdale from parish to parish. Risdale's crimes were known to the bishop and familiar to other members of the committee. But by his own account, Pell never inquired why this priest was always on the move. In giving evidence from Rome to the royal commission, Pell admitted the pattern of Ridsdale's movements between parishes was "somewhat unusual," even by the "standards of the time." Cardinal Pell maintained he was never told about Ridsdale's offending. "It probably would be possible to imagine a greater deception but it's a gross deception," he told the royal commission (Whitsunday Times, 2016).

In May 2015, Gerald Risdale gave video link evidence to the Australian royal commission – he revealed that the Catholic Church was aware of his abuse from the early 1960s, more than a decade earlier than previously thought. When however counsel pressed repeatedly him to admit that he must have told church officials about his abuses, Risdale responded with a litany of claimed memory failings: "I can't remember any of this. . . . I don't know. I don't think so. I can't remember. . . . I've got no recollection of it. . . . I probably would have, but I don't remember anything – anything specific about it" (Australian Broadcasting Corporation [ABC], 2015).

When "Jason," one of Risdale's many victims, by then in his early 20s, finally tried to reveal to his family that he had been repeatedly raped by Ridsdale, his father and brother walked out in disbelief (Astbury, 2013). Bill White, the judge in the final case concerning Father Ridsdale, reflected that the Church's strategy of moving him from parish to parish paradoxically provided him with even more opportunities to sexually abuse children (Astbury, 2013).

The full extent of the Catholic Church's crisis was revealed in February 2017 when it was announced 7% of priests in Australia's Catholic Church were accused of sexually abusing children between 1950 and 2010. Commissioners surveyed Catholic Church authorities and found that between 1980 and 2015, 4,444 people reported they had been abused at more than 1,000 Catholic institutions across Australia, said Gail Furness, the lead lawyer assisting the commission. The average age of the victims was 10.5 for girls and 11.5 for boys. The average time it took between a victim being abused and reporting it, or seeking redress, was reported as 33 years (The Telegraph, 2017). The worst-offending institutions, by proportion of their religious staff, were shown to be the orders of brothers, who often run schools and homes for the most vulnerable of children. Over 40% of the members of the Brothers of St John of God had allegations of child sexual abuse made against them from 1950 to 2010. For other orders the percentages were Christian Brothers (22.0%), Salesians of Don Bosco (21.9%), Marist Brothers (20.4%), and De La Salle Brothers (13.8%). The worst dioceses in Australia in terms of the weighted average of priests accused of being perpetrators were Sale in Victoria (15.1%), Sandhurst in Victoria (14.7%), Port Pirie in South Australia (14.1%), Lismore in New South Wales (NSW) (13.9%), and Wollongong NSW (11.7%) (Blumer, Armitage, & Elvery, 2017). Forty percent of the victims who gave private testimony to the royal commission stated they had been sexually abused by clergy/representatives of the Catholic Church. Another 20% described being abused by individuals associated with other religious groups.

Ms Furness revealed the Holy See had declined a request to hand over documents involving Australian priests accused of abuse. "The Royal Commission hoped to gain an understanding of the action taken in each case," she stated. "The Holy See responded, on July 1, 2014, that it was 'neither possible nor appropriate to provide the information requested" (Bowling, 2017).

In a revolutionary recommendation regarding the relationship between church and state, the Australian royal commission in mid-December 2017 advised that legislators in Australian states and territories should enact laws to specifically overrule the confessional seal, a recommendation that would require mandatory reporting to police from priests who hear confessions concerning child abuse (Royal Commission into Institutional Responses to Child Sexual Abuse, 2017).

Greg Thompson resigned in 2017 as Anglican Bishop of Newcastle, NSW. As a 19-year-old youth, he had been sexually abused by a previous Bishop of Newcastle, Ian Shevill (McCarthy, 2015, 2017). Bishop Thompson had set out to properly investigate accusations of pedophile rings operating for many years within his diocese. The opposition he and his coworkers encountered was extraordinary, but for those familiar with institutional dynamics, sadly predictable.

One of Bishop Thompson's coworkers, ex-policeman Michael Elliot, on national television said, "I would say what I've seen in the Anglicans has been worse than what I've seen in the Catholics." He described massive intimidation by those with reputations to protect, "There was a period where I moved house five times within a 12-month period. And each time, they found me and within a very short period of time, two to three weeks, began targeting me again." A fellow investigator John Cleary, stated, "I was subject to a death threat just before I was due to give evidence in the Supreme Court, which on advice from the police and with the support of the Church's insurer, they agreed to relocate me and my family for a period of two weeks . . . Yeah, I have no doubt that it put pressure on my marriage and my family life." Bishop Thompson observed, "What's particularly distinctive about the story of abuse in this diocese is the habituated protection of perpetrators and the undermining of survivors as they came forward. It was like a religious protection racket" (ABC, 2016).

Opponents of Bishop Thompson used the Royal Commission to try to advance a novel ploy. A group of leading members of the diocese, which included a former Newcastle Lord Mayor and solicitor Robert Caddies, wrote to the senior Royal Commissioner, Justice Peter McClellan, questioning why Bishop Thompson had taken many years to disclose the fact that he had been sexually abused by clergy as a teenager, and thus by extension, placing others at risk by taking so long to come forward.

There was a torrid exchange at the royal commission between Justice McClellan and Caddies, the group's solicitor.

Mr Caddies was probed about the letter signed by him and sent to the royal commission earlier in 2016 raising "grave concerns" about Bishop Thompson. "Can we cut to the chase, you were seeking to have him removed, weren't you?" asked commission chair, Justice Peter McClellan.

Mr Caddies acknowledged that there was "certainly a great unhappiness" and some of that related to the defrocking of his friend, former 13th Anglican Dean of Newcastle Graeme Lawrence in 2012. While Mr Caddies contributed to fund-raising efforts, organized by some church members to help Mr Lawrence fight his defrocking, he admitted to the commission that in line with the evidence, he now accepted that Mr Lawrence abused children (Marchese, 2016). Brian Farran, the then Anglican Bishop of Newcastle in September 2012 defrocked three Anglican priests, Graeme Lawrence, Bruce Hoare, and Andrew Duncan, over allegations of child sexual abuse dating back more than 30 years (ABC, 2012). Another abuser, teacher Greg Goyette, was permanently banned from teaching.

The royal commission heard that Mr Lawrence groomed and sexually abused a boy in 1981, after his first abuser, Anglican priest Andrew Duncan, told him that Mr Lawrence was "part of the family." The man (who can only be identified as CKH) gave public evidence at the royal commission that he was 15 years old when he was first sexually abused by Graeme Lawrence, and that he was abused by a number of Mr Lawrence's associates, going back to age 14. CKH said Bishop Farran did not want to defrock Mr Lawrence. "He was in tears about the difficulty of his decision, and the effect it would have on the parishioners." While giving evidence at the royal commission, a sullen, angry Lawrence stonewalled for two days, denying any sexual relationship had ever occurred with CKH. The evidence revealed the opposite. Counsel presented a number of sexually explicit letters and cards with pictures of naked men, and depicting sex acts, that either Lawrence or Goyette had sent to CKH. Included was a card from Lawrence which had a photo of a young man touching his erect penis and captioned, "Thank heavens for little BOYS! For LITTLE BOYS GET BIGGER EVERY DAY . . . " In Lawrence's handwriting was a message, "Now isn't that true?! Enjoy the card. Thank Heavens! Much love G" (Manne, 2017).

In 2015, Bishop Thompson had issued an historic apology to child sexual abuse victims in the Newcastle/Hunter region. He said the diocese believed more than 30 child sex offenders had abused children over a period of decades. Graeme Lawrence had led a Griffith group of child sex offenders to the Hunter. The royal commission heard that Lawrence, was in a "gang of three." The other two were defrocked priest Bruce Hoare and Peter Mitchell (who had been subsequently jailed for stealing nearly $200,000 from the diocese). This group protected a notorious and sadistic Hunter pedophile priest, Peter Rushton, who frequently abused children in the company of fellow abusers. Rushton moved to the Hunter region in 1963 and died in 2007 without ever being charged. Rushton's record was littered with complaints of sexual assault spanning 40 years (Smith, 2016). From the 1980s to the 1990s, Graeme Lawrence, Bruce Hoare, and Peter Rushton were part of the leadership team in the diocese (McCarthy, 2016).

A witness at the Royal Commission, CKH, reported he was 14 years old when first sexually abused by church deacon Andrew Duncan and 15 years old when he was first sexually abused by Graeme Lawrence, and that via Lawrence he was to be sexually abused by Greg Goyette, Bruce Hoare and Graeme Sturt. CKH's abuse allegations were finally sent to a church hearing. CKH told the Commission that Newcastle Bishop Farran did not want to defrock Mr Lawrence, stating, "He was in tears about the difficulty of his decision, and the effect it would have on the parishioners", but Lawrence, Duncan, and Hoare were ultimately defrocked (Cox, 2016b).

The commission heard that Mr Keith Allen, diocesan council member and solicitor, was stood down by Bishop Thompson because he was in a group that sought to defend the accused priests. The commission heard how Allen fraudulently, had one sadistic abuser, Hatley Gray, write a predated resignation letter so that he could be "in good standing" with his bishop at the time of his resignation and could thus go to another diocese.

> Justice McClellan asked him, "And what you sought to defend was, do you accept now, indefensible?"
>
> Mr Allen replied, "Probably indefensible."
>
> Justice McClellan put to him: "That's because it was a 'do nothing and a cover up and protect the church' approach, wasn't it? And you were part of that practice, weren't you?"
>
> Mr Allen responded, "Yes." (Cox, 2016a)

On July 7, 2014, the British government, under sustained pressure from various politicians, and appreciating growing public concern, announced an unprecedented public inquiry into the processes that resulted in minimal or no investigation of the alleged organized sexual abuse of children involving 10 current and former MPs. A second broader inquiry was established to examine how for decades there was an apparent suppression of allegations of child abuse involving public officials (Middleton, 2015). These inquiries have staggered, faltered, and still not fully taken shape to offer smooth and effective functioning. The first two chairs, Baroness Butler-Sloss and Fiona Woolf, stepped down in response to concerns related to their perceived closeness to institutions and individuals they would be investigating. There were concerns too regarding the limited scope of the inquiry and the lack of ability to compel witnesses to testify. On February 4, 2015, Dame Lowell Goddard was named as the new chair, the existing panel was disbanded, and the enterprise was given new powers as a statutory inquiry. By August 2016 Goddard had resigned, citing among other reasons, the inquiry's "legacy of failure which has been very hard to shake off" (Laville, 2016). Professor Alexis Jay became the inquiry's fourth chairman, inheriting a role that was being dubbed as being "the most toxic job description in public life" (Coleman, 2016).

The first public hearings of the British inquiry commenced in February 2017 and were focused on the post war child migration programs. One victim, David Hill, who became both chairman and managing director of the Australian Broadcasting Corporation had been sent, along with his twin brother and older brother to the Fairbridge farm school in Molong, NSW. He gave evidence that in his estimate 60% of the children sent to the school were sexually abused there (Laville, 2017).

By June 2017, the group *Survivors of Organised and Institutional Abuse* announced their withdrawal from the inquiry, stating it was "not fit for purpose" and that it had become a "very costly academic report writing and literature review exercise" (*The Guardian*, 2017a). Giving evidence to the Independent Inquiry into Child Sexual Abuse, former British Prime Minister, Gordon Brown, in July 2017 said the mass transportation of 130,000 British children overseas between the 1940s and 1970s amounted to "government-enforced trafficking" and that the program probably represented the country's "biggest national sex abuse scandal" (*The Guardian*, 2017b).

In 2014, a commissioned report by Professor Jay had found that at least 1,400 girls in Rotherham, some as young as 11, were left unprotected from abuse by gangs of men, mostly of Pakistani origin, over a 16-year period, as authorities were too afraid to reveal the existence of a race issue. More than a third of the children were already known to child protection authorities (Brooke & Infante, 2014), another example of the sort of institutional betrayal focused on by Freyd and her colleagues (Freyd & Birrell, 2013; Smith & Freyd, 2013, 2014).

The capacity for dissociation enables the young child to exercise their innate life-sustaining need for attachment in spite of the fact that principal attachment figures are also principal abusers. Those who abuse long term, frequently extend their abusive activities to include fellow abusers, who in turn exert additional pressures on their victims to maintain silence. Such structures, whether they be familial multigenerational networks or based around work mates, churches or other institutions, pedophile rings or child prostitution businesses, may be difficult to fully document, let alone disassemble, due in part to the victim's strong attachment to their principal perpetrator. This apparent loyalty speaks of a real need to understand the complex dynamic involving the abuser and the abused, a dynamic in which an appreciation of attachment theory, the coconstruction of self-perception and identity, the nature of shame and its capacity to erode selfhood to the point that any form of assertive action gives way to dutiful compliance, the psychology of betrayal, and the ways in which sexuality can become a very live issue for the therapist, are pivotal concerns.

We are informed by a history in which abuser–abused dynamics have been central to the cyclical pattern of much domestic violence, where making public utterances about presumed abuse that go beyond the available data has proven to be immensely problematic, and yet where we need to be very nuanced in understanding the history of much of society's reflex denial, a denial voiced loudly by many abusers but also on occasions by the abused, and those who witness, or know of the violation. This book tackles such issues.

We are very grateful to our authors for grappling with this complex topic and for the depth and creativity of their thinking, to Jennifer Freyd and the *JTD* for allowing us to produce the original special double issue, to the Cannan Institute for its generous support, and to Routledge for hosting the publishing of this book, derived from the *JTD* Special Double Issue. We very much hope that this edited book will inspire further thinking, debate, and research into the thorny complexities of relational abuse.

References

American Psychiatric Association. (1968). *Diagnostic and statistical manual of mental disorders* (2nd ed.). Washington, DC: American Psychiatric Association.

Astbury, J. (2013, July). Child sexual abuse in the general community and clergy-perpetrated child sexual abuse: A review paper prepared for the Australian Psychological Society to inform an APS Response to the Royal Commission into Institutional Responses to Child Sexual Abuse.

Australian Broadcasting Corporation (ABC). (2012, September 10). Lateline – presented by Emma Alberici. Three Anglican priests defrocked. Retrieved from http://tinyurl.com/bu9vlqt

Australian Broadcasting Corporation (ABC) (2015, May 27). 7:30 Report hosted by Leigh Sales. Retrieved from http://tinyurl.com/yd748rqa.

Australian Broadcasting Corporation (ABC) (2016, July 20). 7:30 Report hosted by Leigh Sales. Retrieved from http://tinyurl.com/ybnwrhvz

Berry, J. (1992). *Lead us not into temptation*. New York: Doubleday.

Bleuler, E. (1911/1950). Dementia praecox or the group of schizophrenias. New York, NY: International Universities Press.

Blumer, C., Armitage, R., & Elvery, S. (2017). Child sex abuse royal commission: Data reveals extent of Catholic allegations. *ABC News*. Retrieved from http://tinyurl.com/hmfwfd5

Bowers, M. K., Brecher-Marer, S., Newton, B. W., Piotrowski, Z., Spyer, T. C., Taylor, W, S., & Watkins, J. G. (1971). Therapy of multiple personality. *International Journal of Clinical and Experimental Hypnosis, 19*, 57–65.

Bowling, M. (2017, February 8). Shocking extent of Church abuse reveal at royal commission. Catholic Leader. Retrieved from http://tinyurl.com/ycyec8sk

Breger, L. (2000). *Freud, darkness in the midst of vision*. New York, NY: John Wiley.

Brewin, C. R., & Andrews, B. (2016). Creating memories for false autobiographical events in childhood: A systematic review. *Applied Cognitive Psychology, 31* (1), 2–23. doi: 10.1002/acp.3220

Brooke, C., & Infante, F. (2014, August 27). Betrayed by the PC cowards. *Daily Mail*. Retrieved from http://tinyurl.com/osjvk2e

Casciani, D. (2011, March 16). "World's largest paedophile ring" uncovered. *BBC News UK*. Retrieved from http://www.bbc.co.uk/news/uk-12762333

Coleman, C. (2016, August 9). Is this the most toxic job in public life? *BBC*. Retrieved from http://tinyurl.com/y76mpslz

Cox, D. (2016a, August 8). Newcastle lawyer did not tell police about abuse allegations against priests, royal commission hears. *ABC News*. Retrieved from http://tinyurl.com/jjs9ptz

Cox, D. (2016b, August 9). Defrocked Dean of Newcastle abused me as a child, royal commission hears. *ABC News*. Retrieved from http://tinyurl.com/jog6jal

DeMause, L. (1998). The history of child abuse. *The Journal of Psychohistory, 25* (3), 216–236.

Dutton, D., G., & Painter, S. L. (1981). Traumatic bonding: The development of emotional attachments in battered women and other relationships of intermittent abuse. *Victimology: An International Journal, 7* (4), 139–155.

Elliott, D. M., & Briere, J. (1995). Posttraumatic stress associated with delayed recall of sexual abuse: A general population study. *Journal of Traumatic Stress, 8*, 629–647.

Ferenczi, S. (1984). Confusion of tongues between adults and the child (J. M. Masson, & M. Coring, Trans.). In J. M. Masson (Ed.), *The assault on truth: Freud's suppression of the seduction theory* (pp. 283–295). London, England: Faber and Faber. (Original work published 1932)

Fliess, R. (1956). *Erogeneity and libido: Addenda to the theory of the psychosexual development of the human: Vol. 1 Psychoanalytic series*. New York, NY: International Universities Press.

Fliess, R. (1973). *Psychoanalytic series: Vol. 3. Symbol, dream, and psychosis with notes on technique*. New York, NY: International Universities Press.

France, D. (2004). *Our fathers: The secret life of the Catholic Church in an age of scandal*. New York, NY: Broadway Books.

Freyd, J. J. (1996). *Betrayal trauma: The logic of forgetting childhood abuse*. Cambridge, MA: Harvard University Press.

Freyd, J. J., & Birrell, P. J. (2013). Blind to betrayal. New York, NY: Wiley.

Herman, J. L. (1981). *Father-daughter incest*. Cambridge, MA: Harvard University Press.

Herman, J. L. (1992a). *Trauma and recovery*. New York, NY: Basic Books.

Herman, J. L. (1992b). Complex PTSD: A syndrome in survivors of prolonged and repeated trauma. *Journal of Traumatic Stress, 5*, 377–391. doi:10.1002/(ISSN)1573-6598

Kempe, C. H., Silverman, F. N., Droegemuller, W., & Silver, H. K. (1962). The battered child syndrome. *Journal of the American Medical Association, 181*, 17–24. doi;10.1001/jama.1962.03050270019004

Kinsey, A., Pomeroy, W., Martin, C., & Gebhard, P. (1953). *Sexual behavior in the human female*. Philadelphia, PA: Saunders.

Landis, C. (1940). *Sex in development*. New York, NY: Harper & Brother.

Laville, S. (2016, August 5). Child sexual abuse inquiry: Rudd vows to press on after Dame Lowell Goddard resignation. *The Guardian*. Retrieved from http://tinyurl.com/hdasrum

Laville, S. (2017, February 28). Man sent as child from UK to Australia tells abuse inquiry: Name the villains. *The Guardian*. Retrieved from http://tinyurl.com/hvnstcb

Manne, A. (2017, May). Rape among the lamingtons. *The Monthly*. Retrieved from http://tinyurl.com/ybslsdo2

Mannix, L., & Donelly, B. (2017, February 20). "It just blows me away": Judge stunned by church's legal aid to paedophile. *The Age*. Retrieved from http://tinyurl.com/jh9l579

Marchese, D. (2016). Child abuse royal commission: Church official denies trying to 'destroy' Newcastle Anglical bishop. *ABC News*. Retrieved from http://tinyurl.com/gu3nvjy

McCarthy, J. (2015, October 26). Anglican bishop Greg Thompson sexually abused by late Bishop Ian Shevill. *Newcastle Herald*. Retrieved from http://tinyurl.com/y8qyswu2

McCarthy, J. (2016, August 2). Newcastle Anglican diocese's defrocked Dean is still influential, the royal commission has heard. *Newcastle Herald*. Retrieved from http://tinyurl.com/y9rdxhm7

McCarthy, J. (2017, May 16). Newcastle Anglican Bishop Greg Thompson resigns after standing up for abuse survivors. *Newcastle herald*. Retrieved from http://tinyurl.com/ycp2ju7x

Marr, D. (2014). *The prince: Faith, abuse & George Pell*. Collingwood, Victoria: Black Inc.

Masson, J. M. (1984). *The assault on truth: Freud's suppression of the seduction theory*. London: Faber and Faber.

Middleton, W. (2013). Ongoing incestuous abuse during adulthood. *Journal of Trauma and Dissociation, 14*, 251–272. doi:10:1080/152999732.2012.736932

Middleton, W. (2014). Parent-child incest that extends into adulthood: A survey of international press reports, 2007–2012. In: Sar, V., Middleton, W., & Dorahy, M. (Eds). *Global perspectives on dissociative disorders: Individual and societal oppression* (pp. 45–64). London, UK: Routledge (Taylor and Francis).

Middleton, W. (2015). Tipping points and the accommodation of the abuser: The case of ongoing incestuous abuse during adulthood. *International Journal for Crime, Justice and Social Democracy* (edited by Salter, M.), *4* (2), 4–17. doi: 10.5204/ijcjsd.v3i2.21

Middleton, W. (2016). Wilhelm Fliess, Robert Fliess, Ernest Jones, Sandor Ferenczi and Sigmund Freud – ISSTD President's Editorial. *Journal of Trauma and Dissociation, 17* (1), 1–12.

Middleton, W., De Marni Cromer, L., & Freyd, J. J. (2005). Remembering the past, anticipating the future. *Australasian Psychiatry, 13* (3), 223–233. doi:10.1111/j.1440-1665.2005.02192.x

Middleton, W., Dorahy, M., & Moskowitz, A. (2008). The concepts of dissociation and psychosis: An historical perspective. In: Moskowitz, A., Schäfer, I., & Dorahy, M. (Eds). *Dissociation and psychosis: Multiple perspectives on a complex relationship* (pp. 9–20). London, UK: Wiley.

Morris-Marr, L. (2015). St Alipius Presbytery in Ballarat holds history of child sexual abuse. *Herald Sun*. Retrieved from http://tinyurl.com/y98cy4hc

Pinker, S. (2011). The better angels of our nature: Why violence has declined. London, UK: Penguin.

Putnam, F. W. (1989). *Diagnosis and treatment of multiple personality disorder*. New York, NY: Guilford.

Ross, C. A. (1989). *Multiple personality disorder: Diagnosis, clinical features and treatment*. New York, NY: Wiley.

Ross, C. A. (2004). *Schizophrenia: Innovations in diagnosis and treatment*. New York, NY: Haworth.

Royal Commission into Institutional Responses to Child Sexual Abuse. (2017). Final Report. Retrieved from https://tinyurl.com/yb89x6ar

Russell, D. E. (1986). *The secret trauma: Incest in the lives of girls and women*. New York, NY: Basic Books.

Şar, V., Middleton. W., & Dorahy, M. J. (Eds.). (2014). *Global perspectives on dissociative disorders: Individual and societal oppression*. Abingdon, UK: Taylor and Francis.

Smith, C. P. & Freyd, J. J. (2013). Dangerous safe havens: Institutional betrayal exacerbates sexual trauma. *Journal of Traumatic Stress, 26*, 119–124.

Smith, C. P., & Freyd, J. J. (2014). Editorial: The courage to study what we wished did not exist. *Journal of Trauma and Dissociation, 15*, 521–526. doi:10.1080/15299732.2014.947910

Smith, R. (2016, August 29). Royal commission hears how senior priest within Newcastle diocese got away with years of sexual abuse. news.com.au. Retrieved from http://tinyurl.com/yddd8otr

Sullivan, A. (2002, March 4). They still don't get it. *Time*, 39.

Sulloway, F. J. (1992). *Biologist of the mind*. Cambridge, MA: Basic Books.

The Telegraph. (2017, June 29). Who is Cardinal George Pell, what is he accused of and how will Vatican respond to Australian sex abuse case? Retrieved from http://tinyurl.com/ybzc2fs9

The Guardian. (2017a, June 14). Inquiry into child sexual abuse 'not fit for purpose', claims victims' group. Retrieved from http://tinyurl.com/ybmpbnkf

The Guardian. (2017b, July 21). Forced migration was UK's worst child abuse scandal, Gordon Brown says. Retrieved from http://tinyurl.com/y98unldn

Whitsunday Times. (2016). Priest's sad story 'not much interest to me' says Pell. Retrieved from http://tinyurl.com/yayyoeyc

Yates, A. (1982). Children eroticized by incest. *American Journal of Psychiatry, 139*, 482–485. doi:10.1176/ajp.139.4.482

Young, L. (1964). *Wednesday's children: A study of child neglect and abuse*. New York, NY: McGraw-Hill.

ARTICLE

Weaponized sex: Defensive pseudo-erotic aggression in the service of safety

Richard P. Kluft, MD, PhD

ABSTRACT

Problematic sexual behaviors are frequently encountered in the treatment of patients suffering Dissociative Identity Disorder and related forms of dissociative disorders. These may include unfortunate patterns of ready acquiescence or submission to overtly or potentially aggressive or sexual approaches/encounters, subtle and/or overt seductive signaling and behaviors, and even overt sexually provocative patterns of verbalizations and actions. This paper discusses the possibility that in some instances, sexual behavior has become weaponized; that is, deployed in circumstances under which assertiveness and/or aggression or other self-protective measures might be expected, probably because such behaviors were not within the range of the possible or were not understood as potentially successful for some victims of trauma. Clinical manifestations are described and discussed. An animal model in which sexual behaviors substitute for aggressive behaviors is described. A speculative hypothesis is offered, postulating that in some cases, such patterns in traumatized humans might represent an epigenetic response to exogenous trauma. Exploration of this model may lead to improved understandings and approaches to trauma victims who manifest such behavior, hopefully destigmatizing them further, facilitating reduction of their shame and guilt, and supporting their recoveries. Clinical interventions are suggested.

Introduction

Patients suffering Dissociative Identity Disorder (DID) and allied conditions frequently manifest problematic sexual behaviors. These may persist in the face of DID patients' clear (but usually rapidly rationalized, denied, and/or dissociated) appreciations of their deleterious consequences. Ranging from mild to quite severe, they may remain refractory to the advices, injunctions, and insights of concerned others and/or mental health professionals. They include disorders of diminished desire and/or aversion; conflicted gender and sexual identities (Stoller, 1973); activities ordinarily classified as perversions (Brenner, 1996); and/or powerfully driven pressures to enact particular sexual scenarios and/or actualize pressures to activate particular patterns of sexual behaviors under particular circumstances (often accompanied with claims that such scenarios/practices are necessary, undertaken without misgivings or conflicts, and in some instances, experienced as immensely pleasurable and satisfying).

Here I will discuss the powerful pressures experienced by a small minority of dissociative women to engage others in sexual activities, even at the cost of disrupting their adult lives and/or their psychotherapeutic encounters. My perspectives are drawn from the study and treatment of women with DID. Some perspectives advanced here are admittedly speculative, presented as food for thought at a moment in time when biological aspects of trauma and the trauma response are subjects of increasing interest.

Novel contributions to the understanding of complex phenomena are merely new chapters in a long, long book, much of which remains to be written. This "chapter" both looks back over 44 years of clinical experience and forward toward developments in branches of molecular biology still in their infancy.

I have spent over four decades working with victims of sexually-exploitive therapists, clergy, and similar figures of authority. I have also worked with offenders. This body of experience has convinced me that the highly censored and politically correct vagueness customary in discussing such situations, the understandable emphasis on the unwanted consequences to the victim, and the unfortunately perfunctory attention paid to the second party apart from condemnation, together contribute to an unfortunate overall failure to communicate the complexity, urgency, and intensity of what might have transpired within the context of the clinical encounter.

Professionals who respond to sexual provocations, however extreme, are indisputably in the wrong. But too often the rapid attribution of blame preempts potentially informative study of what transpired in the minds and actions of both individuals and the occurrences within the relational dyad antecedent to, during, and subsequent to boundary violations. Neither an avoidance of the potentially prurient, militant defense of the victim, nor passionate excoriation of the perpetrator promotes nuanced understanding.

Antecedents to such transgressions are studied by psychoanalysts (e.g., Celenza, 2007; Gabbard, 1995; Gabbard & Lester, 1995). However, among traumatologists, similar explorations of the relational contexts of such incidents are often derailed by strident sexual politics. Recently I presented the same clinical material to psychoanalytic and trauma meetings only months apart. The former group was receptive, but among the latter some rapidly adopted a hostile attitude, accusing me of misogyny quite early in my presentation.

Withholding detailed descriptions to appease those who find them odious squanders educational opportunities advantageous to the welfare of actual and potential victims of exploitation. Three examples follow.

First, assuming the desirability of reducing mental health professionals' misunderstanding and/or making inappropriate responses to such provocations, and of enhancing their sensitivity to such behaviors, from subtle to extreme, it seems wise to provide them with anticipatory socialization and desensitization, reducing the likelihood of dysfunctional therapist behaviors. In 1971, before my residency group was either taught the rudiments of sex therapy or assigned actual sex therapy patients, we were required to spend two full days watching and discussing tapes of incredibly intimate and detailed sexual acts of all varieties in order to deprive these acts of their potentials for prurience, shock, and arousal. Thereafter, we could view and/or listen to clinical material involving such activities with minimal countertransferential arousal/distress responses.

Second, clinicians' failures to explore these materials openly may increase the likelihood that their first intense and overt exposures to such provocations may find them unprepared, vulnerable to becoming over-stimulated, deskilled, and overwhelmed.

Third, an aversion to exploring these situations denies the clinician the vicarious opportunity to learn from others how to see such situations begin to emerge, anticipate the likely next steps, and nip them in the bud. Luborsky's symptom context studies (Luborsky & Auerbach, 1969; Luborsky & Mintz, 1974) demonstrated that the triggers for symptoms emerging in sessions can usually be found in a transferential reference within the several hundred words antecedent to the onset of the symptoms. I use this method to identify and interdict as many of these episodes as possible.

Given that the small minority of patients to whom I refer often express an inability to control their sexual behaviors, I will characterize such circumstances, and ask if we can attempt to understand driven, compulsive, dysfunctional sexual enactments as determined, in some instances, at least in part, by more or less involuntary neuropsychobiological phenomena. Finally, I will share what I have learned about the psychotherapeutic management of unwanted sexual provocations in the consulting room.

Preliminary considerations

My interest in the driven dysfunctional sexuality of DID patients began with a patient who reported abuses so similar to those described in *Sybil* (Schrieber, 1973) that I assumed she had read the book, notwithstanding her denial. Astonishingly, both parents confirmed her allegations. Her mother assured me that she had been psychotic when she mistreated her daughter. Now she knew she suffered paranoid schizophrenia and took her medication conscientiously. Her father explained he had not intervened because raising children was "the women's work."

Perhaps preoccupied by processing the acknowledged maternal brutality, our work had not addressed her claims of sexual abuse by a male relative, or perhaps I overlooked relevant indicators. One evening I did not recognize the individual sitting in my waiting room, wearing a clinging, low-cut "little black dress." Assuming she was someone else's patient, I had turned to leave the room before she called out, "Afraid of me, Doc? I don't bite!"

Thus began my first encounter with a flagrant, over the top sexually aggressively alter presenting me with a confrontational, provocative, and challenging seductive relational field. I had never understood why my patient had been fired from a series of demanding jobs. Soon it became clear she had repeatedly seduced her immediate supervisors so flamboyantly that her resignation was demanded.

I had been taught that if a person incessantly repeats a behavior, however dysfunctional, something within that person was driven to bring these recurrences about; that is, at some level (conscious, unconscious, or both) the person "wanted" such outcomes, or was compelled to repeat problematic behaviors in the service of mastery. Yet when I tried to interpret such understandings to my first traumatized dissociative patients, anger, mortification, self-harm, suicidal impulses, and even suicide attempts/overdosing to drive away pain, were not uncommon. I rapidly arrived at the then-controversial conclusion that such lines of thinking situated both blame and shame within the victim in a rather simple-minded and unproductive manner (Kluft, 2016).

In 1973–1974, there was much to learn, but little guidance or precedent.

The literatures of trauma and dissociation had yet to flower. In desperation, I began to study revictimization. It would be years before the burgeoning literature of feminist thinkers and the contributions of early explorers of therapist/patient sexual exploitation (e.g., Gartrell, Herman, Olarte, Feldstein, & Localio, 1987; Herman, 1981; Pope & Bouhoutsos, 1986) would become available. My early efforts taught me only that such situations were best approached by applying the empathic and interpretive perspectives of Kohut (1971, 1977), with attention to selfobject transferences.

In studying a cohort of men and women who had experienced therapist–patient sexual exploitation, I found that all proved to be victims of parent–child incest and suffered diagnosable dissociative disorders (Kluft, 1989, 1990). Of course, the unlikely conjunction of these three factors was a sampling artifact due to my referral streams at the time rather than a firm basis for more general understanding.

I was forced to reconsider the role of classical Oedipal dynamics. Had Oedipal triumph fixated these male and female patients into a repetitive pattern of seducing/accepting seduction by authority figures, such as therapists, physicians, clergymen, and the like? Clinical experience demonstrated diverse rather than uniform dynamics at play. Pope and Bouhoutsos (1986) published a complex list of dynamic formulations, to which I added some others (Kluft, 1989; 1990; see also Celenza, 2007; Gabbard & Lester, 2005).

Even when my patients' sexualized behaviors demonstrated profound commonalities, their underlying unconscious dynamics showed surprising diversity. My conclusion was that their vulnerability to revictimization resided largely in the persistence of instrumental behaviors that had served these patients well within the contexts of their abusive childhoods, but contributed to recursive cycles of dysfunctional and life-disrupting actions in their adult lives.

The more I worked with traumatized patients the less erotic their expressed sexuality appeared to be. They rarely demonstrated either erotic desire or responsiveness as these terms are normally understood. This contributed to my describing "the sitting duck syndrome" (Kluft, 1989, 1990), the perversion of many aspects of normal coping and relatedness, including sexuality, into patterns designed to maximize safety and minimize damage and distress in dangerous and abusive environments.

It was helpful to understand their "sexual" issues as instrumental, as tactical and strategic enactments in the service of trauma-perverted concepts of safety. But what optimized damage control in environments in which at any second they might become the helpless targets of aggression, sexualized, or otherwise, sabotaged them and diminished their safety in other settings. What created primary gain in abusive settings occasioned substantial secondary loss in others, resulting in ongoing vulnerability to revictimization, compromised object relations, and a diminished quality of life.

The concept of such weaponized sex/instrumental pseudo-erotic behavior as other than genuinely erotic may be easier to grasp when compared with a different but more familiar form of aggressive nonerotic sexual behavior, rape. Rape involves the enactment of sexual behaviors driven by self-gratifying destructive aggression enacted in the service of power, domination, and sadism rather than in the service of mutual affection and shared erotic engagement.

Weaponized sex encompasses a wide and sophisticated array of strategies that utilize sexual behaviors or the implication of possible imminent sexual behaviors to seek safety, to cope with a threatening interpersonal world (and sometimes a world of internalized object relations as well) in which strong unambivalent committed attachments are not firmly established. In weaponized sex, processes and interactions that at first glance appear flagrantly sexual have minimal erotic significance or meaning. Nonetheless, these behaviors (and usually the insistence that they are erotic) are profoundly valued and clung to with desperation as coping and survival strategies.

Clinical encounters with weaponized sex/instrumental pseudo-eroticism

A professional woman from a conservative religious background believed that having angry feelings made a person evil; she deemed this emotion completely unacceptable. After many years of therapy, angry affect began to emerge. Shortly thereafter, she went into an altered state during session, exposed her breasts, and struggled to force my hands upon them. Despite my best countermeasures, this behavior recurred in over a dozen consecutive sessions, always both disremembered and denied. We slowly came to understand that these behaviors expressed both (1) the emergence of an intolerable wish to murder me (her abusive father in the transference); (2) her reenacting defending herself against her homicidal impulses and her father's/my possible reactions to them by offering herself sexually; and (3) erotic feelings toward me. She had dissociated several efforts to kill her brutal father, after which he had nearly beaten her to death. In her contemporary life, this pattern was demonstrated in rapid acquiescence to sexual approaches by powerful men, and in smiling and beginning to unbutton her blouse if a powerful man began to express anger toward her. She never had consensual sex with a lover, but she had become sexually involved with many of the men under whom she had trained or worked, all such experiences banished from memory by amnesia.

My efforts to share my findings about such situations did not fare well in the heated gender-sensitive atmosphere of the 1990s. I was attacked for "blaming" the patients and "excusing" various perpetrators. Few besides my recovered and recovering patients were ready to consider that working with these episodes actually generated non-shaming and effective clinical interventions that restored the health, dignity, and functionality of victimized women, often even allowing them to lay claim to their healthy sexuality for the first time in their lives.

Hence, the importance of providing colleagues with sufficiently detailed illustrations to facilitate the process of bringing the study of this matter out of the shadows and subjecting it to the circumspect thought and study it deserves. Left inadequately characterized and censored beyond recognition under the aegis of political correctness, this important topic can neither be understood nor explored in a meaningful and reasonably objective manner.

Vignette 1

My adolescent friends and I spent years infatuated with one particularly beautiful young woman who would walk along "our" beach, oblivious to us. She became involved with any number of "biker types," but took no notice of us college/professional students. Naturally, we called her "The Girl from Ipanema" after a line from Jobin's song: "Every day when she walks to the sea, She looks straight ahead, not at me"(Jobim, de Moraes, & Gimbel, 1964).

Flash forward 25 years. A new patient was referred by a senior and respected colleague. He ended our conversation with, "Rick, you're holding my career in your hands."

I quickly learned that this patient had been sexually involved with the referring psychiatrist, she suffered a dissociative disorder, and she was "The Girl from Ipanema."

By the end of my first conversation with this beautiful but unfortunate woman, her erotic appeal had vanished. Her over-the-top sexuality had been no more than the desperate strategy she discovered helped her cope with the vicissitudes of her tragic life. She came to believe that she was nothing more than a slut, and that readily offered sex provided her only guarantee of semi-safety and semi-acceptance.

When she perceived that a man was angry or displeased with her, an alarmingly aggressive sexual pattern was triggered, during which she went into an altered state, often started to undress, and/or might began to touch the man. This had occurred with two previous therapists. One had just expressed his frustration over her lack of progress, the other had just begun to push her to pay a higher fee. Other aspects of her situation are discussed elsewhere (Kluft, 1987, 1990).

I conducted her entire therapy with a kind smile on my face. I helped her see that what she thought was her nymphomaniac out-of-control promiscuity with "bad boys" was her automatic submission to any man she experienced as actually or potentially threatening. Both her DID and her weaponized sex became things of the past.

Vignettes 2 and 3

When I describe rather dramatic instances of weaponized sex (because they are the most difficult to manage and pose the greatest threat to patient, therapist, and therapy alike), my efforts to convey that the most common expressions of weaponized sex are passive, subtle, and difficult to discern are easily overlooked or misunderstood. More frequently, the patient begins to respond to what she perceives as cues that another person is expecting/encouraging/inviting/demanding the sexualization of their relationship. This may take the form of elaborating material with seductive potential, responding to what she believes are hints that sex is expected, and encouraging/escalating physical contacts that begin innocently enough (not overtly sexual), but progress toward more dangerous ground. They can build upon what are ostensibly expressions of a more conventional positive transference, be expressed as responses to a therapist's remark/behavior that may have a countertransference-based double entendre, or simply occur in reaction to some ostensibly neutral interaction capable of being interpreted, idiosyncratically, in a sexualized manner.

Thoughtful patients have educated me by sharing their insightful self-observations. One woman hugged me impulsively at the end of a consultation we thought would be our only meeting. When she became my patient years later, she hugged me again. I thought she would feel unduly rejected if I set limits at that point. Session-ending hugs remained brief and perfunctory for nearly a decade. Then she began to press one, and then both breasts against me quite firmly. Before I succeeded in finding a tactful way to broach this subject, she took the initiative.

"Dr. Kluft, I'm realizing that some of the others are trying to seduce you. I'm sure you've noticed what I've been doing. And something's making me want to grind against you, down below. Please don't push me away. Some of the others wouldn't understand. They'd feel rejected. The rest of us will get this under control. I think they really do believe that you are my father, and they have to make sure you'll love them enough so you will feed them. They think if they don't please you, you'll tie them up and shock them. If they don't get you to have sex, they're afraid you'll really hurt them and let them starve for days. They just came into the therapy. I guess we finally felt safe enough to let them out. I thought they understood who you are .... We didn't realize they didn't understand us. They didn't believe you were really safe, and they were going too far. They were sure they were doing what you wanted them to do."

Often sexualized communications transpire without being recognized by other alters and without the therapist's either comprehending them or being able to find a way to discuss them. Sometimes therapists find themselves in situations in which they feel compelled to make confrontations that may make no sense and/or even may prove offensive to the parts at the surface at the time confrontations are made.

I generally walk my patients to the office door at session's end. One woman who had shown no previous aggressive sexual behaviors suddenly turned and tried to kiss me on the lips. I was so caught off guard that I pulled away only at the last moment. She acted as if nothing had happened. Later I referred to this instance and suggested that we talk about it. She insisted that it never had happened, that I must be having sexual fantasies about her or mistaking her for someone else. Five years later the memories of the involved alters leaked into the awareness of the others.

Vignettes 4, 5, 6, and 7

Often emergent weaponized sex can be identified and addressed before it achieves behavioral expression. Four years ago, in a single morning, three consecutive female patients who had been exploited by prior therapists boasted that all the men they had been with told them that they gave the best oral sex in the world. They were not sexually aggressive in their behavior, but the way they discussed their expertise resembled a fisherman's attempts to present the precisely correct bait to the fish he is trying to catch.

One patient's therapy was quite advanced. Our relationship was very warm and friendly. She found she was experiencing increasingly strong loving feeling toward me, including strong erotic desires. These parts were coming close to both acknowledging their transference fantasies and mourning the impossibility of realizing them. At the same time, other parts felt unable to trust me. They feared that acknowledging affection toward me would facilitate inevitable betrayal and mistreatment. Simultaneously, some protective parts (who had taken the brunt of the sexual mistreatment and developed strategies of damage control that involved taking the lead to influence which sexual acts took place) had decided to preempt my inevitable unveiling as an abuser by seducing me.

Sensing but certainly not understanding her distress, I intervened to explore and found myself in conversation with parts prepared to become more aggressive. "You're no better than any other man," one said. "I'll show them what a bastard you are. Then they won't let you get anywhere near them." I did not attempt reassurance. Instead, I responded by encouraging their protective vigilance. I neither set limits nor overtly rejected their ideas or proposed action plans. We kept the matter conversational. Her treatment is nearing a successful conclusion.

In the second, the moment I spoke, my patient switched into an alter unaware of what had been said moments before. She was shocked and outraged by what I tried to share. Finally, I said, "At this moment I am talking to you while you are in a state of mind that has no recollection of what was just said. I know that in this state of mind you would prefer that I let the whole matter drop. But I can't. Something was going on that prompted the conversation I remember, and you say you don't recall it. If I don't try to deal with it, it may be pretty crazy making for those among your system who do remember it. So, let me say that something must have happened, or may have been triggered, that led to that conversation. I suspect that it was something that made some parts of your mind think they were in a sexual or potentially sexual situation. They are not. I think something scared them, and in some way what some of you have blocked out was designed to get me to think about letting you do something sexual to avoid something far worse."

My patient switched and responded, "He always wore black slacks. Why are you wearing black slacks? You never wore black slacks before. When he wore black slacks …." Some of her patterns of thought identified me as a perpetrator who wore black slacks and treated her brutally, a man whose cruelty often could be diverted if she took the lead and provided fellatio.

The third patient arched her back and pushed her chest forward when I spoke to her. She was firmly convinced that I would only give her really good therapy if I really liked her, and that the only clear proof that I liked her would be my complimenting her sexual prowess on the basis of first-hand experience. She held fast to this conviction for over a year. Interestingly, her husband was her prior therapist.

At times, this sort of "fishing" with milder expressions of weaponized sex points directly toward previously unrecognized or unshared transgressions. After 2 years of treatment, one patient began to slip into a younger adolescent state. She attempted to present herself as confident, sexually inviting, and receptive, but her fearfulness undermined the power of her pretensions. "But if you fucked me, I would never tell anyone. Really! I promise!" Material gradually emerged concerning exploitation by a mental health professional who had treated her during her teens.

Vignette 8

Although dramatic and sustained instances of weaponized sex are encountered infrequently, when they do occur they can present significant management challenges. A small number of patients have disrobed completely or partially. A smaller number have (while clothed or unclothed) masturbated to orgasm while verbalizing sexual invitations, and fewer still have even raped/stimulated themselves with objects despite my efforts to contain these situations. Recently, some younger individuals have sent me erotic "selfies" although most alters had remained oblivious to these "communications." Many such situations initially require psychiatric management and first aid rather than insight-oriented interventions.

The following vignette depicts a chaotic situation lurching toward disaster. Fortunately, it proved workable. The patient is a skilled professional whom I will call Elizabeth. She has had affairs with two and possibly three prior therapists, with several of her professors, and with supervisors both during her training and subsequently. She knows I know some of these individuals.

Prior to the interaction recounted below, Elizabeth had alluded to sexual mistreatment by a family member. She rapidly withdrew her remarks and tried to evade exploring what had transpired. When I renewed my request that we discuss what had happened, things changed rather dramatically. Elizabeth did not switch completely, but other alters surged up near the surface, and/or were copresent.

"Do you fuck all of your patients, Dr. K., or just the ones who make it clear they want you? Don't you think people really have to make love in order toreally know one another?" *(Elizabeth leaned forward.)* I bet I can figure out a better use for that couch. What would you do if I just started to take off my clothes? *(I omit several minutes of subsequent lubricious verbalizations and gestures. Finally, Elizabeth put her hands to the buttons of her blouse.)* What will you do if I start to unbutton my blouse?"

"As I ask you what you are trying to communicate by that kind of gesture, I will be throwing those Afghans over there on top of you, one after another, hoping to help you begin a treatment rather than start up some kind of sexual flying circus. I hope what's happening now will give way to a reasonable conversation."

"And if I don't stop ...."

"When I run out of Afghans, I walk out of the office and will have nothing further to do with you."

"I'm not accustomed to men refusing me. But then maybe you're not a man?"

"The world is full of possibilities. But my working with you while you shed your clothes is not among them."

"Think of what you are missing."

"I'll take your word for it."

"OK, OK. You got around some of us. I had to try to see if there was another way to get the upper hand. You haven't convinced me yet. So what do you think?"

"I'm sorry. What do I think about what?"

"These." *(Elizabeth had her hands under her breasts, and lifted them.)*

"Oh. I think that you are misusing them, trying to turn them into weapons you can point at me to intimidate me. Let me put it this way.... You seem on the one hand to be coming for help, after years of unsuccessful therapy with many therapists, some excellent, some not so excellent, and some ... Who knows? On the other hand, you are very much afraid of the therapy you say you want to receive. You are already serving notice that you haven't quite made up your mind, consciously, unconsciously, and everything in between, that you are ready to address what you need to address. You forced yourself to open a door, slammed it shut, and then you turned your efforts toward disrupting our ability to communicate in, shall we say, a more traditional way?"

"OK. So you're not turned on at all?"

"By what?"

"By all ... you know."

"Elizabeth, what I have seen is a very scared woman trying to reassure herself that she can survive in this office and distract our work from what scares her the most. Whether that's to continue to avoid something you feel can't be faced, or whether you're testing me to see whether you can be safe in here and ultimately reach what you need to reach, I don't know. But someonewho's scared, sad, and using sexuality to 'whistle in the dark' is not conveying a powerful sexual message, at least not to me."

I left unsaid that anyone who would present in such an over-the-top manner must have endured some regrettable experiences to have developed such a coping style. Some therapists who claim patients have seduced them have mistaken dysfunctional action defenses for what they describe, at least in their trials or ethics hearings, as libidinal messages of compelling power.

Vignette 9

I do not pretend to have a complete understanding of a phenomenon I will describe as "weaponized sex in the service of the ego." While it could be argued that all patient activities serve a communicative and potentially therapeutic purpose, here I refer to a conscious, controlled, and quite deliberate effort to place sexual matters before the therapist in the effort to facilitate recovery.

A patient had made incredible advances but persisted in one florid risk-taking behavior. For example, every night at a particular hour she did her hair and make-up to perfection, put on high heels but no other apparel, and paraded back and forth in front of the all-glass wall and sliding glass door of her apartment for over half an hour, visible to many neighbors and passersby. We made little headway addressing this behavior. She became convinced I could never understand the remainder of her problems unless I knew the truth of the experiences she was unable to communicate in words. I expressed confidence in our ability to work through the remainder in standard therapy. For the first time in our work together, she disagreed with me, quite vehemently.

Several weeks later she brought in some pictures she said might explain important concerns. We sat side by side to view and discuss them. The first few simply depicted her apartment with its glass wall and sliding door. As I came to a deeper appreciation of the extent of the risks she was taking and began to express my concern, she rapidly flipped through a series of pictures she had taken of her own body as she had felt forced to reenact what she could not let herself share in words, depicting horrible mistreatments of her breasts, her face and hair smeared with feces, and her mouth full of fecal material and toilet paper. Caught off guard, I could not avoid seeing them.

"This is what you have to help me with. Parading naked by that window was just to draw them in. We were shooting a porn film in the red light district of Amsterdam. But this," she said, pointing to the terrible degrading pictures, "this is what I had to deal with." She vomited over and over into my wastebasket. "Sorry, but this is the only way I could tell you."

Our therapeutic alliance was sufficiently powerful to allow us to move right on through this material. My patient told me that while she had no doubt that her naked body would turn me on, and she acknowledged a degree of concern that I might find her torture and degradation so stimulating that I would want to enact it with her, she trusted our warm regard for one another and my many years of not reacting in a predatory manner to the incredibly provocative and stimulating material she had presented. Our relationship, she said, would allow the situation to be safe, and help her carry out what she had concluded was her only path to recovery.

Would we have been able to access this material without such a radical display? She thought not, I thought we could. After showing me these pictures, her dangerous behaviors ceased immediately, and the remainder of her trauma work was completed rapidly. Perhaps she was the wiser member of the therapeutic dyad, but I can find no ethical way for a therapist to propose the deliberate use of such material. She is nearing the termination of a very successful psychotherapy.

A naturalistic model of weaponized sex

Confronted with numerous instances of an unexpected phenomenon that did not seem to share common dynamic underpinnings, but did seem to be an adaptation that once facilitated survival and minimized rejection and physical brutalization, I searched the literature for information and found little. There were many thoughtful studies that offered overall explanations based on the study of individual cases, but having found dynamic diversity rather than commonality among my "weaponized sex" patients, I found these authors' generalizations from particular cases or presentations in terms of *a priori* theoretical assumptions profoundly unconvincing. Certain models encompassed the dynamics and structures of particular instances quite well, but in my opinion the driven, forceful aggressiveness of many of these severe behaviors eluded satisfactory explanation.

Another literature, however, contained thought-provoking observations. Scientists were studying recently discovered tribes in a certain area of Africa whose members engaged openly in both heterosexual and homosexual behaviors and erotized their young. They resolved virtually all threat and conflict situations by engaging in sexual behaviors. Arguments over food were addressed by joining in erotic practices, and then sharing the edibles in contention. When one tribe encountered another with territory or food at stake, the two sides rushed toward one another, often led by the most dominant females, and engaged in sexual intercourse and other erotized activities with their putative opponents, ending the confrontation.

The conflict resolution and acculturation patterns described above are those of the bonobo (Pan paniscus), the most recently discovered and the most diminutive of the great apes (see Blount, 1990; de Waal, 1988, 1995, 1997; Furuichi, 1989; White, 1996). Bonobos may be described as promiscuous, polymorphous-perverse hominids that engage in missionary position sex, French kissing, oral sex, bisexual activities, and the erotization of their young. They are unusually empathic and supportive to one another, clearly reading and responding to one another's emotional states. They seem to have the rudiments of a conversational language. They can learn to recognize and use computer programs to express over 500 human words (de Waal, 1988). Their females have prolonged estrus cycles and enormous clitorises. Their vulvae become engorged quite rapidly. While the females in other great ape genera come into estrus for rather limited periods of time, bonobo females have much more prolonged periods of sexual activity and receptiveness to sexual approaches. They do not form exclusive dyadic bonds. They affiliate rapidly with new individuals or groups of individuals by engaging in sex. Violence among bonobos in integrated groups is infrequent, relatively mild, and transient. It is rarely sustained sufficiently to result in injury. By human standards, what is normative in the society of bonobo, the so-called "make love, not war" ape, might appear to represent a complex series of sexual deviations and an ongoing attachment disorder.

Bonobo behavioral patterns differ dramatically from those of the other great apes; that is, gorillas, orangutans, and chimpanzees (de Waal, 1995; White, 1996). Chimpanzees (Pan troglodytes), for example, are known for their aggressive and violent behavior and their proclivity to resolve conflicts among either individuals or groups with destructive aggression. Individuals or groups may injure, drive off, or kill opponents. Orangutans are usually relatively solitary due to their enormous feeding demands, occasionally coming together. When adult males encounter one another, aggressive displays, aggression, or avoidance usually occurs. With adult females, aggressive displays, avoidance, or rarely bonding may occur. Sexually, there are two male subtypes. The flanged, or larger variety, has massive jowls and other secondary sexual characteristics females find attractive, and easily finds willing sexual partners. The smaller subtype is less combative with its peers, but usually mates by raping a female. Gorillas live in small groups headed by a dominant male. Some males live solitary lives. The most typical aggressions occur when a solo male tries to defeat a dominant male and take charge of his group of females. When a new male takes over a group, infanticide to bring the females into estrus has been reported.

Some have attempted to debunk the "myth" of bonobo peacefulness, citing instances of bonobo aggression. However, notwithstanding these "mythbusting" efforts, demonstrations of bonobo versus bonobo aggression remain uncommon. They usually are observed among young bonobo males who were not raised in integrated bonobo societies, separated by zookeepers or naturalists from naturalistic bonobo groups, especially from adult females, the powerful bonobo matriarchs. Similar breakdowns occur in other normally nonaggressive species subsequent to the undermining of their customary social structures and hierarchies (i.e., murderous attacks on rhinoceros by young male elephants raised without the influence of mature bulls and dominant females).

The species-wide distribution of this unique manner of conduct suggests it is likely to have a genetic basis. Intact bonobo society normatively makes assertive use of a pattern of sexual practices in a manner unique to their species to address and resolve many of the conflict areas for which sexually traumatized human DID patients deploy weaponized sex/instrumental pseudo-erotic behaviors.

This raises an intriguing if highly speculative line of thought: Might it be instructive to consider the possibility that what is normally genetically determined in the bonobo might develop in the wake of epigenetic changes in the traumatized human organism?

Both bonobos and traumatized humans who deploy such sexual strategies eschew violence. Sexual behaviors serve to establish, strengthen, and maintain connections. They enable individuals to both assert themselves and exert damage control. In both instances, sex both replaces and deflects destructive aggression. In the case of bonobo society, this strategy is effective and promotes the safety of individuals and the well-being of the species. However useful during horrific human childhoods, it is dubious that the deployment of these strategies by adult human females is either effective or useful to promote the safety of individuals and the well-being of the species.

From the normal bonobo to weaponized sex/instrumental pseudo-erotic behaviors: Stepping stones toward a testable hypothesis

Epigenetics concern potentially heritable changes in gene expression that do not involve changes to underlying DNA sequences. Therefore, such changes may create a change in phenotype without involving a change to the genotype. Epigenetic changes may occur naturalistically, but can also result from aging, disease, environmental factors, and changes in lifestyle. Implicit in these bland terms is the impact of trauma. Several processes have been identified that initiate and/or support such changes. When we are changed by factors in our lives, epigenetic changes underlie our transitions to new adaptations, for better or for worse.

Years ago, Ernest Rossi (1986, 1993, 2002) explored the likelihood that many physical and psychological problems might result from epigenetic changes, and hypothesized that treatments that succeeded in affecting them might have to exert their impact on a similar level. He sensitized the field of hypnosis to such considerations and is regarded as a brilliant pioneer by hard science geneticists (e.g., Muenke, 2015).

Compelling evidence that epigenetic change can affect massive alterations in the types of phenomena considered crucial by developmentalists and traumatologists is available in the work of Michael Meaney and his colleagues (e.g., McGowan & Szyf, 2010; Meaney, 2001; Meaney & Szyf, 2005; Weaver et al., 2004, 2005). They have demonstrated that exogenous stressors may inactivate dominant genetically programmed maternal behaviors and/or activate elements that drive behavior in very different directions. Genetic lines have been developed that enhance and minimize nurturing behaviors of mothers rats. The enhanced positive maternal behaviors of genetically high nurturing female rats can be inactivated by the application of exogenous stress, and replaced by a pattern of less nurturing behaviors that had been "bred out" of expression in the more nurturing genetic line. Further, such trauma-altered expressions will manifest themselves in the traumatized rats' female offspring, their genetic loading not withstanding. They will be less nurturing as mature mother rats. However, if they are raised by a nurturing surrogate mother rat, their genetically driven high nurturing behavior patterns are reactivated. If litters of rat pups from the two genetically divergent strains are divided, and equal numbers of genetically high nurturing rats and low nurturing rats are combined into two mixed litters, a high nurturing rat mother will raise a mixed litter in which all of the female pups, notwithstanding their genetic heritage, will mother their own pups in a highly nurturing manner. Conversely, the female pups in the mixed litter raised by the low nurturing mother rat will demonstrate low nurturing behavior.

If trauma can inactivate normative attachment patterns and allow the emergence of less desirable alternatives, could it facilitate the emergence and elaboration of the strategies I have described as weaponized sex? Ritualized submissive gestures are not uncommon within the animal kingdom. They often include the submissive/defeated animals allowing itself to be mounted by the dominant/victor animal (Sagan & Druyan, 1992). Could the complex pattern of dysfunctional pseudo-erotic relatedness reflect the activation or disinhibition of usually suppressed/inactivated genetically driven or facilitated strategies, including those of related to submission and affiliation?

Further, could the allostatic load of traumatization overwhelm the body/brain/mind's capacity to remain stable by changing adaptively (McEwen, 2000; McEwen & Steller, 1983), resulting in ongoing toxic genetic–environmental interactions that lead to breakdown and dysfunctional changes along the lines proposed by Meaney, McEwen, and their colleagues? Research in such areas invariably would veer toward complexity theory in that (1) it involves many interacting factors and systems; (2) the dynamics of importance may have subtle cause and effect connections that do not necessarily remain constant; and (3) the degree and nature of the relationships between/among various components are imperfectly known. Consequently, overall outcomes/behaviors are difficult to predict even when components are well known. Small changes in input or parameters may result in large changes of behavior (developed from P. Ferreira, October, 2001).

Such perspectives might help us understand how a psychodynamically diverse population exhibits a range of behaviors that have much in common, raising the possibility that diverse triggers may activate a common and often refractory epigenetically altered behavioral pathway.

While work like Meaney's cannot be replicated with human subjects, man's inhumanity to man at times provides a crude albeit unsettling laboratory. Yehuda's work (Yehuda & Bierer, 2009; Yehuda et al., 2013, 2014) has demonstrated trangenerational epigenetic changes in the families of Holocaust victims. The prospects for inducing epigenetic change via therapy are being explored in a pilot study of cancer patients by Munoz (2015), whose work appears to demonstrate that targeted hypnosis can alter the expression of certain genes.

The possibility of researching genetic and epigenetic apsects of instrumental pseudo-erotic behaviors may not be far over the horizon. The genomes of humans, bonobos, and chimpanzees have been mapped and compared (Prüfer et al., 2012). The gene loci associated with bonobo affiliative behavior have been identified (Staes et al., 2014), and the higher presence of the Dup-Beta allele and certain other features in a critical area appears to be related to the differential affiliative patterns among bonobo, chimpanzees, and humans. Not surprisingly, oxytocin metabolism is involved. Further exploration and comparison of relevant genomic sequences, their operation, inactivation, and modification may yield useful insights.

On the treatment of weaponized sex phenomena

My treatment of patients with instrumental pseudo-erotic behavior makes use of the full array of therapeutic approaches and techniques. Here I mention only what may not appear in more standard discussions of the treatment of traumatized and dissociative patients.

The most important emphasis of my own clinical work with instrumental pseudo-erotic behaviors or weaponized sex, whether in my practice or in consulting to others, is the cultivation of an unabashed alertness to and vigorous pursuit of the meaning of the patient's communications in profound detail, including both physical metacommunications and reported sensory experiences. Tracking such details facilitates my ability to anticipate of the emergence of problematic sexualized behaviors. Pressing for detail that is not immediately apparent facilitates effective trauma processing (Kluft, 2013). Applying approaches analogous to the symptom context method (Luborsky & Auerbach, 1969; Luborsky & Mintz, 1974; Luborsky & Mintz, 1974) and Core Conflictual Relationship Theme (CCRT) analysis (Luborsky & Crits-Cristoph, 1990) often allows me to see such problems developing *in statu nascendi* and prevent/interrupt alloplastic difficulties.

Shortly after writing the above words, I saw relatively new DID patient with a pattern of withdrawal followed by outrageous and usually disremembered behaviors around men. The previous week she had retreated into a corner, curled up, and went silent except for inaudible muttering. I learned that during the half hour it took to break through to her she had been fighting off urges and instructions to take off her clothes. Within moments, she denied this admission. I added her mentioning, glancing at, or moving toward the corner to the list of indicators I tracked.

In the next session, the day I was writing, she started from her seat toward the corner. "Before you go any further," I said, "I wonder if I could talk to the one who will probably try to get you all to take off your clothes once you get to that corner." The patient stopped, switched, and started to dance suggestively, her hands moving to the buttons of her top.

> "Mommy says my big breasts are what all the men like. Wanna see them?"
>
> "Your mommy taught you to dance like this?" *(I replied.)* "Was she a good dancer?"
>
> "Better than me."
>
> "I want to know more about how and why your mother taught you to dance like this."
>
> "She said men would like it."
>
> At this point it was clear that her aggressive sexuality, a pervasive and self-destructive force throughout her life, was largely driven by a young alter groomed for exploitation. "Did your mommy teach you about …" I asked about normal childhood games and activities. She shook her head "No."
>
> "Was it hard for you to play with the other kids?" She became tearful, returned to her seat, and wept several minutes before discussing crucial material.

Tracking of several indicators and intrusive inquiries allowed me to interdict a pattern of behavior that had played a role in her sexual engagements with at least two previous mental health professionals, and speak to her underlying pain. While the devil may be in the details, often the best therapeutic interventions reside there as well.

Consistent with the above, the second approach I find useful is to build my understanding of a patient up from what the patient brings rather than down from what abstract theory might predict. As useful as theory may be, assuming it is applicable for any individual case risks inflicting an indignity upon the uniqueness of the individual, overlooks the importance of subjectivity, and invites stereotypic misunderstandings (e.g., Kluft, 2016).

The third method, foreshadowed in the anecdote above, is to interrupt with dialog and diversion whatever appears to be headed toward a problematic sexual display (see fifth technique also). I have found it productive to say, "So, as you rush to make things sexual, you deprive yourself the opportunity to be understood as a person, and you deprive me of encountering who you truly are, rather than confronting me with just one of the ways you can be. How about letting me get to know the human being you really are before deciding to try to push things further?" The follow-up can be challenging, and require many exchanges, but usually prevents escalation, even in midstream; for example, "I'm going to give you this Afghan. Cover yourself up, and let's continue to discuss why you think having sex right now is such a good idea." Expect a battle, but expect to win it.

Fourth, I avoid voicing shock, value judgments, and condemnations, preferring inclusionism in their place; for example, "Wait a minute. This sex stuff is designed to protect you or some of you from something. Protecting you all is my job, too. Whether you realize it or not, we're on the same side. Stop and think for a minute. A few weeks or months from now, we're going to have a good laugh about the misunderstandings that are pushing you to act today."

Fifth, notwithstanding the incredibly complicated implications and innumerable pitfalls inherent in what am about to say, I follow the lead of Lenore Terr (1992), who observed that persistent traumatic play does not lead to mastery, and must be interrupted. Accordingly, there are many Afghans in my office. If a patient will not desist, I enfold the patient in one or more Afghans, and contain them as best I can, much as I would a child in a refractory tantrum. As I do so, I speak calmly and supportively, explaining my best understanding of why what is happening is happening.

Sixth, in the event such behavior comes as a complete surprise to me and I am either stunned, outmaneuvered, or conclude I am either incapable of or unwilling to physically intervene, I regard it as a learning experience rather than a defeat. My most challenging encounter involved a patient exploited by several medical and mental health professionals who, when I declined her advances, pulled down her underwear, and masturbated with both hands, coating them with vaginal fluids before she reached out to me. I sat immobilized and utterly flabbergasted. The second time this pattern began I was prepared, throwing Afghans over her body as I rushed to contain her at its inception. After some 20 minutes of physical containment, the patient finally could be reoriented, but had no recollection of what transpired. She asked me why her pants were down! I planted the hypnotic suggestion that hereafter, no matter what, at a given signal, all alters would hear me. On the third occasion, as I contained her, I gave that signal, and began a sportscaster's description of what was transpiring. Other alters took over, and that behavioral pattern has not recurred subsequently.

Seventh, I am very cautious about using humor in addressing these situations, and will not unless I am sure that the patient and I have both a relationship that can tolerate humor and a sufficiently shared sense of what is funny to allow me to proceed. I respect Kubie's (1971) caution that all humor may convey latent hostility, and conceivably may prove hurtful to the patient. It is best to appreciate that the overall patient is likely to be very upset and mortified about this aspect of her behavior even if some parts pursue it with apparent gusto, and to proceed with the utmost sensitivity and respect. When in doubt, compassionate efforts to avoid humiliation should trump the most apposite wit.

Eighth, beware lest compassion and empathy without interdiction in word and/or deed be misread as or distorted into implicit encouragement. Keep in mind that such behavior has been understood to promote both survival and safety. The patient may believe that the therapist's efforts to discourage it is a test, and that she dare not be distracted from her efforts lest she incur terrible punishment.

The above has been helpful to me. Hopefully, the future will bring the prospects of new and more effective understandings and interventions.

Discussion

Weaponized sex/instrumental pseudo-erotic behavior involves the suggestion of, the attempt to initiate, and/or enactment of sexual behaviors in the service of coping, safety, propitiation, and survival, often serving as a substitute for assertiveness, establishing one's strength, and/or aggression. Such actions are consistent with an attack other shame script for defense against and/or undoing humiliation (Nathanson, 1992). Weaponized sex differs from similar actions within the scope of normal bonobo coping in that erotic gratification is often nominal at best and that erotic stimulation/arousal conveys very different communications. The occurrence of erotic arousal or even orgasm, although part of some patients' scenarios, is incidental and not necessarily relevant to the underlying dynamics of whatever actions are taking place. In some, however, the patients may follow the pattern described by Middleton (2013, 2017), in which blurring of the boundaries of self between a father–daughter incest dyad cause the daughter to believe that her orgasmic capacity belongs to and is controlled by her father.

Weaponized sex so defined refers to a compulsive, driven, characterologic style over which the enactor experiences less than complete control of her actions, and sometimes becomes a horrified, mortified, or defensively enthusiastic witness of unwanted events as they unfold. Unless interrupted, they often take on a quality of progressive automaticity. A woman suffering an extreme expression of these phenomena had to be physically restrained from her efforts to sexualize our relationship. She had lived a very promiscuous life, but had never experienced voluntary involvement with a sexual partner of her own choosing.

This type of characterologically, compulsively, reenactment, and defensively driven aggressive sexuality has little if anything to do with sexual aggressiveness deliberately deployed in a strategy designed to achieve a chosen goal, to cope with a unique extreme situation, or to pursue the gratification of a strong sexual drive or a sexual perversion. One woman in my practice told me that she was unconflicted about and very confident in her ability to seduce any man if she wanted to or felt she had to, "but you'll have to take my word for it. I'm here for therapy." She demonstrated no aggressively seductive behaviors during her successful treatment. Another found herself in a situation in which she was absolutely sure she was about to be raped by an aggressive man, and turned the tables on him. She was confident that doing this interrupted the full expression of the brutal approaches the man had begun. She understood her efforts to be deliberate, in the service of damage control. While both of these examples describe instrumental uses of sexual aggression, neither has the cardinal qualities of weaponized sex as defined above.

While therapists rarely have difficulty in appreciating how a sexually traumatized individual might be motivated to avoid sexual stimulation and sexual encounters, the enactment of sexually chaotic/problematic behavior by such a person is often more troublesome to manage and treat within the transference/countertransference matrix of the therapeutic dyad.

The observations and ideas communicated here have informed approaches that many of my patients believe have facilitated their treatment, abolished intolerable elements of shame that had proven refractory, and helped them to distinguish between sexuality as a normal aspect of human life and the use of dysfunctional sexualized aggression and sexualized defenses against mistreatment that had confused their understanding of their sexuality and disrupted their capacity for the types of intimacy that involve sexual relatedness.

Therapists who work with DID patients often are both impressed and exasperated by the persistence of dysfunctional sexual behavior patterns despite prolonged and energetic treatment efforts. Herein may reside a major value of bearing the bonobo model and possible epigenetic etiology in mind. Appreciating these phenomena as a driven and desperate problem resolution strategy offers intriguing insights into why the potential to generate behaviors appearing at first glance so repugnant, shaming, and dysfunctional may persist within our recessive/inactivated heritage of biological/psychological survival strategies.

What we as therapists see as revictimization and severe dysfunction is sometimes seen as such by our patients, but often is perceived as the contrary, at least by some alters. Many dissociative disorder patients and other traumatized individuals find security, strength, and reassurance in the power of their sexual behaviors (even when this acknowledgment is restricted to some rather than all alters in complex chronic dissociative disorders).

"It was something that gave me power." "It was the only way I could control/protect/etc." "That was how I knew loved me." "I could always get him to prove that he loved me." "That was the only way I could stop him from hurting me/my sisters/my mother." "It was the one thing I knew I could do well, that got me praise, that got me fed, etc." All of these verbalizations might be described as assertions of triumphant submission. The patients who voiced them genuinely believed (in some or all alters when dissociative) that their sexuality was the most powerful weapon at their disposal in the horrific worlds of their childhoods. And those who gave voice to these expressions were often genuinely puzzled over why, as adults, these strategies backfired as often as they succeeded, and why when they succeeded, the success was transient or brought undue and unwanted complexity into their lives.

To the enacting person or parts, weaponized sex has long appeared to be a win-win situation, achieve desirable goals in the moment, and often rewarded by some sense that their partner is pleased as well. Both parties to such an encounter emerge with a split perception of mastery; each believes he or she is victorious, that he or she has defeated or contained and gotten what he or she wants from the other.

On one level, appreciating that these often refractory patterns may have a hard-wired component due to the interaction of genetics and environmental pressures (which exert a powerful force that may not be blunted until treatment has advanced far enough to affect such processes) offers the therapist a way to approach these problems less judgmentally and with greater patience and compassion. Further, it allows the therapist to wonder whether the explanations being expressed by the patient are ex post facto rationalizations for what they find themselves doing. All too often adult rationales are offered for behaviors documented since childhood.

All in all, these behaviors invite us to pose a fascinating question—Is the refractory and difficult to disable repetition compulsion an epigenetic phenomenon in whole or in part?

Such a powerful albeit rather illusory arsenal is unlikely to be abandoned willingly until therapy has provided the patient with the strength and assertiveness to use other strategies effectively. As such, weaponized sex as an overall strategy is not an easy target to address early in the course of the therapy. Vigorous attempts by the therapist to do so run the risk of initiating a hurtful and blaming sadomasochistic dynamic between therapist and patient. In my experience, gentle exploration aimed at clarifying the patient's subjective experience and perceived understanding and motivation is more helpful in paving the way for later change.

Although weaponized sex may emerge quite rapidly in some therapist patient dyads and enter the treatment in short order, it may remain unknown and/or intractable and/or inaccessible to therapeutic intervention until it becomes expressed in the transference in a manner that the patient can both appreciate and explore without undue disruption, and until treatment has begun the process of altering brain function, and possibly epigenetic pathways, in a salubrious manner.

The concept of "weaponized sex" is not advanced as an novel, heroic, and/or complete approach to understanding some aspects of the dysfunctional patterns of DID patients and other related forms of dissociative disorder. It is not meant to replace or displace other models of understanding. It is put forward as a biopsychosocial hypothesis that nests more comfortably with complexity theory than with more familiar linear "this is what causes that" models of thinking. However, to the extent that it contributes to a more nuanced approach to behavior that if approached simplistically may lead to a patient's experiencing heart-rending guilt and shame in psychotherapy as well as in life, to blunting unfortunate countertransference reactions and therapist participation in the enactment of misadventures, to helping therapists reduce patients' vulnerability to either episodic or apparently unending cycles of retraumatization, and to suggest some therapeutic approaches that might otherwise not be considered in improving such patients' quality of life, it may make a modest useful contribution. To the extent that it reminds us that the best of our theories and models are incomplete, and may obscure our vision in some ways even as they sharpen it in others, it may offer a mild disincentive to intellectual hubris.

Acknowledgments

My thanks to Maximillian Muencke, M.D., Chief and Senior Investigator of the Medical Genetics Branch of the National Institute of Mental Health, for his insightful comments on several crucial issues. My thanks to Sophia Miryam Schüssler-Fiorenza Rose, M.D., Ph.D., Research Fellow at the Spinal Cord Injury Service, Veterans Affairs Palo Alto Health Care Center, for her clarifications of complexity theory and the concept of allostatic load.

References

Blount, B. (1990). Issues in bonobo (*Pan paniscus*) sexual behavior. *American Anthropologist, 92* (3), 702–714. doi:10.1525/aa.1990.92.issue-3

Brenner, I. (1996). On trauma, perversion, and "Multiple Personality." *Journal of the American Psychoanalytic Association, 44*, 784–814.

Celenza, A. (2007). *Sexual boundary violations*. Lanham, MD: Aronson.

de Waal, F. (1988). The communicative repertoire of captive bonobos (*Pan paniscus*) compared to that of chimpanzees. *Behaviour, 106*, 183–251. doi:10.1163/156853988X00269

de Waal, F. (1995). Bonobo sex and society. *Scientific American, 272*, 82–88. doi:10.1038/scientificamerican0395-82

de Waal, F. (1997). *Bonobo: The forgotten ape*. Berkeley, CA: University of California Press.

Ferreira, P. (2001, October). *Tracing complexity theory*. Presentation in ESD.83, Research Seminar in Engineering Theory, at Massachusetts Institute of Technology, Cambridge, MA. Downloaded from the Internet July 31, 2015.

Furuichi, T. (1989). Social interactions and the life history of female *Pan paniscus* in Wamba, Zaire. *International Journal of Primatology, 10*, 855–875. doi:10.1007/BF02735199

Gabbard, G. (1995). *Love and hate in the analytic relationship*. Northvale, NJ: Jason Aronson.

Gabbard, G., & Lester, E. (1995). *Boundaries and boundary violations in psychoanalysis*. New York, NY: Basic Books.

Gartrell, N., Herman, J., Olarte, S., Feldstein, M., & Localio, R. (1987). Reporting practices of psychiatrists who knew of sexual misconduct by colleagues. *American Journal of Orthopsychiatry, 57*, 287–295. doi:10.1111/j.1939-0025.1987.tb03539.x

Herman, J. (1981). *Father-daughter incest*. Cambridge, MA: Harvard University Press.

Jobim, A., de Moraes, V., & Gimbel, N. (1964). The girl from Ipanema. In Creed Taylor (Producer), *Getz/Gilberto*. New York, NY: Verve Records.

Kluft, R. (1987). The parental fitness of mothers with multiple personality disorder. *Child Abuse and Neglect, 11*, 273–280. doi:10.1016/0145-2134(87)90067-6

Kluft, R. (1989). Treating the patient who has been sexually exploited by a previous psychotherapist. *Psychiatric Clinics of North America, 12*, 483–500.

Kluft, R. (2013). *Shelter from the storm*. North Charleston, SC: Kindle Independent Publishing Platform.

Kluft, R. (2016). You have to be carefully taught: Dignity considerations in clinical practice, scholarship, and trauma treatment. In S. Levine (Ed.), *Dignity matters: Psychoanalytic and psychosocial perspectives* (pp. 141–158). London, UK: Karnac Books.

Kluft, R. P. (1990). On the apparent invisibility of incest: A personal reflection on things known and forgotten. In R. P. Kluft (Ed.), *Incest-related syndromes of adult psychopathology* (pp. 11–34). Washington, DC: American Psychiatric Press.

Kohut, H. (1971). *The analysis of the self.* Chicago, IL: University of Chicago Press.

Kohut, H. (1977). *The restoration of the self.* Chicago, IL: University of Chicago Press.

Kubie, L. (1971). The destructive potential of humor in psychotherapy. *American Journal of Psychiatry, 127*, 861–866. doi:10.1176/ajp.127.7.861

Luborsky, L., & Auerbach, A. (1969). The symptom-context method – Quantitative studies of symptom formation in psychotherapy. *Journal of the American Psychoanalytic Association, 17*, 68–99. doi:10.1177/000306516901700106

Luborsky, L., & Crits-Cristoph, P. (1990). *Understanding transference: The core conflictual relationship theme method.* New York, NY: Basic Books.

Luborsky, L., & Mintz, J. (1974). What sets off momentary forgetting during a psychoanalysis? Investigation of symptom-onset conditions. *Psychoanalysis and Contemporary Science, 3*, 233–268.

McEwen, B. (2000). Allostasis and allostatic load implications for neuropsychopharmacology. *Neuropsychopharmacology, 22* (2), 108–124. doi:10.1016/S0893-133X(99)00129-3

McEwen, B., & Steller, E. (1983). Stress and the individual: Mechanisms leading to disease. *Archives of Internal Medicine, 153*, 2093–2101. doi:10.1001/archinte.1993.00410180039004

McGowan, P. O., & Szyf, M. (2010). The epigenetics of social adversity in early life: Implications for mental health outcomes. *Neurobiology of Disease, 39*(1), 66–72.

Meaney, M. (2001). Maternal care, gene expression, and the transmission of individual differences in stress reactivity across generations. *Annual Review of Neuroscience, 24*, 1161–1192. doi:10.1146/annurev.neuro.24.1.1161

Meaney, M., & Szyf, M. (2005). Environmental programming of stress responses through DNA methylation: Life at the interface between a dynamic environment and a fixed genome. *Dialogues in Clinical Neuroscience, 7* (2), 103–123.

Middleton, W. (2013). Ongoing incestuous abuse during adulthood. *Journal of Trauma & Dissociation, 14* (3), 251–272. doi:10.1080/15299732.2012.736932

Middleton, W. (2017). Extreme adaptations in extreme and chronic circumstances: The application of "Weaponized Sex" to those exposed to ongoing incestuous abuse. *Journal of Trauma and Dissociation, 18* (3).

Muencke, M. (2015, October). *The genetic basis of hypnotizability.* Lecture presented at Annual Meeting of the Society for Clinical and Experimental Hypnosis, Orlando, FL.

Munoz, F. (2015, October). *Mind-body epigenetic technique's (MET) potential to modulate Arc and Zif-268 gene expression in breast cancer patients.* Poster presented at the Annual Meeting of the Society for Clinical and Experimental Hypnosis, Orlando, FL.

Nathanson, D. (1992). *Shame and pride.* New York, NY: Norton.

Pope, K., & Bouhoutsos, J. (1986). *Sexual intimacy between therapists and patients.* New York, NY: Praeger.

Prüfer, K., Munch, K., Hellmann, I., Akagi, K., Miller, J., Walenz, B., … Paåbo, S. (2012). The bonobo genome compared with the chimpanzee and human genomes. *Nature, 486*, 527–530.

Rossi, E. (1986). *The psychobiology of mind-body healing.* New York, NY: Norton.

Rossi, E. (1993). *The psychobiology of mind-body healing: New concepts of therapeutic hypnosis, revised edition.* New York, NY: Norton.

Rossi, E. (2002). *The psychobiology of gene expression: Neuroscience and neurogenesis in hypnosis and the healing arts.* New York, NY: Norton.

Sagan, C., & Druyan, A. (1992). *Shadows of forgotten ancestors*. New York, NY: Ballantine Books.

Schrieber, F. (1973). *Sybil*. New York, NY: Henry Regnery.

Staes, N., Stevens, J., Helsen, P., Hillyer, M., Korody, M., & Ens, M. (2014). Oxytocin and vasopressin receptor gene variation as a proximate base for inter- and intraspecific behavioral differences in bonobos and chimpanzees. *PLoS One*, *9* (11), e113364. doi:10.1371/journal.pone.0113364

Stoller, R. (1973). *Splitting: A case of female masculinity*. San Antonio, TX: Quadrangle.

Terr, L. (1992). *Too scared to cry*. New York, NY: Basic Books.

Weaver, I., Cervoni, N., Champagne, F., D'Alessio, A., Sharma, S., Seckl, J., … Meaney, M. (2004). Epigenetic programming by maternal behavior. *Nature Neuroscience*, *7*, 847–854. doi:10.1038/nn1276

Weaver, I., Champagne, F., Brown, S., Dymov, S., Sharma, S., Meaney, M., & Szyf, M. (2005). Reversal of maternal programming of stress responses in adult offspring through methyl supplementation: Altering epigenetic marking later in life. *Journal of Neuroscience*, *25*, 11045–11054. doi:10.1523/JNEUROSCI.3652-05.2005

White, F. (1996). Comparative socio-ecology of *Pan paniscus*. In W. C. McGrew, L. F. Marchant, & T. Nishida (Eds.), *Great ape societies*. Cambridge, England: Cambridge University Press.

Yehuda, R., & Bierer, L. (2009). The relevance of epigenetics to PTSD: Implications for DSM-5. *Journal of Traumatic Stress*, *22*, 427–434. doi:10.1002/jts.20448

Yehuda, R., Daskalakis, N., Desarnaud, F., Makotkine, I., Lehrner, A., Koch, E., … Bierer, L. (2013). Epigenetic biomarkers as predictors and correlates of symptom improvement following psychotherapy in combat veterans with PTSD. *Frontiers of Psychiatry*, *4*, 118. doi:10.3389/fpsyt.2013.00118

Yehuda, R., Daskalakis, N., Lehrner, A., Desarnaud, F., Bader, H., Makotkine, I., … Meaney, M. (2014). Influences of maternal and paternal PTSD on epigenetic regulation of the glucocorticoid receptor gene in Holocaust survivor offspring. *American Journal of Psychiatry*, *171*, 872–880. doi:10.1176/appi.ajp.2014.13121571

Extreme adaptations in extreme and chronic circumstances: The application of "weaponized sex" to those exposed to ongoing incestuous abuse

Warwick Middleton, MB, BS, FRANZCP, MD

ABSTRACT

This paper examines Kluft's construct of "weaponized sex" through the prism of long-term clinical and research involvement with individuals subjected to ongoing sexual abuse during adulthood, a group that by definition has been exposed to more sexual abuse and for longer than any other defined victim population. Examples of the same sort of phenomena described by Kluft are repeatedly observed in therapy with members of this population, but usually not in a dramatic form. As might be anticipated, in order to survive, when an individual is closely attached to a long-term and extreme abuser, the sort of enduring ambivalence carried by the victim towards their primary abuser is manifested in compartmentalized states that wish their abuser dead, while other states in equally compartmentalized ways maintain the attachment via the use of sex—by continuing to be sexually involved with their primary abuser (usually their father), by fantasizing about sex with their abuser, by being sexually involved with those who co-abused with their father, or by staging reenactments with individuals whose sexual behavior re-evokes the abuse by the absent (or deceased) father. The process of healing means that inevitably some manifestations of the responses to such abuse spill over into therapy.

Introduction

As I was finalizing the draft of this paper, an individual, one of ten women examined in my paper, "Ongoing incestuous abuse during adulthood" (Middleton, 2013b), sent me a link to a new press report titled, "Parents' 'sickening' sexual and psychological abuse of daughter," an account by journalist Janet Fife-Yeomans, which appeared in The Daily Telegraph, October 27, 2016. My patient stated, "I found this story this morning… Shockingly, this would have to be the closest thing I've read to my own childhood situation, wouldn't you agree?" The Fife-Yeomans article starts,

"A YOUNG girl was repeatedly tied up and locked in the garden shed or a plastic box in the garage and abused by her parents in what police have described as one of the most sickening cases they have seen.

The father and mother are today due to be sentenced in the District Court in Sydney after being convicted over the years of sexual and psychological abuse which began when the girl was only five and ended when she was 18.

The couple were both highly regarded professionals but cannot be named because it would identify their daughter who had been a promising athlete. The girl would spend up to 3 days tied up and restrained by barbed wire in the former chook shed and the sexual abuse meted out by her father has left her genital area "abnormal", the court was told.

He also forced her to bend double to fit into the box where he kept his diving gear in the garage and locked her in. Her mother told her that he 'always tries to be a good father'. She was also sexually assaulting the girl who was the youngest daughter in the family.

Meanwhile her father told her: 'I can do what I want to you. I own you. I'll make you suffer. I'll leave you tied up in the shed and let you rot.'

The father was convicted earlier this year by a jury, of 73 child sex offences and the mother, of 13 counts including indecent assault after a 12-week trial. After the girl went to police in 2012, detectives found the words she had scratched into the wood framework of the shed with a nail at the age of 11: 'trapped', 'Dad' and 'mum is coming'."

The young woman's 59-year-old father was given a 48 year jail term, while her 51-year-old mother received a 16 year sentence. The presiding judge said that the parents had "hoodwinked" the community around the family and that their victim now suffered with posttraumatic stress disorder and dissociative identity disorder (Carter, 2016).

Kluft's paper, "Weaponized Sex: Pseudo-Erotic Aggression in the Service of Safety" (Kluft, 2017), is a timely and important paper for multiple reasons, and I thought that I would offer an exploration and extension of its key points. This perspective is formed through the lens of a clinician who has made a particular focus of research, the dynamics, and phenomenology of those subjected to ongoing incestuous abuse that extends into adulthood. It is very apparent that there are far more individuals subjected to this form of extreme abuse than have been apparent from the sparse scientific literature that had even acknowledged their existence. In one sense, this group represents the fullest expression of a complex trauma syndrome that incorporates dissociative identity disorder (DID). As such, they have had to make the most extreme of adjustments to survive in a world where the extent of their sexual (and other) abuse is on average greater than that seen with more generally defined populations of individuals with DID. It is apparent that to be even still be alive and to have not died by suicide or been murdered, surviving that adults subjected to this form of unending abuse have had to make multiple adjustments and to have compartmentalized certain aspects of behavior and experience associated with sexuality to an extreme degree.

Having becomes aware of the existence of this subgroup of individuals with DID whose incestuous abuse extended into adulthood, early research on this population indicated that they may represent something in the order of around one in eight of the DID population (Middleton & Butler, 1998). The global interest in the Josef Fritzl case, which came to light in 2008, saw many broadly similar cases of ongoing incest during adulthood being reported by the popular press around the world. These press reports, congruent with the recent one authored by Fife-Yeomans (2016), became the basis for unassailably establishing the widespread nature of this form of abuse as well as outlining common characteristics (Middleton, 2013a). Such reports, verified by court rulings and police statements, formed the foundation for reporting a clinical series (Middleton, 2013b). This series focused in a detailed manner on ten such individuals. It demonstrated that what is commonly reported in press accounts about such abuse is very congruent with what is found clinically. Historical or recent accounts of extreme abuse in this spectrum have continued to surface and to be referred to in an ongoing series of publications (Middleton, 2011, 2013a, 2013b, 2013c, 2013d; Middleton, 2014a, 2014b; Middleton, 2015a, 2015b). Books written by, or about, the survivors of such abuse have become mainstream and prominent (e.g., the account written by Katherine & Smethurst, 2015). Katherine X who was abused for 30 years and had four children to her father paints a typical picture in describing unrelenting abuse incorporating violence and repeated death threats: "Any sense of self I had was gone and I was completely under my father's control. He behaved like a tribal leader, the chief who lorded it over the slaves" (Katherine & Smethurst, 2015, p. 127). Katherine recounted, "If his drinking mates were around he'd parade me in front of them and tell them I was his 'little slut' (p. 95)."

Background

By way of orienting the reader, in respect to the 10 women reported on in the published clinical series (Middleton, 2013b), all had been sexually abused by their fathers and also sexually abused by many others. The majority (80%) reported having been sexually abused by one or more grandparents. Forty percent reported being sexually abused by a sibling and 60% by an uncle. The mean age at which sexual abuse was recalled as commencing was 2.7 years, with progression to full intercourse by 3.8 years. The incestuous abuse on average went on for 31 years. The mean estimated number of sexual abuse episodes was 3,320, a figure which approximated the estimated number of abuse episodes to which Elisabeth Fritzl was subjected. The great majority reported some version of multi-generational/extended family sexual abuse. All ten women were serially sexually abused in organized groups closely linked with their father. Such groups included family members, church colleagues/fellow cult members, work colleagues, pedophile networks, or commercial prostitution with the father in the role of pimp.

There is a general tendency in human affairs to seek out individuals who share similar interests or proclivities and inevitably associations form. With sufficient numbers and individuals with ambition, such associations take on the structures of institutions. All institutions bring with them hierarchical structures and pathways for individuals to build influence. Such power is always accompanied by the potential for it to be used to abuse and exploit others. Many such individuals in positions of power manufacture a display of empathy for others, while in fact they have none. The only restraint that they show in acting out their sexual proclivities is one dictated by self-interest in response to potentially being publicly exposed. They utilize the traditions and power structures of institutions (including one called "the family") to intimidate their victims and to make it apparently obvious that even if they wished to, there is no way that, they have any significant chance of being believed, or having their allegations acted upon (Middleton, 2015b).

Such individuals found that manipulation of an abused daughter's sexual arousal assists in conditioning an enduring (sexualized) attachment, while the induction of fear and shame can be very effectively used in achieving compliance and silence. Their victims have high indices of self-harm and suicidality and are initially at least, at high risk of placing themselves in dangerous reenactment scenarios.

Such female victims experience being "fused" to their father, and they generally did not feel that they owned their own body. Their mother was generally reported as being an active participant in the sexual abuse or at the very least as failing to provide protection for their daughter. Accompanying a propensity to use or threaten violence to their daughters, these women's fathers were or usually had been, stably married, productively employed, and financially comfortable, while half were closely involved with a church. Suicide and murder were reported within first or second-degree relatives of these women at a high rate.

Ongoing incestuous abuse during adulthood is predicated on a dynamic where both parental figures are sexually abusing children in their care or that at least, the primary abuser is passively supported by the other parental figure who never takes effective initiatives to protect her (or sometimes his) child/children. While mothers repeatedly adamantly deny that abuse has been and is occurring, one virtually never encounters a victim of such abuse by the father/step-father where the mother did not on occasions visualize the sexual abuse, while more usually she on occasions played a role as a co-abuser, and in a minority played the leading role as a sexual abuser of her child/children. A victim of this variant of ongoing incestuous abuse described her particular defensive adaptation: "We can manipulate [Mother] so she feels sorry for us [and therefore less violent]. We know how to… survive. You make sure you don't feel anything."

The cases I have seen clinically resemble closely those proven cases internationally featured in many news and court reports (Middleton, 2014a). Many referred individuals carried documented internal injuries and external scars related to their abuse (as with the case described by Fife-Yeomans). For some, the injuries are extreme. A number have in their possession, photographs indicating past and ongoing abuse. Some have accessible close relatives who corroborate details of the abuse, while the majority have been, or remain, associated with police investigations involving prominent abusers. On occasions substantial corroboration of abuse is obtained where one has the opportunity to interview siblings, children, or spouses (e.g., in respect to one individual, her sister had been similarly abused, as had all her children).

A particular woman subjected to ongoing incestuous abuse during adulthood and who had the largest number of dissociative identity states, and the most complex alter system was congruently the one who had been subjected to the greatest estimated number of sexual abuse episodes. Somewhat against the odds, "Betty" as I will call her, approached stable integration twenty-two and a half years after she was first diagnosed. At that time, she was a married woman with three children and she had tried to suicide due to the ongoing incestuous abuse by her father. A few days after her plight was first uncovered, a younger colleague, and I had occasion to converse at length with both her parents. Her mother sat silently and rigidly beside the father. When given free range to expand on the issues concerning his daughter, he spontaneously floated a theory that it was her husband, his son-in-law that was the family abuser, one who he claimed had been sexually abusing all her children. With his story un-contradicted, he elaborated, claiming he had been observing the sinister nature of his daughter's husband's behavior toward his grandchildren over an extended period of time. At this point, this author posed the logical question—given his claimed longstanding serious concerns about the safety of his grand children, what had he actually done to protect them? Instantly caught out in an impasse of logic, the father and his still silent wife made a hasty exit. I saw him one more time the following week and referenced the conversation we had had. He flatly denied the discussion had ever occurred, an illustrative insight into why a child would need to dissociate to endure in his realm. "Betty" described the relationship between her parents: "She was dominated by him… She did whatever he said." Almost 20 years later and with her father then well into his seventies, in the middle of the night, four pieces of cheap jewelry were dropped in his daughter's and her husband's letter box. They were inscribed with "It's Your Fault," "Daddy's Girl," "I Mean What I Say," and "Your mine and only mine." Nearly, a quarter century since she had been in regular contact with any members of her family of origin she was to say of her violent and dissociative father, someone she reported having observed when she was a child, having sex with his own mother, "The day he dies, I'll be free."

Nothing in the statements or behaviors of alleged primary abusers that I have met has given me any significant reason to doubt the main thrust of the detailed and consistently stated accounts of their victims—some of whom I have known over many years. In the case of a particular individual whose life experience contained more violent deaths of friends/relatives and suicides of relatives than any other, newspaper articles had described a number of such deaths/murders. At least four such individuals that I have worked with whose abuse is in this spectrum, thus far, have given evidence in closed sessions of the Australian Royal Commission into institutional aspects of child sexual abuse. The closed and highly controlled nature of this spectrum of family centered abuse leads one to reflect on Hassan's conceptualization of "mini-cults" consisting of anywhere from two to twelve people with the leader being "a husband or a wife, a teacher, a therapist, or even a client" (Hassan, 2015, p. 19).

In addition to the 10 individuals referenced in the published clinical series cited above (Middleton, 2013b), this writer has had substantive clinical contact with 13 other individuals in the years 2011–2016 that had been or continued to be sexually abused by a parent or parents into their adult years. Of these 23 individuals (22 female, one male), I had ongoing close clinical involvement with 16, while with seven the contact was briefer or limited to a single detailed assessment. The 23 include a male sexually abused by his father and three females whose primary sexual abuser was their mother. The clinical observations associated with this group of individuals are incorporated here, as is reference to many other such patients seen in past years.

The central tenets of the "weaponized sex" construct

In order to orientate the reader, I have broken down Kluft's eloquent and at times confronting paper into paraphrased key points concerning patients with DID and allied conditions who fit the Weaponized Sex construct. Key observations made by Kluft about "weaponized sex" can be summarized:-

(1) Patients with DID and allied conditions frequently manifestly problematic sexual behaviors and they range from diminished desire through to particular behaviors associated with high degrees of sexual arousal and orgasmic release.

(2) Some patients continue to engage in problematic sexual behaviors even to the point of jeopardizing adult relationships or undermining therapeutic encounters.

(3) Notions of "political correctness," gender sensitivity or a tendency to accusations of misogyny, may carry with them an inbuilt tendency for shaming and have hampered our ability to objectively and sensitively engage with a real phenomena—the sexual (and frequently defensive) adaptations engaged with, on the part those who have been severely sexually abused in earlier life.

(4) Patients with DID are particularly vulnerable to finding themselves in sexual relationships with therapists, but before we categorize this as a moral/legal/professional issue and remove ourselves, we need to also better understand the dynamic.

(5) In order to be effective therapists and open to dealing sensitively with the material that with great difficulty, they are trying their best to share, we need to personally be relatively desensitized to the sort of material that will inevitably arise in therapy when we are engaging patients who have suffered extreme sexual abuse. They did not create the dynamic they have found themselves in. It is helpful to empathically and calmly engage with sexualized parts including pointing out their underlying protective functions.

(6) Given the extreme compartmentalization of their sexual responses, patients often struggle with the real prospect that they will switch into an identity state, which will manifest sexualized behavior in the therapy room that is deeply shaming or will precipitate the termination of therapy.

(7) When a patient is provocatively seductive, it is not about the erotic appeal of the therapist, but a manifestation of a long-standing adaptation to potential and real past abusers. Some individuals have projected a highly eroticized interface with the world from early in their development, offering sex as a reflex response in multiple situations—some that encompass obvious threat, but in many that outwardly don't, where acceptance is the principal driver. At the core of the expressed eroticism of severely sexually abused individuals, there is the vulnerability of the very abused and repeatedly rejected individual epitomized by Kluft's description of "the sitting duck syndrome" (Kluft, 1990).

(8) "Weaponized sex" is not about actual eroticism but is about calling upon and reenacting a sexualized role, encapsulated in a particular dissociative identity state (or states) that in the past has proven to be in some way protective in situations where none of the other options was preferable. Many dissociative disorder patients find security, strength, and reassurance in the power of their sexual behaviors.

The occurrence with some patients of erotic arousal or even orgasm is incidental to the primary function of "weaponized sex" which is compulsive and can escalate to progressive automaticity.

(9) Those who have experienced engaged, empathic, and non-blaming therapy can make a clear distinction between a stance ordained by notions of "political correctness" and a willingness on the part of the therapist to understand and share in the processing of sheer awfulness—including the extremes of sexual abuse and the repetition of psychological strategies that encompass some variation of its reenactment in multiple scenarios.

(10) The most effective way in which to engage with colleagues about the actual realities of the circumstances that give rise to "weaponized sex" is by providing clinical examples that therapists can relate to and which can stimulate circumspect thought rather than reflex dismissal.

(11) The very sexually abused individual, based on past experience, in order to not be caught out and experience some very negative outcome, responds to cues or perceived cues that suggest at least to him/her that sex is expected.

(12) Any accessible memory of sexualized behavior may be quarantined by particular alters such that the patient in more accessible states will deny any knowledge of it.

(13) It may be late in therapy that dissociative parts exhibit seductiveness, paradoxically because this aspect can be safely revealed, but also encompassing a transference-based relationship fantasy.

(14) Seemingly innocuous aspects of the therapist's demeanor, utterances, or appearances can trigger in a particular patient who is cued by their unique sexual abuse experiences, an instantaneous switch into a particular sexualized identity state—one that offered sex in order to avoid some worse trauma.

(15) Offers to be sexually involved with the therapist and to keep it secret are a strong clue to that patient having been sexually abused by a previous therapist.

(16) On infrequent occasions some dramatic and sustained instances of "weaponized sex", such as attempts to disrobe or masturbate in the therapy room, etc. can present significant management challenges. While such outwardly sexually aggressive actions require sensitive but firm boundary setting, at their core they represent a desperate avoidance strategy on the part of a scared individual. Occasionally the therapist has to improvise when confronted with a patient locked in a persistent and sexually aggressive alter state, but does so while all the time providing explanation and speaking calmly and supportively. Problematic sexualized behaviors may frequently be headed off before

they actually emerge by using dialog or diversion to interrupt their development.

(17) With the occasional patient, sudden extreme sexualized behavior can accompany a dissociative switch cutting off the options to preempt, deflect, or empathically deescalate. Rather than view such episodes as defeats, it is more helpful to view them as learning experiences and preplan ways to avoid their repetition.

(18) Some very traumatized individuals will take a risk and use unconventional, even dangerous, sexualized mechanisms to convey the details of a sexual trauma that they are otherwise incapable of initially describing directly.

(19) The various processes associated with "weaponized sex" coalesce around an adaptation that facilitates survival and minimizes rejection and physical brutalization. Existing dynamic models fall short in encompassing the diversity of this adaptation, and none has sufficiently accounted for the driven, forceful aggressiveness of many of the more severe behaviors.

(20) When dealing with pseudo-erotic behaviors or "weaponized sex" as a therapist, being alert to a patient's meta-communications and sensory experiences allows one to anticipate the emergence of problematic sexualized behaviors, while actively seeking clarification of detail facilitates effective trauma processing.

(21) A patient is more usefully understood by focusing on the material they bring than by trying to make them fit a predetermined theory.

"Weaponized sex" in the clinical context

Writing directly about the sexualized behavior of very traumatized dissociative individuals seems to be for many a fraught enterprise. There are several ways in which even professionals who see themselves as having a particular interest in trauma will raise opposition to hearing about such things. The subject matter may be avoided as being too upsetting or confronting. Or the motives of those who write or speak about such things are questioned. Are they going out of their way to shock or confront their audience? Is their interest in seeking to understand the defensive sexualized behaviors of traumatized individuals, indicative of some personal voyeuristic interest in the subject matter? Kluft challenges the use of notions of political/gender correctness as a mechanism for avoiding approaching, let alone seeking to understand, a set of psychological processes that goes to the heart of understanding what unremitting sexual and associated abuses does to an individual long term.

Given the sort of opposition clinicians face in speaking about this subject area, one can understand why those who have actually had to live through the abuses that produce these sexualized responses have picked up long ago that the subject area is shame filled and not to be talked of. I suspect that not every clinician hangs in there throwing Afghans over a disrobed patient in a switched state rather than succumbing to some form of self-rationalizing panicked abandonment, and an inevitable outcome of which will be that the patient will be further shamed.

My very regular clinical contact with patients who have experienced ongoing incest that extended into adulthood is congruent with the weaponized sex construct. There were many aspects associated with the sexual functioning of this group that no reading of past texts had prepared me for. Indeed, no systematic scientific research on this group had previously ever been done. This poses an interesting question: given that we now know that such abuse is far from rare, how was it that in the past, scientific engagement with this group was limited to the odd clinical anecdote or single case study? The resistance to dealing with the traumas of such individuals is not limited to the patients. That which professionals seemingly avoid can only add to the shame and to reinforcing fear on the part of the victim. Much, in the estimation of such traumatized individuals, can never be safely revealed. And the world in the case of most has remained oblivious to what is happening to them or to having any understanding of what drives extreme responses that for the most part are only occasionally tripped over by the people in their lives.

I will state the challenge. There are profound effects from being brought up in a closed environment which encompasses being regularly sexually abused from an early age by a primary abuser who will almost inevitably then share his child victim with one or other sort of groups of abusers. Congruent with what Yates reported in a classic but orphan paper, "Children eroticized by incest" (1982), we frequently fail to take account of the extreme sexual conditioning a child may experience and how it impacts on all subsequent sexual functioning. "In my experience, many incestuous children are uncommonly erotic. They are easily aroused, highly motivated, and readily orgasmic. The degree of eroticization seems closely related to the intensity and duration of the incestuous union. The original mode (e.g., heterosexual or homosexual, oral-genital, extra-genital) remains highly cathected. These observations are consistent with the observation that sexual responsiveness is a learned behavior (Yates, p. 482)."

Essentially fused to their primary abuser and with so little sense of self that they do not feel they own their own body, such women frequently have a father who has likewise been traumatized as a child and who frequently manifests marked dissociative switching. Repeatedly sexually stimulated from an early age the child becomes orgasmic at a very young age—typically around 6. Adding a further conditioned complexity is the fact that the primary abuser from an early age has imposed on the child victim commands that she should initiate sex (Middleton, 2013b). Their abuser, almost invariably highly controlling in nature, usually makes a particular point of controlling their victim's orgasm—some to an extreme degree where orgasm is "owned" by the abuser and bestowed in certain circumstances—not infrequently linked to some repetitive acts of sadism. With some, the attachment to the abuser is made even more complex as they experience him switching back and forth between variations of "Good Daddy" and "Bad Daddy."

I cannot remember encountering any woman subjected to this sort of ongoing incestuous abuse, where the sexual abuse by the father was brought to an end because they managed to effect a minimum of separation by actually getting married. Congruent with Yates' findings, many as adults had their long-term sexual conditioning set in such a way that it was difficult, if not virtually impossible to experience sexual arousal, let alone orgasm, in circumstances that did not involve their primary abuser, his associates, or someone whose behaviors and utterances closely resembled their familiar abusers. For many, sexual abuse by the father represented the closest facsimile of what passed for emotional closeness or opportunity for approval in what was a chronically unsafe and rejecting family.

Even when the father is not present or is dead, many abused adult daughters are driven in dissociative states, to reenact sexual abuse with individuals, frequently strangers, who are likely to be rough and degrading, a form of treatment cued to conditioned arousal. Treated in this way, it is much easier in fantasy to experience the absent father. Frequently, the shame associated with such compulsive reenactments, and the dynamics associated with sexual arousal achieved in such ways is such that the sexual activity is consigned to a particular dissociative identity state, with other states remaining amnesic (see Kluft, this volume). It is a challenging transition when the amnestic barrier begins to come down, and there is a more general awareness that a past abuser the patient had been at pains to avoid and was being sought out by a particular dissociative part in order to reengage with that abuser or representative of the absent father. It is likewise challenging in therapy to confront a whole range of experiences of a sexual nature that are deeply laced with shame and easily associated in the patient's mind with unique badness rather than being a totally anticipated experience or response when one is accustomed to the familiar dynamics of this form of extreme abuse. Within this group of sexual abuses or responses to abuse that patients had reasoned, on past experience, were "never to be spoken of," and include being forced into sexual contact with dogs or other animals, being forced as a child to have sexual contact with other children, being automatically sexual with other children, being sexually degraded by abusers forcing contact with excrement, being forced as an adult to do sexual things to one's children, or as a substitute to contact with the primary abuser, having compulsions to watch violent/hard core pornography.

My clinical observations are that Kluft is entirely correct in suggesting that when one gently removes the sexual façade that is on occasions erected, one is not engaging with someone joyfully celebrating erotic sensuality—the opposite in fact. Yet in a life where options have been few, they have learned to use sex to decrease danger, pacify potentially violent abusers, to on occasions exert some form of control, or to eke out some sort of substitute for esteem or emotional closeness. For example, "Lucy" a 40-year-old survivor of sexual abuse by three generations of her family, as she approached the processing of particular aspects of her sexual abuse, switched briefly to "Kitty," who announced she was "the seductress" and made the suggestion, "I sort of want to play in here…" "Kitty's" role in carrying most sexual functioning, and dealing with the constant arousal associated with her early and ongoing abuse, an area that was avoided by other alters, was validated along with the message that she was safe and that nothing would be happening aside from hearing what she had to say. She departed with the words, "You're no fun…" In other identity states, there were a variety of perspectives regarding "Kitty" including, "I think she's on a path to sabotage my therapy by doing something inappropriate," "My body lets me down. It's like a punishment." In subsequent discussions "Kitty" further defined her role —"It's about having that power—not about enjoyment. [I have] the power to seduce someone—get them very worked up and then leave!… I just want to give it back to these a—holes!" "Kitty" acknowledged repeatedly engaging with the challenge of having the power to seduce any man, prefacing this reflection by saying, "I wore my best underwear for you…" Other parts responded to the interpretation that such sexualized adaptations reflected a conditioned defense evolved out of sheer awfulness, and one that "Kitty" was not usually capable of following through to completion before all the triggers precipitated a switch. "It really sucks changing halfway through. I feel guilty when they come out. I've created something they have to endure." Other parts offered a congruent reflection, "Why would she set us up like this?.. Why couldn't "Kitty" stay and deal with it?"

Some in the spectrum of abuse that I have focused on here when first seen are outwardly seemingly highly sexualized to the point where on first meeting they say something along the lines of, "Would you like to have sex with me?" Indeed, sexuality has almost literally become the major currency of conversational relatedness. Others present a very non-sexual demeanor. It was a surprise when "Betty" after many years of therapy, suddenly one day asked that identical question. It was not asked in a particularly seductive way. As with many that Kluft refers to, "Betty" had been previously sexually abused by a health professional. He was one of a multitude of abusers. It seemed that she asked the question of me, when she was internally convinced that there was no risk of such a thing happening. Some years later, with seemingly nothing overtly sexual ever happening previously, in a switched state and whilst fully clothed, she started gently stroking in the region of her genitals. Again the identity state was one who contained memories of abuse by a therapist. Her "communication" was dealt with in a dignified manner, with no surprise or alarm conveyed. This speaks to Kluft's point to the desirability of therapists desensitizing themselves to what superficially passes for eroticism. "Weaponized sex" is not a response that remotely incorporates the equality of two unattached individuals getting to know each other.

In comparing Kluft's observations to my experiences with my own patient group, I reflect that even with the extremely abused group subjected to ongoing incestuous abuse during adulthood, the number manifesting particularly challenging aspects of "weaponized sex" has been relatively few. Not many have ever gone beyond a fairly perfunctory offer of sex or a non-dramatic discussion of concerns that approaching certain matters could trigger a switch to a sexually aggressive identity state. A couple has touched themselves in sexual ways when in identity states that were associated with handling past sexual abuse by therapists. (One of these two women was to reflect years later that her trust increased immediately at the point where that very sexualized alter was able to reveal herself—"You weren't going to let anything happen and she didn't get out of control. It's good you don't feel less of me because of her.") Only one individual in my experience stated she was going to strip off her clothes in my office. At the time, over two decades ago, perhaps not very expertly, I calmly said that if she continued with what she was threatening to do, it would mean therapy was terminated. Without drama she desisted. I sensed, in a somewhat extreme way she was testing safety. I have never routinely hugged any patient. With some, there is an understood shaking of hands at the end of therapy sessions. This seems to be an unambiguous, non-sexual but supportive point of physical contact and for some seems to convey a sense of non-shaming acceptance beyond that which words can communicate.

As is the case with vignettes in Kluft's paper, I am endlessly, in the group I have particularly focused on, grappling with individuals burdened with the enormous weight of being the essentially powerless victim of extreme sexual sadism. There is simply no way to discretely contain the psychological impact of such extreme abuses, and it is inevitable that the sequelae will enter the therapy in some or other form (e.g., by the testing of the therapist, as a flashback, pronounced switching, and by the emergence of alters explicitly created in the context of such abuses—to contain such memories and/or to find a way of surviving by joining with the abuser).

Expanding on "weaponized sex" from the perspective of ongoing incest during adulthood

Typically the victims of ongoing incest during adulthood referred to here, all of whom had developed DID, had multiple alters that represented some aspect of their abuse by their primary abuser, with the number of alters and the complication of their alter system overall frequently approximating polyfragmented DID (Kluft, 1991).

Statements of ownership and extreme sexual objectification by the fathers of women endlessly incestuously abused are endless, for example, "He's always told us he owns us"—("Leanne", age 47); "My gender being female, father would say I belong to him"—("Tracy"); "You've got a c–t. What else do you expect"—("Bonnie")? Her father's ownership of her body for "Susan" meant, "That I would do what he said, that I'd respond how he wanted, that he was with me all the time. Even if not there he could still see me. He knew—anything that came out of my mouth, he'd know. He said, he could even read my thoughts. He said the only way I could escape was by being dead. He said my being dead would solve all my problems."

The fusion involving such victims and their primary abusers is apparent in statements such as, "I don't know where I ended and my father started" ("Mary"). Another stated, "My life is and has always been tied to his. He owns my body and my soul. He continues to have the power of life and death over me." Yet another reported her father telling her, "We won't be separated. Not even death would separate us."

Exemplifying the enduring attachment that individuals who have never known an abuse-free existence "Susan's" stated wish is poignant and typical—"I so miss my dad. I wish you could understand that and why I want to be with him."

In the complex nature of their ongoing attachment to their psychologically abusive father who has dominated virtually all aspects of their lives, repeatedly one finds, as these men become terminally ill, their abused daughters express anticipatory grief in part, via experiencing strong urges to have sex with their fathers. One is reminded that which has not been able to be resolved in life is hardly likely to be quickly resolved by death. As Ross and Halpern (2009) emphasize, the attachment to the perpetrator is frequently intense. As Kluft adroitly points out, frequently the most effective way in which to convey perspectives about sensitive sexual issues is by way of clinical examples:-

"Jenny" in her early 50's sexually abused and extruded by her previous therapist who terminated the abuse with a text ("Therapy has ended. Good luck"), shunned by the Church she had been attending, never effected separation from her father (a Vietnam veteran by then in his late 80's who she believed had himself been sexually abused and who was highly dissociative). I witnessed a text from this then 85-year-old abusing father along with texted old photos of his 52-year-old victim as a naked child. The text stated, "If you talk, I will skin you alive. PROMISE." Despite his terminal illness, he continued with what had been lifelong severe abuse. "Jenny" observed of her father, "Everybody that meets him thinks he's charming." She was to say, "Of course he misses me—he's my father! He loves me! He owns me!"

The onset of sexual abuse by her previous therapist is chronicled: "It became obvious he was interested. He talked about sex all the time. He'd ask, 'Who is the one who flutters her eyelids at me/' Then he asked, 'What would you think if I came around to your place?' I thought—here you are, you bastard! Others were flattered.." She reflected on the similarities between her father and her previous abusive therapist, "You know, they're the same people really." She reasoned that if she had sex with her therapist, he'd be less bored and she'd be less likely to be abandoned, though such abandonment inevitably happened after around 5 months. "He broke 'Harold' completely. ['Harold' is an alter.] When 'Harold' said he had feelings for Dr 'Smith', Dr 'Smith' cut him cold... He still believed in Dr 'Smith'... 'Harold' was the one that got the text message... He rang Dr 'Smith' straight away. He got no reply."

The sort of dilemmas associated with this intense conditioned lifelong sexualized attachment is reflected in the nature of a few short illustrative text messages that also at times poignantly include different alters' perspectives on sex with a therapist.

> "Can't see out one eye. Her father spent that night here. Happy about what happened but beating to reinforce [keeping her] mouth shut. Leave it."

> "Happy snap—early 60's. Note unusual self-photo lead and knob on his lap. Girl forced near crotch. 'Amber'."

> "All the ugliness, corruption and evil in this world flow from me. I am a dangerous contagion. 'Amber'."

> "Some out there been following her photographically for decades. Swap images with each other. Sick f——g world."

> "Too much talking. Sorry to disappoint doctor. No more salacious stories to get you hard."

> "Daddy loves me and cares about me. You don't. Go away."

> "You never cared because you never f—-d us."

> "Her Daddy is dying and many times a day messages his little f—k girls. They know what to do."

When he finally died, Jenny wrote, "I'm numb. People had to stand at the service, so many came. After they played the Last Post all the veterans came and placed a poppy on the flag-draped coffin... I had to speak in front of mourners. No one told me that was expected. Relatives know me as [the] mad, ungrateful, unloving daughter. I'm numb. I'm numb." Among a range of communications in the following days was, "Will you be my Daddy? .., F—k me, hit me, make me bleed. Be new Daddy. Kill me. F—k me Daddy."

"Harriet" acknowledged that a past overdose requiring life-support in ICU followed on from pressure from her gun-owning father that she suicide. "He threatened one of my parts—if we spoke about him anymore—about what we do with him and what he does with Jenny [a younger sister]—someone will get hurt." She reflected, that on both sides of her family, the only "normal" person was her maternal grand mother, adding, "And she was murdered…"

> "Harriet" acknowledged that there was nothing in her life that her father didn't seek to control, adding, "I've never been safe in my life." She had for years remained fearful of father forcing her into suicide "so he won't get into trouble."

When her father developed bowel cancer, "Harriet" in her early thirties, having finally, against much internal opposition (from dissociative parts aligned with the father) and external opposition (from all members of her very fractured immediate family) secured (via unequivocal hard evidence collected by police) an Aggravated Violence Order (AVO) against her father, prohibiting him coming near her or otherwise making contact with her. Shortly thereafter her father was diagnosed as being terminally ill with cancer. His illness coming as it did, occasioned renewed guilt, with some parts reasoning, that because "they hadn't been good to him sexually" he had become sick, with some adhering to a belief that if they were again to have sex with their father, they could "cure" him.

The dissociative father had throughout her existence chronically switched into sexually violent states (a common experience for women subjected to chronic ongoing incest during adulthood), in contrast to the "Good Dad" who was seemingly gentle and caring in his behaviors. Yet it was the violent and sadistic father that was associated predominantly with her distressing and intense sexual arousal as she contemplated his imminent death—anticipating the loss of the dominant individual of her life, one she was both deeply fused with and highly sexually conditioned by, as well as one that she had repeated wished dead. As with "Jenny", "Harriet" also described her father actively creating dissociative identity states within her, including states whose primary role was to report back to the father anything of significance that had been divulged to anyone and to take an active role in disposing of incriminating evidence—threatening text messages and the like, as well as warning of likely Police visits. She reflected on a constantly reinforced message, "He said that when he dies he'll be inside me forever."

A century ago Freud drew attention to the difficulties of resolving the loss of the ambivalently loved object (1917) and though he and other prominent early analysts were sexually abused as children (Middleton, 2016), he had not conceptualized the extreme dilemma individuals such as "Jenny" and "Harriet" face when he wrote, "The loss of a love-object is an excellent opportunity for the ambivalence in love relationships to make itself effective and come into the open. Where there is a disposition to obsessional neurosis, the conflict due to ambivalence gives a pathological cast to mourning and forces it to express itself in the form of self-reproaches to the effect that the mourner himself is to blame for the loss of the loved object, that is, that he has willed it (Freud, pp. 250–251). Vaillant observed (1986) "Grief hurts, but does not make us ill. We forget that it is the inconstant people in our lives who drive us mad, not the constant ones who die."

This paper extends Kluft's elucidation by expanding on the extent to which abusers in the spectrum I am particularly focused on, make inducing orgasm on the part of their child victim, a strategy central to their dominance and psychological manipulation, and a process embarked upon usually when the victim was little more than an infant (Middleton, 2013b). Allied with physical threats, it is also a powerful device in further silencing their victim through shame. One woman in her early 40's, in a child identity state, put it this way, "He always told me I enjoyed it. If I didn't want it, I wouldn't enjoy it and this wouldn't happen. He always made me orgasm. It meant that I liked it… It was Daddy's way of showing how much he loved me… and I loved him because he could make me feel special. Daddy said, 'It makes you feel good doesn't it?' Daddy tells us it makes us feel good—makes us feel special. We loved it when he does it. It can't be naughty because we like it." Typical of this sort of controlling and sadistic abuser, her father would lay down conditions for sexually abusing his young daughter to orgasm, such as, he would perversely turn it into a "reward" and inflict the abuse, "when I was a very good girl and did what I was told." The same man brutally exposed her to repeated sexual assaults by his group of drinking buddies and would exhibit extreme rage and violence if thwarted. If as an adult she would try to report the ongoing abuse, he would force from her a recantation. Like so many, her sexually conditioned, but deeply ambivalent attachment to her abusive and now deceased father was such that details of her reenactments of very rough sexual treatment via surviving members of his group of co-abusers, was the province of a couple of identity states, who kept the existence of this activity well compartmentalized (akin to a case mentioned by Kluft, this volume).

A form of "seductive" enactment I have encountered with women in the spectrum of ongoing incest as adults, that falls outside the spectrum of "weaponized sex" is where the primary abuser commands his victim to actively attempt to seduce her therapist, as he is discomforted by the possibility of his victim revealing too much and taking matters to the point of making a police report. It thus makes sense to terminally compromise the therapist by doing what he can to pressure his adult daughter/step daughter to seduce her therapist. While it is unlikely that the abuser is going to confirm this is happening, I have had enough encounters with such abusers over the years, to believe that such scenarios are authentic. I have experienced one such abusive father literally text pictures to me of him actively sexually abusing his daughter accompanied by a less than friendly commentary. Most such women report their primary abuser in one way or other taking an active role in creating identity states predicated to performing particular tasks. Such cases illustrate a paradoxical scenario where sex is "weaponized' by the abuser rather the abused.

"Weaponized sex" provides a foundation for further explaining and expanding the understanding of relational dynamics in those exposed to systematic and ongoing abuse. As the Catholic Church, allied as it is with a policy of celibacy in respect to its clergy, has demonstrated in multiple sexual abuse scandals, it is very problematic to expect that any human being will be able to deny himself/herself any form of sexual expression. Some severely sexually abused women will maintain a conditioned hyper-aroused state particularly focused on their primary abuser and akin to the premature sexualized state that was imposed on them as a child. With others, any tendency toward any form of sexual expression seems outwardly to have been entirely suppressed. However, I expect that the basic biological drive cannot be extinguished. One such highly traumatized woman, although married, maintained what seemed total sexual avoidance, except when, as conveyed by her husband, she on rare occasions, switched into an identity state that assertively initiated sex. I don't think of this as an expression of "weaponized sex", but rather the limited and highly dissociated expression of an innate sexual drive that could not be entirely eradicated, but which being as it was, so associated with triggers, and could not be consciously integrated.

Conclusions

Working with those individuals where incestuous abuse extends into decades, one reflects anew on the psychological tasks that in various permeations are incorporated into the functioning of sexualized alters. Variously they have to compartmentalize sexual responses that were conditioned by abusers and where the options for not complying were all dire, they may incorporate the limited power and tenuous esteem that comes from being the seductress, and they may incorporate behaviors that facilitate complicated responses to the loss or threatened loss of a primary abuser for whom a strong (but ambivalent) attachment has literally been lifelong. They may be the repository of strong arousal feelings that have been a part of their endless sexual conditioning (associated with particular sexual acts and particular individuals or sorts of individuals) dating from early childhood and which are an enduring source of shame and internal conflict, and they may as a consequence of very negative past experiences exhibit a defensive reflex compliance with any sexual offer or demand—even to the point of preempting the question by spontaneously offering sex. On occasions, advances by sexualized alters may be used to test safety in the therapy situation and in respect to therapists who fail their patient by becoming sexually involved until the inevitable betrayal; it is not unlikely that the patient will try to ward off abandonment by trying to be sexually seductive, really the only card they have to play in the circumstances. Some sexualized alters are crafted or actively created, by the primary abuser who, when he is aware of the active involvement of a therapist may instruct them to sexually compromise that therapist.

In order not to overwhelm the individual, many of the activities of sexualized alters are shrouded in amnesia and this is congruent with the un-tethered nature of utterances or behaviors that may be encountered, particularly when accessed or tripped over in circumstances where there has not been a lot of preparation in setting up the communication and in preemptively enlisting the help of other alters in maintaining safety. Some responses of triggered sexualized alters are probably best conceptualized as flashback phenomena.

The illusionary nature of true eroticism in those who have to use "weaponized sex" is born out in the rapidity with which an individual in the throes of an exaggerated display of seductiveness can almost instantly switch to another state overwhelmed with shame and/or fear.

Kluft has challenged us with a frank and psychologically nuanced discussion about matters concerning "sexualized" behaviors by dissociative individuals in therapy that are rarely so closely examined by others. Reflecting on his observations regarding "weaponized sex" through the prism of long-term clinical experience with that subgroup of DID patients who continue to be incestuously abused during adulthood, it is apparent that his clinical observations redefine such matters as material the grounded and aware therapist seeks to understand and work with, at the same time as maintaining sound boundaries, building a therapeutic alliance, and minimizing the patient's experience of shame—something they already have in abundance.

References

Carter, L. (2016). *NSW parents sentenced to lengthy jail terms for sexually abusing, torturing daughter*. ABC News. Retrieved from http://tinyurl.com/hwzmez2

Fife-Yeomans, J. (2016). *Parents' 'sickening' sexual and psychological abuse of daughter*. The Daily Telegraph website. Retrieved from http://tinyurl.com/j3vn537

Freud, S. (1917). Mourning and melancholia. In J. Strachey (Translated), *The standard edition of the complete psychological works of sigmund freud* (Vol. 14, pp. 243–258). London, UK: Vintage. (1914–1916).

Hassan, S. (2015). *Combating cult mind control: 25th anniversary edition*. Newton, MA: Freedom of Mind.

Katherine, X., & Smethurst, S. (2015). *Behind closed doors*. Cammeray, NSW: Simon & Schuster.

Kluft, R. (1990). On the apparent invisibility of incest: A personal reflection on things known and forgotten. In R. P. Kluft (Ed.), *Incest-related syndromes of adult psychopathology* (pp. 11–34). Washington, DC: American Psychiatric Press.

Kluft, R. P. (1991). Clinical presentations of multiple personality disorder. *Psychiatric Clinics of North America, 14* (3), 605–629.

Kluft, R. P. (2017). Weaponized sex: Pseudo-erotic aggression in the service of safety. *Journal of Trauma and Dissociation, 18* (3).

Middleton, W. (2011, August 24–28). *Always daddy's little girl': Incestuous abuse during adulthood.* Invited plenary paper, World Congress for Psychotherapy, "World Dreaming", Sydney Convention and Exhibition Centre, Darling Harbour, Sydney, NSW, Australia.

Middleton, W. (2013a). Parent-child incest that extends into adulthood: A survey of international press reports 2007–2011. *Journal of Trauma and Dissociation, 14* (2), 184–197. doi:10.1080/15299732.2013.724341

Middleton, W. (2013b). Ongoing incestuous abuse during adulthood. *Journal of Trauma and Dissociation, 14* (3), 251–272. doi:10.1080/15299732.2012.736932

Middleton, W. (2013c). Ongoing incestuous abuse during adulthood. *European Society for Trauma and Dissociation Newsletter, 3* (3), 9–12.

Middleton, W. (2013d). Response to Commentary by Adah Sachs on "Parent-child incest that extends into adulthood: A survey of international press reports", and, "Ongoing incestuous abuse during adulthood". *Journal of Trauma and Dissociation, 14* (5), 580–583. doi:10.1080/15299732.2013.799110

Middleton, W. (2014a). Parent-child incest that extends into adulthood: A survey of international press reports, 2007–2012. In V. Sar, W. Middleton, & M. Dorahy (Eds.), *Global perspectives on dissociative disorders: Individual and societal oppression* (pp. 45–64). London, UK: Routledge.

Middleton, W. (2014b). Nicht endender Inzest: Die Fritzl-Analogie. *Trauma: Zeitschrift Für Psychotraumatologie Und Ihre Anwendungen, 12* (4), 34–42. (Unending incest: The Fritzl analogue. Invited paper for journal special issue, ZPA, edited by Vogt, R.).

Middleton, W. (2015a). Tipping points and the accommodation of the abuser: The case of ongoing incestuous abuse during adulthood. *International Journal for Crime, Justice and Social Democracy, 4* (2), 4–17. (edited by Salter, M.). doi:10.5204/ijcjsd.v3i2.21

Middleton, W. (2015b, November 27–29). *Child sexual abuse: Organized and unending.* Plenary paper, presented at ISSTD Bi-National Regional conference, "Broken Structures, Broken Selves: Complex Trauma in the 21st Century", Westin Hotel, Sydney.

Middleton, W. (2016). Wilhelm Fliess, Robert Fliess, Ernest Jones, Sandor Ferenczi and Sigmund Freud – ISSTD president's editorial. *Journal of Trauma and Dissociation, 17* (1), 1–12. doi:10.1080/15299732.2015.1064289

Middleton, W., & Butler, J. (1998). Dissociative identity disorder: An Australian series. *Australian and New Zealand Journal of Psychiatry, 32*, 794–804. doi:10.3109/00048679809073868

Ross, C. A., & Halpern, N. (2009). *Trauma model therapy: A treatment approach for trauma, dissociation and complex comorbidity.* Richardson, Texas: Manitou Communications.

Vaillant, G. E. (1986, May). *Attachment, loss and rediscovery.* The Samuel G. Gibbs Award Lecture delivered at The American Psychiatric Association Annual Meeting, Washington, DC.

Yates, A. (1982). Children eroticized by incest. *American Journal of Psychiatry, 139*, 482–485. doi:10.1176/ajp.139.4.482

Conflicts between motivational systems related to attachment trauma: Key to understanding the intra-family relationship between abused children and their abusers

Giovanni Liotti, MD

ABSTRACT
Research on disorganization of infant attachment provides evidence that it can be caused not only by violent aggression or very early sexual abuse, but also by covert maltreating behavior, which includes the abdication of the caregiver's responsibility to soothe the infant's distress. This paper argues that both overtly abusive caregivers and merely "abdicating" caregivers may cause disorganization of infant attachment through a simultaneous and conflicting activation of the motivational systems governing attachment and survival defense in the infant.

Other inborn motivational systems—regulating caretaking, competitiveness, and sexuality—are disorderly activated, during personality development, within the intra-family relationships of children whose infant attachment has been disorganized. The paper argues that conflicts and abnormal tensions between different motivational systems explain some paradoxical features of the interactions between abusers and abused, and allow for a better understanding of the interpersonal processes involved in the surfacing and exacerbation of dissociative symptoms in the abused.

Children who grow up in families whose adult members abuse them face an unsolvable conflict between two inborn and powerful dispositions: the tendency to ask for soothing and help (regulated by the attachment system: Bowlby, 1969) and the impulse to protect themselves through fight-flight responses (regulated by the survival defense system: Cantor, 2005). This conflict, it will be argued in the first section of this paper, underpins the disorganization of infant attachment both when the caregivers are overtly maltreating, and when they express emotional vulnerabilities that severely hinder their capacity to protect and soothe their children.

Children who have been disorganized in their infant attachments develop, before school age, complex relational strategies, called disorganized/controlling. The genesis of these strategies can be understood on the basis of a multi-motivational theory compatible with the Darwinian foundations of attachment theory (Bowlby, 1969; Cortina & Liotti, 2014). This evolutionary multi-motivational theory will be outlined in the second section of the paper. The third section argues that the activation of motivational systems different from attachment in the controlling strategies protects abused or neglected children and abusive or neglecting parents from the experience of disorganization (linked to the operations of the disordered attachment system in the children and of the disordered care giving system in the parents). This protection, however, comes at a high cost, because it involves abnormal tensions and conflicts between different motivational systems—between attachment and caretaking, attachment and competitiveness, and attachment and sexuality—that add to the basic conflict of disorganized attachment between attachment and survival defense. The multiple abnormal tensions and conflicts between different basic motivational systems, it will be argued in the fourth and fifth sections of the paper, explain some paradoxical features of the interactions between abusers and abused, and allow for a better understanding of the interpersonal processes involved in the surfacing and exacerbation of dissociative symptoms in the abused.

Infant attachment disorganization as an unsolvable conflict between the defense and the attachment systems

The main cause of disorganization in infant attachment behavior is to be found in specific untoward responses of the caregiver to the infant's expressions of distress. Genetic factors play a modulating role between these types of untoward caregiving and disorganization of the infants' attachment behavior (for a review, see Lyons-Ruth & Jacobvitz, 2008). Antecedents of infant attachment disorganization are caregivers' behaviors that are either overtly hostile and maltreating or frightened and helpless. The latter is the more frequent antecedent of infant attachment disorganization (Solomon & George, 2011).

Overtly aggressive parental behavior activates the inborn survival defense system (fight-flight) in the infant, leading to a conflict between the tendency to approach the parent for soothing and help (regulated by the inborn attachment system) and the tendency to flight from danger regulated by the defense system. This conflict is unsolvable because the distress prompts infants, unavoidably, to ask for the abusive parents' protective attention through cry and approaching behaviors. The source of danger is the same as the source of soothing. Main and Hesse (1990) described this conflict between the attachment and the defense system as fright without solution, because each of the two inborn strategies to deal with fear—care seeking and flight from danger—impedes the other.

The same type of simultaneous and inefficient activation of both the attachment and the defense system is also the consequence of parental behavior which is not overly aggressive, but so frightened or helpless as to cause what Solomon and George (2011) called "abdicating the responsibility of protecting and soothing the infant." Since a human infant can neither escape nor fight danger, any threat perceived by the infant automatically activates not only the survival defense system but also the attachment system in search for the necessary help and protection. If the attachment figure responds properly to the infant's cry for help, the defense system is deactivated in the infant. If, however, helpless attachment figures do not respond to the baby bids for help, then both systems, attachment and survival defense, remain strongly activated, and the baby experiences the same lack of solution to his fear that characterizes the interaction with a straightforwardly maltreating parent.

According to polyvagal theory (Porges, 2007), the dorsal nucleus of the vagus nerve is activated in the face of impending danger whenever fight/flight defensive responses are impossible and help asked for through the activation of the attachment system is not predictably forthcoming. The activation of the dorsal vagus brings forth collapsed body posture, loose muscular tone, low heartbeat and respiratory frequency, numbing and a deep feeling of helplessness. It can lead to the vagal syncope and the condition called feigned death, which has been related to dissociative detachment from reality (Schore, 2009). For these reasons—simultaneous conflicting activation of the attachment and the defense systems, and setting dissociative processes into motion—infant disorganized attachment can be regarded as an early relational trauma (attachment trauma) even when it is not caused by overt aggressive behavior of the caregivers (Schore, 2009). This analysis of infant attachment disorganization as the outcome of the simultaneous and conflicting activation of attachment and survival defense may explain why, according to two longitudinal research studies (Dutra, Bureau, Holmes, Lyubchik, & Lyons-Ruth, 2009; Ogawa, Sroufe, Weinfield, Carlson, & Egeland, 1997), infant attachment disorganization predicts dissociative tendencies throughout the developmental years both when it is linked to parental overt abuse and when it is not.

The idea of an unsolvable relational conflict underpinning infant attachment disorganization paves the way to understanding a typical phenomenon: children who have been disorganized in their infant attachment interactions develop a tendency to control the relationship with their attachment figures through dominant aggression and/or care-giving behaviors (inverted attachment). This understanding is based on an evolutionary approach to the inborn basis of human relatedness, which is the theme of the following section.

Attachment and other systems underpinning interpersonal behavior

The attachment theory is firmly grounded in evolutionary psychology (Bowlby, 1969). Contributions from social psychology (e.g., Kenrick, Nieuweboer, & Bunk, 2010), neuroscience (Panksepp & Biven, 2011), and clinical psychology (Cortina & Liotti, 2014; Liotti & Gilbert, 2011) further elaborated the idea, first advanced by Bowlby (1969), that human relatedness is organized by multiple psychobiological systems based on inborn tendencies that are the outcome of evolutionary processes. All these systems are composed by a universal inborn disposition to act in view of a specific biosocial goal (e.g., care-seeking, sexual mating, defining the rank of dominance in social groups), and by individually acquired structures of memory and expectation that regulate specific behavioral strategies for achieving the system's goal. For instance, infants construct different structures of memory and expectation on the basis of the different attitudes of the caregivers' (sensitive, rejecting, ambivalent, hostile or utterly helpless and abdicating parental responsibilities) in responding to their bids for help and soothing. Bowlby (1969) called these structures Internal Working Models (IWM) of attachment.

Besides attachment and survival defense, four other motivations with an inborn basis must be considered in the study of the abuser-abused relationship: care giving, sexuality, competitiveness and predatory aggression. The care-giving system is not simply the outcome of childhood memories in the adult of how requests for soothing and help were met by early attachment figures. It is based on a specific inborn tendency, just as the attachment and the defense systems are. The inborn basis of the care-giving system is shown by the fact that in every species of mammals nurturing tendencies are represented in a specific brain area different from the one related to the attachment system, and are influenced by specific brain chemicals (Panksepp & Biven, 2011). George and Solomon (2011) masterfully explored the cognitive, emotional and behavioral characteristics of the care-giving system. The operations of the sex system are also mapped onto different brain areas and operate through different brain biochemistry compared with the attachment and care-giving systems (Panksepp & Biven, 2011). This functional independence of the sex system from those regulating attachment and care-giving explains why the complex dynamics linking harmoniously attachment to sexuality in the interaction between adult sentimental partners are quite different from the conflicting ones involved in the interactions between a child and a sexually abusive although not violent adult caregiver. The abnormal tensions between attachment, care giving and sexuality lie at the ground of the psychopathological consequences of childhood sexual abuse within the family.

The goal of the competitive system is to define the hierarchies of dominance-submission in social interactions: for this reason it is also called the social ranking system. The specific type of behavior controlled by the ranking system is called by ethologists ritualized aggressive behavior, because competitive aggression is not aimed at damaging another living being (as are both predatory and survival defense types of aggression) but rather at forcing the opponent to submit (Gilbert, 1989, 2000). It is of obvious importance for clinicians dealing with children raised in maltreating families to be able to distinguish ritualized aggression (e.g., spanking children to achieve obedience) from malignant aggression—the latter being a predator-like form of aggression aimed at damaging or killing the victim and able to activate in the victim the survival defense system.

Another evolution-based motivational system must be mentioned here because of its importance to psychotherapy. This system regulates cooperative behavior and is involved in the construction of the therapeutic alliance (Cortina & Liotti, 2014). Tomasello and his collaborators (Tomasello, 1999, 2009; Warneken, Chen, & Tomasello, 2006) provided theoretical arguments and empirical studies supporting the hypothesis that the tendency to cooperate on equal grounds exceeds by far in humans the capacity for egalitarian cooperation observed in other mammal species. They argued that the Darwinian adaptation responsible for the huge development of cooperativeness in humans is the link between the biological and the cultural evolution of our species. The ability to point at an object with the intention of sharing attention to it with a mate, an ability that is observed in human infants, in every culture, at the same age (about the tenth month of life) is the hallmark of the inborn basis of the cooperative system (Tomasello, 1999; for a treatise of the anthropological and philosophical reflections, over the centuries, on the uniquely human ability to use the pointing finger, see Tallis, 2010).

It should be emphasized that predation and survival defense were not selected by evolutionary processes for the regulation of social behavior. Members of our species, however, can direct predatory aggression and survival defense to other human beings. Very rarely activated in the social interaction of other animal species, in humans the operations of the survival defense and the predation systems must be considered key in most interactions between the abused and the abused.

Some typical emotions and specific behaviors involved in the operations of the above mentioned systems—those primarily interpersonal and those that albeit not selected by evolution to regulate social behavior become pathologically involved in traumatic interactions between human beings—are listed in Table 1. The table's contents should not be regarded as exhaustive, given the complexity of the topic: they only aim at providing readers with a bird' eye view of the landscape of evolutionary and neuroscience approaches to

Table 1. Evolution-Based Motivational Systems in Humans.

SYSTEM	FUNCTION	BEHAVIORS	AFFECTS	BRAIN
Survival defense	Alert to danger. Protect self from threats to life	Freezing. Fight/flight. Feigned death (vagal syncope). Killing a predator.	Fright. Destructive rage. Helplessness.	Brain stem (orthosympathetic and vagal systems)
Attachment	Care-eliciting. Seeking for protective proximity, help and soothing	Separation cry. Approaching and clinging to a caregiver.	Separation anxiety. Sadness for the loss. Joy at reunion.	Limbic system
Care-giving	Protecting kin from danger. Soothing their distress	Nurturance. Comforting hugs.	Anxious solicitude. Protective tenderness.	Limbic system
Ranking (Competitive system)	Defining the social rank of dominance and submission	Ritualized aggression (competitiveness). Yielding responses (submissiveness). Dominance.	Anger. Shame. Pride.	Limbic system
Sex	Reproduction and sexual mating	Courting behavior. Sexual intercourse. Maintaining sexual couple.	Lustful wishes and pleasure. Romantic love	Brain stem. Limbic system
Cooperation	Sharing goals. Alliance.	Pointing finger. Shared attention and plans.	Sharing. Egalitarian feelings.	Limbic system. Frontal cortex.
Predation	Getting food	Destructive aggression	Power excitement.	Brain stem.

motivation, emotion and goal-directed behavior. For more details on the emotions and behaviors involved in the operations of the motivational systems mentioned in Table 1, (see Cortina & Liotti, 2014; Gilbert, 1989; Panksepp & Biven, 2011).

An important aspect of the multi-motivational theory based on evolutionary principles is that the intense activation of a motivational system tends to inhibit the concurrent operations of the other systems. Thus, for instance, when the activation of the attachment system is regulated by a secure IWM and an attachment figure is available to help, an infant's defense system that has been activated by perceived danger is promptly inhibited and even totally deactivated. If the activation is less intense, there can be a smooth, harmonious interaction between two motivational systems, for instance when a caregiver simultaneously displays care-giving and dominant behavior in gently but firmly forbidding a child to engage in dangerous actions. There are, however, also less harmonious, conflicting and even seriously disordered interactions between motivational systems, such as those involved in infant attachment disorganization and in the controlling strategies.

The disorganized/controlling strategies

The conflict between the two evolved systems, attachment and defense, which characterizes attachment disorganization in infancy is rather regularly followed, during early childhood, by the untoward activity of two other systems: ranking and care giving. There is robust evidence (Lyons-Ruth & Jacobvitz, 2008) that infants who are disorganized in their attachments tend to become either bossy children who strive to obtain dominance by exerting aggressive ranking competitiveness toward the caregiver (controlling-punitive strategy), or children who invert the attachment relationship and display precocious care giving toward their parents (controlling-caregiving strategy). A major cause of the controlling-caregiving strategy is the relationship with a vulnerable, helpless parent who encourages the child to invert the normal direction of the attachment-caregiving interaction between children and adults. Parents who perceive their children as powerful and evil, and tend to take a submissive attitude toward their displays of ranking aggressiveness, may unwittingly foster the development of a controlling-punitive strategy (for examples, see Hesse, Main, Abrams, & Rifkin, 2003).

The controlling strategies seem to compensate for disorganization in the child-parent interactions: they allow for *organized* interpersonal exchanges with the caregivers, thus reducing the likelihood of dissociative processes during these exchanges (Liotti, 2011). This organization, however, is not based on a harmonious interaction between the child's different motivational systems (attachment, ranking, and care-giving): rather, it is achieved through the compulsory substitution of the attachment system's operations with the activities of another system. Therefore, organization in the interpersonal exchanges between the child whose infant attachment has been disorganized and the abdicating or maltreating caregiver comes at a high price: a controlling-caregiving strategy that follows infant attachment disorganization increases the risk for developing internalizing disorders during childhood, while a controlling-punitive strategy is a risk factor for externalizing disorders (Moss, Smolla, Cyr, Dubois-Comtois, Mazzarello, & Berthiaume, 2006). Moreover, controlling strategies are liable to collapse in the face of traumas, pain, threats of separation or other life events that intensely activate the child's attachment system (Hesse et al., 2003). During episodes of collapse of the controlling strategies the child's thoughts and behavior suggest that dissociative processes are at work, presumably because of the reactivation of the disorganized IWM that links attachment to defense in a conflicting way (Hesse et al., 2003; Liotti, 2004, 2009, 2011).

Disorganized infant behavior and the disorganized/controlling strategies exemplify an untoward occurrence that is also typical of every interpersonal exchange between the abused and their abusers: disharmony in the shifting from the activity of a motivational system to the activation of a different one. The abuser-abused relationship is not only characterized by unbearable mental pain inflicted by the abuser to the abused: it is also a disorder in the complex dynamics between the multiple inborn dispositions that allow human relatedness to proceed along healthy pathways.

Disordered tensions between motivational systems in the abused

A harmonic shift between the attachment and the defense systems takes place, for instance, when attachment becomes a motivational priority *after* infants are exposed to severely distressing events that activate their survival defense system. An example of a disordered or disharmonic shift between attachment and survival defense is provided by the still face procedure (Adamson & Frick, 2003; Tronick, 2003). During the 3-minute interaction with a mother who remains immobile and with her face totally unexpressive, the fright and the bodily collapse (hypoarousal) observed in the infant can be ascribed to an abnormal shift from the activity of the attachment system to the activation of the survival defense system (Schore, 2009). The harmonic order of activation of attachment and survival defense (attachment is activated *after* defense) is typically violated in disorganized attachments, either by the abdicating caregiver's behavior or by the eruptions of violent behavior that interrupt caregiving. If violent behavior (from wild shouting to physical attack) erupts in the middle of a parent's behavior, which until then has been more or less caring, this is very likely to be appraised by the infant's brain as akin to a predator's howls, roars, and physical aggression. This appraisal inverts the sequel of survival defense and care-seeking that constitutes the normal order of activation of the two systems predicated by evolutionary processes.

Violent behavior that interrupts parental caretaking and severely hurts children illustrates also another kind of abnormal shift between basic motivational systems. Usually predator behavior is not addressed to members of the same animal species. In the technical terminology of ethological science, there is either no inborn *action rule* that activates the predation system within social interactions between members of the same species, or there is a *stopping rule* that usually puts a brake to aggressive behavior in social interactions before it reaches the extremes of predatory aggression (for the technical definitions of action rules and stopping rules in ethology, see Dawkins, 1976, p. 42). Only in humans these action and stopping rules are often violated, as tragically testified by so many instances of humans' physical violence aimed at damaging or even killing other human beings.

The disorganized/controlling strategies are further instances of violation of the rules governing the activation of the evolution-based motivational systems. Care-giving and competitive aggression are normally primed by, respectively, another member of the social group requiring help/comfort or displaying the ritualized type of aggression aimed at defining the dominant or the submissive rank in the interaction. The inborn action rules of these systems do not comprise the *previous* activation of the attachment (care-seeking) system. From an evolutionary point of view, it would obviously be non-adaptive if any inborn action rule that predicates the need of seeking care would be a pre-condition for engaging competitive aggression or nurturance in social interactions. The disorganized/controlling strategies involve exactly such a maladaptive sequence: first the activation of the attachment system in the child, and immediately thereafter the activation of either the competitive (controlling-punitive strategy) or the care-giving (controlling-caregiving) systems.

Physical abuse perpetrated by attachment figures on children who have been disorganized in their infant attachments causes malignant variants of the disorganized/controlling strategies. Physical abuse, even when it involves competitive (ranking) and not predatory aggression, primes in the children the activation of the ranking system in its yielding, submissive subroutine (rather than in the dominant subroutine observed in the controlling-punitive strategy), in the attempt to pacify the perpetrator's aggression. In addition to the yielding subroutine of the ranking system, sexual abuse involves the untoward activation of the child's sexual system. When the perpetrator's violence exceeds the limits of ritualized aggression characteristic of the ranking system, and is sadistically aimed at inflicting physical damage or at killing—i.e., when the perpetrator's aggression is an expression of the activation of the predation system—the violation of the inborn order regulating the shifts from one motivational system to another tragically reaches its climax.

A clinical vignette illustrates how the analysis of the abuser-abused relationship according to an evolutionary multi-motivational theory may work in clinical practice. Carla, a 28-year-old married woman suffering from dissociative identity disorder, reported during her psychotherapy memories suggesting an infant disorganized attachment to her mother, later episodes of physical abuse suffered at the hand of the mother and possibly of sexual abuse in the relationship with her father. Before these abuses, Carla (an only child) developed a controlling-caregiving strategy toward her mother who was obviously suffering from depression. The activation of Carla's caregiving system during daily interactions with the mother displaced and inhibited the expression of straightforward care seeking behavior. This prevented the manifestation, in the form of clear dissociative symptoms, of the underlying dissociative processes linked to the IWM of disorganized attachment, but at a heavy price: the development of an internalizing disorder manifested as anxiety, depression and an atypical anorexic pattern during Carla's late childhood. After the episodes of physical abuse in the interaction with her mother, the shifts from attachment to care giving were complicated by shifts also from the abnormally activated care-giving system (inverted attachment) to the ranking system operating in the submissive sub-routine in order to pacify her mother's aggression. The childhood habit of denigrating herself while expressing admiration for the mother ("How beautiful and clever are you, mummy, while I am such an ugly and stupid little girl!") developed during adulthood into self-attacking beliefs and emotions of shame and guilt. Shame is linked to the yielding subroutine of the ranking system (Gilbert, 1989), while guilt is linked to the activation of the caregiving system when an inability or unwillingness to soothe the suffering of a beloved person is perceived (for more detailed information concerning this clinical case see Liotti, 1995).

Disordered tensions between the abuser's motivational systems in the relationship with the abused

The multiple disordered shifts between different motivational systems in the abused during interactions with an abusive attachment figure make up a complex scenario. This is matched by a similarly disordered sequence in the activation of motivational systems in the abuser. The case of Carla's mother provides an illustration of this assertion. Carla's mother was chronically depressed, very likely as a consequence of the unresolved loss of both parents during her childhood. Unresolved losses involve the chronic and unsuccessful activation of the attachment system in the sufferer (Bowlby, 1980). The operations of a parent's chronically activated attachment system may be unwittingly directed toward a child—a possibility that may explain the disorganization of the infant's attachment in the relationship with parents who, although not violent toward their children, are suffering from unresolved losses and traumas (Main & Hesse, 1990; for references to more recent studies on parental helplessness and emotional distress as a cause of infant attachment disorganization see George & Solomon, 2011). On this basis, we can infer that both Carla and her mother very often experienced, in themselves and in their relationship, an abnormal dynamic tension between attachment (care-seeking) and care giving. Moreover, when the attachment rather than the care-giving system is active in a parent and directed toward an infant or a child, the stage is set for possible outbursts of impulsive aggression. In a famous paper, Bowlby (1984) argued that aggression is normally evoked during the operations of the attachment system when the need to be soothed is not met by a proper response from the person to whom the need is addressed (a child's competence in taking care of a parent is obviously very limited). Needless to say, the abrupt rage of an adult who is taking care of a child is perceived by the child not as the expression of the adult's behavior being motivated by the intrusion of care-seeking motivations, but rather as a threat that can activate either the child's ranking system or the survival defense system. In turn, the child's responses linked to the ranking system (either competitive aggression or submissive yielding) can activate the same system in the parent, while freezing, fight or flight responses expressing the operations of the child's defense system may evoke the activation of the defense or even the predation system in the parent. This line of reasoning allows for the inference that during their daily interactions not only Carla's, but also her mother's behavior and subjective experience shifted very often and in a very disorderly manner (indeed, without rhyme or reason) between the manifestations of different motivational systems: care-seeking, care-giving, competitive aggression or yielding, defense and at least on one occasion even predatory-like behavior—systems that normally do not operate simultaneously or in quick succession in any human relationship.

One memory of particularly severe physical abuse, among many others reported by Carla, illustrates these abnormal shifts between different motivational systems. Howling "horrible words", the mother was expressing her disapproval of Carla's "absent mindedness": Carla, then 5 years old, had failed in the always-difficult task of helping her mother as she requested (the request and rage expressed by the howl were very likely linked to operations of the mother's attachment system). Carla reacted by freezing (her evolved brain automatically appraised the howl as akin to a predator's roar, and responded with the activation of her survival defense system). The mother seemingly appraised Carla's freezing as a sign of defiance, and abruptly pushed her daughter to the ground (possibly an automatic response of the mother's ranking system). Carla cried for help from her father (who very rarely responded to Carla's attachment cries, and did not on this occasion) and tried to flee (a response of the survival defense system). At this the mother, who was wearing a wooden-soled sandal, hit Carla's head with a kick: a behavior linked to the predation system. With her head bleeding, Carla's cry now became directed toward her mother (attachment behavior now mixed with the persisting activation of the defense system, as is typical of attachment disorganization). This cry seemed to succeed in activating the mother's care-giving system: while still enraged and bitterly reproaching her daughter for her absent-mindedness (ranking system, dominant subroutine), the woman dressed Carla's wound.

Another tragic memory reported by Carla illustrates what may be the rule rather than the exception in families where infant attachment disorganization is followed by abuse during childhood: the disordered shifts between different motivational systems in the relationship with the abusive parent may extend, albeit usually in a different pattern, to the relationship with the other parent. Sometimes the pattern of disordered motivational shifts in the interaction with the formerly non-abusive parent pave the way for further abuse even in this relationship, as it was true in Carla's relationship with her father.

When she was 10-year-old, Carla was worried by her parents threatening to break their marriage. She wished to protect her obviously depressed mother from the further suffering of foreseeable divorce. She also felt solidarity toward her father, whom she imagined to feel sexually deprived because she had witnessed the mother's explicit rebuttal of sexual intercourse during the frequent conjugal quarrels at home. While Carla's care-giving system underpinned these protective attitudes toward both her parents, her attachment system was also active and dictated the wish to maintain the protection she felt in having two attachment figures at home, however feeble and uncertain this was. Thus, with this care-giving state of mind, Carla readily accepted her father's increasing requests for companionship and affection after the mother decided to sleep alone in another room. During the evening, she began to spend hours in the conjugal bedroom where the father was alone. On at least one occasion, Carla's father misinterpreted his daughter's caring attempts to soothe his distress and loneliness, and responded to them as if they were sexual approaches. Carla reacted to this misinterpretation with a frankly dissociative episode involving dissociative amnesia: in the psychotherapy sessions dealing with this episode she vaguely remembered heavy petting, but could not say how the father's sexual approach ended (very likely shortly before penetration). The disconcerting activation of the sexual system, in a scenario where the quick transitions between the attachment and the care-giving systems were already quite abnormal, enormously complicated the already quite disordered shifts between the attachment and the care-giving systems in both father and daughter.

There are obviously dramatic differences between histories of attachment disorganization followed by controlling strategies but not by overt abuse (where the shifts are between attachment, survival defense and either care-giving or competitive ranking), and histories of abuser-abused relationships where incest and/or episodes of predator-like aggression are also present. There is, however, a common thread between these different types of traumatic relationships: it is a seriously disordered pattern of activation of different motivational systems that violates the inborn rules governing the transition between motivational systems in both the abused and the abuser.

Concluding remarks

This paper has applied the evolution-based, multi-motivational theory of human relatedness to the analysis of the abuser–abused relationship, when the abuse takes place within the family and is accompanied by attachment disorganization. This theory may have important implications for understanding the genesis of dissociation in family contexts. It predicts that the emergence of clinically latent dissociative tendencies in the form of clear cut dissociative symptoms is quite often contingent upon the strong and durable activation of the disorganized attachment system in the context of the interaction between the child and the caregiver, the mediating mechanism being the collapse of the interpersonal controlling strategies (Liotti, 2011). It also suggests the possibility that the origins and inner structure of reciprocally dissociated ego states can be traced back to basic motivational systems, whose function cannot be integrated with the function of other systems because of disordered shifts between them—a suggestion compatible with the tenets of the theory of structural dissociation of the personality (Van der Hart, Nijenhuis, & Steele, 2006). In this perspective, the characteristics of each relationship between the abuser and the abused play a key role in both the origins and the structure of dissociated ego states.

References

Adamson, L. B., & Frick, J. E. (2003). The still face: A history of a shared experimental paradigm. *Infancy*, *4*, 451–473. doi:10.1207/S15327078IN0404_01

Bowlby, J. (1969). *Attachment and Loss* (Vol. 1). London, UK: The Hogarth Press.

Bowlby, J. (1980). *Attachment and Loss* (Vol. 3). London, UK: The Hogarth Press.

Bowlby, J. (1984). Violence in the family as a disorder of the attachment and caregiving systems. *The American Journal of Psychoanalysis*, *44*, 9–27. doi:10.1007/BF01255416

Cantor, C. (2005). *Evolution and posttraumatic stress*. London, UK: Routledge.

Cortina, M., & Liotti, G. (2014). An evolutionary outlook on motivation: Implications for the clinical dialogue. *Psychoanalytic Inquiry*, *34*, 864–899. doi:10.1080/07351690.2014.968060

Dawkins, R. (1976). Hierarchical organization: A candidate principle for ethology. In P. P. G. Bateson, & R. A. Hinde (Eds.), *Growing points in ethology* (pp. 7–54). New York, NY: Cambridge University Press.

Dutra, L., Bureau, J., Holmes, B., Lyubchik, A., & Lyons-Ruth, K. (2009). Quality of early care and childhood trauma: A prospective study of developmental pathways to dissociation. *The Journal of Nervous and Mental Disease*, *197*, 383–390. doi:10.1097/NMD.0b013e3181a653b7

George, C., & Solomon, J. (2011). Caregiving helplessness. In J. Solomon, & C. George (Eds.), *Disorganized attachment and caregiving* (pp. 133–166). New York, NY: The Guilford Press.

Gilbert, P. (1989). *Human nature and suffering*. London, UK: Erlbaum.

Gilbert, P. (2000). The relationship of shame, social anxiety and depression: The role of the evaluation of social rank. *Clinical Psychology & Psychotherapy*, *7*, 174–189. doi:10.1002/(ISSN)1099-0879

Hesse, E., Main, M., Abrams, K. Y., & Rifkin, A. (2003). Unresolved states regarding loss or abuse can have “second-generation” effects: Disorganized, role-inversion and frightening ideation in the offspring of traumatized non-maltreating parents. In D. J. Siegel, & M. F. Solomon (Eds.), *Healing trauma: Attachment, mind, body and brain* (pp. 57–106). New York, NY: Norton.

Kenrick, D. T., Nieuweboer, S., & Bunk, A. P. (2010). Universal mechanisms and cultural diversity: Replacing the blank slate with a coloring book. In M. Schaller, S. Haine, A. Norenzayan, & T. Kameda (Eds.), *Evolution, culture and the human mind* (pp. 257–272). Mahwah, NJ: Erlbaum.

Liotti, G. (1995). Disorganized/disoriented attachment in the psychotherapy of the dissociative disorders. In S. Goldberg, R. Muir, & J. Kerr (Eds.), *Attachment theory: Social, developmental and clinical perspectives* (pp. 343–363). Hillsdale, NJ: The Analytic Press.

Liotti, G. (2004). Trauma, dissociation and disorganized attachment: Three strands of a single braid. *Psychotherapy: Theory, Research, Practice, Training, 41*, 472–486. doi:10.1037/0033-3204.41.4.472

Liotti, G. (2009). Attachment and dissociation. In P. F. Dell, & J. A. O'Neill (Eds.), *Dissociation and the dissociative disorders: DSM-V and beyond* (pp. 53–66). New York, NY: Routledge.

Liotti, G. (2011). Attachment disorganization and the controlling strategies: An illustration of the contributions of attachment theory to developmental psychopathology and to psychotherapy integration. *Journal of Psychotherapy Integration, 21*, 232–252. doi:10.1037/a0025422

Liotti, G., & Gilbert, P. (2011). Mentalizing, motivation and social mentalities: Theoretical consideration s and implications for psychotherapy. *Psychology and Psychotherapy, 84*, 9–25.

Lyons-Ruth, K., & Jacobvitz, D. (2008). Attachment disorganization: Genetic factors, parenting contexts and developmental transformations from infancy to adulthood. In J. Cassidy, & P. R. Shaver (Eds.), *Handbook of attachment 2nd ed.*, (pp. 666–697). New York, NY: Guilford Press.

Main, M., & Hesse, E. (1990). Parents' unresolved traumatic experiences are related to infant disorganized attachment status: Is frightened and/or frightening parental behavior the linking mechanism? In M. T. Greenberg, D. Cicchetti, & E. M. Cummings (Eds.), *Attachment in the preschool years* (pp. 161–182). Chicago, IL: Chicago University Press.

Moss, E., Smolla, N., Cyr, C., Dubois-Comtois, K., Mazzarello, T., & Berthiaume, C. (2006). Attachment and behavior problems in middle childhood as reported by adult and child informants. *Development and Psychopathology, 18*, 425–444. doi:10.1017/S0954579406060238

Ogawa, J. R., Sroufe, L. A., Weinfield, N. S., Carlson, E. A., & Egeland, B. (1997). Development and the fragmented self: Longitudinal study of dissociative symptomatology in a nonclinical sample. *Development and Psychopathology, 9*, 855–879. doi:10.1017/S0954579497001478

Panksepp, J., & Biven, L. (2011). *The archaeology of mind: Neuroevolutionary origins of human emotions*. New York, NY: Norton.

Porges, S. W. (2007). The polyvagal perspective. *Biological Psychology., 74*, 116–143. doi:10.1016/j.biopsycho.2006.06.009

Schore, A. N. (2009). Attachment trauma and the developing right brain: Origins of pathological dissociation. In P. F. Dell, & J. A. O'Neil (Eds.), *Dissociation and the dissociative disorders: DSM-V and beyond* (pp. 107–141). New York, NY: Routledge.

Solomon, J., & George, C. (2011). Disorganization of maternal caregiving across two generations: The origins of caregiving helplessness. In J. Solomon, & C. George (Eds.), *Disorganized attachment and caregiving* (pp. 25–51). New York, NY: The Guilford Press.

Tallis, R. (2010). *Michelangelo's finger*. London, UK: Atlantic Books.

Tomasello, M. (1999). *The cultural origins of human cognition*. Cambridge, MA: Harvard University Press.

Tomasello, M. (2009). *Why we cooperate*. Cambridge, MA: The MIT Press.

Tronick, E. Z. (2003). Things still to be done on the still face effect. *Infancy*, *4*, 475–482. doi:10.1207/S15327078IN0404_02

Van der Hart, O., Nijenhuis, E. R. S., & Steele, K. (2006). *The haunted self: Structural dissociation and the treatment of chronic traumatization*. New York, NY: Norton.

Warneken, F., Chen, F., & Tomasello, M. (2006). Cooperative activities in young children and chimpanzees. *Child Development*, *77*, 640–663. doi:10.1111/cdev.2006.77.issue-3

Through the lens of attachment relationship: Stable DID, active DID and other trauma-based mental disorders

Adah Sachs, PhD

ABSTRACT
Some people with DID, despite years of DID-specific therapy (using the three-phase approach, ISSTD, 2011), seem unable to get better. In particular, they seem unable to remain physically safe ("Phase One") and report continued exposure to abuse. As every fresh hurt causes fresh dissociation, their DID becomes further entrenched over time. Moreover, as dissociation makes the person more vulnerable to being re-abused, they become caught up in a vicious cycle, which further obstructs their efforts toward recovery. In this paper, I propose the existence of two distinct presentations of DID, a Stable and an Active one. While people with Stable DID struggle with their traumatic past, with triggers that re-evoke that past and with the problems of daily functioning with severe dissociation, people with Active DID are, in addition, also engaged in a life of current, on-going involvement in abusive relationships, and do not respond to treatment in the same way as other DID patients. The paper observes these two proposed DID presentations in the context of other trauma-based disorders, through the lens of their attachment relationship. It proposes that the type, intensity and frequency of relational trauma shape—and can thus predict—the resulting mental disorder. It then offers an initial (partial) classification of trauma-based attachment modes and their corresponding symptomatic sequels. The analysis and formulations presented in this paper are based on attachment theory and extensive clinical observations.

There is growing evidence that, by and large, DID is amenable to psychotherapy along the lines of the *Three Phase Approach* (Phase-Oriented Treatment Approach; Brand, Loewenstein, & Spiegel, 2014; Brand et al., 2013, 2012; Dorahy et al., 2014; International Society for the Study of Trauma and Dissociation, 2011; Lloyd, 2016). In this paper, however, I would like to draw attention to a minority group where this treatment method fails to lead to improvement. Observing and analyzing the characteristics of this group will be used to place it in the context of other trauma-based mental disorders.

Stable and active did: Clinical observations

The process of a phase-oriented therapy is described in detail in *The Haunted Self* (Van der Hart, Nijenhuis, & Steele, 2006). Very briefly, it can be outlined as follows: at the start of therapy (*Phase One)*, the emphasis is on establishing trust between patient and therapist, stabilization of symptoms and improving safety in the person's life. This is done through psycho-education regarding DID; techniques for reducing acute stress (e.g., EMDR), learning to recognize unsafe relationships, high-risk behavior and triggers, and the overall responsible, predictable and supportive stance of the therapist. Although the ISSTD guidelines (2011) do not use attachment terminology explicitly, these are the very components of *a secure attachment* within the therapy relationship, with the result of greater safety in the patient's life and growing capacity for learning.

When Phase One is largely reached, it becomes safe to start processing the patient's traumatic history *(Phase Two)*. This history is largely dissociated and held by many alters. Trauma work may be lengthy and destabilizing, and all the resources obtained through *Phase One* are relied upon to help the person through this stage.

As the pain of the traumatic memories starts to reduce, alters become able to share more of their awareness with each other, which indicates the emergence of *co-consciousness* (as part of *Phase Three*). The relationships between alters gradually deepen and improve, as they all start to recognize their shared wish to survive, to be safe and maybe even to be happy. Where full *integration* is reached, alters no longer experience themselves as separate people, but as different states of mind of the same person, in much the same way that non-dissociative people experience themselves.

This journey is invariably complex and challenging, but for some patients, it proves to be insurmountable. Despite all their efforts, and while receiving therapy as described above, they do not improve. They may seem to develop some significant insights and to make deep contact with the therapist, but their overall symptom picture remains largely unchanged, especially with regard to their physical safety. These patients come to their sessions reporting—or bearing evidence of—fresh hurt: bruises, burn marks, missing nails, missing teeth or broken limbs. Both men and women report rapes; women report rape-induced pregnancies (Bentovim, 1995; Chu, 2011; Middleton, 2013a; Miller, 2012; Ross, 2004; Salter, 2013).

These incidents are sometimes said to be "accidents"; sometimes, they are explained as punishment (by their abusers) for telling secrets in their therapy sessions, with an implied accusation of the therapist; sometimes they are confessed to be self-harm, or the patient is unable to recall how or when the injuries happened. Very disturbingly, with some patients such incidents occur repeatedly and frequently, and nothing that the therapist offers, explains or does seems to have any effect on their reoccurrence. *Phase One* seems impossible to reach: rather than gradual stabilization and improved safety, these patients accumulate an ever-growing history of fresh hurt between their therapy sessions and maybe even as a result of these sessions.

Such cases inevitably raise much anxiety in therapists, as well as clinical and ethical questions: does the therapy actually help the person or does the therapist convey to the patient a stance of passivity, indifference, helplessness or even condoning of the abuse? Therapists thus often stipulate that unless the person is able to stop their involvement in abusive relationships; the therapy cannot continue (Richardson, 2012).

The repetition of ***Rona's***[1] *abusive contact with her family had already destroyed several of her attempts at therapy. Sometimes it was Rona who held back, because she was afraid of being punished by her family or of appearing repulsive to the therapist; and sometimes the therapist had become exasperated with her inability to stay away from abuse and ended the work. Yet Rona, desperate as she was to be free of hurt, has never been able to stop these incidents; and, as she was largely dissociated from these occurrences, she could never really explain to the therapist why.*

Therapists of people like Rona struggle with on-going anxiety regarding the usefulness, quality and ethical grounds of their clinical practice. They also struggle with constant worry regarding the safety of their patient, and the frustration of their repeated failures to reach Phase One.[2]

I would like to suggest that the success or failure to achieve stability and safety in the life of some DID patients is due to the presence of two different presentations of DID, a *stable* and an *active* ones, which do not respond to treatment in the same way. While the Three Phase Approach works well for the *stable* presentation, it fails to establish contact with people with the *active* presentation.

I further suggest that the differences between the two presentations lies in the differences between their *attachment modes*,[3] which, in turn, are based on the *type, intensity* and *frequency* of trauma in their attachment relationship. This "lens" will later be applied to other trauma-born mental disorders.

Stable DID

I suggest the term "*Stable DID*" for those cases where the childhood trauma that caused the DID has stopped. This could have occurred through a variety of changes in the patient's life (e.g., the abuser died or left. See discussion of Table 1, below). These patients struggle daily with the dangers of dissociation (e.g., amnesia to traumatic experiences resulting in ignorance of danger

Table 1. Linking trauma, attachment and symptomatic sequels.

		Key characteristics of relational trauma	Resulting attachment mode	Symptomatic sequels
Decreasing severity.	**A**	**Type**: Ongoing, life-threatening, sadistic abuse by multiple attachment figures in a group context. Abuse started in early childhood and never stopped **Intensity**: very high **Frequency**: almost constant **Attachment figure dependency**: very high, almost constant	IAc	-Active DID **Therapeutic prespective**: High dependency perpetuates traumatic relationships and inhibits change.
	B	**Type**: Prolonged and severe childhood abuse, now ended. Harm may continue via agent who *symbolizes* the original perpetrator (e.g., a violent partner, abusive alters, self- harm, "accident proneness") **Intensity**: high **Frequency**: intermittent **Attachment figure dependency**: high, intermittent	IAs, possibly with some IAc features	-Stable DID -Other DDs -Other trauma-based disorders including BPD, eating disorders & self-harm **Therapeutic prespective**: Gaps in dependency states may allow changes.
	C	**Type**: Long-term relational trauma, but no overt abuse. Attachment figure deeply preoccupied with death, mentally unwell or otherwise dysfunctional **Intensity**: moderate **Frequency**: continual **Attachment figure dependency**: varied	"Classic" disorganized attachment, "caregiving disorganized" (Liotti) IAs.	-Disorders mimicking the attachment figure (e.g., depression) -High-risk behavior -PDs -Self-harm -No clear disorders **Therapeutic prespective**: Deficiency in sense of Self.
	D	**Type**: Non-relational trauma (e.g., terrorist attack, violent crime, serious accident, natural disaster). **Relational Intensity**: mildly elevated due to elevated needs. **Frequency**: episodic **Attachment figure dependency**: mildly elevated	No effect on attachment mode (attachment remains as it was before the trauma)	-PTSD -No Disorders **Therapeutic prespective**: Trauma specific.

signals), as well as with the chaos of a life run by a group of separate alters. These patients are also highly vulnerable because of the susceptibility to re-traumatizing triggers, which can appear, innocently enough, in their lives in the present, and can never be fully avoided.

Jim, *a man who as a toddler was often locked up in a small cupboard as punishment, was "triggered" by getting stuck in a lift, at the age of 35. When the lift doors opened ten minutes later, Jim was found lying on the floor of the lift, sucking his thumb, wet, and unable to speak. In subsequent sessions, he was able to recall his terror of dying alone in the dark and airless cupboard of his childhood.*

Helen *walked up to a bearded man with a red tie that she saw in the street near my practice and said to him that she was a good girl and would come with him without any fuss. The red tie and the beard, resembling her uncle's, were a trigger for a child alter who used to surface when she was taken by that uncle to be abused by a group of men. Mercifully, the man she met in the street kindly offered to walk her to where she was going, and brought her to my office.*

Such triggers are extremely distressing. They are debilitating to one's capacity to lead a normal life and can be dangerous (e.g., the man in the red tie might have accepted my patient's sexual offer). However, the danger is incidental: The person's life is not centered around harmful relationships or dangerous situations. The therapy, therefore, can focus on reducing the impact of triggers or on "stabilizing of symptoms" (Phase One); on processing the original trauma (Phase Two); and finally on recovery.

Active DID

By contrast, I suggest the term "*Active DID*" for those cases where the person, like Rona, is still actively involved in a life of abuse, which they are unable to stop. This may not be initially apparent:

Forty-year-old Paula had told me, at the start of her therapy that she had lost all contact with her abusive family over 20 years ago that no family member knew where she now lived and that her last visit to her mother's home was at her 16th birthday party. However, after a few months of therapy it transpired that while Paula, who initiated the therapy, was indeed estranged from her family, many of her alters were visiting home regularly, some spoke to her mother on the phone every day, and the family was certainly aware of her phone number and home address. Furthermore, specific alters were responsible for telling her mother everything that had been said in therapy, which explained how her mother knew when to punish Paula for telling the family secrets. After years in which Paula believed that the family had magic powers, she realized that their accurate knowledge of her whereabouts had always been facilitated by her own alters. She also realized that the many injuries on her body, including pregnancies and abortions, corresponded with family holiday gatherings.

Paula, at that point, had never really left home, though she had a flat of her own. She was actively connected to her family, where being abused—as well as abusing others—was part of the family culture. Indeed, over time she has recalled many occasions in which she, or, rather, some of her alters, had abused other people. And because the abuse she was part of as a victim, a witness and a perpetrator was too unbearable to keep in mind, she dissociated, over and over again, with new alters being created and her DID becoming further entrenched.

Paula was not able to stop the abuse in her life at an early point of her therapy (i.e., in "Phase One"). She was not even able to explain how or why these incidents occurred, and, most critically, what was the power that kept bringing her back into family gatherings, which she dreaded. I suggest that this power was her *attachment mode.*

Attachment modes

Attachment is our most basic survival instinct (Bowlby, 1958, 1988), and it works by making the baby of every species cling to an adult, the *attachment figure* [4] and stay within the orbit of that adult's attention. While the "clinging" or *attaching* to a specific adult is instinctive (Bowlby, 1958), the way to engage the full attention of a *particular* human adult is unique: it is shaped, individually, by the responses of that specific adult, and needs to be learned. Some attachment figures respond to cries; others to a smile or to baby being very quiet. As the engagement of the adult with the baby is crucial for the baby's survival, the baby learns very quickly how to invoke it (Suttie & Suttie, 1932). The behavioral patterns which succeed in engaging the attachment figure most fully become the *attachment mode* of the baby: his or her lifelong blueprint of relatedness.

Elements shaping the attachment mode: Type, intensity and frequency of distress

I suggest that three elements shape the baby's (and later, the adult's) attachment mode: the *type* of distress-behavior which engages the attachment figure; the *intensity* of the distress in the attachment relationship and the *frequency* of distress episodes that the baby is exposed to.

Type

The type of distress signals (i.e., attachment behavior) which engages a particular attachment figure can vary greatly, from the most natural expression of distress (e.g., a cry) to highly complicated clusters of distress signals. The behavior itself, as well as the type of response that it elicits from the attachment figure, creates a *type* of interaction which spells safety and closeness in the child's mind: In other words, they become the child's *attachment mode.*

While all attachment modes aim to increase safety and chances for survival, they are not all equally useful for survival or for healthy mental development. This is because some attachment figures respond only to attachment behavior which is dangerous or harmful to the child, thus increasing (rather than reducing) the distress and danger in the child's life. Where harmful behavior is the deepest way in which the child can engage the attachment figure, the child's *attachment mode* will be thus shaped.

Intensity

The degree of fear, pain or emotional devastation that the child experiences in the attachment relationship determines the intensity of attachment needs: The more severe the trauma, the more urgent and overwhelming are the attachment needs, and the more frantic the striving toward the attachment figure. In these moments, the child experiences complete *dependency* on the attachment figure, which makes him or her ready to assume *any type* of attachment behavior, including highly dangerous or painful ones (see *type*, above).

Frequency

The significance of the *frequency* of relational trauma (Schore, 1994, 2001) is not primarily in the quantity of traumatic events, but in the number and length of the ***gaps between*** the high intensity, high dependency traumatic episodes. These gaps are the windows of opportunity that the child has to develop relationships with people other than the attachment figure; to experience moments of independence; to be able to absorb and process other (nontraumatic) input; to have and make choices; and to develop a Self.

The longer these gaps are, the more opportunities for development and learning the person has. Children who grow up with very small or no gaps between high-intensity trauma and attachment needs are the least able to allow distance from their attachment figure and subsequently to develop and learn. For the same reason, they are also the least able to establish therapeutic relationships which will enable them to heal from trauma.[5]

Type, intensity and frequency of relational trauma across different modes of attachment

Secure attachment

Babies who can engage their attachment figures, predictably and consistently, through their most natural reactions to pain or fear (e.g., a cry), develop *secure attachment.* This is because their attachment figures are ready to respond when needed and are *attuned* to the baby's own ways of indicating distress. The *type* of behavior which alerts the attachment figure to baby's needs is baby's natural affect. The fact that this natural affect engages another person in a positive, helpful and loving way fosters the development of a Self, as the baby senses, wordlessly: I feel bad. I cry. Help comes. I feel good and strong. I am good. I'm loved.

Both the *intensity* and *frequency* of distress in this relationship are low (regardless of any distress that may exist outside the relationship), as the attachment figure is attentive and responsive to the baby's needs.

The degree of baby's *security* determines the extent of the baby's ability to increase the physical distance from the attachment figure and to explore the environment (Ainsworth, Blehar, Waters & Wall, 1978; Main, 1995). The freedom to go and explore, the capacity to be alone (Winnicott, 1958) and the pleasure of returning to the "secure base" (Bowlby, 1988) form the basis of the ability to learn and to play (Winnicott, 1967, 1971), and to continue to develop the Self (Kohut, 1977; Mollon, 1993)—all of which are necessary for a normal mental development.

Insecure attachment

Insecurely attached babies (both ambivalent and avoidant) have to modify their natural behavior (e.g., *not* to cry) in order to attract the attachment figure's attention. This may have long-term negative effects. Because the *type* of behavior that engages their attachment figure did not reflect their true affect or "true self" (Winnicott, 1960), their self-perception, confidence or ability to communicate openly may suffer. Nonetheless, this is a functional attachment mode, as their early ability to engage their attachment figure when in distress and to receive help had never been compromised. The *intensity* as well as the *frequency* of distress in such an attachment relationship is moderate (rather than low), because the attachment figure only responds once the baby has adjusted into the "required" type of attachment behavior.

Disorganized attachment

Sadly, some attachment figures do not respond to baby's attachment calls by reliably attending to safety. To start with, their responses appear to be unpredictable: the same attachment behavior (e.g., a cry) may sometimes elicit a hug, sometimes a beating (De Zulueta, 1993) and sometimes no response at all (see *Abdicating of Parental Role*, Liotti, this volume). For such a baby, it is difficult to establish a reliable way to call the attachment figure, leaving baby constantly alert to moment-by-moment clues about which behavior may bring safety *now*. This chaotic and stressful existence is disorganized attachment (Main & Solomon, 1986, 1990).

The *type* of behavior which engages the attachment figure is constantly changing; and when the child "gets it wrong" the response to the distress signals may be harmful (e.g., beating), or no response at all, forcing the child to keep trying. The *intensity* of distress in the relationship is high. The *frequency* of distress is also high, as distress episodes often do not get resolved.

Instead of having the attachment figure attuned to baby's needs, disorganized babies are, by necessity, constantly focused on the attachment figure. This means that they have little space—and no help—to learn about their environment or develop a Self. These developmental impairments carry into adulthood and are evident in many forms of mental disorders, including DID, where the Self becomes fragmented.

Furthermore, the behavior types which attract the attachment figure's attention may in themselves be dangerous or harmful (e.g., self-harm). Such attachment behavior increases, rather than reduces, the danger in the child's life. As increasing risk contradicts the very purpose of attachment behavior, such attachment behavior is clearly dysfunctional. Indeed, the new *reactive attachment disorder* classification (DSM-5: American Psychiatric Association, 2013, p. 265) views many clinical symptoms as disordered forms of attachment behavior.

Zooming in: Subgroups within disorganized attachment

I would like to propose that the disorganized category of attachment is grossly over inclusive and needs to be examined in more detail.

The disorganized category covers a very wide range of behavior and a very wide range of type, intensity and frequency of distress. It is generally thought of as a perpetual state of random chaos. This does not fit what we know about the lives of children who grow up in even the most pathological households: These children *do* learn how to reach their attachment figures and have modes of behavior which are not random (e.g., the appearance of specific alters in specific situations). This is because attachment behavior,

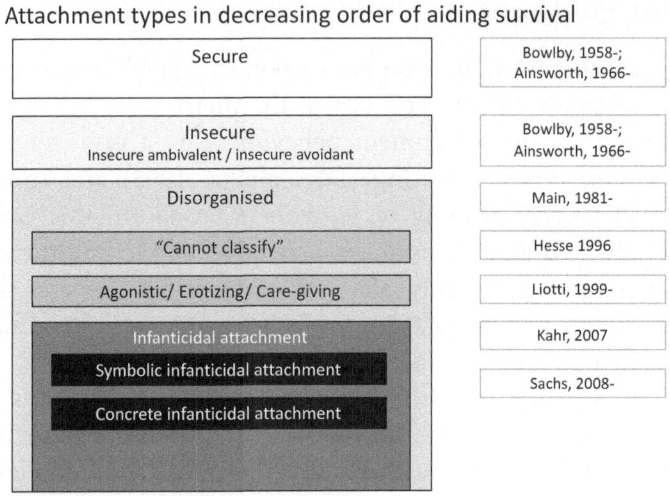

Figure 1. Attachment types in decreasing order of aiding survival.

however chaotic or dysfunctional, is never random. It always follows, reflects and matches the mental state and reaction patterns of the attachment figure. As attachment needs are crucial for survival, children and even babies soon "learn the signs" of their attachment figures; however, obscure these may be; and they find ways—however difficult and costly—to engage their attachment figure. I propose that these specific ways of engaging constitute distinct sub-groups within the seemingly formless, "disorganized" group. These sub-groups are shown in Figure 1, in the contexts of previously defined attachment modes. We may say that they are light rays or the "method within the madness" of disorganized attachment.

The first notion of differentiation within disorganized attachment was proposed by Hesse (1996) in his seminal paper on the emergence of a new and "can't classify" category. Hesse described an attachment behavior that did not match any of the then defined attachment categories, including the disorganized one. In this group, Hesse observed, "there appears to be a collapse in discourse strategy at a global (versus local) level" (Hesse, 1996, p. 5). He also found that the severity and scope of their trauma were particularly high. Both the scope of trauma and the scope of inconsistency of discourse strategy are evident in dissociative disorders (Dorahy, Middleton, Seager, Williams, & Chambers, 2016). Most importantly, these findings highlight the need for more meticulous differentiation within the chaotic, "disorganized" category.

Liotti (1999) subsequently described three forms of attempting to engage a highly dysfunctional attachment figure, who does not respond to ordinary attachment calls: The *erotizing type* engages through erotized behavior and may develop in a child whose attachment figure could only become fully engaged through sexual communication. The *agonistic type* engages through heated conflicts or violence; and the *care-giving* type fulfills attachment needs through offering care to a needy parent. In these attachment patterns, attachment needs masquerade as sexual, aggressive or care-giving behavior (see also Liotti, in this volume).

Kahr (2007) defined *Infanticidal Attachment* as the attachment behavior of a child whose attachment figure is deeply preoccupied with death, especially with regard to the child (unconscious infanticidal ideation). Such a child, aiming to engage their attachment figure, is constantly compelled to "brush against death": self-harm, high risk behavior, eating disorders, depression, addictions or suicide attempts[6] can be seen as attachment behavior for this attachment type, as the child strives to act in ways that are the most meaningful to the parent.

Sachs (2007) describes *Symbolic Infanticidal Attachment (IAs)*, where the attachment figure has no wish to harm the child—on the contrary, he or she may be extremely anxious to "save" the child. The child's attachment behavior (e.g., high-risk behavior) is thus not a death wish, but an attempt to engage the parent through their deepest preoccupations, which are grief, illness or death. Green (1986) describes a similar dynamic between a mother who is engrossed in loss and grief, and her child, whose life is governed by the need to compete with a dead person for the love of his mother. Sachs (2008) describes this attachment mode (IAs) in families of Holocaust survivors.

The damage that such self-representation causes to the development of a child is profound, because the child's depression, illness or looming death engages the attachment figure more than the child's live and developing Self. These children are thus forced to constantly hover between their natural aliveness and their parent's preoccupation with loss and death, causing profound disorganization.

However, the damage to the child is not caused directly by the attachment figure, but through the child's striving to represent or to *symbolize* for the parent that which the parent is most preoccupied with.

Some attachment figures, however, become fully engaged not through anxiously contemplating the possible death of the child, but through the concrete act of inflicting life threatening, sadistic abuse on the child. As in all attachment modes, the child strives toward the attachment figure by acting in the ways that most deeply engage him or her; in this case, by being fully cooperative with the most severe and extreme forms of abuse. This was termed *Concrete Infanticidal Attachment* (IAc) (Sachs, 2007, 2011, 2013). People with this attachment mode strive toward, rather than away from, severe pain or near-death abuse, because these are the only moments in which they feel truly held in the mind of the attachment figure, safe and loved. In IAc, full submission is necessary for reaching the attachment figure (see discussion of Table 1).

This attachment mode is the most severe type of attachment disorder, as it is entirely based on sadism and murderousness, which most obviously contradict the purpose of attachment.

Relational trauma and mental disorders: Initial classification

The notion that there is a close link between chronic childhood trauma and a long list of mental disorders is widely shared.[7] Howell (2005) states: "Chronic trauma...that occurs early in life has profound effects on personality development and can lead to the development of dissociative identity disorder (DID), other dissociative disorders, personality disorders, psychotic thinking ... anxiety, depression, eating disorders, and substance abuse" (p. iv).

I would like to suggest that this link is not random (see Nijenhuis, 2015),[8] but that the type of mental disorders which develops out of relational trauma can be largely predicted, using the lens of *type, intensity* and *frequency* of relational trauma and their impact on the attachment mode. Furthermore, I suggest that much of the symptom picture of trauma-born mental disorders is actually the person's attachment behavior.

For example, where the attachment figure only became fully engaged through sexually abusing the child (i.e., *type* of relational trauma), sexualized behavior is likely to become a central element in the child's (and later the adult's) behavior whenever he or she is in distress, that is, their attachment behavior. The symptom picture of a subsequent mental disorder (if any) will include a sexual component (e.g., promiscuity) or a reaction against it (e.g., self-harm).

The *severity* of the trauma will determine the intensity of attachment needs, and thus the level of dependency on the attachment figure for fulfilling these needs. High dependency maximizes the adherence to the *type* of attachment behavior that can engage the attachment figure and bring relief. In the example of sexualized attachment behavior, this will mark the difference between a person who is inappropriately flirtatious and a person whose behavior when distressed is a clinical symptom of mental disorder (e.g., pedophilia).

Frequent high-dependency moments in childhood allow very little opportunity for freedom from attachment needs and the development of other aspects of personality and Self. For example, in a family where sadistic violence is widely practiced and involves all members of the family (as victims, perpetrators or witnesses), fear is always present, and the (dysfunctional) attachment behavior is thus constantly activated. A person who grows up in such conditions is hard to engage in a thoughtful way, where violence is not present. This causes major challenges in the therapeutic relationship, as will later be discussed in relation to the treatment of people with *Active DID*.

A dysfunctional attachment mode is a reflection of the actual relationship between a child and his or her attachment figure. An attachment relationship which involves high levels of physical and mental harm (i.e., relational trauma) leads to attachment behaviors which involve high levels of physical and mental harm (i.e., mental disorder symptoms), which are shaped in the image of the original trauma. This forms the link between chronic childhood traumatization (relational trauma) and specific mental disorders.

Clinical discussion of Table 1: Four patient groups

Table 1 presents a preliminary classification of some trauma characteristics and their mental health sequels. Stable and Active DID are viewed in the context of other trauma-born mental disorders.

Group A

The most severely affected group consists of patients who are in an ongoing attachment relationship with their *original abusers*, which they have never left, and cannot leave, because the intensity of fear and dependency has never allowed any distance from the attachment figure(s).

The trauma described by Group A patients typically includes a life-long involvement in violent, sadistic and life-threatening abuse as a victim, a witness and a perpetrator. Importantly, the abuse occurs in the context of a group to which the person belongs, willingly or otherwise; and the group, as a whole, is the person's attachment figure (note the attachment plurality, mirrored in the structure of DID). Such a group may be a family, a religious sect, a care home, a military offshoot, a concentration camp, a pedophile ring or any other setting which has full control over the person's life and in which fear is high and constant. Within the group, severely abusive criminal acts (e.g., sex with children, torture) are deemed normative, moral or even virtuous (if not legal).

From an attachment perspective, the significance of the group context is manifold: While a child who is abused by one person may also have the experience of some safe relationships, the child who is brought up in an abusive group setting has no real notion of any safe relationships. Furthermore, an abusive group creates a cultural context, an "us", a sense of an exclusive belonging (e.g., Mafia families). The knowledge that the acts of the group are illegal in the wider society only increases the dependency on the group, as it enhances the sense of alienation from society and reduces the potential for making significant relationships "outside."

The intensity of the dependency is related to the person's perception of the power, size and cohesiveness of the group as a whole, as well as to the level of pain, fear and sadism which has to be endured. People who perceive their group to be large, well organized and possessing extraordinary powers (e.g., a Satanist cult) are thus the least able to distance themselves from their attachment figure (the group).

In particular, those of Group A who recall having abused others find it the hardest to connect to "outsiders", as their own perception of their loss of humanity makes them feel incapable of making a deep link with people who have not committed abuse. In therapy, these feelings find expression in comments such as "you must think I'm a monster (i.e., only in my family am I 'normal')"; "don't look at me, it will make you dirty"; "God will never let me get better, it's my punishment."

The inability to be distant from the attachment figure obstructs the person's capacity to explore, learn and develop a sense of Self; and the weakness of the Self perpetuates dependency on the (abusive) attachment figure. And because the abuse (perpetrated on the person and/or by the person) is unbearable in its intensity, the person dissociates, over and over again. Their DID is thus *active*, continues to develop (e.g., with new alters being created) and becomes further entrenched over time.

For people in Group A, a sense of safety and closeness (i.e., secure attachment) can only be reached through highly abusive engagement; anything else is experienced as superficial, cold or irrelevant. This presents the therapist who works with this group with an extraordinary challenge.

Group B

People in group B have suffered severe and prolonged abuse by an attachment figure, from a young age, and the presence of fear in their lives was high. Engaging their attachment figure required subordination to further abuse (Infanticidal Attachment), which required frequent use of dissociation as a defense. The high level of fear locked the child into a high dependency on the attachment figure; and the dysfunctional mode of parental response to the fear forced the child into subordinating to, or even seeking, abuse.

However, people in this group have disengaged from their abusing attachment figure at some point. This can happen where there were sufficient *gaps* between high intensity of attachment needs. For example, where the attachment figure was only intermittently abusive; where the abuser was not the child's main attachment figure (e.g., a teacher, a priest, a nanny); or where the abuser died or left when the person was still young. Critically, the child had at least one other important relationship who provided some notion of safety.

Susie was the daughter of a prostitute, father unknown. She lived with her mother in a one-room flat on a rough estate and was regularly abused by her mother and her mother's clients, physically and sexually. Remarkably, Susie did manage to have a decent life. Although riddled with depression, constantly self-harming and occasionally dabbling in prostitution, she ended up marrying a supportive man and taking good care of her children. In therapy, she remembered the afternoons she had spent with an older prostitute, a neighbor, who used to make her grilled-cheese toast and call her poppet. "Her room smelt of toast and coffee. I was happy and safe with her. I think she really liked me. I used to pretend she was my mother," Susie said.

Having at least one safe attachment means a reduction in fear, which allows some exploration and the forming of new attachment relationships. The quality of new attachment figures varies, and the person may maintain a life of self-harm, vulnerability to grooming, involvement in crime or choosing abusive partners. These unconscious (or dissociative) choices demonstrate that the person, when distressed, still strives to engage their attachment figure through being hurt. However, while engagement in a harmful life may continue, it includes a level of symbolization because the new attachment figure only mimics, that is, symbolizes the original one, rather than *being* it. Furthermore, abuse inflicted by a secondary figure is less terrifying than abuse by the original figure, at a younger age and with higher dependency. The reduction in fear and dependency that has been achieved makes positive new relationships (including the therapy relationship) more likely.

Mental symptoms typical of this group include deep guilt, shame and self-loathing for loving the abuser (Dorahy, 2016), which often manifest in severe depression, suicidality, eating disorders or self-harm. Where the intensity of the relational trauma (and the subsequent helpless dependency) was particularly high, a full-blown dissociative disorder is likely. The person could maintain their subordination to abuse or the active seeking of it through the aid of amnesia, depersonalization/derealization or stable DID.

Group C

This group has suffered profound, but not abusive, relational trauma. Their attachment figures are likely to have also suffered severe trauma and pervasive losses and are deeply preoccupied with grief, illness, danger or death (De Zulueta, 1993; Green, 1986; Kahr, 2007; Niederland, 1961; Pines, 1993; Sachs, 2008, 2013; Shefet, 1994; Sigal, 1971). The only way to reach the attachment figure was through sharing this preoccupation or playing a role in it.[9]

The symptomatic picture of people in this group may include persistent suicidal ideation (but rarely actual attempts); a "tendency" for accidents or illnesses; a high-risk life style; eating disorders or other forms of self-harm. Their symptoms can be understood as their attachment behavior, that is, their keenest attempts (when distressed) to engage an attachment figure who is deeply preoccupied by death, illness or potential loss. It also includes depression, which mirrors the emotional state of the attachment figure.

The striving toward danger or death in order to engage their attachment figure is the hallmark of *Infanticidal Attachment*. However, the damage to the person is not caused directly by the attachment figure, but by the striving to *symbolize*, represent or play a role in the attachment figure's preoccupation. It thus falls under *Symbolic Infanticidal Attachment (IAs)*. The fact that any actual physical hurt is done by the person him or herself is crucial, because it signifies a level of agency, which differs from the utter helplessness of being hurt by others. It should be noted that in the more serious cases, where the symptoms include dissociation, the person may be unaware that self-harm is caused by their own hands. These cases may show a symptom picture which overlaps with group B.

Group D

Non-relational trauma (e.g., a natural disaster) does not alter the nature of the person's attachment mode,[10] because it does not link trauma with attachment. The person's attachment mode will thus remain as it was before the trauma, and any symptomatic sequels of the traumatic event will be linked only to the trauma itself (amnesia to parts of the event, flashbacks, phobia of triggers) but not to other (relational) aspects of the person's life. A person who had secure attachment before the trauma would be more likely to recover well, as he or she is better able to be comforted and regain a sense of safety, while a person who had insecure or disorganized attachment prior to the trauma would be more likely to develop PTSD (Escolas et al., 2012; MacDonald et al., 2008; Nye et al., 2008).

Summary: Active did, therapeutic considerations

Returning to the start of this paper, we have observed that patients with Active DID do not respond well to treatment as per the three-phase approach. In particular, they seem unable to relinquish their involvement in a life of abuse and thus reach any semblance of safety or stabilization of symptoms (Phase One). Their therapy is thus forever focused on survival of endless emergencies. Additional stress is caused when the unstable patient suddenly discloses extremely traumatic material, while alters unfamiliar to the therapist threaten to hurt the patient (or the therapist) as a result of the disclosure. The therapist is no more able to slow down these disclosures (which would normally be processed as part of Phase Two) than to reach Phase One; and the on-going sense of danger, worry and stagnation stifle the therapeutic process.

I would like to point out that, despite our wish to have a solid treatment protocol, this state of affairs is not particularly uncommon. In a much neglected passage, Van der Hart et al. (2006, p. 217) observe:

> Phase-oriented therapy may be applied in a simple, straightforward way in less complicated cases.... However, in most cases, ... the phase-oriented model takes the form of a spiral (Courtois, 1999; Steele et al., 2005; Van der Hart et al., 1998). This implies that as needed, Phase 2 treatment will be periodically alternated with Phase 1; and later ... Phase 2 and even Phase 1 work will again be alternated with Phase 3.

The authors do not explain the reasons for the need to work "out of sequence," why (or if) this alteration to the basic model ultimately helps, or what this need tells us about the patient. Based on the formulations that this paper has offered, I would like to suggest the following, very brief explanation.

A person with IAc (see Table 1) finds comfort and reduction of distress while being abused by their attachment figure, because this is when their attachment figure is fully engaged. And as the abuse causes severe distress, the needs of the child to be comforted are extremely intense and pressing, leading to intense dependency on the attachment figure, who can only be reached through further subordinating to harm. This vicious cycle is at the heart of this attachment mode, and the motivating power of the *Active DID* presentation.

For people with this attachment mode, being abused at the hand of their attachment figure is a *necessity*, because it is their only way to engage it. For these people, what most of us call "safety"—that is, the absence of any serious threat (as in a good therapy session)—means renouncing all attachment needs; and attachment needs cannot be renounced.

For this group, the ability to reject abuse can only be reached through a profound change to their attachment mode, a change that would make them able to fulfill their attachment needs in a different way. As attachment modes are enduring structures, such a change (if it were possible) would be the highest achievement of their therapeutic journey. It could certainly not be reached early in their treatment, as "Phase One". Until this stage is reached, we would need to *attune* (Stern, 1998) with the affective discourse of a person whose life is riddled with horrors and fears that we cannot alleviate, and whose attachment behavior forces us to face.

No reassurance or soothing can comfort the person with IAc in their distress, only further abuse. And as we are not able to offer them the awful potion which they crave, it falls to us to watch the magnitude of their distress and feel our helplessness in the face of atrocity. This attunement is the first step toward a secure attachment.

Notes

1. The clinical examples in this paper are drawn from my extensive clinical work as a therapist, supervisor, case manager and an expert witness to the court. To preserve anonymity, all identifying details have been changed and the short vignettes used as illustrations are amalgamations of frequently seen examples. The one exception is the case of Paula, which, at her own request, is reported with only minimal changes.
2. Van der Hart et al. (2006) also remark on this difficulty, see p. 217.
3. The term "attachment mode" is used throughout this paper in preference to the more widely (and interchangeably) used "attachment style," "attachment pattern" or "attachment type".
4. In some species, where the offspring have no direct connection to the parents (e.g., most fishes), the attachment is to the group of siblings, which offers "security in numbers".
5. An example of minimal gaps between high intensity episodes is children who are abused by multiple perpetrators, in a "culture" of abuse and where their contact with the rest of society is restricted. These children are at the highest risk of remaining involved in a severely abusive relationship which continues into their adulthood (Middleton, 2013a)
6. Kahr even considers some cases of schizophrenia to be expression of infanticidal attachment, because the confusion of the schizophrenic discourse complies with the parental need to hide the cause of terror (the parent's murderousness) from the world.
7. (Bowlby, 1979, 1984; Brand et al., 2013; Chu, 2011; Courtois, 2010; Dorahy et al., 2014, 2016; Hesse, 1996; Kahr, 2007; Laing & Esterson, 1964; Lidz, 1973; Main & Solomon, 1986; Middleton, 2013b; Ross, 2007; Van der Hart et al., 2006; to name but a few).
8. Nijenhuis (2015), too, suggests that the link between trauma-related structural dissociation of the personality (TSDP) and mental disorders is not random, but is ordered according to what he calls "a dimension of severity": "TSDP postulates that the dissociation of the personality is severe in major DID, marked in most cases of minor DID, moderate in spirit possession disorder, complex PTSD... significant in simple PTSD... [and] absent to insignificant in patients with other mental disorders and in mentally health individuals" (p. 135).
9. For full discussion of the complexities of attachment in these circumstances, see Sachs, 2008 on second-generation Holocaust survivors.
10. Some non-relational trauma (e.g., imprisonment) may become relational over time, as attachment relations may develop with one's captors.

References

Ainsworth, M., Blehar, M., Waters, E., & Wall, S. (1978). *Patterns of attachment: Assessed in the strange situation and at home*. Hillsdale, NJ: Erlbaum.

American Psychiatric Association. (2013). *Diagnostic and statistical manual of mental disorders* (5th ed.). Arlington, VA: American Psychiatric Association.

Bentovim, A. (1995). *Trauma-organized systems: Physical and sexual abuse in families*. London, UK: Karnac Books.

Bowlby, J. (1958). The nature of the child's tie to his mother. *International Journal of Psycho-Analysis, 39*, 350–373.

Bowlby, J. (1979). On knowing what you are not supposed to know and feeling what you are not supposed to feel. *Canadian Journal of Psychiatry, 24*, 403–408.

Bowlby, J. (1984). Violence in the family as a disorder of the attachment and caregiving systems. *The American Journal of Psychoanalysis, 44*, 9–27. doi:10.1007/BF01255416

Bowlby, J. (1988). *A secure base: Parent-child attachment and healthy human development.* Abingdon, UK: Routledge.

Brand, B. L., Loewenstein, R. J., & Spiegel, D. (2014). Dispelling myths about dissociative identity disorder treatment: An empirically based approach. *Psychiatry, 77* (2), 169–189. doi:10.1521/psyc.2014.77.2.169

Brand, B. L., McNary, S. W., Myrick, A. C., Classen, C. C., Lanius, R., Loewenstein, R. J., … Putnam, F. W. (2013). A longitudinal, naturalistic study of dissociative disorder patients treated by community clinicians. *Psychological Trauma: Theory, Research, Practice and Policy, 5*, 301–308. doi:10.1037/a0027654

Brand, B. L., Myrick, A. C., Loewenstein, R. J., Classen, C. C., Lanius, R., McNary, S. W., … Putnam, F. W. (2012). A survey of practices and recommended treatment interventions among expert therapists treating patients with dissociative identity disorder and dissociative disorder not otherwise specified. *Psychological Trauma: Theory, Research, Practice and Policy, 4*, 490–500. doi:10.1037/a0026487

Chu, J. (2011). *Rebuilding shattered lives* (2nd ed.). Hoboken, NJ: Wiley.

Courtois, C. A. (1999). *Recollections of sexual abuse: Treatment principles and guidelines.* New York, NY: Norton.

Courtois, C. A. (2010). *Healing the incest wound* (2nd ed.). New York, NY: Norton.

De Zulueta, F. (1993). *From pain to violence.* London, UK: Whurr Publishers.

Dorahy, M., Brand, B. L., Sar, V., Krüger, C., Stavropoulos, P., Martínez-Taboas, A., … Middleton, W. (2014). Dissociative identity disorder: An empirical overview. *Australian and New Zealand Journal of Psychiatry, 48*, 402. doi:10.1177/0004867414527523

Dorahy, M., Middleton, W., Seager, L., Williams, M., & Chambers, R. (2016). Child abuse and neglect in complex dissociative disorder, abuse-related chronic PTSD, and mixed psychiatric samples. *Journal of Trauma & Dissociation, 17*, 223–236. doi:10.1080/15299732.2015.1077916

Escolas, S. M., Arata-Maiers, R., Hildebrandt, E. J., Maiers, A. J., Mason, S. T., & Baker, M. T. (2012). The impact of attachment style on posttraumatic stress disorder symptoms in postdeployed service members. *U.S. Army Medical Department Journal, July/Sept. 2012*, 54–61.

Green, A. (1986). The dead Mother. In A. Green (Ed.), *On private madness.* London, UK: Hogarth.

Hesse, E. (1996). Discourse, memory, and the adult attachment interview: A note with emphasis on the emerging cannot classify category. *Infant Mental Health Journal, 17*, 4–11. doi:10.1002/(ISSN)1097-0355

Howell, E. (2005). *The dissociative mind.* Mahwah, NJ: Analytic Press.

International Society for the Study of Trauma and Dissociation. (2011). Guidelines for treating dissociative identity disorder in adults, third revision. *Journal of Trauma & Dissociation, 12*, 115–187. doi:10.1080/15299732.2011.537247

Kahr, B. (2007). Infanticidal attachment. *Attachment: New Directions in Psychotherapy and Relational Psychoanalysis, 1*, 117–132.

Kohut, H. (1977). *The restoration of the self.* New York, NY: International Universities Press.

Laing, R. D., & Esterson, A. (1964). *Sanity, madness and the family.* London, UK: Tavistock Publication.

Lidz, T. (1973). *The origin and treatment of schizophrenic disorders.* New York, NY: Basic Books.

Liotti, G. (1999). Understanding the dissociative processes: The contribution of attachment theory. *Psychoanalytic Inquiry, 19* (5), 757–783. doi:10.1080/07351699909534275

Lloyd, M. (2016). Reducing the cost of dissociative identity disorder: Measuring the effectiveness of specialized treatment by frequency of contacts with mental health services. *Journal of Trauma & Dissociation, 17* (3), 362–370. doi:10.1080/15299732.2015.1108947

MacDonald, H. Z., Beeghly, M., Grant-Knight, W., Augustyn, M., Woods, R. W., Cabral, H., ... Frank, D. A. (2008). Longitudinal association between infant disorganized attachment and childhood posttraumatic stress symptoms. *Development and Psychopathology, 20* (2), 493–508. doi:10.1017/S0954579408000643

Main, M. (1995). Recent studies in attachment: Overview, with selected implications for clinical work. In S. Goldberg, R. Muir, & J. Kerr (Eds.), *Attachment theory: Social, developmental and clinical perspectives* (pp. 407–474). Hillsdale, NJ: Analytic Press.

Main, M., & Solomon, J. (1986). Discovery of a new, insecure-disorganized/disoriented attachment pattern. In M. Yogman, & T. B. Brazelton (Eds.), *Affective development in infancy* (pp. 95–124). Norwood, NJ: Ablex.

Main, M., & Solomon, J. (1990). Procedures for identifying infants as disorganized/disoriented during the Ainsworth strange situation. In M. T. Greenberg, D. Cicchetti, & E. M. Cummings (Eds.), *Attachment in the preschool years: Theory, research and intervention* (pp. 121–160). Chicago, IL: University of Chicago Press.

Middleton, W. (2013a). Parent-child incest that extends into adulthood: A survey of international press reports, 2007-11. *Journal of Trauma and Dissociation, 14*, 184–197. doi:10.1080/15299732.2013.724341

Middleton, W. (2013b). Ongoing incestuous abuse during adulthood. *Journal of Trauma & Dissociation, 14*, 251–272. doi:10.1080/15299732.2012.736932

Miller, A. (2012). *Healing the unimaginable.* London, UK: Karnac Books.

Mollon, P. (1993). *The fragile self: The structure of narcissistic disturbance.* London, UK: Whurr Publishers.

Niederland, W. (1961). The Problem of the survivor. In H. Krystal (Ed.), *Massive psychic trauma* 1968. New York, NY: International Universities Press.

Nijenhuis, E. R. S. (2015). *The trinity of trauma: Ignorance, fragility, and control Volume I & II.* Göttingen, Germany: Vandenhoeck & Ruprecht.

Nye, E. C., Katzman, J., Bell, J. B., Kilpatrick, J., Brainard, M., & Haaland, K. Y. (2008). Attachment organization in Vietnam combat veterans with posttraumatic stress disorder. *Attachment & Human Development, 10* (1), 41–57. doi:10.1080/14616730701868613

Pines, D. (1993). The impact of the holocaust on the second generation. In D. Pines (Ed.), *A woman's unconscious use of her body – A psychoanalytical perspective.* London, UK: Virago.

Richardson, S. (2012). in First Person Plural (Producer) (2012). *A logical way of being: The reality of dissociative identity disorder (DVD).* Wolverhampton, UK: First Person Plural.

Ross, C. A. (2004). *Schizophrenia: Innovations in diagnosis and treatment.* New York, NY: The Haworth Maltreatment and Trauma Press.

Ross, C. A. (2007). *The trauma model: A solution to the problem of comorbidity in psychiatry.* Richardson, TX: Manitou Communications.

Sachs, A. (2007). Infanticidal attachment: Symbolic and concrete. *Attachment: New Directions in Psychotherapy and Relational Psychoanalysis, 3*, 297–304.

Sachs, A. (2008). Intergenerational transmission of massive trauma: The holocaust. In J. Yellin, & O. Bedouk-Epstein (Eds.), *Terror within and without: Attachment and disintegration: Clinical work on the edge* 2013. London, UK: Karnac Books.

Sachs, A. (2011). As thick as thieves, or The ritual abuse family: An attachment perspective on a forensic relationship. In V. Sinason (Ed.), *Attachment, trauma and multiplicity* (2nd ed.). Hove, UK: Brunner-Routledge.

Sachs, A. (2013). Still being hurt: The vicious cycle of dissociative disorders, attachment and ongoing abuse. *Attachment: New Directions in Psychotherapy and Relational Psychoanalysis, 7*, 90–100.

Salter, M. (2013). *Organised sexual abuse.* Abingdon, UK: Routledge.

Schore, A. (1994). *Affect regulation and the origin of the self: The neurobiology of emotional development.* Mahwah, NJ: Erlbaum.

Schore, A. (2001). The effects of early relational trauma on right brain development, affect regulation and infant mental health. *Infant Mental Health Journal, 22*, 201–269. doi:10.1002/(ISSN)1097-0355

Shefet, R. (1994). Filial commitment as an impossible task in the children of Holocaust survivors. *Sihot-Dialog, 9*, 23–27.

Sigal, J. (1971). Second-generation effects of massive psychic trauma. In H. Krystal, & W. Niederland (Eds.), *Psychic traumatisation.* Boston, MA: Little Brown & Company.

Steele, K., Van der Hart, O. & Nijenhuis, E. R. S. (2005). Phase-oriented treatment of structural dissociation in complex traumatisation: Overcoming trauma-related phobias. *Journal of Trauma and Dissociation, 6*(3), 11–53.

Stern, D. (1998). *The interpersonal world of the infant.* London, UK: Karnac Books.

Suttie, I., & Suttie, J. (1932). The mother: Agent or object? *British Journal of Medical Psychology, 12*, 199–233. doi:10.1111/j.2044-8341.1932.tb01075.x

Van der Hart, O., Van der Kolk, B. A., & Boon, S. (1998). Treatment of dissociative disorders. In J. D. Bremner & C. R. Marmar (Eds.), *Trauma, memory, and dissociation* (pp. 253–283). Washington, DC: American Psychiatric Press.

Van der Hart, O., Nijenhuis, E. R. S., & Steele, K. (2006). *The haunted self.* New York, NY: Norton.

Winnicott, D. (1958). The capacity to be alone. In D. Winnicott (Ed.), *The maturational process and the facilitating environment (1990).* London, UK: Karnac.

Winnicott, D. (1960). The theory of the parent-infant relationship. *International Journal of Psycho-Analysis, 41*, 585–595.

Winnicott, D. (1967). Mirror role of mother and family in child development. In D. Winnicott (Ed.), *Playing and reality.* London, UK: Tavistock Publishing.

Winnicott, D. (1971). *Playing and reality.* London, UK: Tavistock publication.

Dying for love: An attachment problem with some perpetrator introjects

Valerie Sinason, PhD MACP M Inst Psychoanal FIPD

ABSTRACT

This paper focuses on some problematic victim-perpetrator dynamics in psychotherapy with patients with Dissociative Identity Disorder where there has been longstanding multi-perpetrator organized abuse described, which also involves family members. Additionally, in this specific sample, there have been reported experiences of serious assaults from attachment figures in which the patient felt close to death. The clinical concern is expressed that only in the nearness of death is a connection felt to the attachment figure and this leads to extra suicidality in the patient and extra vulnerability to secondary traumatization for the therapist. This group faces not only relational betrayal dynamics with their reported external abusers, who provide toxic "love", but with internal perpetrators, victim-perpetrators, and victims too. The impact of an incestuous and rivalrous civil war in the body and mind that replicates the external system and is projected into the therapeutic encounter poses particular problems for therapists and patients. There are different problems for the treatment according to how the perpetrator-identified dissociative system is in need of a near-death connection.

Dying for love

Ninety percent of adults with dissociative disorders reported abuse in early childhood by an attachment figure (Fonagy & Target, 1995). They are also likely to have a disorganized attachment and an experience of an earliest care-giver as frightened or frightening. As Sachs and Galton (2008) state, there is an intrinsic forensic aspect to their condition in that, however it happened, their psychological predicament and identity is mainly there because of a crime. "Whether through commission or omission, cruel planned intent or appalling unintentional neglect, they are victims of a crime in which their earliest right and needs for nurture and nourishment and safety have been betrayed" (Sinason, 2015).

Developmentally, a young child does not have the cognitive or emotional capacity to manage an abusive environment (Fairbairn, 1952). The child cannot run away from abusive attachment figures and therefore a major form of survival and defense, with or without the additional defense of dissociation, is for the child to perceive himself as bad rather than have bad attachment figures. It was the British psychoanalyst Fairbairn who particularly showed the way in which by taking all blame and/or seeing himself as bad, the traumatized child succeeds in making his attachment figures externally and internally appear good (Fairbairn, 1952).

For a child to maintain the hope that a parent really is good allows some sense of a future. Hiding from the reality that his parents are bad objects allows the child to support the illusion that there is hope for him in the future, and that by behaving in a different manner he will be able to find the key to his parents' love. Conversely, if the child were able to realize that his key attachment figures were indeed bad objects who rejected him and failed him through cruelty, perversion, mental illness, and then his entire universe could collapse (Sinason, 2014)

How is this defensive belief dealt with when the nature of the reported abuse from that attachment figure is of the utmost severity? How is the attachment pattern impacted on when the child or adult experiences or perceives they have experienced deliberate near-death episodes within the context of incestuous betrayal trauma. This paper will explore these complex relational issues drawing on insights from clinical material.

Defenses, identification with the aggressor, and introjection

The traumatized child needs the ordinary defenses of identifying with the aggressor (Freud, 1936) and introjecting (Ferenczi, 1909) as part of the building of identity. By identifying ourselves with an attachment figure, a parent, we learn how to anticipate the change in time and our slow transformation from a little person to an adult. The more adverse the circumstances the greater the chance of splitting in which part of the self can project onto another part or object all the hatred and disgust it has internalized. This explains the ubiquitous childhood popularity of the English nursery song "I am the King of the Castle and you're the dirty rascal". The loved child from a good-enough attachment experience in a safe-enough society can enjoy "playing" both roles, knowing that reality is a different place from the poles of idealization and denigration. However, what happens when the only safety can come from your main attacker?

Josef (not his real name), a former holocaust survivor, told me of his pain at witnessing other Jewish children in the concentration camp walking about making Hitler salutes (personal communication, 1986). I explained what a natural defence that was and emphasized that it was normal for a child to want to be part of the master race ("king of the castle") as a defense against the terrible helplessness of being the small victim ("the dirty rascal"). Only then could the man weep and tell me he was that child. Each time he goose-stepped or saluted in order to survive he felt he was attacking the disgusting small weak Jewish body he could not bear the pain of. The badness that was projected into him he could only cope with by taking on as his own. This is what Fairbairn (1952) termed the "moral defence".

As Clarke (2012, p. 204) explained,

> The child seeks to purge his objects of their badness by taking this badness upon himself and is rewarded by the sense of security that an environment of good objects confers. However, this outer security is purchased at the price of inner security as his ego is henceforth left at the mercy of a band of internal persecutors. The bad objects the child internalizes are unconditionally bad and, since the child has internalized them, and thus identifies with them, then he is unconditionally bad. In order to be able to redress this unconditional badness the child internalizes his good objects, which assume a super-ego role.

On one occasion, Josef was given some breadcrumbs by a guard amused by his attempts to look like a Nazi. The guilt he felt at his pride and pleasure at this "compliment" was so corrosive that it reinforced his need to exist on a daily loop of internal shame and pain.

Anya, a holocaust survivor with a history of promiscuity and unsuccessful marriages to older men revealed how she first gained food in a concentration camp by exposing a breast to an older guard. Her excitement at the process, a deflection of the terror of dying, fuelled her anorexia and self-injury for decades after. She felt shamed to be called a "gold-digger", a woman who used her beauty and sexuality to attract a wealthy older man. It was a re-enactment that she kept repeating. To give up the defense that she felt had led to her survival was not possible for her.

For some, Stockholm Syndrome (i.e., a form of identification with the aggressor/s) allows a slight lessening of guilt, for others it does not. Nevertheless, psychoeducation is important for a whole range of patients and their therapists, and it can provide some hope for the most deeply entrenched in closed systems to understand why this is so. Stockholm Syndrome and holocaust survivors provide examples where identification with the aggressor is evident, dissociative identity disorder (DID) provides another. Introjection is one of the pathways the Hungarian psychoanalyst Ferenczi pioneered (1909) and this was developed further by Fairbairn.

In relational therapy for DID, Howell (2011) emphasized the importance of including Fairbairn's work because the processes of splitting and projection that he describes in detail underpin our ordinary mental systems when anything traumatic happens and are further exacerbated within a DID system. This exacerbation is because the nature of the splits intensifies as a result of disorganized attachment and cumulative trauma. Amnesic barriers are formed, whether subjective or objective (Morton, 2012; Sinason & Morton, 2014).

Morton (2012) has been undertaking memory tests with adults with a DID diagnosis and has identified a rare sample in which the subjective amnesia reported by some dissociative states can be validated as also being objective in that there is no leakage between states. Sinason and Morton (2014) referred to this level of amnesia as quaternary structural dissociation and hypothesize that with this condition different personality states were deliberately created rather than being a creative defensive choice. Whether quaternary or tertiary structural dissociation is indicated, they are both largely the results of disorganized attachment and cumulative relational trauma.

Perhaps most pertinent to this work with all levels of DID is Fairbairn's (1958) understanding that the maintenance of the internal world as a closed system was "the greatest of all sources of resistance" (p. 380). This adds to the concepts from van der Hart, O., Nijenhuis, E. R. S., & Steele, K. (2009) on the phobic response to making links or Mollon's (2002) use of the concepts of destructive narcissism. Finnegan and Clarke (2012) are also amongst a very small number who have explored "resistances that derive from the maintenance of ties to bad objects and the wish to preserve the inner world as a closed system."

For example, in the field of intellectual and physical disability, a young woman was referred who had been abused by a care worker whilst in respite care. She was visually impaired, and had severe epilepsy. Despite the level of terror in her presentation and the enormous amount of weight she had lost, those close to her were more concerned by her animation when she declared she was "talking to the man", the abuser. In her assessment (Sinason, 2010) she described how she begged him to stop hurting her. "Don't you worry, I wouldn't go near you again with a barge pole", he reportedly said in a sneering way (p. 251). Each time she considered she was ready to make a police statement she could not do it. Indeed, her eyes lit up in an animated way. "I can't. He's here. He will go away if I say what happened". I said she was frightened that if she said what had happened and the police saw it, Mr X might go away to prison, and for punishment the Mr X she kept seeing in her head would also leave her. "Yes. Then I'd be alone with nothing." In other words, without this abusive attachment figure to whom she was linked by pain, terror, sexuality and shame, she would feel emotionally orphaned. The closed system with its permanent repetition of abuser/abused was preferred.

How can you then move in therapy when your defenses and energies are dedicated to keeping a closed system with pre-existing abusive attachments running efficiently? And if the forces of sexuality and violence are linked together internally and externally how does that impact in the therapy room? What does it mean if the point of contact is a constellation of deliberate near-death attachment, sexuality and shame?

Key issues

In this paper the focus is on extreme victim-perpetrator states in a small group of patients with dissociative disorders where the nature of suicidal ideation is stronger even than with DID generally (Foote, Smolin, Neft, & Lipschitz, 2008). Indeed, it is more homicidal against the self than suicidal. We have found that in a descriptive sample of eight such patients out of a larger group of one hundred and twenty now being evaluated there are certain characteristics in common. Seven out of the eight were female and all eight were white, middle class and aged between forty to fifty. They were considered by their own report and by their psychotherapists to have a continued external and/or intrapsychic involvement in ongoing abuse and a history of complaints and "trigger-happy" volatile responses to apparently small slights or perceived injustices

Regardless of the nature or level of the dissociation, to survive the long-term impact of living in an abusive family a small child may rely on identification with the aggressor as well as internalizing or introjecting perpetrator. The problem that faces the therapeutic alliance is then compounded by the impact of these abuser introjects.

We consider that where such patients may have a "quaternary" structural dissociation (Miller, 2012; Sinason & Morton, 2014) in which most of the alters were forcibly and deliberately created (Miller, 2012; Vogt, 2015), the therapeutic process will be more problematic if there is an attachment to near-death as victim, perpetrator or victim-perpetrator as there will be less chance of leakage of any states of mind on the side of life and attachment. On the other hand, if the main personalities have a stable relationship with the therapist, there can be greater success. With tertiary structural dissociation the stability of the relationship and attachment to the therapist determines outcome (Sachs, 2017; van der Hart, O. et al., 2009).

It is important to note that treatment can still be viable within the most vulnerable group. However, we need to note the possibility of failure if the balance in the system is overloaded in favor of destroying life, hope, and the therapy. Concern for the pain of suffering patients can at times lead to a minimizing of both the dangers some patients are in and the dangers they present to the therapist. When working with a relational attachment-based template it can be particularly hard to accept the level of states with a totally destructive mission.

Vogt (2015, p. 59) highlighted,

> they are viciously dominant and obstruct any development. The destructive core of perpetrator introject does not aim for survival but aims for the deliberate oppression of new victims. One of their long-term goals can also be to ensure the abuse can go on indefinitely and to set back any progressive developments.

This is a development of his earlier awareness (2013, p. 12) that parts of such patients can

> carry the traumatic imprint of their perpetrators with them and these parts try to obstruct or even destroy therapy…find fault with the therapist for every little mistake or inconsistency, slander the therapeutic work in front of others and in a worst case scenario may even sue the therapist for malpractice.

His Somatic-Psychological-Interactive Model (SPIM) explicitly names and measures the strength of such perpetrator introjects (2015). He sees these aspects of self as driven "by a perceived social threat or by envy when the supposedly favored person is perceived to gain power". Such a projection is often rooted in the terrible consequences of incest between siblings and parents. This can fan the mother's jealousy for the "favored" daughter who is the subject of her partner's attention as well as the sibling jealousy as to who has been "chosen" for abuse (Vogt, 2015).

Here are some amalgamated examples that come regularly from work with such dissociated states:

> You said you would see me every week but 2 weeks ago I was not out and you did not call me out. So you lied to me. I can tell your insurers and your accrediting bodies.

Another scolded,

> You told that pathetic inside child you would ring her care-co-ordinator on Thursday and you still haven't. I have a note of it.

Another threatened,

> You liked that little fatface-Stupid Little Shit-you spent more time with her than me. Perhaps I will kill her this week.

Finally, another,

> You worried when that pathetic cow went out for the night. But that was her fun. You are just her little bit of soft. You don't understand a thing. (Sinason, 2015)

Unlike other aspects of dissociative systems, the switch here is particularly complex. It oscillates between three states: an extreme infanticidal victim mode to a homicidal defensive mode to a murderous mode. In infanticidal mode, the dissociative part sees the psychotherapist as Kali, the death-dealing Mother who has to be appeased or surrendered to. In homicidal mode the therapist must be attacked viciously and destroyed to preempt the violence that the patient fears will come from her. Finally, in the perpetrator introject the psychotherapist is in the presence of a chilling abuser. I use the image of the Goddess Kali deliberately as the reported murder of fetuses and small babies is endemic to this group (Sinason, 1994).

In order to maintain the abusive attachment such states of mind will remove any information that contradicts the slander and betrayal projections onto the therapist. It will depend on the particular nature of the psychotherapist as to whether the abuser introjects or the victim states are more difficult to work with. Usually both states co-exist. The impact of abusive enculturation lasts for years and any concept of short-term treatment needs to be robustly critiqued. Whilst there are successful treatments with this group of patients we also need to be prepared for failure, even after several years of initial success.

A case illustration

This is an amalgam of the experiences of many of the personalities who fit this subject matter. I will name this amalgam "Allura" in honor of Fairbairn's crucial concept of the alluring rejecting object who is desperately sought for, even more so as a result of rejection.

Allura – hanging on to life

Allura was middle-aged, a tired woman with a long history of psychiatric in-patient periods and multiple conflicting diagnoses, each of which correctly represented an alter personality. It took her 7 years to gain a correct diagnosis. All she wanted was "peace". She considered, to her relief, that any further pregnancy would now be unlikely and that removed an ongoing trauma over the reported loss of her babies in utero or at term. She reported lifelong incestuous relationships with her parents and siblings and others but said she could never go to the police as she was "part of the filth" in carrying on with it. She was quiet and undemanding. Her particular expressed difficulty in therapy concerned her sister Lara who was their mother's favorite. Allura, as her father's favorite, which she had no wish to be, knew that she incurred her mother's hatred because of this. She longed for her mother's approval. Some of her most shame-filled moments were knowing Lara's sense of triumph in witnessing their mother's attacks on her. At the same time she felt protective of Lara when Lara was coldly rejected by the father. Such families regularly promoted a murderous Abel and Cain rivalry between their children and with each other.

Whilst Allura dressed androgynously to aid male personalities the only splash of color in an otherwise drab presentation, was around her neck. She had a range of scarves of many noticeable colors and textures. Sometimes this was to cover bruises that came from auto-asphyxia and external "consenting" sadomasochistic games, and sometimes it was to draw attention to the part of her body which was the altar onto which all her relationships played out, the place where life and death issues were enacted.

On arrival at one session, after sitting uncomfortably, drawing the therapist's attention to the implications of such discomfort, a "switch" of state occurred into a pseudo- orgasmic child, Little Swan. "What do you want me to do?" she would whisper seductively, removing the colored scarf and angling her neck, expecting the sight of it would be a murderous sexual aphrodisiac.

She would combine an intense seductive stance with a reawakening of remembered pain. Even when she could hardly walk or move and her body movements were evocative enactments of electric shocks, her fusion of sexuality and pain were a complex transference for her therapist. Her attachment was to the men and women family members who praised her for not crying and doing what they wanted in such a superlative way. She clearly sought and expected a sexual and violent response from the therapist and could not understand why it did not happen. "Aren't I good enough? What am I doing wrong? I will be in trouble if you don't want me".

Only momentarily would "Ugly Duckling" appear, a child the same age as Little Swan who experienced only the terror and pain. Whenever her therapist felt a moment of protectiveness toward Ugly Duckling there would be a switch to Big Swan, an aggressive late adolescent, and her orgasmic excitement at being near death. "They hurt me last night", she emphasized, posing her body and looking seductively at the therapist. " Hanged me. Oooh-(said with sensuous relish).. will my foot touch the stool in time? Will they let me? Oooh-Mumma…Mumma!"

In such moments the therapist is made to be the voyeuristic spectator in the triangle, witnessing a sadomasochistic lethal duel but with no power to change things. The moment the hurt is registered, the sexualizing of pain comes in, the Russian roulette of life and death and, ultimately, the near-death moment of connection with the primary betraying incestuous object-the mother. Only by offering herself as a sexual object and live sacrifice is there any connection. Anything outside of that is "grey", unreal. Big Swan and Little Swan can only feel truly alive in the second of limbo between life and death, sexualizing their necessary surrender to their primary attachment figures. The only relief from their surrender was murderous rivalry experienced toward the twin, Lara, and projected onto other females whether colleagues of the therapist or others.

Just once, with unusual vulnerability, Big Swan described how, after a violent physical attack on her in which she felt certain she would die, her mother stroked her hair and masturbated her and welcomed her back to life.

Trying to evoke this intensity in her "ordinary" life in order to meet this connection can destroy multiple therapies as well as leading her into more and more dangerous one-night stands with strangers. Being on the verge of death is her identity, her 911 and it is the transference she seeks in treatment. Where the therapist makes a boundary against joining in, the hatred that cannot be expressed to the abuser is transferred.

Vulture, a perpetrator alter modeled on Allura's grandfather, could only connect to the therapist or indeed other alter personalities through sadism and death-threats. "Shall I eat a Little Ugly Duckling for supper? Such an easy neck to break, such small ribs to slice. Do you have children? Is this where you live?"

A dissociative state called Messenger took pride in texting the therapist on all the occult dates when the Swans would be "out" being abused, implying that if the therapist did not respond they would be responsible for their death and therefore implicated in murder.

All links to the therapist were made on the crucible of torture or death

Incestuous murder and victimhood

It was Fairbairn (1944) who believed that the infant's subjective sense that his mother, upon whom he depends utterly, is unable to love him generates "an affective experience which is singularly devastating" (p. 113). For an older child, the experience of loving the mother who is experienced as unloving and unaccepting of his love is one of "intense humiliation" (p. 113). "At a somewhat deeper level (or at an earlier stage) the experience is one of shame over the display of needs which are disregarded or belittled" (p. 113). Hidden under all the sadism and threats of perpetrator alters is the unbearable pain of an unloving mother who is herself too traumatized to contain her child or children. As a result of the lack of any secure attachment, sibling rivalry, real or projected, also becomes more murderous, intensified where there are reports of family incest.

In addition, internal parts/states cannot link because of the projected sibling murderous rivalry. Whether in face-to-face work or in responding to an emergency text or email from one suicidal alter, the therapist can then be overwhelmed by ten more all expressing either fury that another has been prioritized as "more important" or expressing worthlessness that they did not merit a response. One part can sexualize watching the internal "self"-injury of another as a reconnection with the role they were given by a parent. Another can perpetrate enormous sadism in identification with the external abuser, not realizing it is on a shared body-for example Vulture's murderous feelings toward Ugly Duckling. Sinason (2008) provided a detailed clinical example of an internal murder.

The near-death or deathly experiences are crucial to this particular dynamic. Alter-personalities are not "playing" at dying. They can do it. Sachs (2007), following Kahr (1994, 2007) on suicidal introjection with schizophrenia and Sinason's work (1994) on the internalized death wish of adults with a disability, has transferred to the context of DID the different levels of verbal or physical threats and actual assaults. She highlights the different situation where a child or adult with DID is dealing with either metaphorical or literal death threats from a parent. The powerful impact of these inevitably affects victim-perpetrator dynamics. In this paper I am referring only to where patients report actual grievous bodily harm to a point where they were expecting death and were informed they would be killed. The longing for the moment when mother has sated her murderous rage and connects for a moment shows itself in the surrender mode of the victim alter, at times sexualized (as with Little Swan and Big Swan) and at times converted to violence (as with Vulture and Ugly Duckling) to deny and cover the terror of annihilation.

When we add to this toxic situation the consequences of long-term incest maintained into adulthood, the problem is heightened. Middleton (2011) has carefully provided an understanding of such long-term effects. Indeed, in his sample the female victims faced death-threats, actual use of weapons, pornography and prostitution. These women introject versions of their fathers within their dissociative systems and have high levels of self-harm. By focusing on proven cases which have made the international media Middleton avoids the dissociative responses that "hearsay" clinical papers can evoke. No-one can deny the terrible reality of these publicly known cases. Middleton is able to show that whilst the majority of patients with DID have experienced abuse, a smaller percentage has experienced abuse consistently into adulthood and it is this group who need to remain more dissociative.

However, with the "hearsay" cases, whose allegations have not yet been researched by police or taken into the courtroom, we have so far found important similarities. No-one is sure of who is the child and who is the parent, the mother, the wife. Perhaps more concerning is the work in progress comparing the narratives of court-proven cases with clinical accounts (Sinason, in press).

Dietz, Hazelwood, and Warren (1990) in their descriptive study of 30 sexually sadistic white male criminals showed that the most striking difference between the causes of death in these murders and the distribution of causes of death among murder victims generally is the relatively high proportion of asphyxia (61%), as opposed to the relatively low proportion of gunshot wounds (25%). This also fits our understanding of the tortures cult victims have reported. Indeed, many, like Allura, resort to auto-asphyxia. Hucker (2009) and Hucker and Blanchard (1992) have similar results. In a paper on sexual sadism awaiting publication, I also underline the point that proven cases of sexual sadism and murder show chilling unexpected resemblances to the narratives provided by this subgroup who have rarely gone to the police (Sinason, in press). It is possible that such similarities will aid the clinical gap between those who cannot face going through a police investigation and those who do.

Indeed, it is forensic psychoanalytic sources which provide theoretical help for this work. In particular, we see that murder and torture can be committed to defend the mind against disintegration (Glasser, 1986) and that sexual arousal can occur to defend the mind against the terror of violence (Glasser, 1986, 1996). Glasser proposed that in such perverse scenarios there is a longing to merge in intimacy which carries the terror of being abandoned as well as the dread of the consequent annihilating engulfment. The sexualization is a process of trying to resolve this conflict by converting aggression into sadism, the aim of which is to keep the object alive but under the control of the perpetrator with this perversion. He called this the "core" complex.

He also proposed (1998) that there were two distinct modes of violence, "self-preservative violence" and "sado-masochistic violence." Self-preservative violence is a primitive response to a threat whether internal or external. The violence aims to end the source of threat immediately, there is no personal significance about the other, apart from being a source of danger that needs to be obliterated. Sado-masochistic aggression comes from sexualizing the self-preservative aggression so that the object is saved but is made to suffer. This form of aggression is proposed to be operative in the perpetrator introject dissociative identities explored in this chapter.

Little Swan and Big Swan, enjoying the titillating moments of asphyxia or auto-asphyxia, were therefore, as female victim-perpetrator introjects, using sadism to control but keep alive Ugly Duckling. Vulture, as a predator, only related to the Ugly Duckling and the therapist in a similar sadistic moment of keeping them alive at a point near death.

Meltzer is another psychoanalyst whose concept of an internal Mafia fits in here as a means of allaying a primitive terrorizing identification. He shows how a destructive part of the self takes hold of a submissive part who accepts it over "the dread of loss of protection against the terror" (Meltzer, 1973, p. 105). Glasser and Meltzer are both aware of the excruciating fear of loss that underpins such behavior. This mirrors the inlaid system of programmed DID as shown by Miller (2012). However, what Meltzer saw as phantasy-the perpetrating groups, both internal and external, take as reality. This leaves the therapist feeling the impact of such cruelty on every level, as psychic narrative, as internal reality and as possible external reality.

Therapeutic challenges

Specialists in the field have long pointed to the positive leadership survival qualities of some perpetrator introjects who are able to be engaged in psychotherapy (van der Hart & Boon, 1997). With an attachment to the therapist, the veneer of violence, sexual excitement or criminal wishes quickly fades in most cases of DID and the therapist works with the leadership quality of the abuse-loyal trauma-bonded state. However, the group I focus on here are very different to the usual abuser-identified states in DID. The introject is criminal and outwardly destructive. It needs to be recognized that some might be unchangeable (Sinason, 2015).

All of us working with extreme DID that comes from organized abuse are used to working with child or adult alter-personalities modeled on abusers who have been given the names or functions that fit perverse criminal activities. In working with systems committed to change, despite all the difficulty and distrust, we quickly find out that "Evil" is really a sad 10 year old child who has been told he is an evil criminal or monster or that the sex kitten Beta, does not really enjoy sex, but will be tortured if she does not smile. Even in our rarest categories we find criminal introjects who are either workable with or who form a minority within an open resourced democratic system where we also feel the hope and pain of the child. It is a familiar dynamic in this work for the therapist to experience the terror of the child's experience in their adult patient (Davies & Frawley, 1994). However, the countertransference from a perpetrator-introject with a homicidal or infanticidal attachment is on a more powerful projected level. Homicidal longings and infanticidal terrors join together in the same system in ways which can leave the clinician reeling.

I am clarifying this as hope is one of the most vulnerable areas in this work and it is painful for survivors and clinicians alike to consider areas of treatment failure. Whilst we state that DID in the end represents the whole person we have to accept that there is a final balance between the perpetrator introjects and the rest of the system and if it is too heavily weighted in favor of the perpetrator parts, where near death is the point of contact, the treatment is extra problematic and the outcome is more prone to failure. This does not mean treatment is never viable but that an assessment needs to be made of the extra risks involved to all.

This is a regular problem we also face in supervision. The therapist becomes vulnerable to secondary traumatization by the intensity and nature of telephone calls, emails and text messages from her dissociative client. For example, a near-ubiquitous situation occurs when alter after alter hints at a suicide act by one dissociative state which was about to happen, or an act of murder by one state against another (who was not aware of the DID and did not realize it was their own body they were attacking) or an alleged punishment rape or torture by outside unknown abusers. The therapist feels that if she did not respond she would be party to the murder/suicide. After spending extra time responding to the different messages and, despite exhaustion, feeling she had averted a crisis, she sits at her desk only to find a new crisis had emerged.

What becomes clearer in such supervisions as well as therapies is that the patient can only feel close to the new attachment figure, the psychotherapist, when there is a near death experience and an empathic response is felt in the therapist. Without the empathic response there would be no hope to destroy.

Outside of that experience there can be a numbness, an absence of feeling. This mirrors earlier relationships in which the child only experienced a connection at the height of abuse in a near-death experience.

Being saved or having the power of life and death is therefore the core of the new relationship and the relational connection heightens this core. In the transference the therapist can become Allura's sibling, gloating in her torture and potential death or the hostile abusive mother wanting to punish Allura, by killing her, for gaining father's attention. Ordinary reflective responses by the psychotherapist are experienced as cold, distancing and dissociative. Whilst Allura remains exhausted, pale and depleted and would never express anger with her therapist, Big Swan and Vulture do so regularly.

> It was really close last night. I was almost dead. Lovely. And then they will really come for you, you stupid therapist. You thought you could help us. No-one will want to see you when I let us get killed.

The therapist can work intensively with one dissociative state who is then internally murdered by another. The therapist, then experiences literally as well as in the transference, the breaking of affectional bonds (Sinason, 2008). Where a child alter is internally murdered by a perpetrator introject the emotional experience for the therapist can indeed be one of witnessing infanticide. Indeed, where there is no direct feeling for the child alter or alters who experience the pain there is more likely to be a negative outcome.

A single therapist facing multiple projections and counter-transferences can be too vulnerable. Some of us have followed Liotti, Mollon, and Miti (2005) and Liotti (2006) in trying to create a team around such patients in order to reduce the toxic power of the maternal transference. A psychoanalytically-oriented combined treatment can consist of two co-therapists, or a therapist and a support worker, or a psychiatrist/psychologist and therapist. It is understood that projective identifications and splitting mechanisms will be activated, involving different members of the therapeutic personnel. It is the task of teamwork to explore and contain transference and countertransference manifestations and not fragment. However, sometimes the team is not strong enough to contain and hold the forcefulness of the projections. Breitenbach's (2015) and Vogt's (2015) worked on perpetrator introjects highlights this.

Conclusion

The group of DID patients under examination here have both entrenched perpetrator and victim identities that manifest from needing to survive enmeshed and organized abuse within their closed family unit and the systems and people that operated around it. The internal world of these patients has them on the one hand needing to control and perpetrate against another to survive their own psychic death and to feel sexually alive, while on the other needing to be near-death to feel attached. This dynamic provides exquisite challenges for the therapist.

With the most violent and despairing patients we enter an emotional space we may never have had to enter before. Secondary traumatization to the therapist needs to be taken very seriously here and we do not consider there is any level of experience or seniority in this work where it is possible to manage without supervision.

Psychotherapists working in the field of trauma, especially those working in a relational way, are sensitively in touch with the pain of the victim, often to their own cost. What has been less adequately chronicled is the impact on clinicians of the abuser-identified dissociative personalities, or, more importantly, the introjected double of an outside abuser. This means that a non-forensic clinician used to working with victims only is finding out that they are dealing with perpetrators.

Whilst all clinicians are aware of the process of identification with the aggressor and the lethal familial attachment patterns that exist in families that abuse, and whilst all clinicians are aware of the appalling predicament of a client who has been forced to perpetrate when this is against their nature and wishes, this is not the same as dealing with a live introject of an abuser with an infanticidal or homicidal attachment.

Clinicians working in the field of dissociative disorders have a deep sense of human rights in that we are working with a population not yet receiving adequate treatment or recognition. We are also working with a group whose narratives meet with media and false memory attacks. This can make it harder to consider that some systems are so lethal. Assessing the level of perpetrator-introjects in an overall system could allow more choice in considering the right treatment options. Perpetrators are not born, they are made, they are constructed. Where groups, including attachment figures, have destroyed a child right from the start with layers of toxic projections it is more surprising that so many courageous survivors of DID have cast away criminality. By understanding the toxic process and by earlier intervention we have the chance of lessening this tragic compound trauma.

References

Breitenbach, G. (2015). *Inside views from the dissociated worlds of extreme violence: Human beings as merchandise*. London, UK: Karnac.

Clarke, G. S. (2012). Failures of the moral defence in the films Shutter Island, Inception and Memento. *International Journal of Psychoanalysis, 93*, 205–212. doi:10.1111/j.1745-8315.2011.00521.x

Davies, J. M., & Frawley, M. G. (1994). *Treating the adult survivor of childhood sexual abuse: A psychoanalytic perspective*. New York, NY: Basic Books.

Dietz, P. E., Hazelwood, R. R., & Warren, J. (1990). The sexually sadistic criminal and his offences. *Bulletin of the American Academy of Psychiatry & Law, 18*, 168–170.

Fairbairn, W. R. D. (1944). Endopsychic structure considered in terms of object-relationships. In Scharff, E.E. & Birtles, E.F. (Eds.), *Psychoanalytic studies of the personality* (pp. 82–136). London, UK: Routledge & Kegan Paul.

Fairbairn, W. R. D. (1952). *Psychoanalytic Studies of the Personality*. London, UK: Routledge & Kegan Paul.

Fairbairn, W.R.D. (1958) On the nature and aims of psychoanalytic treatment. *International Journal of Psycho-Analysis, 39*, 374–385.

Ferenczi, S. (1909). Introjection and transference. In Jones, E. (Ed. & Trans.), *Sex in psycho-analysis* (pp. 35–57). New York, NY: Basic Books.

Finnegan, P., & Clarke, G. (2012). Evelyns PhD in Wellness—A Fairbairnian understanding of the therapeutic relationship with a woman with DID. *Attachment, 6*, 51–68.

Fonagy, P., & Target, M. (1995). Dissociation and trauma. *Current Opinions in Psychiatry, 8*, 161–166. doi:10.1097/00001504-199505000-00006

Foote, B., Smolin, Y., Neft, D., & Lipschitz, D. (2008). Dissociative disorderand suicidality in psychiatric outpatients. *Journal of Nervous and Mental Disease, 196*, 29–36. doi:10.1097/NMD.0b013e31815fa4e7

Freud, A. (1936). *The ego and the mechanisms of defense* (Vol. 2). London, UK: Karnac.

Glasser, M. (1986). Identification and its vicissitudes as observed in the perversions. *International Journal of Psycho-Analysis, 67*, 9–17.

Glasser, M. (1996). Aggression and sadism in the perversions. In I. Rosen (Ed.), *Sexual deviation, 3rd edition* (pp. 279–299). Oxford, UK: Oxford University Press.

Glasser, M. (1998). On violence: A preliminary communication. *The International Journal of Psychoanalysis, 79*, 887–902.

Howell, E. (2011). *Understanding and treating DID a relational approach*. London, UK: Karnac.

Hucker, S. J. (2009). Manifestations of sexual sadism: Sexual homicide, sadistic rape and necrophilia. In F. Saleh, J. Bradford, & D. Brodsky (Eds.), *Sexual offenders*. Oxford, UK: Oxford University Press.

Hucker, S. J., & Blanchard, R. (1992). Death scene characteristics in 118 fatal cases of autoerotic asphyxia compared with suicidal asphyxia. *Behavioral Sciences and the Law, 10*, 509–523. doi:10.1002/bsl.2370100407

Kahr, B. (1994). The historical foundations of ritual abuse, an excavation of ancient infanticide. In V. Sinason (Ed.), *Treating survivors of Satanist abuse* (pp. 45–56). London, UK: Routledge.

Kahr, B. (2007). The infanticidal attachment. *Attachment, 1*, 117–132.

Liotti, G. (2006). A model of dissociation based on attachment theory and research. *Journal of Trauma and Dissociation, 7*, 55–74. doi:10.1300/J229v07n04_04

Liotti, G., Mollon, P., & Miti, G. (2005). Dissociative disorders. In G. Gabbard, J. Beck, & J. Holmes (Eds.), *Oxford textbook of psychotherapy*. Oxford, UK: Oxford University Press.

Meltzer, D. (1973). *Sexual states of mind*. Perthshire, UK: Klunie Press.

Middleton, W. (2011, August). *Always daddy's little girl: Incestuous abuse during adulthood*. Plenary Paper presented at "Trauma & Healing" Themed Day: World Congress For Psychotherapy, "World Dreaming", Sydney Convention & Exhibition Centre, Australia.

Miller, A. (2012). *Healing the Unimaginable, Treating Ritual Abuse and Mind Control*. London, UK: Karnac.

Mollon, P. (2002). The dark dimensions of multiple personality. In V. Sinason (Ed.), *Attachment, trauma and multiplicity, working with dissociative identity disorder* (pp. 177--194). London, UK: Routledge.

Morton, J. (2012). Memory and the dissociative brain. In V. Sinason (Ed.), *Trauma, dissociation and multiplicity, working on identity and selves* (pp. 65–78). London, UK: Routledge.

Sachs, A. (2007). Infanticidal attachment: Symbolic and Concrete. *Attachment Journal, 1* (pp. 297–305). London, UK: Karnac.

Sachs, A. (2017). Stable vs. Active DID: Clinical observation and analysis. *The Journal.*

Sachs, A., & Galton, G. (Eds.). (2008). *Forensic aspects of psychotherapy.* London, UK: Karnac.

Sinason, V. (1994). *Mental handicap and the human condition.* London, UK: Free Association Books.

Sinason, V. (2008). When murder moves inside. In A. Sachs, & G. Galton (Eds.), *Forensic aspects of dissociative identity disorder* (pp. 100–107). London, UK: Karnac.

Sinason,V. (2010). *Mental handicap and the human condition: An analytic approach to intellectual disability, Second updated edition.* London, UK: Free Association Books.

Sinason, V. (2014). Fairbairn: Abuse, trauma, and multiplicity. In G. S. Clarke, & D. E. Scharff (Eds.), *Fairbairn and the object relations tradition* (pp. 197–208). London, UK: Karnac.

Sinason, V. (2015). *Identifying with an Abuser and relating to a Perpetrator Introject: A particular complex attachment pattern in dissociative identity disorder.* Talk given 10th October 2015 at 14. München, Germany: Internationale Bindungskonferenz.

Sinason, V. (in press). *Sexual sadism.* London, UK: Karnac.

Sinason, V., & Morton, J. (2014 October). *Quaternary Structural Dissociation.* Presented at the Quaternary Structural Dissociation Symposium, 31st ISSTD Conference, Longbeach, CA, USA.

van der Hart, O., & Boon, S. (1997). Treatment strategies for complex dissociative disorders. *Dissociation, 10,* 157–165.

van der Hart, O., Nijenhuis, E. R. S., & Steele, K. (2009). *The haunted self: Structural dissociation and the treatment of chronic traumatisation.* New York, NY: W.W. Norton.

Vogt, R. (2013). *Perpetrator introjects psychotherapeutic diagnostics and treatment models.* Kröning, Germany: Asanger Verlag.

Vogt, R. (2015). *SPIM 30 treatment model for dissociative trauma disorders.* Kröning, Germany: Asanger Verlag.

Predicting a dissociative disorder from type of childhood maltreatment and abuser–abused relational tie

Christa Krüger, MBBCh, MMed(Psych), MD, FCPsych(SA) and Lizelle Fletcher, BCom(Econometrics), Honours(Mathematical Statistics), MSc(Mathematical Statistics), PhD(Statistics)

ABSTRACT

We investigate the types of childhood maltreatment and abuser–abused relational ties that best predict a dissociative disorder (DD). Psychiatric inpatients (*n* = 116; mean age = 35; F: M = 1.28:1) completed measures of dissociation and trauma. Abuse type and abuser–abused relational ties were recorded in the Traumatic Experiences Questionnaire. Multidisciplinary team clinical diagnosis or administration of the SCID-D-R to high dissociators confirmed DD diagnoses. Logit models described the relationships between abuser–abused relational tie and the diagnostic grouping of patients, DD present (*n* = 16) or DD absent (*n* = 100). Fisher's exact tests measured the relative contribution of specific abuse types. There was a positive relationship between abuse frequency and the presence of DD. DD patients experienced more abuse than patients without DDs. Two combinations of abuse type and relational tie predicted a DD: childhood emotional neglect by biological parents/siblings and later emotional abuse by intimate partners. These findings support the early childhood etiology of DDs and subsequent maladaptive cycles of adult abuse. Enquiries about childhood maltreatment should include a history of emotional neglect by biological parents/siblings. Adult emotional abuse by intimate partners should assist in screening for DDs.

Introduction

The etiological role of complex, chronic, relational early childhood maltreatment in the development of DDs is well known (Dalenberg et al., 2012; Dorahy et al., 2014; Dorahy & Van der Hart, 2007; Van der Hart, Nijenhuis, & Steele, 2006). The roles of specific types of childhood maltreatment and the specific abuser–abused relational ties that place the victim at the highest risk of developing a DD are less well known.

Along with sexual and physical abuse, emotional abuse has been receiving increased attention in the literature. Emotional abuse has been associated with or may predict dissociative *symptoms* in various populations, including adult psychiatric patients with various diagnoses (Mueller-Pfeiffer et al., 2013), adolescent psychiatric outpatients (Sar, Önder, Kilincaslan, Zoroglu, & Alyanak, 2014), female psychiatric inpatients with posttraumatic stress disorder linked to childhood maltreatment (Haferkamp, Bebermeier, Möllering, & Neuner, 2015), patients with borderline personality disorder (Watson, Chilton, Fairchild, & Whewell, 2006), and patients with schizophrenia spectrum disorders (Schäfer et al., 2006).

Emotional abuse has also been associated with or may predict pathological *dissociative disorder* (DD). Emotional abuse, sexual abuse, and physical neglect are significant predictors of a DD diagnosis in women (Sar, Akyüz, & Dogan, 2007). A study by Simeon, Guralnik, Schmeidler, Sirof, and Knutelska (2001) compared patients with depersonalization disorder to healthy control subjects and identified emotional abuse as the most significant predictor of a depersonalization disorder diagnosis.

Emotional neglect, as a facet of emotional abuse, has been studied less frequently. Sar, Akyuz, Kugu, Ozturk, and Ertem-Vehid (2006) demonstrated that emotional neglect (but not emotional abuse) predicted a DD diagnosis in college students. Ozcetin et al. (2009) found that emotional abuse and emotional neglect were significantly higher in women with pseudoseizure-type conversion disorder than in healthy controls. More recently, Kilic et al. (2014) demonstrated that childhood emotional neglect predicted somatoform dissociation in women with fibromyalgia or rheumatoid arthritis. Similarly, Vogel et al. (2009) found an association between childhood neglect and adult dissociation in schizophrenia inpatients.

In addition to abuse type, the specific abuser–abused relational ties may also predict a DD. Identifying abuser–abused relational ties can be complex. Perpetrators of childhood abuse are not always a parent or father (Ross et al., 1991; Sandberg, 2010). Where a strong relationship between DD and childhood sexual abuse was recorded, the specific relational ties are not always identified (Farley & Keaney, 1997; Israel & Stover, 2009). Mueller-Pfeiffer et al. (2013) found that *peri- and extrafamilial* maltreatment, but not intrafamilial maltreatment, predicted dissociative symptoms in adult psychiatric patients. Plattner et al. (2003) found significant correlations between *intrafamilial* trauma and the presence of a DD in delinquent juveniles. Similarly, Simeon et al. (2001) found that the majority of perpetrators of emotional abuse were one or both parents.

The relationships between types of childhood maltreatment and specific abuser–abused relational ties and their influence on DD have never been addressed simultaneously. Mueller-Pfeiffer et al. (2013) came close when they studied three variables simultaneously (abuse type, familial relationship, and developmental stage) in relation to dissociative *symptoms* as measured by the DES Taxon score. We investigate the specific types of childhood maltreatment and the associated specific abuser–abused relational ties that are the best predictors of a DD. Identifying important risk factors associated with DD may assist in screening high-risk patients.

Methods

Design

This quantitative study forms part of a broader mixed-methods research project. The objectives included screening for patients with DDs among psychiatric inpatients, exploring differences between patients with and without DDs, describing local variations in the clinical picture of the DDs, monitoring treatment progress and outcome in patients with DDs, evaluating available local non-public-mental-health services for patients with DDs, and generating hypotheses for future research. The design and methods were described elsewhere (Krüger, 2016).

This specific cross-sectional quantitative study investigated if types of childhood maltreatment and the associated relational tie between the abused and the abuser could predict the grouping of psychiatric patients as either having or not having a DD.

Setting and sampling

This study was conducted at two clinical facilities: Weskoppies Hospital (WKH) (a specialized state psychiatric hospital in Pretoria, and an academic training hospital at the University of Pretoria) and Tshwane District Hospital (TDH) (a regional general hospital in Pretoria that renders primary level psychiatric care).

The 116 participants (58 patients from each of the 2 hospitals) were consecutive psychiatric admissions who fulfilled the set of inclusion and exclusion criteria. The inclusion criteria were an age of 18 years or older and the ability to read and write English sufficiently to complete self-report questionnaires. The exclusion criteria were severe neurological or general medical conditions, or severe psychiatric impairment that precluded the patient's ability to complete self-report questionnaires.

Instruments and procedures

Participants completed the following self-report questionnaire scales: Dissociative Experiences Scale (DES) (Bernstein & Putnam, 1986; Carlson & Putnam, 1993), Multidimensional Inventory of Dissociation (MID) (Dell, 2006), and Traumatic Experiences Checklist (TEC) (Nijenhuis, 1999/2004). The TEC was chosen for its broad coverage of traumatic experiences (Nijenhuis, 1999/2004). Demographic and clinical data were also collected.

DD was diagnosed in 16 patients according to a combination of the following: scores of >30 on both the DES and MID, discussion with the relevant multidisciplinary treating team, consulting the clinical records, conducting clinical psychiatric interviews, and administering the Structured Clinical Interview for DSM-IV Dissociative Disorders—Revised (SCID-D-R) (Steinberg, 1994a, 1994b). The SCID-D-R was administered in nine cases to confirm the clinical diagnosis. The proportion of patients with a DD was 13.8% of the 116 participants.

Twelve patients who had scores of >30 on both the DES and MID were lost to follow up after their discharge from hospital. The reasons were nonfunctional mobile phone numbers or relocations, and two patients who declined future contact after the questionnaire scales. The diagnosed proportion of patients with a DD in this study could have been greater if these lost-to-follow-up patients had been fully assessed.

Analysis

The scale scores between patients with and without a DD were compared using *t*-tests for two independent samples.

Logit models using TEC data were constructed to identify the significant abuser–abused relational tie predictors of a DD diagnosis. Degrees of association between abuser–abused relational tie and a diagnosis of a DD were investigated by compiling cross-tabulations and expected frequencies, and calculating Fisher's exact test statistics.

Thirty-four individually recorded and coded relational ties were grouped into eight categories: (1) biological parents, (2) biological siblings, (3) other biological relatives, (4) step-parents, (5) step-siblings, (6) intimate partners, (7) friends or family friends, and (8) community members (including teacher, neighbor, colleague, manager, pastor, police officer, stranger, or a combination of various people). These eight categories were further consolidated in three categories based on closeness or accessibility to the victim. Biological parents have the greatest accessibility; other relatives (including other biological relatives, biological siblings, step-parents, and step-siblings) have intermediate accessibility; and friends/others (including friends, family friends, partners, and community members) have the least accessibility. Abuser–abused relational ties for five different types of maltreatment (emotional neglect, emotional abuse, physical abuse, sexual harassment, and sexual abuse) were compared between patients with and without a DD based on these three categories.

Abuser–abused relational tie associations with maltreatment were further compared between patients with and without a DD using *all biological relatives* (i.e., parents and other biological relatives, representing a *given* life-long, and often a close relationship between abuser and abused) and *intimate partners* (a category that emerged prominently from the raw data and that represented a usually close, yet *chosen* relationship between abuser and abused) as relationship categories. These distinctions were based on the idea that "closeness" does not depend on familial bond (Schultz, Passmore, & Yoder, 2003). Step-relatives, friends, family friends, school mates, and community members (i.e., nonbiological relational ties) were excluded from these analyses, even though these might be close relationships. These relationships are usually not chosen by the victim. Further comparisons between different biological relatives were conducted. All biological relatives were divided into biological parents versus other (non-parental) biological relatives to gain a deeper understanding of the role of different relational ties.

We considered if the *type* of abuse may predict a DD diagnosis or alternatively play a mediating or moderating role in the relationship between the abuser–abused relational tie ("abuser relation") and the presence of a DD. The TEC's five trauma area presence scores (for emotional neglect, emotional abuse, bodily threat, sexual harassment, and sexual abuse) are not only based on experiences of abuse. Specifically, the trauma area presence score for bodily threat includes a count of physical abuse experiences and a count of traumatic experiences that might be considered less relationally abusive or non-abusive, including intense pain (e.g., from an injury or surgery), threat to life from an unknown person (e.g., during a crime), and bizarre punishment. The score for bodily threat could therefore not be used as a pure indicator of physical abuse.

The focus then shifted to the raw item data of the TEC. Individual TEC item scores were also used in the analyses. Note, though, that many of the individual TEC items contain information not only about the type of abuse but also about the relational tie between abuser and abused.

Ethical considerations

Ethical clearance was granted by the Research Ethics Committee of the Faculty of Health Sciences, University of Pretoria, reference number 121/2012. Written informed consent was obtained from all participants after adequately explaining the study's procedures to them. Questionnaire data were collected anonymously to protect participants' identities.

Results

A total of 116 patients participated in this study. Of those, 16 (13.8%) were diagnosed with a DD. WKH contributed 58 patients, with 6 (10.4%) DD diagnosed patients, and TDH contributed 58, with 10 (17.2%) DD diagnosed patients. The 16 DD patients had a mean age of 34.3 (±11.1) years, a female: male ratio of 3:1, and a race distribution of 69% White, 19% Colored, 13% Black, and 0% Indian, according to the standard presentation of formal South

African governmental demographic statistics. The 100 non-DD psychiatric patients had a mean age of 35.4 (±10.8) years, a female:male ratio of 1.13:1, and a race distribution of 72% White, 18% Black, 8% Colored, and 2% Indian. The DD patients did not differ statistically from non-DD patients with respect to age, sex, or race.

According to DSM-5 (APA, 2013), 11 of the 16 DD patients (69%) had dissociative identity disorder (DID) (3 primarily of the possession type), 3 patients (19%) had other specified dissociative disorder (chronic or recurrent mixed dissociative symptoms that approach, but fall short of, the diagnostic criteria for DID), 1 (6%) had dissociative amnesia with fugue, and 1 (6%) had conversion disorder/functional neurological symptom disorder (with seizures). The patient with a primary diagnosis of conversion disorder was included in the DD sample on the basis of the ICD-10's and planned ICD-11's inclusion of conversion disorders among DDs (WHO, 1992).

The majority of DD patients ($n = 11$; 69%) had a comorbid mood disorder. Four DD patients (25%) had a comorbid conversion disorder (with seizures). Two DD patients (13%) had a comorbid personality disorder. The 100 non-DD patients' primary psychiatric diagnoses included mood disorders (74%), psychotic disorders (9%), substance-related disorders (9%), personality disorders (4%), cognitive disorders (2%), anxiety disorders (1%), and eating disorders (1%).

DD patients had significantly higher scores on all the scales (DES, MID, TEC) administered (Table 1). All 95% bootstrap confidence intervals indicate a significant difference between the scale scores of DD and non-DD patients ($p < 0.05$).

The frequency of occurrence of maltreatment type according to different abuser relations was recorded in the TEC (Table 2). Biological parents (and to a lesser degree biological siblings and other biological relatives) were the most frequently recorded abusers among DD and non-DD patients.

Table 1. Comparison of scale scores between patients with and without dissociative disorders ($N = 116$).

	Other psychiatric disorder (n = 100)		Dissociative disorder (n = 16)		
	Mean	Standard deviation	Mean	Standard deviation	95% Bootstrap confidence intervals
DES[1]	22.8	16.8	52.6	15.7	(21.27; 38.76)*
DES taxon	14.3	14.9	45.6	23.0	(19.31; 43.79)*
MID	21.5	18.5	49.4	14.7	(19.57; 36.13)*
TEC total score[2]	9.5	4.9	14.0	5.1	(1.94; 7.48)*

[1]DES: Dissociative Experiences Scale; MID: Multidimensional Inventory of Dissociation; TEC: Traumatic Experiences Checklist.

[2]The TEC total score represents a count of all potentially traumatic experiences listed in items 1–29 of the scale, which include not only experiences of abuse but also non-abusive traumatic experiences that often form a part of everyday life, e.g., loss of a family member, or threat to life from an accident. For TEC subscores, see Table 4.

*Statistically significantly different on bootstrap analyses at the 5% level.

Emotional neglect, emotional abuse, and physical abuse were predominantly associated with biological parents (Table 2). Sexual harassment and sexual abuse were equally dominantly associated with community members and biological relatives (Table 2).

DD patients recorded more maltreatment experiences than non-DD patients. All DD patients (100%) reported emotional neglect and emotional abuse, 81% reported physical abuse, and 56% reported sexual harassment and sexual abuse. Of the 100 non-DD patients, 71% reported emotional abuse, 67% reported emotional neglect, 50% reported physical abuse, 43% reported sexual abuse, and 32% reported sexual harassment.

The logit model identified a significantly higher probability of a DD diagnosis in patients who experienced emotional abuse associated with abuser relation of "intimate partner" (Table 3). The abuser relation of intimate partner was associated with a DD diagnosis for all abuse types (Table 3), but these predictions were not significant. Fisher's exact tests gave the same statistical results when biological relatives were divided into biological parents and other (non-parental) biological relatives.

Fisher's exact tests compared TEC trauma area presence scores between DD and non-DD patients. *Emotional neglect* was strongly associated with a DD diagnosis ($p = 0.003$, Table 4). *Bodily threat* and *sexual harassment* also associated significantly with a DD diagnosis ($p < 0.05$) while *emotional abuse* had moderate evidence of association with a DD ($p < 0.10$).

Fisher's exact tests compared TEC individual items for different abuser relations between DD and non-DD patients. The individual TEC items relating to the trauma area presence scores are arranged according to the different types of abuse (while allowing for the combination of abusive and non-abusive experiences under "bodily threat") (Table 4). DD patients had higher frequencies ($p < 0.001$) of "*emotional neglect (e.g., being left alone, insufficient affection) by your [biological] parents, brothers or sisters*" than non-DD patients. DD patients had higher frequencies of emotional neglect ($p = 0.039$), emotional abuse ($p = 0.049$), and sexual harassment ($p = 0.035$) by more distant (biological) relatives than non-DD patients (Table 4). DD patients had higher frequencies of sexual harassment ($p = 0.023$) by nonfamily members than non-DD patients (Table 4).

More complex logit analyses assessing multiple predictors for abuser relation categories and the probability of a DD diagnosis could not be performed due to the sparseness of the data.

Discussion

Childhood emotional neglect by biological parents/siblings

Self-reported emotional neglect was most strongly associated with a diagnosis of a DD in our study. All patients with a DD reported emotional neglect,

Table 2. Frequencies of abuser–abused relational ties in various forms of maltreatment (TEC data) (N = 116).

	All participants (N = 116)	% of 116	Other psychiatric disorder (n = 100)	% of 100	Dissociative disorder (n = 16)	% of 16
Emotional neglect by						
No one	33	28	33	33	0	0
Biological parent/s	52	45	42	42	10	63
Next degree biological relative/s	11	9	8	8	3	19
Biological sibling/s	8	7	7	7	1	6
Intimate partner	6	5	5	5	1	6
Friend/s or family friend/s	4	4	4	4	0	0
Community member/s	1	1	1	1	0	0
Step-parent/s	1	1	0	0	1	6
Step-sibling/s	0	0	0	0	0	0
Emotional abuse by						
No one	29	25	29	29	0	0
Biological parent/s	39	34	34	34	5	31
Friend/s or family friend/s	12	10	10	10	2	13
Next degree biological relative/s	11	10	9	9	2	12
Intimate partner	10	9	7	7	3	19
Biological sibling/s	7	6	7	7	0	0
Step-parent/s	4	3	2	2	2	13
Community member/s	3	3	2	2	1	6
Step-sibling/s	1	0	0	0	1	6
Physical abuse by						
No one	53	46	50	50	3	19
Biological parent/s	23	20	18	18	5	32
Intimate partner	12	10	9	9	3	19
Friend/s or family friend/s	9	8	8	8	1	6
Biological sibling/s	6	5	5	5	1	6
Next degree biological relative/s	5	4	5	5	0	0
Step-parent/s	5	4	4	4	1	6
Community member/s	2	2	1	1	1	6
Step-sibling/s	1	1	0	0	1	6
Sexual harassment by						

(Continued)

Table 2. (Continued).

	All participants (N = 116)	% of 116	Other psychiatric disorder (n = 100)	% of 100	Dissociative disorder (n = 16)	% of 16
No one	75	65	68	68	7	44
Community member/s	12	10	9	9	3	18
Next degree biological relative/s	8	7	6	6	2	13
Friend/s or family friend/s	7	6	6	6	1	6
Biological parent/s	5	4	4	4	1	6
Step-parent/s	4	3	4	4	0	0
Biological sibling/s	2	2	2	2	0	0
Intimate partner	3	3	1	1	2	13
Step-sibling/s	0	0	0	0	0	0
Sexual abuse by						
No one	64	55	57	57	7	44
Community member/s	15	13	12	12	3	19
Friend/s or family friend/s	10	9	10	10	0	0
Next degree biological relative/s	10	9	8	8	2	13
Biological parent/s	7	6	6	6	1	6
Intimate partner	4	3	2	2	2	12
Step-parent/s	3	2	3	3	0	0
Biological sibling/s	2	2	2	2	0	0
Step-sibling/s	1	1	0	0	1	6

Table 3. Abuser relation as predictor of dissociative disorder diagnosis in various forms of maltreatment (TEC data) (*N* = 116).

	All participants (N = 116)	% of 116	Other psychiatric disorder (n = 100)	% of 100	Dissociative disorder (n = 16)	% of 16	Logit Model (p)
Emotional neglect							
Biological relatives	70	60	56	56	14	88	
Intimate partner	6	5	5	5	1	6	0.8442
Emotional abuse							
Biological relatives	54	47	49	49	5	31	
Intimate partner	11	10	7	7	4	25	0.0278*
Physical abuse							
Biological relatives	34	29	28	28	6	38	
Intimate partner	11	10	8	8	3	19	0.4912
Sexual harassment							
Biological relatives	15	13	12	12	3	19	
Intimate partner	2	2	1	1	1	6	0.3725
Sexual abuse							
Biological relatives	19	16	16	16	3	19	
Intimate partner	2	2	1	1	1	6	0.2795

*Statistically significant at the 0.05 level.

most frequently perpetrated by *biological parents.* When individual TEC items were analyzed, we identified *emotional neglect (e.g., being left alone, insufficient affection) by your parents, brothers or sisters* as the strongest individual predictor of a diagnosis of a DD.

Our findings support earlier studies that suggest that an *abuser–abused relational tie of a close biological relative (parent or sibling)* might be the greatest risk factor associated with developing a DD (Plattner et al., 2003; Simeon et al., 2001). The findings reported here support Freyd's (1994) betrayal trauma theory. The betrayal of trust that occurs when child victims are abused by their primary caregivers is considered pivotal in the pathogenesis of DDs (Freyd, 1994, 1997; Haferkamp et al., 2015; Schultz et al., 2003).

These results were obtained from a self-report questionnaire, completed by people suffering from a DD and other non-DD psychiatric disorders. Patients diagnosed with DD may possibly dissociate from other forms of abuse that could have even greater traumatic impact. This abuse would then be underreported. The high frequency of abuse and high scale scores (Table 2) indicate clear differences between DD and non-DD patients. Emotional neglect and emotional abuse were the most *reported* forms of abuse by DD patients, thus possibly exaggerating the strength of their predictive roles.

Table 4. Comparison of frequencies of types of abuse between patients with and without dissociative disorders ($N = 116$).

		Other psychiatric disorder (n = 100)	% of 100	Dissociative disorder (n = 16)	% of 16	Fisher's exact test (p)
TEC trauma area presence scores[1]						
Emotional neglect		64	64	16	100	0.003**
Bodily threat[2]		85	85	16	100	0.026*
Sexual harassment		33	33	9	56	0.029*
Emotional abuse		75	75	15	94	0.068
Sexual abuse		45	45	9	56	0.125
TEC individual items endorsed:[3]						
Item 14a	Emotional neglect by parents/brother/sister	53	53	16	100	<0.001**
Item 15a	Emotional neglect by more distant relatives	24	24	8	50	0.039*
Item 16a	Emotional neglect by nonfamily members	39	39	10	63	0.103
Item 22a	Physical abuse by nonfamily members	31	31	9	56	0.086
Item 23a	Bizarre punishment	19	19	6	38	0.109
Item 10a	Intense pain	53	53	12	75	0.113
Item 20a	Physical abuse by parents/brother/sister	30	30	7	44	0.386
Item 21a	Physical abuse by more distant relatives	11	11	3	19	0.408
Item 9a	Threat to life	43	43	9	56	0.419
Item 26a	Sexual harassment by nonfamily members	22	22	8	50	0.023*
Item 25a	Sexual harassment by more distant relatives	11	11	5	31	0.035*
Item 24a	Sexual harassment by parents/brother/sister	9	9	2	13	0.635
Item 18a	Emotional abuse by more distant relatives	21	21	7	44	0.049*
Item 19a	Emotional abuse by non-family members	44	44	11	69	0.051
Item 17a	Emotional abuse by parents/brother/sister	55	55	12	75	0.176
Item 29a	Sexual abuse by nonfamily members	33	33	9	56	0.081
Item 28a	Sexual abuse by more distant relatives	13	13	4	25	0.233
Item 27a	Sexual abuse by parents/brother/sister	13	13	2	13	1.0

[1]TEC trauma area presence scores: These scores represent a count of different types of abuse.
[2]Bodily threat: The score for this trauma area subsumes not only a count of physical abuse experiences, but also a count of non-abusive traumatic experiences including threat to one's life, intense pain, or bizarre punishment.
[3]The list of individual TEC items reported here includes only the items of abuse and the three items that are included in the scale's defined score for bodily threat alongside the physical abuse items (i.e., threat to one's life, intense pain, and bizarre punishment).
*Statistically significant at the 0.05 level.
**Statistically significant at the 0.01 level.

Later emotional abuse by intimate partners

This study found a strong association between emotional abuse by an intimate partner and the diagnosis of a DD. Where emotional neglect by biological relatives may be a childhood phenomenon, emotional abuse by an intimate partner is often an adult or teenage phenomenon. The TEC records traumatic experiences during the respondent's entire lifetime. Identifying different perpetrators usually indicates abuse during specific life stages even though no differentiation is made between childhood abuse and abuse during adulthood. Intimate partners were more frequently recorded as perpetrators of emotional abuse in patients with a DD than biological parents or other biological relatives. More recent memories of adult emotional abuse by intimate partners could possibly dominate older memories of childhood emotional abuse while the TEC was being completed.

DD patients reporting that intimate partners are the most frequent perpetrators of emotional abuse do not detract from the traumatic childhood etiology of DDs. High frequencies of emotional abuse perpetrated by intimate partners may lend support to Sach's concept of a vicious cycle of DDs, attachment, and ongoing abuse. Severe early (childhood) abuse may activate both a passive dissociative reaction and an active attachment reaction, both of which may contribute to (adult) situations of repeated abuse as time goes on (Sachs, 2013). Emotional abuse by intimate partners might not be the *cause* of the DD, but this is how it often *turns out* for adult patients with a DD. The fact that emotional abuse was self-reported may exaggerate its predictive role.

Conflation of information in, and scoring of the TEC

The conflation of information regarding abuse types and the abuser–abused relational tie in the individual items of the TEC, as well as the confounding of information in the trauma area presence scores of the TEC, complicated the analyses of the TEC data.

We addressed these issues by returning to the raw data of the TEC. Mueller-Pfeiffer et al. (2013) followed a different approach by devising a new scoring system in their German adaptation of the TEC (Schumacher et al., 2011). Mueller-Pfeiffer et al. (2013) also parsed out early life stress and adult life stress separately in an attempt to circumvent the TEC's conflation of various life stages in the original design of the scale.

Our study differs further from the Mueller-Pfeiffer et al. (2013) study in that their study used the 8-item DES Taxon for measuring pathological dissociation, whereas our study distinguished between DD and non-DD patients. Our study was limited by the diagnostic distinction and the resultant small subgroup of patients with a DD. The small sample limited the statistical analyses but differentiating between the groups had the benefit of emphasizing the clinical relevance of the findings.

Mueller-Pfeiffer et al.'s (2013) study did not find a relationship between the development of dissociative symptoms after childhood maltreatment and developmental stage or family context at the time of maltreatment. Their study found a strong association between peri-/extrafamilial maltreatment and dissociative symptoms. In contrast, our study offers support for *both an early childhood etiology of the DDs and subsequent maladaptive cycles of abuse in adulthood.* Conflation of different kinds of data may have been an issue in Mueller-Pfeiffer et al.'s study (2013). Our approach of returning to the raw data of the TEC has possibly allowed for the clear emergence of two separate scenarios.

Additional limitations

This study was limited by sample size. The scales used here and in the broader project took some time to administer, and a limited number of 116 participants could be recruited. Of the 116 patients who took part in the study, a clinically significant proportion of patients were diagnosed with DD (13.8%). This proportion's relatively small size in comparison with the rest of the patients with other psychiatric disorders constrained the statistical analyses and resulted in low statistical power, especially when the subsets of the different abuse types were considered. The relatively small subgroup of patients with a DD also contributed to the logit models' and logistic regression analyses' not reaching a solution. Even though mixed psychiatric samples have several benefits (see also Simeon et al., 2001), the proportion of patients with a DD in such mixed psychiatric samples will always remain relatively small in statistical terms, which would inhibit and/or complicate any predictive analyses.

The logit models with accompanying cross-tabulations and Fisher's exact tests used in this study did contribute useful information, supporting the widely accepted theory that complex, chronic, relational *early childhood abuse* leads to the development of DDs, while at the same time helping to interpret how adult abuse fits into the picture.

Future research directions and clinical implications

Future research might benefit from the use of alternative scales that measure childhood traumatic events, e.g., the Childhood Trauma Questionnaire/CTQ (Bernstein et al., 2003), although even the CTQ purportedly has problems of a psychometric nature (Haferkamp et al., 2015). Future development of scales of childhood maltreatment and other traumatic experiences should differentiate clearly between the different types of maltreatment, the ages of the victim at the time of each type of maltreatment, and the perpetrator/s of each type of maltreatment separately, *at that specific time*—and should allow for all possible permutations. Such refinement will enhance the clinical applicability of studies such as ours.

Health- and other professionals who encounter children or adolescents should be especially vigilant to recognize the presence of *emotional neglect by biological parents or close biological relatives*. Emotional neglect may be interlinked with other types of abuse and children who suffer in this way may be at high risk of developing a DD. Such children should be referred for a full assessment for the presence of a DD and given the appropriate treatment as needed. Likewise, mental health professionals who assess or treat adult psychiatric patients should enquire about a *childhood history of emotional neglect by their biological parents or close biological relatives*, as part of the routine enquiry about a history of childhood maltreatment. Enquiring about *adult emotional abuse by intimate partners* might also assist in screening for DDs among adults.

Conclusions and recommendations

DD patients reportedly experienced more abuse than patients without DDs. Two combinations of abuse type and abuser–abused relational tie predicted a DD: *childhood emotional neglect by biological parents or siblings*, as well as *later emotional abuse by intimate partners*.

These findings support the early childhood etiology of the DDs, i.e., that complex, chronic, relational early childhood abuse leads to the development of DDs. At the same time, these findings help us to interpret how adult abuse fits into the picture, by lending support to the concept of subsequent maladaptive, attachment-based cycles of abuse in adulthood.

A childhood history of emotional neglect by biological parents or siblings should form a part of the routine enquiry about a history of childhood maltreatment. Enquiring about adult emotional abuse by intimate partners might also assist in screening for DDs among adults.

Acknowledgments

The authors are grateful to Mrs J Sommerville of the Department of Statistics, University of Pretoria for her assistance with electronic data management and statistical analyses; to Mr BB Versfeld, Ms R Liprini, and Ms L Meiring (research assistants in the Department of Psychiatry, University of Pretoria) for their assistance with questionnaire-based data collection and data management to Dr. C Tosh for language editing; and to the patients for their willingness to participate in this research study.

Funding

This research was funded by grants from the South African National Research Foundation, as well as the Department of Psychiatry and Faculty of Health Sciences of the University of

Pretoria. These sponsors had no role in the study design; in the collection, analysis, and interpretation of data; in the writing of the report; or in the decision to submit the article for publication.

Declaration of interest

There are no conflicts of interest.

References

American Psychiatric Association (APA). (2013). *Diagnostic and statistical manual of mental disorders, 5th ed. (DSM-5)*. Washington, DC, USA: American Psychiatric Association.

Bernstein, D. P., Stein, J. A., Newcomb, M. D., Walker, E., Pogge, D., Ahluvalia, T., ... Zule, W. (2003). Development and validation of a brief screening version of the childhood trauma questionnaire. *Child Abuse & Neglect, 27*, 169–190. doi:10.1016/S0145-2134(02)00541-0

Bernstein, E. M., & Putnam, F. W. (1986). Development, reliability, and validity of a dissociation scale. *The Journal of Nervous and Mental Disease, 174* (12), 727–735. doi:10.1097/00005053-198612000-00004

Carlson, E. B., & Putnam, F. W. (1993). An update on the dissociative experiences scale. *Dissociation, VI* (1), 16–27.

Dalenberg, C. J., Brand, B. L., Gleaves, D. H., Dorahy, M. J., Loewenstein, R. J., Cardeña, E., ... Spiegel, D. (2012). Evaluation of the evidence for the trauma and fantasy models of dissociation. *Psychological Bulletin, 138*, 550–588. doi:10.1037/a0027447

Dell, P. F. (2006). The Multidimensional Inventory of Dissociation (MID): A comprehensive measure of pathological dissociation. *Journal of Trauma & Dissociation, 7* (2), 77–106. doi:10.1300/J229v07n02_06

Dorahy, M. J., Brand, B. L., Şar, V., Krüger, C., Stavropoulos, P., Martínez-Taboas, A., ... Middleton, W. (2014). Dissociative identity disorder: An empirical overview. *Australian & New Zealand Journal of Psychiatry, 48* (5), 402–417. doi:10.1177/0004867414527523

Dorahy, M. J., & Van Der Hart, O. (2007). Relationship between trauma and dissociation: A historical analysis. In E. Vermetten, M. J. Dorahy, & D. Spiegel (Eds.), *Traumatic dissociation: Neurobiology and treatment* (pp. 3–30). Washington, DC, USA: American Psychiatric Publishing, Inc.

Farley, M., & Keaney, J. C. (1997). Physical symptoms, somatization, and dissociation in women survivors of childhood sexual assault. *Women & Health, 25* (3), 33–45. doi:10.1300/J013v25n03_03

Freyd, J. J. (1994). Betrayal trauma: Traumatic amnesia as an adaptive response to childhood abuse. *Ethics & Behavior, 4*, 307–329. doi:10.1207/s15327019eb0404_1

Freyd, J. J. (1997). *Betrayal trauma: Traumatic amnesia as an adaptive response to childhood abuse*. Cambridge, MA: Harvard University Press.

Haferkamp, L., Bebermeier, A., Möllering, A., & Neuner, F. (2015). Dissociation is associated with emotional maltreatment in a sample of traumatized women with a history of child abuse. *Journal of Trauma & Dissociation, 16* (1), 86–99. doi:10.1080/15299732.2014.959149

Israel, E., & Stover, C. (2009). Intimate partner violence: The role of the relationship between perpetrators and children who witness violence. *Journal of Interpersonal Violence, 24* (10), 1755–1764. doi:10.1177/0886260509334044

Kilic, O., Sar, V., Taycan, O., Aksoy-Poyraz, C., Erol, T. C., Tecer, O., … Ozmen, M. (2014). Dissociative depression among women with fibromyalgia or rheumatoid arthritis. *Journal of Trauma & Dissociation, 15* (3), 285–302. doi:10.1080/15299732.2013.844218

Krüger, C. (2016). Variations in identity alteration – a qualitative study of experiences of psychiatric patients with dissociative identity disorder. In A. P. van der Merwe, & V. Sinason (Eds.), *Shattered but unbroken: Voices of triumph and testimony* (Chapter 6, pp. 133–161). London, UK: Karnac Books.

Mueller-Pfeiffer, C., Moergeli, H., Schumacher, S., Martin-Soelch, C., Wirtz, G., Fuhrhans, C., … Rufer, M. (2013). Characteristics of child maltreatment and their relation to dissociation, posttraumatic stress symptoms, and depression in adult psychiatric patients. *The Journal of Nervous & Mental Disease, 201* (6), 471–477. doi:10.1097/NMD.0b013e3182948096

Nijenhuis, E. R. S. (1999/2004). *Somatoform dissociation: Phenomena, measurement, and theoretical issues.* New York, NY: WW Norton & Co.

Ozcetin, A., Belli, H., Ertem, U., Bahcebasi, T., Ataoglu, A., & Canan, F. (2009). Childhood trauma and dissociation in women with pseudoseizure-type conversion disorder. *Nordic Journal of Psychiatry, 63* (6), 462–468. doi:10.3109/08039480903029728

Plattner, B., Silvermann, M. A., Redlich, A. D., Carrion, V. G., Feucht, M., Friedrich, M. H., & Steiner, H. (2003). Pathways to dissociation: Intrafamilial versus extrafamilial trauma in juvenile delinquents. *The Journal of Nervous & Mental Disease, 191* (12), 781–788. doi:10.1097/01.nmd.0000105372.88982.54

Ross, C. A., Miller, S. D., Bjornson, L., Reagor, P., Fraser, G. A., & Anderson, G. (1991). Abuse histories in 102 cases of multiple personality disorder. *Canadian Journal of Psychiatry - Revue Canadienne de Psychiatrie, 36* (2), 97–101.

Sachs, A. (2013). Still being hurt: The vicious cycle of dissociative disorders, attachment, and ongoing abuse. *Attachment: New Directions in Psychotherapy and Relational Psychoanalysis, 7*, 90–100.

Sandberg, D. A. (2010). Adult attachment as a predictor of posttraumatic stress and dissociation. *Journal of Trauma & Dissociation, 11* (3), 293–307. doi:10.1080/15299731003780937

Sar, V., Akyüz, G., & Dogan, O. (2007). Prevalence of dissociative disorders among women in the general population. *Psychiatry Research, 149*, 169–176. doi:10.1016/j.psychres.2006.01.005

Sar, V., Akyuz, G., Kugu, N., Ozturk, E., & Ertem-Vehid, H. (2006). Axis I dissociative disorder comorbidity in borderline personality disorder and reports of childhood trauma. *The Journal of Clinical Psychiatry, 67* (10), 1583–1590. doi:10.4088/JCP.v67n1014

Sar, V., Önder, C., Kilincaslan, A., Zoroglu, S. S., & Alyanak, B. (2014). Dissociative identity disorder among adolescents: Prevalence in a university psychiatric outpatient unit. *Journal of Trauma & Dissociation, 15* (4), 402–419. doi:10.1080/15299732.2013.864748

Schäfer, I., Harfst, T., Aderhold, V., Briken, P., Lehmann, M., Moritz, S., … Naber, D. (2006). Childhood trauma and dissociation in female patients with schizophrenia spectrum disorders: An exploratory study. *The Journal of Nervous & Mental Disease, 194*, 135–138. doi:10.1097/01.nmd.0000198199.57512.84

Schultz, T., Passmore, J. L., & Yoder, C. Y. (2003). Emotional closeness with perpetrators and amnesia for child sexual abuse. *Journal of Child Sexual Abuse, 12* (1), 67–88. doi:10.1300/J070v12n01_04

Schumacher, S., Martin-Soelch, C., Rufer, M., Pazhenkottil, A. P., Wirtz, G., Fuhrhans, C., … Mueller-Pfeiffer, C. (2011). Psychometric characteristics of the German adaptation of the Traumatic Experiences Checklist (TEC). *Psychol Trauma, 4*, 338–346. doi:10.1037/a0024044

Simeon, D., Guralnik, O., Schmeidler, J., Sirof, B., & Knutelska, M. (2001). The role of childhood interpersonal trauma in depersonalization disorder. *American Journal of Psychiatry*, *158*, 1027–1033. doi:10.1176/appi.ajp.158.7.1027

Steinberg, M. (1994a). *Interviewer's guide to the structured clinical interview for DSM-IV dissociative disorders - Revised (SCID-D-R)* (2nd ed.). Washington, DC: American Psychiatric Press.

Steinberg, M. (1994b). *Structured clinical interview for DSM-IV dissociative disorders – Revised (SCID-D-R)*. Washington, DC: American Psychiatric Press.

Van der Hart, O., Nijenhuis, E. R. S., & Steele, K. (2006). *The haunted self: Structural dissociation and the treatment of chronic traumatization*. New York, NY: WW Norton & Co.

Vogel, M., Spitzer, C., Kuwert, P., Möller, B., Freyberger, H. J., & Grabe, H. J. (2009). Association of childhood neglect with adult dissociation in schizophrenic inpatients. *Psychopathology*, *42*, 124–130. doi:10.1159/000204763

Watson, S., Chilton, R., Fairchild, H., & Whewell, P. (2006). Association between childhood trauma and dissociation among patients with borderline personality disorder. *Australian & New Zealand Journal of Psychiatry*, *40*, 478–481. doi:10.1080/j.1440-1614.2006.01825.x

World Health Organization. (1992). *The ICD-10 classification of mental and behavioural disorders: Clinical descriptions and diagnostic guidelines*. Geneva, SZ: World Health Organization.

Victim–perpetrator dynamics through the lens of betrayal trauma theory

Kerry L. Gagnon, MA, Michelle Seulki Lee, MA, and Anne P. DePrince, PhD

ABSTRACT

Interpersonal trauma exposure is linked with a host of seemingly disparate outcomes for victims, such as psychological distress, post-trauma appraisals (e.g., alienation, shame), poor cognitive functioning, expectations of harm in relationships, and revictimization risk. The presence of interpersonal trauma alone may not fully explain this range of outcomes. The current paper applies Betrayal Trauma Theory (BTT), which was originally articulated two decades ago as a framework for understanding memory disruptions following interpersonal trauma, as a framework to understand the diverse outcomes that can occur when interpersonal trauma is perpetrated by a close other. Implications for clinical work and future research are considered.

Maureen seeks therapy for occasional bouts of depression and anxiety as well as problems in relationships, and reports that she has a hard time maintaining relationships and frequently feels taken advantage of by people. She describes feeling cut off from people and disruptions in her sense of self. In addition to reports of child abuse by a parent, she recently disclosed that she was abused by her intimate partner. While she says she is committed to therapy, she is often late for or misses scheduled sessions. She reports she is on the verge of losing her job after her employer has complained repeatedly about her problems with attention to detail and spacing out.[1]

Interpersonal trauma exposure (including physical, sexual, psychological, and family abuse) has been linked to a broad range of mental and physical health consequences, such as dissociation, post-traumatic stress disorder (PTSD), depression, sexually transmitted diseases, and chronic pain (e.g., Black, 2011; Briere & Jordan, 2009; Campbell, 2002; Coker et al., 2002). The presence of interpersonal trauma exposure alone, however, does not account for the range of issues that clients, such as the composite client Maureen, bring to therapy (e.g., DePrince & Freyd, 2002). We propose that Betrayal Trauma Therapy (BTT) (Freyd, 1994, 1996), which was originally articulated two decades ago as a framework for understanding memory disruptions following interpersonal trauma in which victims are dependent on their abusers (for reviews, see

DePrince et al., 2012; Freyd, DePrince, & Gleaves, 2007), offers an important theoretical lens through which to consider diverse outcomes of clinical importance. Where a growing body of work has focused on BTT and mental health symptoms (e.g., dissociation; Freyd et al., 2007), this review focuses on empirical findings that illustrate BTT as a useful framework with which to understand links between abuse by a close other and post-trauma appraisals (i.e., alienation, shame, self-blame), cognitive function (i.e., executive function (EF)), and alterations in relationship schemas.

Overview of betrayal trauma theory

BTT emphasizes the importance of social relationships in understanding post-traumatic outcomes. Specifically, BTT predicts that abuse perpetrated by someone on whom a victim depends will lead to different outcomes relative to traumas that do not evoke betrayal or involve harm in close relationships (DePrince et al., 2012; Freyd, 1999, 2001, 2008; Freyd et al., 2007). Additionally, BTT proposes that betrayal traumas vary in their degree of betrayal. Further, the degree of betrayal is related to how the traumatic event is processed and remembered, and consequently, how the trauma affects psychological well-being. Indeed, researchers have demonstrated that traumas high in betrayal are linked with greater severity of PTSD, anxiety, dissociation, alexithymia, and depression symptoms relative to traumas low in betrayal (Goldsmith, Freyd, & DePrince, 2012).

BTT suggests that dependence in the victim–perpetrator relationship puts pressure on the victim to adapt to the abuse in ways that preserve the relationship. A child who is abused by a caregiver, for example, cannot simply leave the relationship because the child depends upon the caregiver for survival (e.g., providing food and shelter). Maintaining attachment to the caregiver despite the abuse may require the child to minimize awareness of the abuse. BTT suggests that betrayal dynamics may, therefore, promote cognitive and emotional processing that inhibit awareness. Dissociation, emotional numbing, and alexithymia, for example, may help victims decrease awareness of abuse-related information, thus supporting maintenance of the necessary attachments to perpetrators (Freyd, 1996; Freyd, DePrince, & Zurbriggen, 2001).

Though responses such as dissociation may be adaptive in the context of the victim–perpetrator relationship, such responses may increase risk for later victimization (DePrince, 2005) and a host of other negative psychological and physical health outcomes (Goldsmith, Chesney, Heath, & Barlow, 2013; Goldsmith et al., 2012). Although BTT does not directly explain the constellation of outcomes, it does provide a theoretical framework to understand these outcomes. Victims who use emotional processing strategies such as dissociation, emotional numbing, and alexithymia to maintain attachment to their abusive caregivers, for example, may be less likely to develop and/or use effective emotion regulation skills over time, which may increase their risk for negative mental health outcomes. Thus, for a client such as Maureen, mental health symptoms may have their roots, at least in part, in emotional processing that was adaptive for surviving the initial abuse, and has also contributed to future risk for psychological distress. Building on this discussion of mental health symptoms, we now turn to consider other outcomes associated with betrayal trauma exposure.

Post-trauma appraisals

While initial conceptualizations of BTT focused on the characteristics of the trauma itself (i.e., the degree of dependence in the victim–perpetrator relationship), more recent work has expanded to consider survivors' meaning-making—which we will refer to as appraisals—of the events and how they relate to outcomes. BTT predicts that victims who are dependent on perpetrators will be less likely to recognize betrayal in those relationships. By extension, victims may be less likely to label their experiences (e.g., physical, sexual, psychological abuse) as involving betrayal. As noted earlier, the theory also implicates dissociative processes in unawareness. Integrating these ideas, recent research with women exposed to domestic violence by intimate partners—a betrayal trauma—found that women with *higher* reported dissociative symptoms were *less* likely to endorse items describing the domestic violence as a betrayal (DePrince, Chu, & Pineda, 2011). In another sample of adults who experienced betrayal traumas (most frequently childhood abuse) and were diagnosed with dissociative identity disorder or PTSD, however, researchers did not replicate this link between dissociative symptoms and betrayal appraisals (DePrince, Huntjens, & Dorahy, 2015). Among other possible explanations (e.g., sample differences), the inconsistent findings across the two studies may suggest that victims of betrayal trauma may use other appraisals, beyond betrayal, in order to maintain attachment with the perpetrator. For example, victims may appraise their experience in such a way that places the focus of the abuse on the self rather than on the perpetrator. Thus, victims may blame themselves instead of the perpetrator (self-blame) or think of themselves as dirty or bad (shame), thereby minimizing a focus on the actions of the perpetrator. Victims may also think of themselves as disconnected from self and others (alienation), which could enable them to create an emotional distance between themselves and the perpetrator. Closer examination of alienation, self-blame, and shame appraisals is warranted in this review because these appraisals have been documented in people exposed to betrayal traumas and are linked with post-traumatic mental health symptoms (DePrince, Zurbriggen, Chu, & Smart, 2010; DePrince et al., 2011; Ehlers & Clark, 2000; Foa, Ehlers, Clark, Tolin, & Orsillo, 1999; Halligan, Michael, Clark, & Ehlers, 2003).

When betrayal traumas occur, alienation—the perception of being isolated and disconnected from people—may arise out of the harm caused in the context of a close victim–perpetrator relationship. Appraisals of alienation, for example, may be adaptive in the context of the abuse; feelings of being separated from others may help victims emotionally distance and detach themselves from an abusive relationship in which they have to physically stay in for survival. As noted by DePrince and colleagues (2011), feelings of alienation may contribute to multiple forms of distress (e.g., depression, dissociation, and PTSD symptoms). For example, disconnection from oneself and others might result in problems of identity in dissociation and isolation in depression (DePrince et al., 2011).

Researchers have also documented associations between betrayal trauma and appraisals of self-blame and shame. Specifically, researchers have found that a history of betrayal trauma predicts greater perceptions of self-blame and shame toward later victimizations and interpersonal threat (Babcock & DePrince, 2012; Platt & Freyd, 2015). From a theoretical standpoint, perceptions of self-blame may help victims of abuse maintain the victim–perpetrator relationship; by blaming themselves, victims remain unaware of betrayal in the relationship and are able to maintain the necessary attachment to the perpetrator. Similarly, victims' shame may refocus the abuse onto themselves in such a way that victims feel humiliated and/or embarrassed by the abuse, rather than feeling betrayed by their perpetrator. Shame may stem from feelings of defeat and helplessness within the victim–perpetrator relationship; the victim is dependent on the perpetrator, and therefore, is unable to escape the abuse (Harper & Arias, 2004). Appraisals of self-blame have been specifically linked to depression (DePrince et al., 2011) and appraisals of shame have been linked to PTSD (Andrews, Brewin, Rose, & Kirk, 2000; DePrince et al., 2011).

Although research is still needed to understand the causal link between betrayal traumas, post-trauma appraisals, and post-trauma symptoms, the extant findings provide a foundation for considering post-trauma appraisals as a mediating factor in the development of various outcomes following betrayal trauma. Researchers have documented that negative trauma-related cognitions mediate change in PTSD and depression symptoms (McLean, Yeh, Rosenfield, & Foa, 2015; Schumm, Dickstein, Walter, Owens, & Chard, 2015), and therefore, provide evidence that negative trauma-related cognitions may be an important target for treatment. Further, as interventions for PTSD vary in degree to which they focus on a range of trauma-related appraisals (e.g., cognitive processing therapy; for a review, see Monson & Shnaider, 2014), clinicians working with clients who have a history of betrayal trauma may find that interventions that target a full range of post-trauma appraisals (e.g., shame, self-blame, alienation) are efficacious in reducing trauma-related distress.

Cognitive functioning

BTT also emphasizes the importance of considering cognitive processes and how these processes affect psychological outcomes and well-being. Emerging research demonstrates a link between betrayal trauma exposure and EF performance. EFs are cognitive skills that control complex goal-directed behavior, such as attention, self-monitoring, remembering and manipulating information in working memory, and inhibiting information unrelated to the task at hand. Existing research suggests that children and adults exposed to betrayal trauma are at greater risk for EF deficits, specifically deficits in working memory, auditory attention, and processing speed, relative to those with low or no betrayal trauma exposure (DePrince, Weinzierl, & Combs, 2009; Stein, Kennedy, & Twamley, 2002; Twamley et al., 2009). While longitudinal data are lacking to answer whether EF deficits are a risk factor for or consequence of betrayal trauma exposure, several potential explanations point to EF deficits as a consequence of betrayal trauma. Victims of betrayal trauma, for example, may engage in cognitive avoidance strategies (e.g., dissociation, emotional numbing) in order to remain unaware of betrayal, and these cognitive strategies may negatively impact the development and utilization of EF strategies, particularly when the betrayal trauma occurs in childhood while the EF system is developing. Indeed, higher levels of dissociation have been linked to EF deficits in children (e.g., inhibition; Cromer, Stevens, DePrince, & Pears, 2006). Another possible explanation for EF deficits resulting from betrayal trauma exposure is that coping with betrayal trauma involves cognitive strategies that deplete cognitive resources from areas of the brain responsible for EF (Schmeichel, 2007).

Deficits in EF can impact an individual's well-being across multiple domains, including academic, psychological, and social functioning. For instance, EF deficits have been associated with poorer mathematical achievement in children (Bull, Espy, & Wiebe, 2008), as well as worse depressive symptoms in adults exposed to betrayal trauma (Fossati, Ergis, & Allilaire, 2002; Hebenstreit, DePrince, & Chu, 2014). Lee and DePrince (2014) found that EF is related to efficacy in obtaining resources (e.g., housing, shelter) following intimate partner abuse. Deficits in EF may, therefore, be an important factor for service providers to consider when working with victims of betrayal trauma. For clients such as Maureen, EF problems may manifest in being late to appointments and seeming disorganized and/or not attending to details at work. From a betrayal trauma perspective, professionals who work with clients like

Maureen may want to consider potential EF disruptions and provide their clients with specific tools for managing EF-related challenges. Giving structured reminders ahead of appointments and providing structure and repetition throughout treatment, for example, may maximize participation in therapy and, in turn, improve psychological outcomes over time.

Alterations in relationship schemas

As proposed by BTT, when abuse is perpetrated by a close and trusted other, a victim must adapt in ways that may have negative implications for future relationships. Betrayal trauma is associated with alterations in the mental representations of relationships that impact thoughts and behaviors in a relationship context, which we will refer to as relationship schemas. According to the interpersonal schema hypothesis of revictimization (Cloitre, 1998; Cloitre, Cohen, & Scarvalone, 2002), interpersonal abuse involving a close other disrupts healthy relationship schemas such that individuals form automatic associations between relationships and harm. A person who was abused by a parent during childhood, such as the composite client Maureen, is more likely to have developed relationship schemas in which close, interpersonal relationships are automatically associated with abuse (e.g., abuse is a way to connect; Cloitre et al., 2002). Automatic associations between relationship and harm may increase the risk for revictimization because victims may be more likely than peers to expect abuse to be a normal part of relationships (Lee, Begun, DePrince, & Chu, 2015). DePrince, Combs, and Shanahan (2009) found that women with multiple experiences of betrayal trauma demonstrate stronger schematic representations of relationships that include harm compared with single or nonvictimized women, suggesting that stronger associations between relationship and harm may increase the likelihood of victimization. Exposure to multiple betrayal traumas may make individuals more likely to "stay in a relationship that becomes violent and/or feel disempowered to leave such a relationship" (DePrince et al., 2009a).

The extant literature also suggests that relationship schemas may play a role in the link between betrayal trauma exposure and future negative outcomes (e.g., revictimization, psychological distress). Future research, however, is needed to understand the development of relationship schemas and how schemas affect outcomes following betrayal trauma. Understanding the course and outcomes of relationship schemas has important implications for treating clients such as Maureen. Treatments such as Cognitive Behavioral Therapy (CBT) that target core beliefs as well as psychodynamic approaches that target relationship patterns could be used to help clients like Maureen identify their relationship schemas.

Future directions and conclusion

Abuse perpetrated by a close other is linked with a host of apparently disparate outcomes. BTT provides a broad and important theoretical framework to understand how these disparate outcomes may share a common underpinning in adaptations made to navigate the victim–perpetrator relationship. This review has focused on emotional and cognitive processes that may be relevant for clinicians to consider when working with clients who have experienced betrayal trauma. A BTT framework, for example, may facilitate developing a case conceptualization for a composite client such as Maureen. Maureen reports a constellation of problems that researchers have linked to betrayal trauma experiences, such as feeling cut off from other people (i.e., alienation). Maureen also describes a history of revictimization that can be understood, in part, as linked to relationship schemas that automatically associate close relationships with harm. Important to treatment efficacy, Maureen is frequently late or misses scheduled sessions. Her lateness may be due to deficits in EF that are linked to betrayal trauma exposure. By using hypotheses from BTT in the development of a case conceptualization, the therapist and Maureen may better understand and integrate the diverse problems she reports, thereby aiding in treatment planning and efficacy. For example, instead of feeling frustrated at Maureen's lateness to scheduled sessions, the client and therapist might hypothesize that EF difficulties linked to betrayal trauma exposure contribute to this problem, and then use interventions to provide greater structure to help Maureen succeed in attending sessions on time. Likewise, understanding links between betrayal trauma, relationship schemas, and revictimization offer new inroads as the therapist and Maureen address expectations in relationships and safety. For example, a BTT conceptualization might lead therapists to consider strategies from cognitive processing therapy to address trauma-related appraisals and/or from interpersonal or behavior therapy to address relationships (for an overview of relevant cognitive behavioral strategies, see Monson & Shnaider, 2014).

In conclusion, the empirical studies reviewed here illustrate how seemingly disparate outcomes—ranging from post-trauma appraisals to cognitive control problems—can be understood through the lens of BTT. BTT research has shown utility in advancing clinical conceptualization of the complex and diverse problems clients experience following betrayal trauma exposure. Future research, however, is still needed to better our understanding of the emotional and cognitive mechanisms that contribute to revictimization and psychological outcomes following abuse perpetrated by a close and trusted other. Future research is also needed to explore the application of BTT in the context of specific trauma-focused interventions.

Note

1. Maureen reflects a composite of women we have heard from in our research on betrayal trauma exposure.

References

Andrews, B., Brewin, C. R., Rose, S., & Kirk, M. (2000). Predicting PTSD symptoms in victims of violent crime: The role of shame, anger, and childhood abuse. *Journal of Abnormal Psychology, 109* (1), 69–73. doi:10.1037/0021-843X.109.1.69

Babcock, R. L., & DePrince, A. P. (2012). Childhood betrayal trauma and self-blame appraisals among survivors of intimate partner abuse. *Journal of Trauma & Dissociation, 13* (5), 526–538. doi:10.1080/15299732.2012.694842

Black, M. C. (2011). Intimate partner violence and adverse health consequences: Implications for clinicians. *American Journal of Lifestyle Medicine, 5* (5), 428–439. doi:1559827611410265

Briere, J., & Jordan, C. E. (2009). Childhood maltreatment, intervening variables, and adult psychological difficulties in women: An overview. *Trauma, Violence, & Abuse, 10* (4), 375–388. doi:10.1177/1524838009339757

Bull, R., Espy, K. A., & Wiebe, S. A. (2008). Short-term memory, working memory, and executive functioning in preschoolers: Longitudinal predictors of mathematical achievement at age 7 years. *Developmental Neuropsychology, 33* (3), 205–228. doi:10.1080/87565640801982312

Campbell, J. C. (2002). Health consequences of intimate partner violence. *The Lancet, 359*, 1331–1336. doi:10.1016/S0140-6736(02)08336-8

Cloitre, M. (1998). Sexual revictimization: Risk factors and prevention. In V. M. Follette, J. I. Ruzek, & F. R. Abueg (Eds.), *Cognitive-behavioral therapies for trauma* (pp. 278–304). New York, NY: Guilford Press.

Cloitre, M., Cohen, L. R., & Scarvalone, P. (2002). Understanding revictimization among childhood sexual abuse survivors: An interpersonal schema approach. *Journal of Cognitive Psychotherapy, 16* (1), 91–111. doi:10.1891/jcop.16.1.91.63698

Coker, A. L., Davis, K. E., Arias, I., Desai, S., Sanderson, M., Brandt, H. M., & Smith, P. H. (2002). Physical and mental health effects of intimate partner violence for men and women. *American Journal of Preventive Medicine, 23*, 260–268. doi:10.1016/S0749-3797(02)00514-7

Cromer, L. D., Stevens, C., DePrince, A. P., & Pears, K. (2006). The relationship between executive attention and dissociation in children. *Journal of Trauma & Dissociation, 7* (4), 135–153. doi:10.1300/J229v07n04_08

DePrince, A. P. (2005). Social cognition and revictimization risk. *Journal of Trauma & Dissociation, 6* (1), 125–141. doi:10.1300/J229v06n01_08

DePrince, A. P., Brown, L. S., Cheit, R. E., Freyd, J. J., Gold, S. N., Pezdek, K., & Quina, K. (2012). Motivated forgetting and misremembering: Perspectives from betrayal trauma theory. In R. F. Belli (Ed.), *True and false recovered memories: Toward a reconciliation of the debate (Nebraska Symposium on Motivation 58)* (pp. 193–243). New York, NY: Springer.

DePrince, A. P., Chu, A. T., & Pineda, A. S. (2011). Links between specific posttrauma appraisals and three forms of trauma-related distress. *Psychological Trauma: Theory, Research, Practice, and Policy, 3* (4), 430–441. doi:10.1037/a0021576

DePrince, A. P., Combs, M. D., & Shanahan, M. (2009). Automatic relationship-harm associations and interpersonal trauma involving close others. *Psychology of Women Quarterly, 33* (2), 163–171. doi:10.1111/j.1471-6402.2009.01486.x

DePrince, A. P., & Freyd, J. J. (2002). The intersection of gender and betrayal in trauma. In R. Kimerling, P. C. Ouimette, & J. Wolfe (Eds.), *Gender and PTSD* (pp. 98–113). New York, NY: Guilford Press.

DePrince, A. P., Huntjens, R., & Dorahy, M. J. (2015). Alienation appraisals distinguish adults diagnosed with DID from PTSD. *Psychological Trauma: Theory, Research, Practice, and Policy, 7* (6), 578–582. doi:10.1037/tra0000069

DePrince, A. P., Weinzierl, K. M., & Combs, M. D. (2009). Executive function performance and trauma exposure in a community sample of children. *Child Abuse & Neglect, 33*, 353–361. doi:10.1016/j.chiabu.2008.08.002

DePrince, A. P., Zurbriggen, E. L., Chu, A. T., & Smart, L. (2010). Development of the trauma appraisal questionnaire. *Journal of Aggression, Maltreatment & Trauma, 19* (3), 275–299. doi:10.1080/10926771003705072

Ehlers, A., & Clark, D. M. (2000). A cognitive model of posttraumatic stress disorder. *Behaviour Research and Therapy, 38*, 319–345. doi:10.1016/S0005-7967(99)00123-0

Foa, E. B., Ehlers, A., Clark, D. M., Tolin, D. F., & Orsillo, S. M. (1999). The posttraumatic cognitions inventory (PTCI): Development and validation. *Psychological Assessment, 11* (3), 303–314. doi:10.1037/1040-3590.11.3.303

Fossati, P., Ergis, A. M., & Allilaire, J. F. (2002). Executive functioning in unipolar depression: A review. *L'Encéphale, 28* (2), 97.

Freyd, J. J. (1994). Betrayal trauma: Traumatic amnesia as an adaptive response to childhood abuse. *Ethics & Behavior, 4* (4), 307–329. doi:10.1207/s15327019eb0404_1

Freyd, J. J. (1996). *Betrayal trauma: The logic of forgetting childhood abuse.* Cambridge, MA: Harvard University Press.

Freyd, J. J. (1999). Blind to betrayal: New perspectives on memory for trauma. *The Harvard Mental Health Letter, 15* (12), 4–6.

Freyd, J. J. (2001). Memory and dimensions of trauma: Terror may be 'all too-well remembered' and betrayal buried. In J. R. Conte (Ed.), *Critical issues in child sexual abuse: Historical, legal, and psychological perspectives* (pp. 139–173). Thousand Oaks, CA: Sage.

Freyd, J. J. (2008). Betrayal trauma. In G. Reyes, J. D. Elhai, & J. D. Ford (Eds.), *The encyclopedia of psychological trauma* (pp. 76). Hoboken, NJ: John Wiley & Sons Inc.

Freyd, J. J., DePrince, A. P., & Gleaves, D. (2007). The state of betrayal trauma theory: Reply to McNally—Conceptual issues, and future directions. *Memory, 15*, 295–311. doi:10.1080/09658210701256514

Freyd, J. J., DePrince, A. P., & Zurbriggen, E. L. (2001). Self-reported memory for abuse depends upon victim-perpetrator relationship. *Journal of Trauma & Dissociation, 2* (3), 5–15. doi:10.1300/J229v02n03_02

Goldsmith, R. E., Chesney, S. A., Heath, N. M., & Barlow, M. R. (2013). Emotion regulation difficulties mediate associations between betrayal trauma and symptoms of posttraumatic stress, depression, and anxiety. *Journal of Traumatic Stress, 26*, 376–384. doi:10.1002/jts.2013.26.issue-3

Goldsmith, R. E., Freyd, J. J., & DePrince, A. P. (2012). Betrayal trauma: Associations with psychological and physical symptoms in young adults. *Journal of Interpersonal Violence, 27* (3), 547–567. doi:10.1177/0886260511421672

Halligan, S. L., Michael, T., Clark, D. M., & Ehlers, A. (2003). Posttraumatic stress disorder following assault: The role of cognitive processing, trauma memory, and appraisals. *Journal of Consulting and Clinical Psychology, 71*, 419–431. doi:10.1037/0022-006X.71.3.419

Harper, F. W. K., & Arias, H. (2004). The role of shame in predicting adult anger and depressive symptoms among victims of child psychological maltreatment. *Journal of Family Violence, 19* (6), 367–375. doi:10.1007/s10896-004-0681-x

Hebenstreit, C. L., DePrince, A. P., & Chu, A. T. (2014). Interpersonal violence, depression, and executive function. *Journal of Aggression, Maltreatment & Trauma, 23* (2), 168–187. doi:10.1080/10926771.2014.872749

Lee, M. S., Begun, S., DePrince, A. P., & Chu, A. T. (2015). *Schema and sexism: Dating violence acceptance among adolescent girls exposed to domestic violence.* Poster presented at the 31st Annual Meeting of the International Society for Traumatic Stress Studies, New Orleans, LA.

Lee, M. S., & DePrince, A. P. (2014, November). *Role of executive function on obtaining resources following intimate partner violence.* Poster presented at the 30th Annual Meeting of the International Society for Traumatic Stress Studies, Miami, FL.

McLean, C. P., Yeh, R., Rosenfield, D., & Foa, E. B. (2015). Changes in negative cognitions mediate PTSD symptom reductions during client-centered therapy and prolonged exposure for adolescents. *Behaviour Research and Therapy, 68,* 64–69. doi:10.1016/j.brat.2015.03.008

Monson, C. M., & Shnaider, P. (2014). *Treating PTSD with cognitive-behavioral therapies: Interventions that work.* Washington, DC: APA Books.

Platt, M. G., & Freyd, J. J. (2015). Betray my trust, shame on me: Shame, dissociation, fear, and betrayal trauma. *Psychological Trauma: Theory, Research, Practice, and Policy, 7* (4), 398–404. doi:10.1037/tra0000022

Schmeichel, B. J. (2007). Attention control, memory updating, and emotion regulation temporarily reduce the capacity for executive control. *Journal of Experimental Psychology: General, 136* (2), 241–255. doi:10.1037/0096-3445.136.2.241

Schumm, J. A., Dickstein, B. D., Walter, K. H., Owens, G. P., & Chard, K. M. (2015). Changes in posttraumatic cognitions predict changes in posttraumatic stress disorder symptoms during cognitive processing therapy. *Journal of Consulting and Clinical Psychology, 83,* 1161–1166. Advance online publication. doi:10.1037/ccp0000040

Stein, M. B., Kennedy, C. M., & Twamley, E. W. (2002). Neuropsychological function in female victims of intimate partner violence with and without posttraumatic stress disorder. *Biological Psychiatry, 52* (11), 1079–1088.

Twamley, E. W., Allard, C. B., Thorp, S. R., Norman, S. B., Hami Cissell, S., Hughes Berardi, K., … Stein, M. B. (2009). Cognitive impairment and functioning in PTSD related to intimate partner violence. *Journal of the International Neuropsychological Society, 15* (6), 879–887. doi:10.1017/S135561770999049X

Shame as a compromise for humiliation and rage in the internal representation of abuse by loved ones: Processes, motivations, and the role of dissociation

Martin J. Dorahy, PhD

ABSTRACT
This paper examines one particular way a person abused may come to internally position themselves and the abuser to understand their abuse experience. It is based on a differentiation and exploration of the dynamic relationship between shame and humiliation associated with complex feelings the abused has to the abuser. Humiliation is described as denoting the naked self exposed *by* another, while shame is described as denoting the naked self exposed *to* another. From this lens, abusive events are conceived as humiliating experiences that come to be represented as shame experiences. Shame is argued to cover over humiliation in order to separate the abused from their internal representation of the abuser (i.e., conceal the self-other object-relationship). This process is facilitated by dissociation and serves several functions, including cloaking hostile feelings (e.g., humiliation fury) toward the abusive (though loved) object. Shame, with the assistance of dissociation, becomes a compromise formation. It punishes the self for the initial humiliation rage directed at the object, protects the object from further attack and blame for the abuse, and obscures awareness of the rage felt toward the object as well as the reparatory guilt possible from it. Dissociation maintains this position by isolating the interpersonal field, the self and object, from the narrative of abuse events. The potential for freedom comes from eroding dissociation, leaving the shame bubble, entertaining the abusive (though loved) object as etiologically significant, and facing the humiliation and humiliation rage that provides the path to reparatory guilt.

"You like it, I can tell," the words deceivingly thrust toward James as a young boy by his much older brother following a further instance of sexual abuse. James did not like it but his brother often used similar sentiments when the physical and emotional pain of the abuse momentarily gave way and his body, biologically wired to respond, appeared to defy him with a pulse of pleasure, a groan of excitement or a flash of stimulation. He felt ashamed that he would react this way, and his brother's words exposed James's body as outside his conscious control and flawed for momentarily responding with pleasure to something he found terrifying, painful, vile, and unwelcome. While his brother's actions and words had the humiliating characteristics of egregiously taking advantage of James's lesser size, power, and status and demonstrated James's inferiority and weakness for them both to see, James recounted the experience not from a place of feeling humiliated by his brother but of being shamed by himself and his behavior. In his view, his brother no longer had a central role to play in the emotional wound that accompanied the memories of these events. Rather, that wound was created by James's own flawed character; his brother was an "extra" in the narrative and relatively free of "sin." James, betrayed by his own body and behaviors, was the sinner. A humiliating event had become a shameful event.

This paper argues that the object-relational interplay between abused and abuser in the torturous dance of chronic attachment-based maltreatment at least in part is shaped, maintained and has its emotional residue in the dynamics of shame and humiliation. Specifically, it is argued that shame covers over humiliation in order to separate the abused from their internal representation of the abuser, thus moving from a self (abused)-other (abuser) explanatory framework to a self-focused explanatory framework. This process is facilitated by dissociation and serves several functions, including cloaking hostile feelings toward the abusive (though loved) object.

Shame and humiliation are closely related and deeply bruising self-conscious affective experiences common in adults with a childhood history of abuse and neglect (Negrao, Bonanno, Noll, Putnam, & Trickett, 2005; Platt & Freyd, 2015). Acknowledgment of, and attention to, them is increasingly understood as important to therapeutically overcoming the lingering outcomes of child maltreatment (Feiring & Taska, 2005; Gilbert, 1998b; Kluft, 2007). A focus of the present paper is the dynamics associated with the translation of humiliation into shame in the service of protecting the abusive (though loved) object (see Fairbairn, 1943, who also explored this process with some reference to shame). It draws on the theory of Davanloo (1987) and stems from reflections about the abused–abuser dyad while working with, and trying to understand the relational dynamics, emotional foundations, and resistances in several long-term cases of familial sexual, emotional, or physical abuse. It is limited to cases where the abuser is a loved other and shame is heavily interwoven in the abuse narrative.

The dynamics and characteristics of shame and humiliation

Humiliation is typically associated with embarrassment and shame (Elison & Harter, 2007; Steiner, 2011; Tomkins, 1963) and they collectively fall under the self-conscious emotions (Tracy & Robins, 2004). Differentiating between two emotions belonging to the same family (e.g., self-conscious emotions) is notoriously difficult and in the current absence of empirically derived and agreed upon discriminatory criteria is prone to the vagaries imposed by language and culture

(Crozier, 2014). The need to differentiate closely aligned emotions like shame and humiliation in the clinical arena seems important only to the degree it has meaningful therapeutic utility. Whilst acknowledging, and not wanting to explore, the literature devoted to whether shame and humiliation are ultimately distinct emotions or simply different manifestations of a common affective experience (Elison & Harter, 2007; Gilbert, 1998a; Tomkins, 1963), the perspective of this paper is that there might be utility in being mindful of differences in shame and humiliation to assist working through central abuse issues involving care-figures.

Shame and humiliation both involve a painful devaluation of, and desire to want to conceal, the vulnerable, exposed self. Yet, they also diverge in important ways. Elison and Harter (2007) propose three central features that characterize an experience as humiliating (1) an intentional action of another to (2) lower the status of a person (3) while other people are observing. The observing others or audience may be internally constructed ("what if others saw me like this") and in reality need to be no bigger than one (i.e., the humiliator; Bigliani, Moguillansky, & Sluzki, 2013). In bringing about its wounding impact, the act of humiliation may target, or create, a particular deficit, disability, or characteristic of the victim, for which they are aware of, and sensitive to, to maximize its effect (Elison & Harter, 2007). This might include being exposed as physically or socially less powerful than the other, as when an adult abusively forces themselves on a child and the child's helplessness and powerlessness is exposed (Lisak, 1994). With regard to the internal experience, Gilbert (1998a) suggests that humiliation entails (1) a directing of attention from the self and onto the other person as bad, to blame, and responsible for causing the pain of humiliation; (2) a sense that the humiliating action of the other was unjust, unfair, or undeserving; and (3) a rage directed toward the other that may manifest as a desire for retaliation. Importantly for humiliation, the lowering of dignity and status created by exposing the weakness or flaw in the self is caused by another not the self (Elison & Harter, 2007).

Contrasted with humiliation, where another or others are bringing negative evaluations onto the self, shame involves negative reflections of the self by the self (Crozier, 2014; Gilbert, 1998a; Lee, Scragg, & Turner, 2001; Lewis, 1971, 1987a; Miller, 1988). In shame, the primary orientation is to the self (Lewis, 1971), in humiliation to the other (Miller, 1988). As Miller (1988) states, "ashamed persons are looking at themselves and judging themselves to be inferior, inadequate or pathetic" (1988, pp. 44–45). Having these deep-seated flaws and inadequacies revealed to self and others (Miller & Tangney, 1994) may lead to rejection or scorn from others whose evaluations are valued (Lewis, 1987a), but they did not maliciously expose them. *In shame, the self is the failure and others may reject or be critical of this exposed, flawed self. In humiliation, others callously expose and reject the flawed self.* Shame cuts a person off from others, creating a crippling sense of seclusion (Dorahy, 2014). "Shame is what one feels one is" (Gilbert, 1998a, p. 248). In adults like

James, it can come to reflect a syntonic representation of the self of which explanations of personal events and the actions of others are filtered through (See Dorahy & Clearwater's (2012) "shame-as-self" construct that captures the enmeshment of shame into the sense of self in abuse victims). With shame, the person comes to believe they deserved it, with humiliation they do not believe it was deserved (Klein, 1991). With humiliation, the other is primarily to blame, while with shame, the self is primarily to blame (Negrao et al., 2005). Shame takes the person out of the interpersonal world and places them in the intrapersonal realm (Bigliani et al., 2013; Miller, 1988). In contrast, humiliation, with its object-directed rage, has the person in the interpersonal; the self and other (Miller, 1988).

The *scars and unhealed wounds* of the humiliating act, visible to the self and perceived as visible to others, may become the content and focus of shame. These wounds, flaws, and deficits may sit close to the surface and drive the shame-prone personality characteristics and interpersonal engagement style of highly traumatized abuse survivors (Chefetz, 2015; Dorahy & Clearwater, 2012).

It should be noted that shame has a long association with anger (Lewis, 1971; Tangney, Wagner, Fletcher, & Gramzow, 1992), but this anger is acute and directed toward another who in the moment touches on shameful feelings (Hejdenberg & Andrews, 2011). It is short (rather than ruminative), intense, and designed to deal with the immediacy of the painful reactivated shame feeling, by transferring it onto the other (Lewis, 1987a; Nathanson, 1992). The rage turned in on the self in shame is briefly turned out. It entertains the other to the point of neutralizing their shaming presence. The aggressive response to shame may reflect the uninitiated rage reaction toward the original etiological (humiliating) figure that was never expressed and was subsequently turned toward the self. But in the dynamic explored here, the connection between that rage and the original humiliating object is obscured and considerations regarding the earlier humiliating experience (e.g., abuse) continue to have the self (rather than the object) as the central etiological figure. Rage is not acknowledged toward the other, or only faintly; so, the original experience/s remain shameful rather than humiliating.

Drawing on the literature differentiating humiliation and shame, this paper understands humiliation as having the weak, defective, flawed, and "naked" self intentionally *highlighted by* another in the presence of real or imagined critical others. Another is blamed for revealing the deficient self such that the self is exposed but another is responsible for the exposure. In shame, the weak, defective, flawed, and "naked" self is *exposed to* real or imagined rejecting appraisals from actual or perceived other/s—the self's inferiority and weakness is to blame, others are more peripheral. There is an inward focus toward flaws, failings, deficits. In short, humiliation captures the naked self exposed *by* another, while shame captures the naked self exposed *to* another. Feelings are directed toward the other in humiliation, making it a more interpersonal, object-oriented experience than shame, which is more intrapersonal on account of feelings being directed toward the self. The object is central to the etiology of humiliation and the target of reactive emotions. The self is central to the etiology of shame and the target of reactive emotions.

In cases of child abuse, the victim is put in the helpless, degraded, and devalued position by the intentional actions of the abuser and may feel in the immediacy (or at some point later) the abuser exposing their vulnerability. In the case of James, his brother's comment exposed what James had wanted to keep hidden, his momentary pleasurable reaction to his brother's maltreatment. In such a situation, James is confronted with two painful points of focus, (1) *his brother's actions toward him* that made his body automatically react in that way, even against his own will and (2) *his body's reaction* to his brother's actions. Focusing on the first is likely to drive humiliation, and appraisals of his brother to blame with reactive rage toward him. Focusing on the second is likely to drive shame, with appraisals of himself as at fault, and reactionary rage directed inward. Often when adults with child abuse histories present for treatment, they have only a tenuous association to the abuser's role in causing the painful feelings of exposure, and rather have their self more as responsible due to some flaw or defect in them that brought about, fostered, excused, or did nothing to stop the abuser's behavior (Darlington, 1996).

Research suggests that self-blame, intimately connected with shame (Lutwak, Panish, & Ferrari, 2003), may be particularly heightened in cases where the abuse started younger, involved a close family member, and included penetration (Barker-Collo, 2001; Feiring & Cleland, 2007). James's exposed flaw was his lack of control over his body's responses and the initial humiliation he felt was transformed into shame so that he, rather than his brother, became the target of reactive rage. Gilbert (1998b) also notes occasions when the victim alternates between object blame and rage, and self-blame and rage. But in cases of abuse in childhood by a loved one, shame may be primed over humiliation for environmental, developmental, and psychodynamic reasons. Environmentally, it may not be safe to express or even feel rage at the abuser, so it is turned in. Developmentally, the idiosyncratic perspective of shame is more consistent with ego-centric views and explanations of children. Psychodynamically, by taking the position of the shameful object, the child preserves the abuser as a good object, providing a sense of security in the external world. In this case, as Fairbairn (1943) notes, "outer security is purchased at the price of inner security" (p. 65). Yet, the movement from humiliation (and its correlates) to shame (and its correlates) arguably also occurs in the service of protecting the object from fantasized attack and the guilt that such an action evokes.

The shame compromise: Humiliation, reactionary rage, guilt, and concern

Child abuse by an attachment figure, caregiver, or family member, in contrast to abuse by a stranger or someone relatively unknown, brings with it the intermingling of complex feelings toward the individual and their object representations. Caring, loving, affectionate feelings mix with anger, pain, and betrayal (Davanloo, 1995; Freyd & Birrell, 2013; Kahn, 2006). The desire for connection, the craving for an attachment bond, and the maintenance of love toward the caregiver (Bowlby, 1958; Fairbairn, 1943) can survive the most chronic and heinous abuse (Hesse & Main, 2000; Sachs, 2013). It has long been understood that feelings of rage toward a loved object evoke unconscious guilt (Davanloo, 1987; Klein, 1940; Lewis, 1987a; Steiner, 1993). Failure to adequately have this guilt managed, contained, or resolved, which may result from a lack of parental attunement, fear, neglect, or the maintenance of rage by ongoing abuse, is thought to produce condemnatory punishment, or what has been labeled persecutory guilt (Hasui, Igarashi, Nagata, & Kitamura, 2008; Money-Kyrle, 1955). This form of guilt lambasts the self for the rageful attack on the loved (though abusive) other, even though the actual reason for the punishment may reside well out of self-awareness (Davanloo, 1987; Freud, 1923; Hepburn, 2012). Persecutory guilt is differentiated from reparatory guilt. Reparatory guilt is associated with acknowledging the damage of the rage on the other and *feeling* the pain of guilt for that rage, without rationalization, deflection, or other forms of resistance (e.g., "they deserved my rage for what they did to me") (Abbass, 2015; Steiner, 2011). Reparatory guilt allows the painful acceptance of the self as perpetrator of hostile (fantasized) attack on the other for the hurt and humiliation they caused. Reparatory guilt aids development and growth by allowing guilt to the felt, while persecutory guilt promotes stuckness and stagnation by punishing the self and blocking the affective experience of guilt (Hepburn, 2012).

Hepburn (2012) argues that persecutory guilt is characterized by the fact that it does not actually belong to the person but rather reflects them taking possession of the guilt of another (e.g., the perpetrator), as a way of gaining agency over the other person's treatment of them (see also Fairbairn, 1943 for a discussion of this process in regard to internalizing "bad" objects). An additional perspective, following Davanloo's (1987) theorizing, is that persecutory guilt does in fact belong to the person and is related to the rage and unconscious (phantasized) attack on the loved (though abusive) other. However, in adult adaptation to child abuse, the shame carried by the victim often seems to belong to the abuser and may reflect a projectively identified affect "given" to the abused by the abuser. James's brother demonstrated the ease with which a subtle, well-timed humiliatory statement (intentionally pointing out James's body reaction) could allow his brother to project his own shame into James, which James then identified with by using the reaction of his own body as a focus and linchpin for the whole episode. Arguably, the carrying of the abuser's shame is held onto, rather than given up, because of the psychological function it comes to serve for dealing with internal chaos created by (among other things) managing the object relationship with the abuser.

Punishment of the self through persecutory guilt is one outcome of the rage directed at a loved (though abusive) object. The current paper draws on Davanloo (1987), who suggests that another outcome is the desire to protect the object (as well as others) from that rage. This desire to protect the object and others may take many symptomatic forms, including dissociation, repression, and conversion of the rage (and other feelings), as well as emotional avoidance of others who may stir up the complex feelings associated with the object (Abbass, Arthey, & Nowoweiski, 2013; Abbass, 2015; Frederickson, 2013). Because of its withdrawal from the object, it seems also that shame may be a potent affect in the protection of the object and others. Persecutory guilt unconsciously operates to punish the self as retribution for the rage directed at the loved (though abusive) object. In this way, it is a true representation of guilt, which Lewis (1971) in her seminal work understood as the aversive feeling associated with a specific action. Yet, it comes to continually admonish the person for who they *are* not simply what they *did*. In this way, persecutory guilt for the unconscious aggressive action begins to reflect shame, an attack on the whole self as defective and weak (Lewis, 1971, 1987a).

As the cognitive components of shame attribute blame and responsibility to the self, and one's own flaws, inadequacies or exposing actions become the focus, feelings toward the other, and the empathic concern for them that mobilizes the punishing guilt (Davanloo, 1987; Gilbert, 1998b; Steiner, 1993) is retreated away from. The self is center stage, unlike guilt and humiliation, where the self and other share the spotlight. What started as unconscious punishing guilt for the rage toward the abusive (though loved) object becomes shaming self-attack for the person's "part" in their own abuse. In this way, shame becomes a potent punisher of the self and a potent protector of the object, shielding them from hostile feelings and fantasies that characterize the self-other intrapsychic interchange of humiliation. With shame blocking access to the feelings toward the object that humiliation allows, there is no room available for exploration of these feelings (e.g., anger), and therefore, no pathway is open for reparatory guilt. Nonetheless, in holding the self accountable and obscuring or neutralizing the abusive role of the other, threats to attachment are attenuated. As Lewis (1987a) notes, "shame is seen as a means by which people try to preserve their loving relationship to others" (p. 2).

Brought together, and within the dynamics of adults abused in childhood by a loved one, shame may become a compromise formation between impulse and defense against it. As such:

(1) It punishes the self for the (unconscious) attack on the object associated with the object's original humiliating abusive actions.
(2) It protects the object from ongoing attack by focusing blame, responsibility, and anger onto the self.
(3) It "protects" the self from the painful realization of the rageful feelings and aggressive fantasies toward the object and the reparatory guilt this afforded.
(4) It allows the preservation of attachment.

Yet, this compromise formation starves the self of the opportunity for growth. The repressive and stagnatory qualities of shame, with attack directed inward and downward at the self, become a means of deflecting humiliation and rage directed at the object which blocks the upward and developmentally-enabling emotional pain of reparatory guilt and remorse.

In summary, it is proposed that based on the definition of humiliation utilized here, abuse in childhood by a caregiving other is an act of humiliation that prompts negative exposure of the self and immediate reactive rage toward the other. The object representation of the other is now damaged by the phantasized attack associated with rage, and the self is thrust into the role of perpetrator (intrapsychically). The love and empathic concern toward the object (despite the abuse they enacted) activates persecutory guilt as a punishment for the attack. This punishes the self and protects the other but maintains an object (i.e., self-other) connection (i.e., self is concerned for the damage to the other). In order to maintain the punishment of self and protection of the object (and other people) from the rage associated with the humiliating abuse, shame comes to replace persecutory guilt, where the whole self is attacked as being defective, weak, and at fault. The rage toward the object is obscured by a retreat into the self and away from object connection and object culpability. This compromise organization "protects" the self from acknowledging rage toward the object that comes from entertaining them and their acts of humiliation. In addition, while attempting to maintain an attachment connection (Lewis, 1987b), this compromise withholds the pain of reparative guilt, which resultantly blocks the emotional path to growth.

The role of dissociation in the shame compromise

When talking about his childhood abuse, James's narrative was organized around his bodily responses and how shameful they were. He spoke in a flat, somewhat detached and emotionally numb manner emphasizing how his body had betrayed him and exposed him to further abuse by his brother. When initially asked about his brother's role in what occurred, he looked somewhat confused, as if he had rarely contemplated this facet of the experience and shifted with little consideration of it back to his monotone description of events from his own self-oriented and self-attacking perspective. Efforts by the therapist to inject his brother into the narrative were typically dismissed subtly or overtly. It seemed that memories of abusive episodes activated for him a construction of events which had him as the primary focus, shame as the dominant affect, and self-blame as the core appraisal cognition. His brother's role in initiating and continuing the abuse appeared to be stripped from the narrative, dissociated away in some other aspect of self that rarely was accessed. This dissociative part of self seemed to also contain feelings of humiliation and rage toward his brother. It appeared to hold the interpersonal field, the self, and object. Chefetz (2015) speaks of the importance of three processes to dissociation: The *isolation* of excluded aspects of the experience, including affects, into their own dissociative parts of self (Van der Hart, Nijenhuis, & Steele, 2006), the continued unconscious endeavor to maintain *exclusion* of the content of this dissociative structure, and the *deflection* of any effort to know what resides in the structure. For James, he isolated his brother's ill treatment of him and the associated reactive feelings (e.g., humiliation, rage). He continued the exclusion of the interpersonal field by the construction and ongoing adherence to a strict shame narrative. Finally, he deflected any effort to draw his brother into the narrative, resultantly avoiding the dissociative content, by shifting back to the shame narrative, defending his brother as a good family man or disavowing any suggestion that his brother was responsible by stating, "that's what my wife [but not me] thinks."

The interpersonal field becomes the target of dissociation and by separating it from central images and memories associated with the abuse shame can dominate the internal landscape, maintaining the compromise formation. Humiliation, object-directed rage, and reparatory guilt associated with rage toward the loved (though abusive) object can be held from self-awareness and self-experience. Thus, while it was argued above that one facet of the unconscious motivation for persecutory guilt and shame was to punish the self and protect the object, the motivation of dissociation in the dynamic described here is for the dilution or cessation of other-directed emotions and cognitions (e.g., pain caused by them, rage toward them, guilt for harming their object representation). Consequently, dissociation facilitates shame and reduces humiliation and object-directed rage. This may also offer a means to minimizing erosion of the attachment relationship.

Case example

For much of her childhood and all her adult life, 50-year-old Ms Y had viewed herself as "poisonous" and held the dominant narrative of responsibility for the emotional and physical abuse she experienced at the hands of her father. Over the previous two and a half years, therapy had made inroads into dismantling the structural dissociation associated with her father's treatment of her, while undermining the processes that maintained it. Ms Y had recently overtly acknowledged feeling like she was dangerous to the therapist and needed to keep emotionally separate to protect him (i.e., transferential protection of object). This provided direct access via the transference to her relationship with her father. Now more able to hold some affect associated with him without resorting to dissociation she recalled memories of him calling her a "burden" and berating her existence as trivial and worthless. Reevoked in her were strong feelings of shame, a desire to be invisible, and perceptions of herself as poisonous and responsible for the strain her father faced. As she reflected on her self-disgust and herself as toxic, she for the first time without active deflection took up the invitation to examine her feelings toward him for what he said. The object had begun to be entertained actively. She described feeling weak, small, and inferior by *his* words and the sense of humiliation brought a blast of intense rage that she recognized but quickly converted into sharp abdominal pain, bloating, and nausea. The humiliation and rage were "distracted" by this debilitating physical pain. When she reverted back to her self-disgust and shame for burdening her father, humiliation, rage toward him, and all forms of physical discomfort subsided. While she was the shameful burden, he was free of responsibility, and any strong negative feelings she had toward him were severed.

Intrapsychically this offered protection to him from her rage activated by any reflection of him humiliating her with intentional mistreatment. As the humiliation rose, she began to be more connected with him as a key protagonist in her abuse memories, re-awaking that dimension of his object inside her, with intense feelings being directed at him. As a result, the rage and desire for revenge (phantasized behavioral urge of the rage) brought sickness and pain as she worked intrapsychically to protect him. This turned her away from her humiliation-rage toward him and triggered the shame she felt for being infected, of danger to him, and responsible for burdening his life. This shut down the object-relational connection of rage, had her retreat back into herself where she was at fault and he was her victim. The shame operated to protect him (object-relationally) from humiliation-rage. It also blocked her from feeling humiliation and object-directed rage that goes with it, which prevented access to reparatory guilt for the reactive rage toward him (Davanloo, 1995).

In the next session, she brought an earlier, more acutely traumatizing memory of waiting at age 4 with excitement for him to visit. Shortly after he arrived, her exuberance was rapidly extinguished by him unpredictably flying into a cold rage and having her kneel on the floor. Standing behind her, seemingly so he was not confronted with her pain, he preceded to whip her on the back with his belt. Her initial retelling of this event brought great shame that her dirtiness and repulsiveness drew this behavior out of him. Yet following the work from the previous week, and the continued breakdown of her dissociated interpersonal field, she began to remember others looking on, which mobilized her humiliation and rage to her father. This time she held more of it emotionally before anxious feelings converted into stomach pain and took her back into herself and away for him. Ms Y was also now more able to intellectualize about the shift from shame to humiliation, which therefore allowed the introduction of the humiliating other and rage toward him, as well as the guilt that existed as a result of her love for him.

In short, as dissociation began is dissolve, Ms Y came to realize that her father abused her (i.e., she entertained the object's role in her childhood experience). She had never forgotten the events but due to dissociative exclusion and deflection had never conceived of them in this way, believing she deserved that particular "attention" from her father because she was disgusting and poisonous. As she began to entertain her father in these memories, she began to see him play a pivotal role in making her feel infected and poisonous. The previous dissociated humiliation and rage toward him began to mobilize and be acknowledged. In the transference relationship, shame began to lift, so she no longer covered her face from the therapist and began to open up physically and emotionally to her feelings toward her father. Shame began to transform into humiliation which brought with it the humiliating father, her rage toward him, her feelings of love and affection for him, and forgiveness of herself via reparatory guilt. Many other aspects of the abuse could then be explored without fear, and the debilitating defenses it brought, of her own intense feelings toward her father. These included his betrayal of her, her profound feelings of loss for the father she wanted but never had, admiring his strength and loathing his abuse of it, and feeling compassion toward him and toward herself.

Conclusion

In cases of abuse from a loved one, the abused must find ways to accommodate their object-relationship with the abuser. Shame with the assistance of dissociation may reflect one compromise formation that corrals the competing forces in operation. These forces include the humiliation felt when being abused, the rage from that humiliation/abuse toward the abusive (though loved) object, and the persecutory guilt for the rage. With shame and its cognitive correlates at the forefront, the self becomes the target of eroding self-punishment for who it is, not simply what it's done. The object is not the focus; so, humiliation and humiliation rage are left out of view. This position is maintained by the dissociation of the interpersonal field (or at least some aspects of it; e.g., object-directed rage), with the person trapped in the shame bubble, dissociated from the object and their role in abuse experiences. What started as humiliation becomes shame and the object is spared the rage now directed at the self. The potential for freedom comes from eroding dissociation, leaving the shame bubble, entertaining the abusive (though loved) object, and facing the humiliation and humiliation rage that provides the path to reparatory guilt.

Acknowledgments

The author would like to thank Drs Richard Chefetz, Donncha Hanna, Henry Luiker, and Catherine Gallagher for valuable comments on earlier drafts of this manuscript.

References

Abbass, A. (2015). *Reaching through resistance: Advanced psychotherapy techniques*. Kansas City, MO: Seven Leaves Press.

Abbass, A. A., Arthey, S., & Nowoweiski, D. (2013). Intensive short-term dynamic psychotherapy for severe behavioral disorders: A focus on eating disorders. *Ad Hoc Bulletin of Short-Term Dynamic Psychotherapy - Practice and Theory, 17*, 5–22.

Barker-Collo, S. L. (2001). Adult reports of child and adult attributions of blame for childhood sexual abuse: Predicting adult adjustment and suicidal behaviors in females. *Child Abuse & Neglect, 25*, 1329–1341. doi:10.1016/S0145-2134(01)00278-2

Bigliani, C. G., Moguillansky, R., & Sluzki, C. S. (2013). *Shame and humiliation: A dialogue between psychoanalytic and systemic approaches*. London, UK: Karnac.

Bowlby, J. (1958). The nature of the child's tie to his mother. *International Journal of Psycho-Analysis, 39*, 350–373.

Chefetz, R. A. (2015). *Intensive psychotherapy for persistent dissociative processes: The fear of feeling real*. New York, NY: Norton.

Crozier, W. R. (2014). Differentiating shame and embarrassment. *Emotion Review, 6*, 269–276. doi:10.1177/1754073914523800

Darlington, Y. (1996). Escape as a response to childhood sexual abuse. *Journal of Child Sexual Abuse, 5*, 77–93. doi:10.1300/J070v05n03_05

Davanloo, H. (1987). Clinical manifestations of superego pathology. *International Jounal of Short-Term Psychotherapy, 2*, 225–254.

Davanloo, H. (1995). Intensive short-term dynamic psychotherapy: Spectrum of psychoneurotic disorders. *International Jounal of Short-Term Psychotherapy, 10*, 121–155.

Dorahy, M. J. (2014). Scham und Täterintrojekte [Shame and the perpetrator introject]. *Trauma: Zeitschrift Für Psychotraumatologie Und Ihre Anwendungen, 12* (4), 16–25. Kröning: Asanger Verlag.

Dorahy, M. J., & Clearwater, K. (2012). Shame and guilt in men exposed to childhood sexual abuse: A qualitative investigation. *Journal of Child Sexual Abuse, 21*, 155–175. doi:10.1080/10538712.2012.659803

Elison, J., & Harter, S. (2007). Humiliation: Causes, correlates, and consequences. In J. L. Tracy, R. W. Robins, & J. P. Tangney (Eds.), *The self-conscious emotions: Theory and research* (pp. 310–329). New York, NY: Guilford Press.

Fairbairn, W. R. D. (1943). The repression and the return of bad objects (with special reference to the "war neuroses"). In W. R. D. Fairbairn (Ed.), (1952). *Psychoanalytic studies of the personality* (pp. 59–81). London, UK: Routledge & Kegan Paul.

Feiring, C., & Taska, L. S. (2005). The persistence of shame following sexual abuse: A longitudinal look at risk and recovery. *Child Maltreatment, 10*, 337–349. doi:10.1177/1077559505276686

Feiring, C. R., & Cleland, C. (2007). Childhood sexual abuse and abuse-specific attributions of blame over 6 years following discovery. *Child Abuse & Neglect, 31*, 1169–1186. doi:10.1016/j.chiabu.2007.03.020

Frederickson, J. (2013). *Co-creating change: Effective dynamic therapy techniques*. Kansas City, MO: Seven Leaves Press.

Freud, S. (1923). The Ego and the Id. In J. Strachey (Ed. & Trans.), *The standard edition of the complete psychological works of sigmund freud, Volume XIX (1923-1925): The ego and the Id and other works* (pp. 1–66). London, UK: Hogarth Press.

Freyd, J. J., & Birrell, P. (2013). *Blind to betrayal: Why we fool ourselves we aren't being fooled*. New York, NY: Wiley & Sons.

Gilbert, P. (1998a). What is shame? Some core issues and controversies. In P. Gilbert, & B. Andrews (Eds.), *Shame: Interpersonal behaviour, psychopathology, and culture* (pp. 3–38). Oxford, UK: Oxford University Press.

Gilbert, P. (1998b). Shame and humiliation in the treatment of complex case. In N. Tarrier, A. Wells, & G. Haddock (Eds.), *Treating complex cases: The cognitive behavioural therapy approach* (pp. 241–271). Chichester, UK: Wiley & Sons.

Hasui, C., Igarashi, H., Nagata, T., & Kitamura, T. (2008). Guilt and its multidimensionality: Empirical approaches using Klein's view. *American Journal of Psychotherapy, 62*, 117–142.

Hejdenberg, J., & Andrews, B. (2011). The relationship between shame and different types of anger: A theory-based investigation. *Personality and Individual Differences, 50*, 1278–1282. doi:10.1016/j.paid.2011.02.024

Hepburn, J. M. (2012). A problem of guilt: An exploration of feelings of guilt as an obstacle to psychic change. *British Journal of Psychotherapy, 28*, 188–200. doi:10.1111/bjp.2012.28.issue-2

Hesse, E., & Main, M. (2000). Disorganized infant, child, and adult attaxhment: Collapse in behavioural and attentional strategies. *Journal of the American Psychoanalytic Association, 48*, 1097–1127. doi:10.1177/00030651000480041101

Kahn, L. (2006). The understanding and treatment of betrayal trauma as a traumatic experience of love. *Journal of Trauma Practice, 5*, 57–72. doi:10.1300/J189v05n03_04

Klein, D. C. (1991). The humiliation dynamic: An overview. *The Journal of Primary Prevention, 12*, 93–121. doi:10.1007/BF02015214

Klein, M. (1940). Mourning and its relation to manic-depressive states. *The International Journal of Psychoanalysis, 21*, 125–153.

Kluft, R. P. (2007). Application of innate affect theory to the understanding and treatment of dissociative identity disorder. In E. Vermetten, M. J. Dorahy, & D. Spiegel (Eds.), *Traumatic dissociation: Neurobiology and treatment* (pp. 301–316). Arlington, VA: American Psychiatric Press.

Lee, D. A., Scragg, P., & Turner, S. (2001). The role of shame and guilt in traumatic events: A clinical model of shame-based and guilt-based PTSD. *British Journal of Medical Psychology, 74*, 451–466. doi:10.1348/000711201161109

Lewis, H. B. (1971). *Shame and guilt in neurosis*. New York, NY: International Universities Press, Inc.

Lewis, H. B. (1987a). Introduction: Shame - the "sleeper" in psychopathology. In H. B. Lewis (Ed.), *The role of shame in symptom formation* (pp. 1–28). Hillsdale, NJ: Lawrence Erlbaum.

Lewis, H. B. (1987b). The role of shame in depression over the life span. In H. B. Lewis (Ed.), *The role of shame in symptom formation* (pp. 29–50). Hillsdale, NJ: Lawrence Erlbaum.

Lisak, D. (1994). The psychological impact of sexual abuse: Content analysis of interviews with male survivors. *Journal of Traumatic Stress, 7*, 525–548. doi:10.1002/(ISSN)1573-6598

Lutwak, N., Panish, J., & Ferrari, J. (2003). Shame and guilt: Characterological vs. behavioral self-blame and their relationship to fear of intimacy. *Personality and Individual Differences, 35*, 909–916. doi:10.1016/S0191-8869(02)00307-0

Miller, R. S., & Tangney, J. P. (1994). Differentiating embarrassment and shame. *Journal of Social and Clinical Psychology, 13*, 273–287. doi:10.1521/jscp.1994.13.3.273

Miller, S. B. (1988). Humiliation and shame: Comparing two affect states as indicators of narcissistic stress. *Bulletin of the Menninger Clinic, 52*, 40–51.

Money-Kyrle, R. E. (1955). Psycho-analysis and ethics. In M. Klein, P. Ileimann, & R. E. Money-Kyrle (Eds.), *Directions in psycho-analysis: The significant of injant conflict in the pattern of adult behaviour* (pp. 421–439). London, UK: Tavistock Publications.

Nathanson, D. L. (1992). *Shame and pride: Affect, sex and the birth of the self.* New York, NY: Norton.

Negrao, C., Bonanno, G. A., Noll, J. G., Putnam, F. W., & Trickett, P. K. (2005). Shame, humiliation, and childhood sexual abuse: Distinct contributions and emotional coherence. *Child Maltreatment, 10*, 350–363. doi:10.1177/1077559505279366

Platt, M. G., & Freyd, J. J. (2015). Betray my trust, shame on me: Shame, dissociation, fear and betrayal trauma. *Psychological Trauma: Theory, Research, Practice and Policy, 7*, 398–404. doi:10.1037/tra0000022

Sachs, A. (2013). Still being hurt: The vicious cycle of dissociative disorders, attachment, and ongoing abuse. *Attachment: New Directions in Psychotherapy and Relational Psychoanalysis, 7*, 90–100.

Steiner, J. (1993). *Psychic retreats: Pathological organizations in psychotic, neurotic and borderline patients.* London, UK: Routledge.

Steiner, J. (2011). *Seeing and being seen: Emerging from a psychic retreat.* London, UK: Routledge.

Tangney, J. P., Wagner, P., Fletcher, C., & Gramzow, R. (1992). Shamed into anger? The relation of shame and guilt to anger and self-reported aggression. *Journal of Personality and Social Psychology, 62*, 669–675. doi:10.1037/0022-3514.62.4.669

Tomkins, S. S. (1963). *Affect, imagery, consciousness. Volume 2: The negative affects.* New York, NY: Springer.

Tracy, J. L., & Robins, R. W. (2004). Putting the self into self-conscious emotions: A theoretical model. *Psychological Inquiry, 15*, 103–125. doi:10.1207/s15327965pli1502_01

Van der Hart, O., Nijenhuis, E. R. S., & Steele, K. (2006). *The haunted self: Structural dissociation and the treatment of chronic traumatization.* New York, NY: Norton & Co.

Knowing and not knowing: A frequent human arrangement

Sylvia Solinski, MB, BS, FRANZCP

ABSTRACT
The paradigmatic system of societal abuse occurs in totalitarian state systems. The relational systems of subjugation that maintain such states of terror must, of necessity, destroy any authentic civic space in which individuals can flourish. Similar dynamics characterize child abuse within families. Survival requires the use of varied strategies, the most extreme of which are dissociative in nature, and that result in marked distortions of developmental trajectories across all psychological domains. Such dynamics are mirrored in dissociative systems that, in the absence of intervention, perpetuate the trauma of non-recognition by subjugation and self-objectification, or by omnipotent denial of others' subjectivity. All abusive systems are facilitated by bystanders, whose awareness of what is disavowed is always partial, resulting in a state of knowing and not-knowing. As dynamics shift, bystanders may behave like victims—passive, helpless, frightened and frozen, or like perpetrators—taking vicarious and voyeuristic pleasure in abuse or actively aiding and abetting the abusers.

Something in the air

When the Korean-American journalist Suki Kim was appointed as an English teacher to an elite school in North Korea, she was cautioned that everything she said and did would be monitored: Her orientation to university teaching included the warning: "Just get in the habit of not saying everything that is on your mind, not criticizing the government and things of that sort, so you won't slip" (Kim, 2014). Continuous censorship left her enervated but she remained a keen observer of her students who, despite being privileged and relatively well-fed members of their society, nevertheless live a restricted routine necessitating perpetual hypervigilance so that they are little better than "soldiers and slaves" (Kim, 2014). The Internet is virtually inaccessible to these privileged students, and what they learn is predicated on Juche, an official ideology that venerates the regime's dynasty as quasi deities whose judgement and wisdom may never be questioned: "There in that relentless vacuum, nothing moved. No news came in or out. No phone calls to or from anyone. No emails, no letters, no ideas not prescribed by the regime" (Kim, 2014).

The ascription to the "Great Leader, Dear Leader, Precious Leader" (Kim, 2014) of everything positive, from the weather to scientific knowledge, is a feature of the only world the students know and terror lies close to the surface of their regimented lives. Any slip, such as a student's admission to liking rock 'n' roll, can constitute a transgression punishable by camp internment: "I had never seen anyone scan the room so fast, and the other students went quiet and looked down at their food" (Kim, 2014). When a "minder" lingered in Kim's office, she "noticed several students at the door, who swiftly recoiled … These were the most garrulous ones from the group, so it was eerie to see how they stiffened at the sight of him" (Kim, 2014). Ultimately, Kim was unable to gauge whether her students' childlike vulnerability reflected an innocence of sorts or whether they were intelligent people forced to stifle their minds. Such uncertainty regarding others discourages any affiliation other than to the state and is characteristic of and demanded by totalitarian rule.

Totalitarianism

Those who live under totalitarian regimes are subject to unprecedented political terror. Soviet Russia and Nazi Germany, totalitarian states that were spawned in the early 20th century, were a qualitatively new form of political organization (Arendt, 1973). The simultaneous existence of "dual states" consisting of a "normative state" in which the norms of state bureaucracy and the judiciary served as a façade for the "prerogative state" enabled the circumvention of civil authority and the establishment of a separate bureaucracy of terror for the unrestricted "measures" of the Leader (Bracher, 1973; Fraenkel, 1969; Wildt, 2009). Thus, a formal state-juridical apparatus lulled both domestic and foreign misgivings during and after the encroachment of the police state, which proved to be a truly revolutionary system of government. The development of such political smokescreens, albeit from entirely different origins, characterized both Soviet Russia (completed in 1923) and Nazi Germany (from 1933). The multiplication of offices and government agencies (including secret services) was used by both regimes with the utmost flexibility for the continual shifting of power; the only things of which people could be sure were that the more visible the agency, the less its power, and that power resided in obscurity. Real power began with secrecy—with the secret police. "In this respect the Nazi and Bolshevik states were very much alike; their difference lay chiefly in the monopolization and centralization of secret police services in Himmler on one hand, and the maze of apparently unrelated and unconnected police activities in Russia on the other" (Arendt, 1973).

The category "objective enemy" is vital to totalitarian regimes whose enemies are defined *ideologically* rather than in terms of what they have done. Accordingly, descendants of the aristocracy in Soviet Russia and the Jews in Nazi Germany were not suspected of hostile action but, in keeping with the regime's ideological tenets, were deemed its "objective" enemies. As ideology changes, new objective enemies need to be found. Hence, the category "enemy" potentially spares no-one; any thought that deviates from the officially prescribed and permanently changing party line is inherently suspect. In a context of ubiquitous spying in which each individual is, effectively, under constant surveillance, all relationships are conducted in the shadow of mutual suspicion (Arendt, 1973). In Soviet Russia: "Informers were everywhere—in factories and schools and offices, in public places and communal apartments. By any estimate, at the height of the Great Terror (1937–38) millions of people were reporting on their colleagues, friends and neighbours…" (Figes, 2007). In "Doctor Zhivago," Pasternak could write: "When the war broke out, its real horrors, its menace of death, were a blessing compared with the inhuman power of the lie, a relief because it broke the spell of the dead letter." The war years would come to be recalled with nostalgia, as a period of spontaneity and vitality, "as an untrammeled joyous restoration of the sense of community with everyone" (Pasternak, 1958).

Total domination, striving to collapse the space between people, is achieved in totalitarian regimes that are mass organizations of atomized, isolated individuals. The concentration and extermination camps of totalitarian regimes are the laboratories wherein people are degraded and exterminated. They serve to eliminate spontaneity and to transform humans into things: "The camp guards understood full well that to choose the moment and the means of one's death is to affirm one's freedom … thus even though the guards killed with such apparent ease, they did everything in their power to prevent people from ending their own lives" (Todorov, 2000). The inmates are sealed off from the world of the living, and this isolation contributes to "the peculiar unreality and lack of credibility that characterize reports from the concentration camps… anyone speaking or writing about their experiences in concentration camps is still regarded as suspect; and, if the speaker has resolutely returned to the land of the living, he himself is often assailed by doubts with regard to his own truthfulness, as though he had mistaken a nightmare for reality" (Arendt, 1973).

Depersonalization is ubiquitous under totalitarianism, and nowhere more so than in the camps. Writing of his experiences in Dachau and Buchenwald, Bettelheim disconcertingly uses the third person singular: "…right from the beginning he become convinced that these horrible and degrading experiences somehow did not happen to 'him' as subject but only to 'him' as an object … this attitude was corroborated by many statements of other prisoners … the prisoners had to convince themselves that this was real, was really happening and not just a nightmare. They were never wholly successful" (Bettelheim, 1943). People who doubt the reality of their own experience and their entitlement to inclusion in the human community merely demonstrate what perpetrators have always known: that the more monstrous the crime the greater the likelihood that the victim will not be believed (Arendt, 1973). As Levi (1984) was the first to note, humanity has already distorted and repressed even this very recent past, and it remains a commonplace that the innocent feel guilty and the guilty feel innocent.

In a totalitarian regime it is possible to distinguish between the unprincipled, obedient automaton, looking out for himself, adopting any convenient motivational camouflage, and the fully informed, monstrous ideologue, whose retreat from truth to evil omnipotence is based on "principle". Both, however, occupy the same moral void (Cohen, 2001). Between perpetrators and victims stand a host of intermediaries occupying a zone that, in one way or another, includes the entire population (Todorov, 2000). The nuances of not knowing, even about mass murder, are well captured by Geras (1998): "These are the people who affect not to know, or who do not care to know and so do not find out; or who do know but do not care anyway, who are indifferent; or who are afraid, for themselves or for others, or who feel powerless; or are weighed down, distracted or just occupied (as most of us) in pursuing the aims of their own lives" (Geras, 1998). Within the atrocity triangle (perpetrator/victim/bystander), bystanders may fear and hate the perpetrators and identify with the victims, or themselves belong to the potential victim group or share the ideology and identity of the perpetrators. The resulting observer reactions are correspondingly various, including feeling helpless and frozen, watching in approving silence, and expressing vociferous encouragement while deriving vicarious and voyeuristic pleasure.

The crucible

Most shockingly, the atrocity triangle flourishes in families who abuse their own. The person who has suffered early abuse is trapped in a totalitarian space in which family members manifest a breathtaking seeming obliviousness to what occurs in their vicinity, whether it constitutes sexual abuse, violence, or plain unhappiness. There is a subterranean level at which everyone knows what is happening, but on the surface there is a permanent "as if" discourse. The family's distinctive self-image underlies the rules that determine which aspects of shared experience can be openly acknowledged and which must remain closed and denied. These rules are governed by the metarule that no-one must either admit or deny that the rules exist (Cohen, 2001). The essence of perpetration is objectification and the systematic undermining of the victim's sense of agency. In a sinister kind of collusion termed "violent innocence," there is a form of denial "in which we observe not the nature of the subject's denial of external perception, but the subject's denial of the other's perception" (Bollas, 1992). Denial is no longer an individual matter; others—family, friends, lovers—are drawn into its field wherein the abuser offers an "innocent gaze" and withholds help, leaving the newly created victim in psychic disarray. With the victim's innocence and obedience at his disposal, the perpetrator finds diverse uses for the victim's mind, body, and spirit that fuel the perpetrator's sense of omnipotence, described by Shaw (2014) as malignant or traumatizing narcissism. The victim may be used to supply gratification for sexual and sadistic urges, to support the perpetrator's economic and status advancement, and to augment the perpetrator's psychological self-regulation. As Grand (2000) points out, perpetrators require endless repetitions of their destructive acts because the relief of displaced tension is always temporary. The unending cycle of perpetration requires a constant supply of victims, collaborators, and thwarted rescuers.

Perpetration reaches its apotheosis when four conditions are simultaneously present: i) survivors have an indelible conviction that they are unredeemable and wish to die; ii) collaborators and bystanders refuse culpability, escalating their victim-blaming and denial while continuing to reap the benefits of perpetration and victimization; iii) perpetrators are immune to constraints, exposure, or prosecution; and iv) interveners are chronically confused about what is actually happening and who can be trusted (Schwartz, 2013). This is entirely consistent with the findings of Middleton (2015) regarding organized abuse of children and ongoing incestuous abuse during adulthood. Middleton found that, for decades, the ability of perpetrators to lead double lives with impunity was facilitated by passive and active collusion across all sectors of society. He cites the experiences of a journalist whose investigation of a high-level pedophile ring was based on 7 years of research: "It was then that I truly entered a parallel universe that encompasses the refined destruction of children along with its cover-up by the very state and federal authorities who have pledged to protect them from the depravity of evil men—a universe where lies masquerade as truth, shadows reflect light and innocence is condemned" (Middleton, 2015). How can a child survive such relentless perversion?

Confusion of tongues and minds

Ferenczi's elaboration of "identification with the aggressor" (1933) countered the prevailing notion that children are *not* innocent victims of sexual abuse. In elucidating the "confusion" regarding the guilt and shame felt by the abused child, he stressed the culpability of the abusing adult: "The weak and undeveloped personality reacts to sudden unpleasure not by defense, but by anxiety-ridden identification and introjection of the menacing person or aggressor… through introjections of the aggressor he disappears as part of the external reality, and becomes intra- instead of extra-psychic." (Ferenczi, 1933). Trauma induces an automatic trance-like state during which the child *instantly* dissociates his own feelings and perceptions, divines the perpetrator's mind "from the inside" (Frankel, 2002) in order to gauge what is imminent and how best to counteract it, and feels and does whatever is necessary to survive.

Identification enables the child to anticipate danger, and dissociation eliminates both unbearable pain or fear, *and* feelings whose expression would pose a threat. "At the same time, he takes into his mind—introjects…" (Frankel, 2002) aspects of the exonerated perpetrator or, rather, of the relational process (Ogden, 1986), while the child feels that *he* is bad and blameworthy. Elaborating the "moral defense" against traumatic relational dynamics, Fairburn (1952) suggested that: "The child would rather be bad himself … taking upon himself the burden of badness which appears to reside in his objects … he is rewarded by that sense of security which an environment of good objects so characteristically confers" (Fairburn, 1952). This psychic rearrangement of the actual abuse obviates the helplessness inherent in being a victim and, vitally, facilitates the maintenance of attachment to the perpetrator. But there is a price to pay: "The sense of outer security resulting from this process of internalization is, however, liable to be seriously compromised by the resulting presence within him of internalized bad objects. Outer security is thus purchased at the price of inner insecurity…" (Fairburn, 1952).

In conceptualizing identification with the aggressor, current attachment theory draws on "enactive procedural representations of how to do things with others" (Lyons-Ruth, 1999). Such unconscious relational knowing of dyadic interactions (internal working models) is developmentally foundational. "When development has gone well these procedural ways of being are connected with one another. Traumatic procedural learning, however, is much more vulnerable to dissociative processes" (Howell, 2014). When mutuality is not based on the needs of the child, all manners of contradictory, abusive, and misattuned behaviors ensue; if the child's negative affects are not acknowledged, integration of conflicting internal working models is not possible (Lyons-Ruth, 1999) and experiences remain dissociated and unlinked.

Inasmuch as internal working models include an expectation of a particular kind of relationship involving the individual, the other and a dominant affect, they are, in effect, self-states. In the reenactment of posttraumatic dominant-submissive relational patterns, a particular sequence develops, alternating between helpless victim and abusive/enraged dissociated self-states. These self-states, which "reenact and embody the relational positions of the victim and the aggressor, become partially or entirely dissociated. Their oscillation appears to be a continual reenactment of the traumatic violation of the relational boundary" (Howell, 2005). Although the terror-filled part of the relationship may not be conscious, it motivates action and viewpoints in powerful ways. Howell (2014) invokes research on mirror neurons and on imitative, anticipatory procedural enactments. She considers that both imitation and anticipation have their neurological counterparts that lead to commonly seen elaborations of identification with the aggressor encompassing a spectrum of conditions that are characterized by the dissociative structure of the mind. These elaborations exact a terrible cost because introjection perpetuates the *experience* of trauma; traumatic responses are continually activated, and the defensive use of "identification with the aggressor and dissociation now becomes habitual and refractory" (Frankel, 2002).

The high cost of living

The assault on the self by the abuser leaves the victim confused about his identity. Shengold (1989) calls this "soul murder" and Shaw (2014) refers to it as the "trauma of unrecognition." The absence of inter-subjectivity results in two modes of defense: "accommodation" and "avoidance" (Meares, 2005). Habitual accommodation and submission to others leads to a personality structure that has been described as a false self. This is characterized by a diminished sense of personal experience that is owned and unique, and by doubts about the veracity and authenticity of personal experience and existence. These may extend to matters of simple and raw experience when the abuser's beliefs supplant those of the victim. Since meaning is other-derived, the abused clings to the traumatic experience and to the familiar (positive) feelings associated with the attachment figure of the abuser. Enactments reinforcing experiences of masochism, shame, self-sabotage, self-harm, helplessness, despair, and numbness soothingly offset the penumbral threat of loss of the abusing other, an abandonment that would engender a sense of annihilation. Other consequences include "a noisy or a very gentle fascism of one's own" (Frankel, 2002) manifesting an intolerance of ostensibly dangerous differences in others, and obsessive-compulsive manifestations that reflect an incapacity to make decisions because there is little ownership of the mind.

Avoidance is a second kind of false self system that is more mask-like than that of accommodation (Meares, 2005). It has been termed "schizoid" by Fairburn and "narcissistic" by others such as Kohut (Howell, 2005). Narcissism entails a self-contained, closed system in which "intense attachment to internal objects contributes to a sense of … omnipotence and grandiosity" (Howell, 2005). In a bid to satisfy attachment needs, an aspect of the self creates illusory sources of protection and comfort and offers the mirroring, admiration, and appreciation that is craved. Concomitantly, marked hyper-vigilance, contempt, rage, or misinterpretation of others' behavior preclude the possibility of inter-subjectivity and circumvent traumatic attachment by eschewing interpersonal relationships.

Hence, abused children who learn both victim and abuser roles may oscillate between a hyper-attached self-state and an attachment-phobic aggressive self-state in order to keep terror at bay. "The rageful self-state can only be maintained briefly before fear of abandonment or annihilation triggers the idealizing self-state which, in turn, can only be maintained for a short while before fear of vulnerability triggers the rageful self-state" (Howell,

2014). Such alternation maximizes avoidance and produces the "stable instability" of borderline personality disorder (Howell, 2014). Bromberg's (1998) views on personality disorders are predicated on his belief that "the experience of being a unitary self is an acquired, developmentally adaptive illusion" (Bromberg, 1998) and that, in the face of trauma, dissociation serves to protect this illusion. He speculates that "the concept of personality 'dis-order' might usefully be defined as the characterological outcome of the inordinate use of dissociation, and that, independent of type (narcissistic, schizoid, borderline, paranoid, etc.), it constitutes a personality structure organized as a proactive defensive response to the potential repetition of childhood trauma" (Bromberg, 1998).

Thwarting an illusion: Nowhere to play

Play occurs in a transitional space that is part real and part illusory. The toddler's play has particular characteristcs that reflect the enabling atmosphere provided by a caregiver, a proto-intimate language that is non-grammatical, replete with analogical, dreamlike associations and is inner-directed rather than communicative, and an absorption "in the activity like an adult who is lost in thought" (Meares, 2005). The field of play "seems necessary to the representation of self" (Meares, 2005); signs that belong to a collective reality are distinguished from symbols that are private, idiosyncratic, and correlated with a burgeoning imagination as co-constructed narratives of the self become increasingly reflective.

The abused child suffers a developmental arrest in transitional experiencing (Winnicott, 1971) resulting in the collapse of inchoate subjectivity and inter-subjectivity. Chronic reliance on dissociation interferes with symbolization thatrelegates emotions and memories to state-dependent somatosensory levels of experiencing (Van der Kolk & Van der Hart, 1989) and that compromises linking functions, reflectivity, and meta-cognitive processes (Fonagy, Gergeley, Jurist, & Target, 2002). The child lives in a world of signs, a concrete zone devoid of spontaneity in which associative connections with other states of mind are quashed and the ability to contextualize experience is minimal (Bromberg, 1998). Hence, the capacity for self-observation, tolerance of ambiguity, and negotiation of social cues is limited; interaction with others becomes a haphazard ordeal as the victim of abuse is lost in a thicket of nuance from which she frantically tries to extricate herself by resorting to her limited repertoire of reflexive responses. The repertoire is stretched to its limits in those with dissociative identity disorder.

Doubling up: Dissociative identity disorder

Internalized perpetration reaches the epitome of traumatic attachment and identification with the aggressor in the intra-psychic architecture of dissociative identity disorder (DID). Dissociated identities, based on the pseudo-delusion of separateness (Kluft, 1984), exist in an inner world dubbed the "third reality" (Kluft, 2006), a closed and somewhat impenetrable system in which events "may be experienced as just as real as events that take place in external reality" (Kluft, 2006). Dissociated parts invoke trance logic (governed by the rule of primary process), inhabit separate compartments of behavior, affect, sensation, behavior, memory, and meaning, and resist acknowledging contradiction. Brittle, defensive self-sufficiency characterizes the dissociative internal landscape with its multiple subjectivities, glaring inconsistencies, and a striking absence of normal intra-psychic conflict (Bromberg, 2011). The dissociative self-system is a house divided, oblivious to the true nature of its internecine inner turmoil. In cases where internalized perpetration has been a significant factor in structuring the victim's dissociative system, aspects of the individual may also be at war with anyone labelled as an enemy by the perpetrator; the designated enemy population usually includes therapists, care-seeking aspects of the self, parts of the self-care system, and parts who turn a blind eye to the situation or who are rendered inert so that they are unable or unwilling to risk transformation without a benign enough interpersonal connection.

The psychological map of DID represents an internalization of the dynamic patterns of intimate interpersonal violence and betrayal. The structure of DID and of the templates of dissociative parts may be considered to conform (Davies & Frawley, 1994; Howell, 2011) to the classic Karpman (1968) drama triangle constituting victim, perpetrator, and rescuer. Child parts who bore the brunt of past abuse are subjected to ongoing abuse by parts whom they perceive to be either the original perpetrators or their agents. Both child and perpetrator parts are disoriented, remaining oblivious to changes wrought by the passage of time. Rescuer parts derive either from the person's past experiences of safe haven (usually tenuous, tentative, and temporary), or from fantasies of restitution. Although rescuer parts tend to be better oriented than other parts, their attempts to intervene are constrained by the logic of a closed system and can only stave off the inevitable rather than circumvent it. Moreover, they are often effete and require external "nudging" to galvanize them to act. "In this notion of cascading permutations of drama triangles organizing the internal world of DID individuals, the unrecognized problem of identification with collusion (ostensibly the fourth side of the trauma square at the intra-psychic, familial and cultural levels) is the strongest factor in driving and sustaining elaborate dissociative self-organization" (Schwartz, 2013). DID can be conceptualized as "a disorder of internalized domination and failed recognition" (Schwartz, 2013) grounded in the misuse of power by caretakers/authorities and potentiated through social complicity. Symptomatology reflects the quintessence of malevolent hierarchy and authoritarian power imbalance (Schwartz, 2000). Social complicity combined with traumatically induced collapse of transitional and dialectical experiencing in both interpersonal and intra-psychic life results in the feigning of a unitary self.

By constructing a dissociative system in order to keep toxic emotional states at bay (Briere, 1995), survivors are held hostage to a protean view of the past. The resources of the abused self "have been devoted to physical and psychological survival, and attachment to the sources of trauma has taken precedence over self-awareness and self-actualization" (Schwartz, 2013). Survivors strive to maintain the semblance of stability that has been achieved through identification with the perpetrator's world view, belief systems, rationalizations, spiritual and political perspectives, and, most importantly, his strategic misrepresentations of the victim. Shame is a potent driver of dissociative adaptation and identification. Survivors, particularly those with a past of coerced perpetration trauma, are vulnerable to multiple vectors of mutually reinforcing shame. These include the internalization and continual reiteration of hateful, degrading messages and threats from the perpetrator(s); survivors can echo these messages, accepting them (even arguing for them) as representing the "real me," without any awareness that "they are vehicles of an unacknowledged form of posttraumatic ventriloquism" (Schwartz, 2013). Personifications and enactments of self-hate replace healthy assertion, differentiation, and normal fantasies of retaliation; living in a kind of tortured isolation where language and communication appear to be only empty lies or tricks, the survivor's longing to communicate dissociative self-experience precipitates internal shaming by other parts of the self (Bromberg, 2011).

Trapped in a Web of internal persecution and egregious displays of pride, indifference, or defensive autonomy, the survivor will often seek comfort by taking refuge in behaviors and attitudes that were reinforced in the original abusive developmental context—helplessness, perfectionism, acquiescence, denial, arrogance, righteousness, boundary violations, and provocative sexuality. Anything that jeopardizes the perpetuation of dissociative adaptations, including any threat to the survivor's attachments to malevolent but "protective" parts, is perceived to be highly threatening (Schwartz, 2013). The survivor's inevitable assaults on the good will of others reinforce the belief that he is contaminated and beyond salvation. The prospect of dismantling their persecutory theater of mind is as difficult and terrifying for survivors as that of sustaining it. If deserving death for wanting life (Grand, 2000) is the solution to the shame of coerced moral transgression, then ongoing punishment and chronic self-hatred become the protective jail in a life sentence without parole.

Conclusion

In describing how scapegoats shoulder the sins and darkest truths of their culture, Grant (1996) notes that "scapegoats end up as either overly domesticated citizens who passively accept social denial systems or as wolves who contemptuously observe life from the margins of society" (Grant, 1996). Saul

Bellow (1970) puts it well: "But he was human, so he could arrange many things for himself. Both knowing and not knowing—one of the most frequent human arrangements" (Bellow, 1970). Frequent and human perhaps, but not always benign. Survivors of the 20th century have learned that the state of "both knowing and not knowing" facilitates terrible deeds. It is equally indispensable to their perpetrators, and to those who disavow any knowledge of them.

References

Arendt, H. (1973). *The origins of totalitarianism*. San Diego, CA: Harvest Books.

Bellow, S. (1970). *Mr Sammler's planet*. London, UK: Weidenfeld & Nicholson.

Bettelheim, B. (1943). Individual and mass behavior in extreme situations. *The Journal of Abnormal and Social Psychology, 38*, 417–452. doi:10.1037/h0061208

Bollas, C. (1992). *Being a character: Psychoanalysis and self-experience*. New York, NY: Hill & Wang.

Bracher, K. D. (1973). *The German dictatorship*. London, UK: Penguin University Books.

Briere, J. N. (1995). Child abuse, memory, and recall: A commentary. *Consciousness and Cognition, 4*, 83–87. doi:10.1006/ccog.1995.1007

Bromberg, P. (1998). *Standing in the spaces: Essays on clinical process,trauma and dissociation*. Hillsdale, NJ: The Analytic Press.

Bromberg, P. (2011). *The shadow of the tsunami and the growth of the relational mind*. New York, NY: Routledge.

Cohen, S. (2001). *States of denial: Knowing about atrocities and suffering*. Cambridge, UK: Polity Press.

Davies, J. M., & Frawley, M. G. (1994). *Treating the adult survivor of sexual abuse: A psychoanalytic perspective*. New York, NY: Basic Books.

Fairburn, W. R. D. (1952). *Psychoanalytic studies of the personality*. London, UK: Tavistock Publications Ltd.

Ferenczi, S. (1933). Confusion of tongues between adults and the child. In M. Balint (Ed.), (1980). *Final contributions to the problems and methods of psycho-analysis*. London, UK: Karnac Books.

Figes, O. (2007). *The whisperers: Private life in Stalin's Russia*. London, UK: Penguin Books.

Fonagy, P., Gergeley, G., Jurist, E. L., & Target, M. (2002). *Affect regulation, mentalization and the development of the self*. New York, NY: Other Press.

Fraenkel, E. (1969). *The dual state: A contribution to the theory of dictatorship*. New York, NY: Octagon Books.

Frankel, J. (2002). Exploring Ferenczi's concept of identification with the aggressor: Its role in trauma, everyday life, and the therapeutic relationship. *Psychoanalytic Dialogues, 12*, 101–139. doi:10.1080/10481881209348657

Geras, N. (1998). *The contract of mutual indifference: Political philosophy after the Holocaust*. London, UK: Verso.

Grand, S. (2000). *The reproduction of evil: A clinical and cultural perspective*. Hillsdale, NJ: The Analytic Press.

Grant, R. (1996). *The way of the mind: A spirituality of trauma and transformation*. Oakland, CA: Robert Grant.

Howell, E. (2005). *The dissociative mind*. Hillsdale, NJ: The Analytic Press.

Howell, E. (2011). *Dissociative identity disorder: A relational approach.* New York, NY: Routledge.

Howell, E. (2014). Ferenczi's concept of identification with the aggressor: Understanding dissociative structure with interacting victim and abuser self-states. *The American Journal of Psychoanalysis, 74,* 48–59. doi:10.1057/ajp.2013.40

Karpman, S. (1968). Fairy tales and script drama analysis. *Transactional Analysis Bulletin, 7,* 39–43.

Kim, S. (2014). *Without you there is no us: My time with the sons of North Korea's elite.* New York, NY: Random House.

Kluft, R. P. (1984). Treatment of multiple personality disorder. *Psychiatric Clinics of North America, 7,* 9–29.

Kluft, R. P. (2006). Dealing with alters: A pragmatic clinical perspective. *Psychiatric Clinics of North America, 29,* 281–304. doi:10.1016/j.psc.2005.10.010

Levi, P. (1984). *The periodic table.* New York, NY: Schocken.

Lyons-Ruth, K. (1999). Two-person unconscious: Intersubjective dialogue, enactive relational representation, and the emergence of new forms of relational organization. *Psychoanalytic Inquiry, 19,* 576–617. doi:10.1080/07351699909534267

Meares, R. (2005). *The metaphor of play: Origin and breakdown of personal being.* Essex, UK: Routledge.

Middleton, W. (2015). Tipping points and the accommodation of the abuser: Ongoing incestuous abuse during adulthood. *International Journal for Culture, Justice and Social Democracy, 4,* 4–17.

Ogden, T. H. (1986). *The matrix of the mind: Object relations in the psychoanalytic dialogue.* Northvale, NJ: Aronson.

Pasternak, B. (1958). *Doctor Zhivago.* London, UK: Wm. Collins Sons and Co. Ltd.

Schwartz, H. L. (2000). *Dialogues with forgotten voices: Relational perspectives on child abuse trauma and treatment of dissociative disorders.* New York, NY: Basic Books.

Schwartz, H. L. (2013). *The alchemy of wolves and sheep: A relational approach to internalized perpetration in complex trauma survivors.* New York, NY: Routledge.

Shaw, D. (2014). *Traumatic narcissism: Relational systems of subjugation.* New York, NY: Routledge.

Shengold, L. (1989). *Soul murder.* New Haven, CT: Yale University Press.

Todorov, T. (2000). *Facing the extreme: Moral life in the concentration camps.* London, UK: Phoenix.

Van der Kolk, B. A., & Van der Hart, O. (1989). Pierre Janet and the breakdown of adaptation in psychological trauma. *American Journal of Psychiatry, 146,* 1530–1539. doi:10.1176/ajp.146.12.1530

Wildt, M. (2009). *An uncompromising generation: The Nazi leadership of the Reich Main Security Office.* Madison, WI: The University of Wisconsin Press.

Winnicott, D. W. (1971). *Playing and safety.* New York, NY: Basic Books.

Mother–child incest, psychosis, and the dynamics of relatedness

Joan Haliburn, MBBS. FRANZCP. M. Med

ABSTRACT

Sexual abuse perpetrated by a parent particularly the mother creates turmoil in the child who has to depend on the very person who betrays their trust. A review of the literature confirms that there are only a few case studies of mother–child incest reported in the psychoanalytic literature; the incidence of such incest, however, is unknown. Considerably, more information is available in the forensic and child abuse literatures along with an increase in research; yet, there is a paucity of data. Child sexual abuse by women as highly prevalent is described in early societies, and that there is a bias in peoples' minds about the capacity of females to sexually abuse children is raised by many writers. The fact of being abused by one's mother brings up specific issues for survivors of maternal incest. Shame and the fear of not being believed, which was the experience of my female patient and a sense of specialness and failure of recognition of incest by the males, created particular difficulties which had to be dealt with in psychotherapy. This paper describes three teenagers, one female and two males who were sexually abused by their mothers. I have condensed several years of treatment to provide an account of the female patient and a summary of each of the males, and I attempt to explore the dynamics of relatedness in the abused and the abuser.

That women do engage in sexual activities with children needs to be acknowledged, as nearly a century of information has become available (Elliott, Eldridge, Ashfield, & Beech, 2010). This lack of acknowledgement has hindered information gathering, recognition, understanding, and support to adults, teenagers, and children who are victims. According to Strickland (2008), research to date has been descriptive in nature and few comparison studies are available. While the literature abounds with descriptions of the male pedophile, rapist, and sex offender, little information is available on the role of gender and sexuality in sex offending (Hayes & Carpenter, 2013). Mother–son incest as well as female pedophilia disorder remain poorly recognized (Lamy et al., 2016). According to Banning (1989), there is an unwillingness to believe that women are capable of such acts and as a result of this gender bias, female sexual crimes are more likely to be obscured, resulting in continuation of the cycle of abuse (Duncan, 2010), to the detriment of victims.

Reports of perpetration of sexual abuse by women have been rare until recently, due most likely to the belief that women would not or could not sexually abuse, especially their own children. As a result, the relative percentage of mothers who abuse their children is unknown (Courtois, 2010). The social construction of women according to Gannon and Cortoni (2010) has decreed that incestuous acts toward their family members is "unthinkable" and this knowledge has often been dismissed. Lifting the silence around maternal sexual abuse allows sons and daughters to be heard and their lives to be reclaimed (Duncan, 2010).

Differences between female and male sex-abusers

Studies of female abusers have found that it is very often the mother or a woman in a maternal role who sexually abuses that child (Kendall-Tackett, 1987). On average, victims of female perpetrated sexual abuse are younger compared with their male counterparts. Courtois (1988) describes that abuse often starts in infancy and continues for 6–11 years and Peter (2009) cites that 92% of female perpetrated sexual abuse victims were under the age of 9 years and female abusers were less likely to discriminate between male and female victims. Females tend to have significant complex personal trauma histories as compared with their male counterparts (Strickland, 2008). In the case of male perpetrators, the taboo of incest, the desire to keep it secret, leads either to coercion or to threat, usually of harm to the child, of not being believed or the certainty of family rupture.

Cross-cultural studies

Cross-cultural studies from the United States, Australia, Canada, England, South Africa, and Sweden document that females commit a broad range of sexual offences across cultures that are both similar to and different from those committed by men (Duncan, 2010). They also point out that female sexual abuse can exact a toll on the victim's physical and emotional health, and ability to function effectively in relationships as is seen in those sexually abused by men.

Mother–child incest

Mother–child incest involves violation of trust and exploitation of the child's affection and dependency needs—a double betrayal. There are mothers who sexually abuse their children even into adulthood and incest is usually shrouded in secrecy. Father–daughter incest is widely written about in the literature, but what of mother–child incest?

Mothers as nurturers

The bond between a mother and a child is considered the quintessential relationship that provides the basis for developing healthy human connections (Bowlby, 1988). The expectation of mothers is one of nurturers, caregivers, and protectors, and infants and children often do not construe their mothers' perpetrating actions as abuse; therefore, subtle behaviors difficult to distinguish from normal caregiving may be overlooked (Courtois, 1988).

Effects of mother–child incest

As with male sexual abuse of young children, victims of both sexes are affected by serious mental health problems, such as self-harm, suicidal ideation, depression, anxiety, personality disorders, and substance abuse (Gannon & Cortoni, 2010). Equally, the child may respond to victimization by becoming avoidant and dissociating emotions or running away (Gannon & Cortoni, 2010). Psychological escape by dissociation may also happen; however, symptoms such as anxiety, phobias, sleep difficulties, eating disorders, and obsessive compulsive behavior may occur. Victims of such abuse feel additional shame and stigma (Courtois, 2010). Feelings of betrayal expressed as feelings of anger and mistrust are a common by-product of incest, and many struggle with issues of sexuality, sexual identity, and difficulties with relationships. When the offender is the child's mother, key additional impacts include significant difficulties in forming a sense of self-separate from the mother, an excessive need to return to the mother so as to validate his or her existence, and enmeshment that can be so extreme as to lead to psychosis (Gannon & Cortoni, 2010). It is necessary to look at the effects separately, in female and male victims.

Effects of mother–daughter incest

We do not have sufficient knowledge of mother–daughter incest, and despite some difference, incest between mother and daughter has been reported to cause after effects similar to those resulting from other forms of incest (Courtois, 2010). As with father–daughter incest, victims are often overcome by feelings of powerlessness engendered by the abuse. This includes a terror of vulnerability and a perceived need to be in control that may sometimes lead to identification with the aggressor and the likelihood of aggression and exploitation toward others. Female victims often feel different, damaged, and defective, as a result of internalization of negative projections of the perpetrator and the inevitable shame and guilt related to the abuse. To be sexually abused by a woman in society which sees such abuse as unusual increases the likelihood of stigmatization and associated shame and guilt (Gannon &

Cortoni, 2010). In addition, women who have been sexually abused by their mothers experience considerable difficulties with the idea of motherhood or the transition to motherhood ambivalence about having children, a fear of repetition of incest, a fear of lack of knowledge about mothering, and an active seeking of support and guidance in parenting (Reckling, 2004).

Whether there are differences in effects between overt and covert incest is unknown.

Effects of mother–son incest

Unlike daughters who have been sexually abused by their mothers, sons abused by their mothers often experience a feeling of specialness, of being an "exception" and even a "king of the world" fantasy, as described by Margolis (1977). Many male adolescents who initially perceive the abuse as benign or even in a positive light tend to be psychologically impaired, developing problematic substance abuse, sexual problems, and self-harming behavior, and as Ogden (1989) pointed out, the male child's psychological development is often foreclosed as a result of overtly sexualized behavior from the mother.

Psychosis

Psychosis involves a loss of contact with reality, with excessive concerns about alteration of "self" (identity diffusion and confusion, perceptual difficulties, thought disorder, and altered experiences of being in the world with others). Experiences of depersonalization and derealization are common in psychosis and in dissociative disorders, and thus differentiation is essential. The capacity for self-observation is lacking and so also is the awareness of mental and emotional processes (De Masi, 2003).

The role of early trauma in the development of psychotic disorders presents us with a challenge. General population studies (Shevlin, Dorahy, & Adamson, 2007, 2008) have demonstrated that there is an association between early trauma and development of both psychotic-like experiences and psychotic symptoms, and that sexual trauma may be an important contributing factor in the development of psychosis for some individuals. In one study, only sexual abuse, of the individual types of trauma, was associated with transition to psychosis, and the association remained when adjusting for potential confounding factors. This longitudinal data suggest a relationship between experiences of sexual abuse and the medium-to-long-term development of a psychotic disorder (Thompson et al., 2014). Similarly, exposure to adverse childhood events was an important determinant of psychotic disorders in the analysis of 18 case-control studies (Varese et al., 2012).

Patients

The three patients explored in this paper experienced a first-episode psychosis for which they received treatment with antipsychotic medication in the acute phase and were apparently stabilized. It is important at this point to mention that antipsychotics "dampen the salience" of these abnormal experiences, and by doing so "permit the resolution of symptoms-they do not erase the symptoms, and provide a platform for psychological resolution" (Kapur, 2003).

They were subsequently seen by the author in psychodynamic psychotherapy. Some details of the female patient and brief summaries of the two male patients are provided. Pseudonyms are used and some information changed in order to maintain their anonymity, without affecting the actual content. All three have given informed consent for their cases to be presented—Prue had no reservations, but Gerry and Ben did not want their therapies to be published and also wished for certain details to be omitted.

Prue

In the third year of therapy, Prue frequently and loudly expressed her hatred toward her adoptive mother, as fragments of abuse emerged. In a loud voice she shouted, "she said I was dirty." This was the first fragment of a long and painful history of sexual, physical, and emotional abuse by her adoptive mother. I later learned that the sexual abuse ended when Prue started menstruating around 9 years of age. I will start at the beginning to put Prue's story in context. Prue was 15 years old when we started twice-weekly therapy. She had experienced a brief psychotic episode that had responded well to antipsychotics.

On first presentation, Prue could be mistaken for a boy. She wore trousers and desert boots, an open-necked collared shirt, and closely cropped and styled hair. With an almost permanent grimace, bowed head, and shuffling gait (not medication induced), she attracted attention. She frequently picked at her skin till it was almost bleeding and offered no eye contact. Her words seemed as if they were being squeezed out of her throat with a shrillness that was disarming. She was thought disordered and frequently and inappropriately said, "sorry, sorry, sorry" in mid-sentence. She was ritualistic and walked back and forth several times through the office doorway before she finally left after a session and would sometimes become almost catatonic. She often talked about dying but was not actively suicidal. She constantly negated herself: "I'm bad—No, I'm not bad; I'm guilty—No, I'm not guilty." She pathologically doubted herself, in an attempt as it were to undo her own thoughts as a way of coping with her confusion. "Object—coercive doubting" (Kramer, 1985) is described where doubts about self, and self and other persist as part of a cognitive style to support knowing and not knowing following early maternal incest.

Transference and countertransference

Prue was most often angry and dismissive and I began to feel an early and traumatic countertransference. I felt like a "dirty" mother and I nearly "hated" her but had to "negotiate this carefully" (Winnicott, 1949). I felt almost overwhelmed by a lack of boundary and struggled to maintain my separateness, which made Prue more angry, because to her, it seemed that I was pulling away. It felt as if she was trying to enter into my body. Forming a safe therapeutic relationship with her was extremely difficult during the first 6 months, while she frequently continued to be filled with rage. I had to bring one session to a premature end, saying to her firmly "I will not allow you to abuse and berate me-we are ending this session now, Prue, but I will be here as usual and would like to see you for our next session." This seemed to bring about some change, though not immediately. She gradually settled and became somewhat more contained, and I began to feel myself again, though there were a few such repetitions later.

I wondered afterward, about my reaction. Was I reacting to her as her mother would? On the other hand, I asked myself, was she behaving toward me as she would in the later years toward her mother? Or was it a repetition of her mother's behavior toward her? I reconciled with trying to accept that it was probably all three, at different times. My countertransference in this therapy as I recollect was mixed-shock, disbelief, anger, hate, disgust, pity, and care, all in quick succession. Prue's lack of boundary (Meares, 2004) due to insufficient separation from her mother and her lack of self-other differentiation called for considerable care in this therapeutic endeavor and, as I usually do, was using my countertransference to guide me.

Progress

By the end of the first year, her skin-picking ceased completely, her grimaces and mannerisms lessened, hallucinations ceased, but she still exhibited what seemed at the time "delusional" ideas about herself. It is important at this juncture to offer an explanation. Delusions are a cognitive effort by the patient to make sense of aberrantly salient experiences, whereas hallucinations reflect a direct experience of the aberrant salience of internal representations (Kapur, 2003).

Therapy

The Conversational Model (Meares, 2012) of psychotherapy, a phasic, integrative, non-interpretive, relational, and trauma-informed model which advocates the use of empathy, simple language, vocal utterances, and nonverbal ways of communication with patients who present in a distressed state, particularly while the therapeutic relationship is being established was the mode of therapy used.

Dissociation

Frequent dissociative episodes occurred as fragments of early memories emerged in the second and third years of therapy. She had no recollection when the abuse started but added "as far as I can remember, she did these things to me." Genital stimulation, and checking and cleaning of orifices, was a regular ritual carried out by her mother. Her grimaces and odd mannerisms reappeared as fresh memories of other abusive acts emerged. Prue's grimaces and mannerisms seemed to be representative of repetitive traumatic responses in the form of troubling body memories. Dissociative episodes, which reduced in frequency, were an attempt at distancing herself from conscious memory of what had happened, as she talked about her experiences. I reassured her of her safety. One day, she expressed with mixed feelings "she must have hated me-what mother would do such things to her child" and added with resignation, "but then I wasn't her child."

Dis-identification

Further memories included those of physical beatings, criticism, and deprivation, after the sexual abuse ceased. Prue repeatedly said, "I don't want to be like her—I often feel like I'm turning into her. I dress in men's clothes from the men's stores so I can be different from her—I want to be different. I am angry, she is inside my skin, I cannot get rid of her. I don't want to be like her. She liked attention. Everything was about her and nobody else. I sometimes think I sound like her."

Prue wanted to dis-identify with her mother's femaleness, contrary to normal female development, where identification with the same-sex parent occurs in adolescence. She continued to doubt her sexuality and her gender. Ogilvie and Daniluk (1995) also describe this need on the part of the patient, to be different. Prue continued to question her identity and expressed a need to change herself completely. For the first time, she was able to put into words what she had been feeling fear of being female. With increased ability to get in touch with feelings and express them, her mannerisms and ritualistic behavior reduced significantly.

She began to express more positive feelings toward me, as she talked about our sessions coming to an end, "You won't be seeing me forever, why would you" she stated rather than ask.

Prue completed her Higher School Examination 2 years later than she would otherwise have and started a course in graphic design which she enjoyed, though she was often paranoid about other females in the college and their "intentions." In this context, she confronted me one day about my own thoughts toward her, "you must think I'm dirty too" and without waiting for an answer, she said, "why would you not?" I almost winced as I replied "you need to be sure that I don't think of you as dirty." Some time later in therapy, she recalled this and apologized profusely, but we were able to talk in more depth about our relationship.

Abandonment

Issues of adoption became prominent in the fifth and sixth years of therapy. Prue was angry at her own mother, for abandoning her to be abused and mistreated. She fantasized what it would have been like if she was never adopted but expressed no desire to seek her birth parents. As fresh memories emerged, she often felt that she would never be able to escape them.

Prue's mother was diagnosed with an aggressive type of cancer and passed away 2 years before we concluded therapy. During the 7 months before she died, Prue visited her weekly. She said she was being grateful. She mourned the loss of her natural mother, and later that of her adoptive mother, but with mixed feelings of anger at abandonment by her natural mother and shame about her adoptive mother's treatment of her. She also experienced for the first time, considerable anxiety at the thought that our sessions would one day come to an end. Her separation anxiety was pervasive; however, she was able to work through it over the next 2 years.

Positive countertransference

I had become quite fond of Prue and aware of my feelings that I could not let her go before she had resolved all her problems. I had misgivings that she had not worked through her difficulties with intimacy; however, at her insistence, we set a date to end therapy. Prue was in a lesbian relationship that scarcely included any physical closeness; however, they were "good friends." A year later, I encouraged Prue to continue her therapy to deal with her fear of intimacy, but she declined. She had maintained the gains she had made and was successfully employed. Her best friends were males with whom she identified and maintained a platonic relationship. She had fought vigorously to dis-identify with everything about her adoptive mother, and intimacy was a threat that she was not yet ready to confront. At no stage in therapy did Prue wish to disclose the abuse to anyone in the family, even after the death of her mother. She felt that no one would believe her but accepted this with resignation.

Gerry

Gerry was 19 years old and was diagnosed with a first episode psychosis, when he became grandiose, belligerent, disorganized, and delusional. When I saw him, his mood was mildly elevated, he was grandiose, chaotic, and slightly thought disordered, though he was taking a moderate dose of antipsychotic.

It became apparent in the third year of therapy that Gerry's relationship with his mother was over-close, as he described considerably seductive behavior on her part, which he said continued to adulthood. His role was very much that of a surrogate husband, which I thought he recognized. Each time he talked about his mother even with a hint of negativity, he was overcome by abnormal physical reactions, difficulties in speaking, severe chest pain (this prompted him to have an electrocardiogram, which was normal), tingling and numbness in his extremities, an inability to sit still, and a need to empty his bladder.

He experienced depersonalization and derealization in the sessions and reported them happening frequently outside. He related feeling suicidal when he attempted as a teenager, to have a girlfriend, but felt he could not betray his mother. He described his father as a rather passive man and later remarked that he "has been castrated by my mother too." Later in therapy, he mourned for the loss of his childhood, his failure to have a girlfriend, and the failure to grow up like most of his friends had done, and though he displayed a marked degree of awareness, he continued to see himself as "special" as he was chosen by his mother in preference to his three older brothers. Both mother–son incest and positive initial perceptions of sexual abuse experiences appear to be risk factors for more severe psychosocial adjustment problems (Kelly et al., 2002).

Gerry moved out of home rather unexpectedly with his father's help in the fourth year of therapy. He began to achieve a degree of separateness from his mother, making decisions for himself, and passively letting her know that he could manage without her. He resumed his studies successfully and found a job. Therapy continued for a further 2 years during which time he revived his interest in the Arts and developed a circle of friends, mainly female; however, he struggled to form an intimate relationship though maintained his desire for the female sex.

Ben

Ben was 18 years old when he was diagnosed with a psychosis which was characterized by deteriorating concentration, thought disorder, increasing anxiety and panic attacks, constant repetitive behavior, talking to himself, quite oblivious of his surroundings. He was also noted to have a number of negative symptoms including passivity, isolation, and indecision along with experiences of depersonalization and derealization.

These dissociative experiences persisted intermittently for about 3 years into the therapy as fragments of memory of sexual contact with his mother and of increasing arousal emerged. The sexual abuse short of penetration appeared to have stopped when he started high school around the age of 13 years. He felt special and positive about his relationship with his mother and had great difficulty separating from her. She was very caring since he became sick. He struggled with anxiety and depression along with active suicidal ideation for quite some time.

In the fifth year of therapy, Ben met a woman of similar age with whom he consummated their relationship (after a number of unsuccessful attempts when he would see his mother's face superimposed on the woman's face). This made him increasingly anxious and guilty. He felt he was betraying his mother and ceased this relationship after a few months. His was a 12-year therapy with a break of 2 years, during which time, Ben left to live in a remote part of the country where he experimented with drugs.

He returned and asked to resume therapy.

Ben was quite narcissistic, which he openly acknowledged. He compulsively entered relationships but was critical and dissatisfied with his partners. We were able to talk about his longing for his mother with whom he communicated frequently. "This narcissistic triumph of the male child, along with associated feelings of omnipotence and grandiosity is achieved at significant cost to the developing child's psychic economy" (Gabbard & Twemlow, 1994, p. 172).

The dynamics of relatedness

The abused child

In discussing the dynamics of relatedness in mother–child incest, early development in the context of the mother–child dyad needs to be considered. The mother constructs the child's world from birth and this becomes his/her reality, as the child's unique dependence on the mother provokes submission and prevents disclosure. Prue distinctly remembered her mother repeatedly saying to her "I'm your mother" as she scuttled away and hid, in order to avoid her, and though she could not recollect how old she was at the time, she was probably of an age when she could reason "like" and "not-like," i.e., between the age of 3 and 6 years when cognitive ability starts to grow. When Prue started to menstruate at the age of 9 years, the sexual abuse ceased, and she remembered her mother harshly turning against her, that she began to fear that she would be returned to the "adoption agency."

We know so little about mother–child incest that the following can only be proposed: in feeling rejected, the narcissistic mother has to deal with earlier developmental rejections and abuse that she may have suffered—these were probably projected. Girls in these situations feel isolated, stigmatized, powerless, and betrayed by the person in whom unbounded trust is placed (Courtois, 1988), reflecting the feeling of "otherness" and "difference" in terms of shame for being sexually abused by one's mother.

Incest with its innumerable permutations makes for psychological complexity. Overt and covert incest has been described (Adams, 1991). When a child becomes the mother's main preoccupation and object of her affection, love, and passion, the boundary between caring and incest is crossed and the child merely exists to meet the needs of the parent. "While the overt incest victim feels abused, the covert victim feels idealised and privileged. The adult covert incest victim remains stuck in a pattern of living aimed at keeping the special relationship going with the opposite-sex parent. A privileged and special position is maintained; the pain and suffering of a lost childhood denied" (Adams, 1991, p. 10). The stage of development when child sexual abuse occurs is important, as the younger the child, the more devastating the consequences (Cole & Putnam, 1992).

Whether intercourse occurs or not, a son seduced by his mother may be overcome by conflicted emotions, especially guilt, desire, confusion, anger, aggression, love, and hate. He may exhibit a dissociative style, have poor social skills, and be mistrustful, insecure, isolated, and uncomfortable with peers, particularly with women (Brodie, 1992). This is increasingly evident in the histories of some narcissistic young men in therapy. In some instances, the son may never grow up and leave his mother, and in some, discomfort may turn to resentment (Justice & Justice, 1979). Schlesinger (1999) described a case of matricide following repetitive mother–son incest. The son may seek therapy for symptoms commonly associated with abuse, without making an association between them and the behavior of his mother (Courtois, 2010). Ben and Gerry came for therapy with what seemed to be unrelated symptoms, and it was not until a later stage in therapy that they became aware that their relationship with their mothers was incestuous. Nevertheless, they could not confront their mothers, even though they strove hard to separate.

The adoptive mother as abuser

It is necessary to take into consideration the fact of Prue's mother not being her natural mother. Did that make a difference? There cannot be a definitive answer; however, the position of such mothers requires to be considered. "Adoptive mothers may also have to deal with problems of inadequacy and failed identity, even though the fault may not lie with them, they tend to take the responsibility" (Schechter, 1970).

The adoptive child is the product of another woman of whom the adaptive mother is envious of and a triangle of conflict between the three is created. A similar triangle of conflict is possible between the adoptive mother, her own mother, and the adoptive child wherein unresolved conflicts play out and are coped with mainly by projection. Would the adoptive baby fulfill the mother's fantasies of her "natural" child if she had one? The adoptive mother must work through, like the biological mother, her expectations and fantasies of motherhood and vicissitudes of her relationship with her own mother. Preexisting rivalry or conflict in the relationship may be intensified, leading to further inadequacy which interferes with the adoptive mother enjoying or providing nurture to her child. The fulfillment of narcissistic needs in order to achieve an identity as a mother, in order to be seen as "whole," may be derailed in some adoptive mothers.

Prue's adoptive mother, whom I have met, could be described as borderline, highly narcissistic, intelligent, extremely self-absorbed, and lacking in empathy. She was extremely rejecting and critical of Prue in my presence, as we met in the initial stages of Prue's treatment. She did not have a major mental illness, but a personality disorder with mixed narcissistic, histrionic, and borderline traits seemed likely. Prue described her father as affectionate toward her and she thought he liked her more than he did her sister. This, Prue thought made her adoptive mother "filled with envy." Envy and the need for dominance may have played a part, as it might have done in her own history. She described Prue as a stubborn and headstrong girl, who, from the moment she "set eyes on her," felt she was going to be a "handful." Prue was adopted at 6 months of age. Prue's mother was the dominant figure in her life and in the life of the entire household and seemed devoid of the capacity for nurture. Prue was fond of her father and pitied him because he would never stand up to her mother. He was well educated, financially comfortable, and successfully employed.

Identification

Stern (1998, p. 125) encapsulates the essence of identification in the parent–child dyad when he notes "an important part of primary relatedness is the ability to identify with your baby. To identify is to mentally slip into your baby's skin or mind, by way of empathy, and then be able to alter your own feelings to conform to those you imagine the baby is having. The end result is that you feel as if you know what it feels like to be the baby (for a moment, anyway), and through this understanding, to get to know your baby better. When you allow this empathic exchange, you establish a special emotional link to your child." What if the mother does not identify with her baby, for some reason or other to do with herself, her history, her environment? A combination of all three factors is more likely, because one would expect that whatever it is that results in failure to identify with her child must arise from some deep-seated place. The child then has to conform with the mother's requirements, to the point where Gerry, during an episode of depersonalization, described "I feel like a woman-my hands look like hers." Negotiating several different self-states clearly indicated the extreme degree of enmeshment, the power of the mother's projections, and Gerry's continuing "identification with his mother during his adolescence" (Blos, 1967).

The capacity to communicate unconsciously is innately present in every individual but achieves a special sensitivity between mother and child—the most crucial aspects of this process are the maintenance of a given reality—the child seems innately programed to collude with his mother's individual view of reality, and his behavior reflects this (Rucker & Mermelstein, 1979). Gerry often felt that he "became" his mother and that she "controlled" everything he did and said. He became increasingly aware of his different self-states when in the third and fourth years of therapy, his face would become contorted whenever he spoke about his mother in slightly negative terms. As he became aware of the reality of their relationship, Gerry described "a dark cloud" coming over him, he felt paralyzed, and on several occasions, he experienced lower limb "seizures" as he spoke. As described by Dutton and Painter (1981), one could describe both Gerry and Ben as "traumatically bonded" with their mothers. Middleton (2013) described women in ongoing incestuous abuse who feel they do not "own" their bodies and experience being "fused" to their father.

Maternal identity

Weldon (1988) describes "dysfunctional sexuality of certain women and the unique power wielded by the mother over her child in certain circumstances leads to physical abuse or incest." The child as rival may be true in the case of Prue who described her father as being very fond of her. Maternal identity involves developing a sense of nurturance, internalization of a protective, and caring relational ability in expectation of the birth of a child and subsequently. It is likely that problems have occurred in the development of maternal identity in each of these three mothers, as a result of early abuse and/or deprivation.

Are incestuous mothers antisocial or psychopathic?

Incestuous mothers appear to be unable to interpret social signals in others, to have an inability to experience empathy, and a disregard for the emotions of their children (as in Prue's case) they lack a Theory of Mind (Ruiz-Tagle, Costanzo, De Achaval, & Guinjoan, 2015). Descriptions of the mothers from these three patients lead me to conclude that narcissism and psychopathy play an important part in their interactions with their children. Prue's mother may also have had antisocial traits in addition, resulting in rather antisocial attitudes toward her child. "The antisocial tendency" says Winnicott (1966) "is linked inherently with deprivation-that the child has experienced trauma at an age when he/she has been far enough developed to be aware, in contrast with environmental disturbance at an earlier stage of emotional development, when it would produce distortions of the personality, resulting in illness, including psychosis. The antisocial tendency relates not to privation but to a deprivation." On a similar vein, Blackburn (2007) writes, "Core personality characteristics of psychopathy are more closely related to narcissistic than to antisocial personality disorder."

Though we don't know enough about incestuous mothers to decide whether they are antisocial or psychopathic, what clearly stood out in the case of Prue was her mother's total disregard and lack of empathy for her daughter's predicament, her need for control, and the complete submission she required from her child, which, when it was not forthcoming, resulted in physical abuse. Gerry and Ben's narcissistic personality traits seemed to be a reflection of similar, but perhaps more entrenched narcissism in their mothers. From their descriptions of their mothers' attitudes, it seemed highly likely that their mothers were narcissistic and psychopathic. The absence of guilt, shame, or remorse in one of the young men's mothers (from the patients' descriptions) was also striking, when he reported having reluctantly and fearfully talked about his relationship with her.

Discussion

In psychoanalytic psychotherapy, the therapist attempts to form a picture of the parent from the perceived experiences that have been integrated within the mind of the child/adult patient. How can we understand the mother–infant relationship and the early stages of development of the mind when mother–child incest occurs? Clearly, these patients were severely damaged to the point where their reality testing was compromised.

There were marked differences in the transference relationship with Prue, which was unlike that with Gerry and Ben. Prue was distrustful of the therapist (same sex) and angry. She exhibited narcissistic, obsessional, and borderline-personality traits with depression and marked dissociative tendencies with at least three different self-states. Gerry and Ben were not distrustful, they idealized the therapist (opposite sex). They exhibited narcissistic, borderline, and dependent personality traits, and their abuse characteristics were different from those of Prue. Perhaps, the presence of multiple types of abuse contributed to the complexity and anger displayed by Prue.

There appears to have been a sense of entitlement and grandiosity in the mothers of the male patients, who also presented with grandiosity. The "experience of omnipotence" is the mother's gift to the infant for just a short while, when she (mother) must adapt (Winnicott, 1965), as a small child will regard caregivers as instruments to provide his/her own needs, but only for a little while, as he/she soon discovers. This feeling of omnipotence and grandiosity in both Gerry and Ben appears to have grown alongside their mother's, though each of the mothers used them for her own gratification. This intertwining of feelings characterizes what is commonly described as enmeshment, a word that does not really capture their almost fused relationships with their mothers.

"Mother-son incest may be considered to be traumatic and central to the pathogenesis of a specific form of narcissistic character pathology characterised by paranoid orientation to others and an expectation of humiliation, punishment, and abandonment that pervades the patient's adult object relations-one pathway to the development of a hyper-vigilant form of narcissistic character pathology" (Gabbard & Twemlow, 1994).

What may seem like a "narcissistic triumph" in Gabbard's words was in fact experienced by Gerry as "a hollow feeling that is there all the time" and described by Ben as "an empty feeling that never goes away". Mother–child incest leaves lasting scars that profoundly affect the child's self-functioning and his internalized other. Both males grappled with the idea of no longer being seen as special, they feared humiliation and abandonment.

I am yet to further process the material of these three therapies, though I have had helpful discussions with a colleague while I was seeing them.

Trauma-informed, development psychotherapy which is non-interpretive and empathic, offers acceptance and understanding, can provide a reality base even from a severely disturbed position.

Conclusion

In presenting the literature on mother–child incest and my experience of working with these young patients, I aim to raise the level of discussion in this area and increase sensitivity among clinicians to its possibility. I have had to draw from my memory because I could not write sufficiently detailed process notes after the sessions which were to do with my own reactions to the material presented. I struggled with the idea of writing up these cases for quite some time but decided to write for several reasons. First, such cases are rarely reported. The reasons for the low number of such cases reported in the psychoanalytic literature may be the low numbers of men who seek psychotherapy, and when they do enter psychotherapy, they do not see maternal seduction and incest as abusive and traumatic, and they do not easily disclose such behavior, perhaps for fear of humiliation or of betrayal of their mothers. This is an important difference between opposite sex abuse in males and females. Second, each case illustrates in its own unique way the difficulties encountered in adulthood, by male and female survivors of maternal incest. Third, the complexity of working psychotherapeutically with such individuals, and finally, the need for increased awareness among mental health clinicians of mother–child incest and the severity of psychopathology that results. This heightened awareness may reduce difficulty accessing treatment, for both the abused and the abusers, and therefore not compound the betrayal that has already been experienced. The frequency with which mental health patients report histories of sexual abuse and neglect as children no longer surprises clinicians; however, when the abuser is female, it is often met with shock and disbelief and a tendency to be dismissive. Unless we move beyond the gender stereotype, the needs of such women and their child and adult victims will not be met.

References

Adams, K. M. (1991). Silently seduced: When parents make their children partners-Understanding covert incest. Clearwater Beach, FL: Health Communications. In C. A. Courtois (Ed.), *Healing the incest wound: Adult survivors in therapy (2010)* (pp. 10). New York, NY: Norton.

Banning, A. (1989). Mother-son incest: Confronting a prejudice. *Child Abuse & Neglect, 13* (4), 563–570. doi:10.1016/0145-2134(89)90060-4

Blackburn, R. (2007). Personality disorder and antisocial deviance: Comments on the debate on the structure of the psychopathy checklist-revised. *Journal of Personality Disorders, 21* (2), 142–159. doi:10.1521/pedi.2007.21.2.142

Blos, P. (1967). The second individuation process of adolescence. *Psychoanalytic Study of the Child, 22*, 162–186.

Bowlby, J. (1988). *A secure base: Clinical applications of attachment theory.* London, UK: Routledge.

Brodie, F. (1992). When 'the other woman' is his mother...Book One: A guide to identifying your mate's child abuse incest, and dissociation. Tacoma, WA: Winged Eagle Press. In C. A. Courtois (Ed.), *Healing the incest wound: Adult survivors in therapy.* New York, NY: Norton.

Cole, P. M., & Putnam, F. W. (1992). Effect of incest on self and social functioning: A developmental psychopathology perspective. *Journal of Consulting and Clinical Psychology, 60* (2), 174–184. doi:10.1037/0022-006X.60.2.174

Courtois, C. A. (1988). *Healing the incest wound: Adult survivors in therapy.* New York, NY: Norton.

Courtois, C. A. (2010). *Healing the incest wound: Adult survivors in therapy, 2nd edition.* New York, NY: Norton.

De Masi, F. (2003). On the nature of intuitive and delusional thought: Its implications in clinical work with psychotic patients. *International Journal Psychoanalysis, 84*(Pt 5), 1149–1169. doi:10.1516/K1Q6-TXWC-7GXU-AWE6

Duncan, K. A. (2010). *Female sexual predators: Understanding them to protect our children and youths.* Santa Barbara, CA: Praeger.

Dutton, D., & Painter, S. L. (1981). Emotional attachments in abusive relationships: A test of traumatic bonding theory. *Violence and Victims, 8* (2), 105–120.

Elliott, I. A., Eldridge, H. J., Ashfield, S., & Beech, A. R. (2010). Exploring risk: Potential static, dynamic, protective and treatment factors in the clinical histories of female sex offenders. *Journal of Family Violence, 25* (6), 595–602. doi:10.1007/s10896-010-9322-8

Gabbard, G. O., & Twemlow, S. W. (1994). The role of mother-son incest in the pathogenesis of narcissistic personality disorder. *Journal of the American Psychoanalytic Association, 42* (1), 171–189. doi:10.1177/000306519404200109

Gannon, T. A., & Cortoni, F. (2010). *Female sexual offenders: Theory, assessment and treatment.* Malden, MA: John Wiley & Sons.

Hayes, S., & Carpenter, B. (2013). Social moralities and discursive constructions of female sex offenders. *Sexualities, 16* (1–2), 159–179. doi:10.1177/1363460712471112

Justice, B., & Justice, R. (1979). The broken taboo: Sex in the family, New York: Human Sciences Press. In C. A. Courtios (Ed.), *(2010) Healing the incest wound, adult survivors in therapy* (2nd ed.). New York, NY: Norton.

Kapur, S. (2003). Psychosis as a state of aberrant salience: A framework linking biology, phenomenology, and pharmacology in schizophrenia. *American Journal of Psychiatry, 160* (1), 13–23. doi:10.1176/appi.ajp.160.1.13

Kelly, R. J., Wood, J. J., Gonzalez, L. S., MacDonald, V., & Waterman, J. (2002). Effects of mother-son incest and positive perceptions of sexual abuse experiences on the psychosocial adjustment of clinic-referred men. *Child Abuse & Neglect, 26* (4), 425–441. doi:10.1016/S0145-2134(02)00317-4

Kendall-Tackett, K. A. (1987). Perpetrators and their acts: Data from 365 adults molested as children. *Child Abuse & Neglect, 11* (2), 237–245. doi:10.1016/0145-2134(87)90063-9

Kramer, S. (1985). Object-coercive doubting: A pathological defensive response to maternal incest. In H. P. Blum (Ed.), *Defence and resistance: Historical perspectives and currrent concepts* (pp. 325–351). New York, NY: International University Press.

Lamy, S., Delavenne, H., & Thibaut, F. (2016). A case of female hyper-sexuality and child abuse and a review. *Archives of Women's Mental Health, 19* (4), 701–703. doi:10.1007/s00737-015-0579-z

Margolis, M. (1977). A preliminary report of a case of consummated mother-son incest. *Annual of Psychoanalysis, 5*, 267–293.

Meares, R. (2004). The conversational model: An outline. *American Journal of Psychotherapy, 58* (1), 51–66.

Meares, R. (2012). Some thoughts about language, In: Meares, Bendit, Haliburn, Korner, Mears & Butt (Ed.), *Borderline Personality Disorder and the Conversational Model—A Clinician's Manual*, pp. 36–44, New York, NY: Norton.

Middleton, W. (2013). Ongoing incestuous abuse during adulthood. *Journal of Trauma & Dissociation, 14* (3), 251–272. doi:10.1080/15299732.2012.736932

Ogden, T. H. (1989). The threshold of the male Oedipus complex. *Bulletin of the Menninger Clinic, 53* (5), 394–413.

Ogilvie, B., & Daniluk, J. (1995). Common themes in the experiences of mother-daughter incest survivors: Implications for counselling. *Journal of Counselling and Development, 73* (6), 598–602. doi:10.1002/j.1556-6676.1995.tb01802.x

Peter, T. (2009). Exploring taboos: Comparing male- and female-perpetrated child sexual abuse. *Journal of Interpersonal Violence, 24* (7), 1111–1128. doi:10.1177/0886260508322194

Reckling, A. E. (2004). Mother-daughter incest: When survivors become mothers. *Journal of Trauma Practice, 3* (2), 49–71. doi:10.1300/J189v03n02_03

Rucker, N. G., & Mermelstein, C. B. (1979). Unconscious communication in the mother-child dyad. *The American Journal of Psychoanalysis, 39* (2), 147–151. doi:10.1007/BF01262920

Ruiz-Tagle, A., Costanzo, E., De Achaval, D., & Guinjoan, S. (2015). Social cognition in a clinical sample of personality disorder patients. *Frontiers of Psychiatry, 6*, 75. doi:10.3389/fpsyt.2015.00075

Schechter, M. D. (1970). About adoptive parents. In E. J. Anthony, & T. Benedek (Eds.), *Parenthood: Its psychology and psychopathology* (pp. 353–371). Boston, MA: Little Brown & Co.

Schlesinger, L. B. (1999). Adolescent sexual matricide following repetitive mother-son incest. *Journal of Forensic Sciences, 44* (4), 746–749. doi:10.1520/JFS14548J

Shevlin, M., Dorahy, M. J., & Adamson, G. (2007). Trauma and psychosis: An analysis of the national comorbidity survey. *American Journal of Psychiatry, 164* (1), 166–169. doi:10.1176/ajp.2007.164.1.166

Shevlin, M., Houston, J. E., Dorahy, M. J., & Adamson, G. (2008). Cumulative traumas and psychosis: An analysis of the national comorbidity survey and the British psychiatric morbidity survey. *Schizophrenia Bulletin, 34* (1), 193–199. doi:10.1093/schbul/sbm069

Stern, D. N., & Bruschweiler-Stern, N. (1998). *The birth of a mother: How the motherhood experience changes you forever.* New York, NY: Basic Books.

Strickland, S. M. (2008). Female sex offenders: Exploring issues of personality, trauma, and cognitive distortions. *Journal of Interpersonal Violence, 23* (4), 474–489. doi:10.1177/0886260507312944

Thompson, A. D., Nelson, B., Yuen, H. P., Lin, A., Amminger, G. P., McGorry, P. D., … Yung, A. R. (2014). Sexual trauma increases the risk of developing psychosis in an ultra-high-risk "prodromal" population. *Schizophrenia Bulletin, 40* (3), 697–706. doi:10.1093/schbul/sbt032

Varese, F., Smeets, F., Drukker, M., Lieverse, R., Lataster, T., Viechtbauer, W., & Bentall, R. P. (2012). Childhood adversities increase the risk of psychosis: A meta-analysis of patient-control, prospective- and cross-sectional cohort studies. *Schizophrenia Bulletin, 38* (4), 661–671. doi:10.1093/schbul/sbs050

Weldon, E. V. (1988). *Mother, Madonna, Whore: The idealization and denigration of motherhood.* London, UK: Free Association Books.

Winnicott, D. W. (1949). Hate in the counter-transference. *International Journal Psychoanalysis, 30,* 69–74.

Winnicott, D. W. (1965). *The Maturational processes and the facilitating environment,* pp 37–75. London, UK: Karnac.

Winnicott, D. W. (1966). Becoming deprived as a fact: A psychotherapeutic consultation. *Journal of Child Psychotherapy, 1* (4), 5–12. doi:10.1080/00754176608254894

Dissociation in families experiencing intimate partner violence

Alison Miller

ABSTRACT
This paper, using an illustrative case study, presents the hypothesis that cyclical spouse abusers suffer from a dissociative condition (or perhaps a personality disorder in which dissociation is a prominent feature) that results from disorganized attachment. The partner of the spouse abuser tries various unsuccessful strategies to appease her spouse in order to change his behavior. If the relationship lasts for years, she adapts by developing a milder but parallel dissociative process, developing chains of state-dependent memory and resultant ego states for the different phases of the domestic abuse cycle. The children suffer from attachment disruption which can potentially continue the process to the next generation.

The intimate terrorist

Various researchers have attempted to classify maritally violent men (Holtzworth-Munroe, 2000; Holtzworth-Munroe & Stuart, 1994; Jacobson and Gottman, 1998). Johnson (2008) makes an important distinction between *situational couple violence* and *intimate terrorism*, the latter described as "coercive control" by Stark (2007). Jacobson and Gottman make a further distinction between "pit bulls" (whose physiological reactions indicate powerful emotional turmoil as they verbally lash out in anger at their wives) and "cobras" (who are physiologically calm as they appear to lose control, and are violent in contexts outside the home). The "pit bulls" show more of a borderline personality organization, whereas the "cobras" are more psychopathic. This parallels the distinction between "fear aggression" and "dominance aggression" well known to dog owners.[1]

Dutton (2007, p. 124) suggests that those spousal abusers who engage in intimate terrorism suffer from a disrupted attachment process. "Men who are abusive experience extreme and disproportionate anger in an intimate context that resembles an infantile tantrum and suggests some 'primitive' (i.e., pre-Oedipal) origin of this anger in an equally intimate relationship." Perlman and Bartholomew (1994) describe four adult attachment styles: secure (low attachment avoidance, low attachment anxiety), dismissing (high avoidance, low anxiety), preoccupied (low avoidance, high anxiety), and fearful (high avoidance, high anxiety). Liotti (2006) and others have connected dissociation with disorganized (what Bartholomew calls "fearful") attachment. I propose that a failure of integration of the personality in infancy because of disrupted early attachment leads to both fearful and preoccupied attachment styles in the same person, each style manifested in one primary ego state which actively takes control of the abuser's body and mind. I shall illustrate this through excerpts and summaries from the journal of "Jane," a university educated woman, who kept a journal during and shortly after the end of her abusive marriage, which began prior to public knowledge about domestic violence, and lasted almost 20 years. Jane, like many victims, and in contrast to popular assumptions about abused women, had experienced no prior physical or verbal abuse. She came from a family with two loving and gentle parents. A confident and assertive person at the start of her marriage, she did not seriously consider ending the marriage for many years because of a religious faith which stressed the permanency of marriage and the duty of loving one's spouse "for better or worse." Jane observed both her husband John's and her own changes over the years. According to Jane, John came from a family with a shaming father, an abusive older brother, and an overwhelmed mother.

Many spouses suggest that their violent partners go through different ego states in a regular cycle, culminating in a rageful abusive state, which is distinctly different from the partner's seemingly normal personality. Recent writers in the area of intimate partner violence have dismissed the notion of a battering cycle, first proposed by Walker (1979). Stark (2007), coming from a feminist perspective, interprets male partner violence or coercive control as an attempt to reinstate male privilege, and accuses the cycle model of perpetuating several myths about abusive violence. Rather than examining the evidence regarding whether a subset of abusers have a cycle, Stark focuses on arguing with Walker's suggestion that victims suffer from what we would now call post-traumatic stress disorder (PTSD). It is possible that abusers have a cycle, but that mutual dissociation rather than PTSD explains some of the victims' behavior. Johnson (2008) ignores the important question of whether spouse abusers have a battering cycle; Dutton (2007) validates the existence of such a cycle in "borderline" abusers. In the present case example, Jane describes a cycle which lasted for years but eventually degenerated into constant abuse.

Psychotherapists working with persons who suffer from dissociative disorders recognize the presence and influence of very young parts who experience life as if they are children undergoing trauma and/or attachment disruption. Such parts, if they take control of an adult, engage in behaviors which may be characteristic of a young child with disorganized attachment (Ainsworth et al., 1978). The constant attention and "mind reading" a spouse abuser demands from his partner is what a toddler needs from his mother, but impossible for an adult to provide for another adult. A mother is also able to set limits on her toddler's acting out behavior, while recognizing his egocentricity and helping him understand others' needs. A woman is unable to set similar limits on her "big-body" abusive partner. I propose that dissociation is key to the attachment disturbance in the perpetrator of intimate partner violence, and it frequently involves intense alternating anxious and angry ego states as well as a seemingly calm "good boy" state.

"Mr. wonderful" ("good boy") outside the home

Jane married a man who presented to her and others a charming and considerate face, which she initially believed to be his nature. Throughout the marriage, John continued to be that man outside the home, and everyone who knew them believed he was indeed a kind and thoughtful person. Jane's attempts at disclosing her ongoing abuse (to her mother, a professor, and an old friend) were misinterpreted as indicating normal marital conflict. She came to realize that the discrepancy between John's public and private faces was so great that no one would have believed her if she told them what was going on behind closed doors.

Jekyll and hyde

During their honeymoon, John began to have periods of withdrawal. His face would become rigid like a mask, and he wouldn't speak to Jane for hours. She felt afraid, and would plead with John to tell her what was wrong. Sometimes he just did not reply, and other times he said (and apparently believed) that she knew what she had done to upset him.

Six weeks after they married, Jane's diary provided a dramatic illustration of her sense of the dissociation between John's gentle and aggressive ego states. "He told me about a dream he'd had, involving him and his older brother Jason and a very large mean cow (John grew up on a dairy farm), which respected Jason because he was harsh, and was out to get John because he was weak and the cow disliked him. I began to wonder about this—if in his sight I am like the cow, and he's afraid to treat me gently in case I hurt him but thinks I will respect harshness. This isn't the case, of course. But I wonder if whenever John is very open and close to me he becomes afraid (…) It's as though he has two personalities, a soft and kind 'John' one and a harsh, keep-your-distance 'Jason' one. Jason, whom he hates, somehow represents for him success in life and safety. After he has been John for a while he retreats into his shell as 'Jason.' He may think something I say or do is the reason, but it is really just the excuse."

Cycle of buildup and discharge

Walker (1979) initially traced the buildup, discharge, and contrition phases in the cyclical spouse abuser. In the buildup phase, the batterer gradually escalates his criticism and emotional abuse of his partner. In the discharge phase, he acts out his uncontrolled rage by battering his partner. After the discharge, he may experience contrition and promise it will never happen again and/or he may justify his behavior on the basis of "stress" or his partner's alleged provocations. Once the rage is fully discharged, the abuser may be relatively pleasant until the buildup begins once more (Miller, 2006, 1998).

Jane's home life, as she described it, was a roller-coaster, based on John's moods, which seemed to follow an internal cycle of their own, which she judged to be about 6 weeks in length on the average. After John dared to risk physical or emotional intimacy, Jane would see him gradually fill up with negativity, and increasingly provoke her by niggling little perfectionistic criticisms and blaming. It felt to her as though there was something very angry and uncontrolled which was trying to find a way out of him. During this buildup period, he would gradually increase his provocation, to get her to react in a way which would justify his becoming angry with her. She would try her hardest not to give him grounds for an explosion, but it never worked.

Jane wrote:

"Usually we have a problem, then are really lovey-dovey for a day or two, then spend several days 'on and off', with John alternately being warm to me and (...) retreating into a kind of defensive shell. During these periods certain tensions build up—misunderstandings—and these explode into a problem when I ask him or he tells me what's wrong. It's always something I did or said that hurt or distracted him. Then I say it didn't mean what he thought it did, and we begin to fight, he accusing me and I weeping and denying malicious intent and showing my hurt from the accusations. After a while I give up saying anything because I know it will only be misinterpreted. I withdraw and he follows me with more accusations. After he has given out enough harshness to shut me up completely and make me despair, he quits, spends some time alone and then comes back all warm and loving. The whole process starts over again. I know he wouldn't agree with this, but I think the whole cycle is somehow contained in him."

I propose that the abusive partner with a disorganized attachment style (alternately preoccupied and fearful) is experiencing an approach–avoidance conflict. He desperately wants closeness with his partner, just as an infant wants to be physically close to the mother when stressed or afraid, so any stress makes him approach her for comfort. But as he gets closer to her, the approach gradient weakens and the avoidance gradient increases more steeply, so he wants to escape her or make her go away. Allison, Bartholomew, Mayseless, and Dutton (2008) studied the attachment styles and behavior of couples who had experienced male violence. They identified two consistent themes associated with partner violence: *the strategy of pursuit* and *the strategy of distancing*. Violence could serve either strategy: it could force engagement of a partner who was perceived to be disengaging, or it could push back a partner who was perceived to be approaching too closely.

Projection of malice onto partner

Jane's journal has many accounts of John's verbal abuse, which primarily consisted of accusations of malicious intent. Jane described John as "a man without skin" who would experience a slight or gentle emotional touch as a blow.

For Jane, one of the worst things about their fights was the interrogation. John would ask her *why* she had done or said a particular thing. Initially she took his inquiry as sincere, but after many such experiences she came to realize that he wanted her to give the answer he had already decided on: that she was deliberately trying to hurt or shame or embarrass or criticize him. If she told the truth, that what she said was not meant that way, he would attack more viciously and keep on asking. Jane was in a double bind: She could lie and say she had been deliberately hurtful (resulting in punishment), or she could tell the truth and say she had not intended to hurt him (resulting in being accused of lying as well as of being deliberately hurtful). John may also have experienced a double bind, as follows: If Jane had malicious intent, he was rejected and unloved, whereas if she had no malicious intent, he must be bad for inferring it, and therefore unloveable, which he could not bear. Better to be unloved than unloveable. Whenever Jane told the truth, that she did not intend to hurt him, it confirmed what he needed to believe: that she did have malicious intent, and did not love him even though he was loveable. John had to avoid shame at all costs.

Needing all initiative to be his

John expected Jane to be available for his needs, like a mother, but was unable to respond to hers. It was very important to John that any kindness he showed to Jane be on his initiative, not hers. Every fight in the later years of the marriage had the same litany of all the times Jane had made decisions, even just for herself, without consulting him, through all the years of their 20-year marriage—proof to him of Jane's lack of commitment and emotional abandonment of him. Jane's interpretation was that John needed all initiative to be his, and couldn't let her make any decisions or really participate in joint decisions. He needed her presence to validate his decisions, but not to have genuine input. Her independent subjectivity was a threat to him.

A very young child is egocentric in a similar way; he does not really recognize the subjectivity of family members or other children, but in the second and third years of life he begins to assert his own will. If his parent respects the child's subjectivity, the child develops both self-respect and the capacity for empathy. But if the parent is constantly intrusive into the child's initiative, and shames the child for noncompliance, the child may develop compliant behaviors, but will not learn genuine cooperation or recognize the value of others' subjectivity, and in addition will feel both shame and anger in the presence of the parent. Dutton summarizes from his research (2007) on childhood antecedents of male partner violence: "If I had to pick one single action by the parent that generated abusiveness in men, I would pick being shamed by the father" (p. 202). When the shamed child as an adult enters an intimate relationship, he has a new potentially threatening attachment figure, and the shamed and angry states from childhood become active. He responds to his spouse as if she were the intrusive, shaming parent. He becomes what Shaw (2014) calls a "traumatizing narcissist," attacking his intimate partner in order to ward off shame. Shaw (p. xv) writes that "the subjectivity of the other … is the target of the traumatizing narcissist's relational system." Shaw goes on to say "The adult traumatizing narcissist is obsessed with maintaining a rigid sense of omnipotent superiority and perfection—of infallibility, self-sufficiency, and entitlement. He defends his conviction of righteousness and justification vigilantly" (2014, p. 34).

Controlling details of partner's and family's behavior

Over the years, John began to control more and more areas of Jane's life. He made her keep a record of every penny she spent. He wouldn't permit her to put photographs in albums, saying they had to do it together. He didn't let her open letters on her own before he came home. He also controlled the children's behavior in minute detail, telling them, for example, how much cereal to put in their bowls and how many squares of toilet paper to use.

Stark (2007) defines such "coercive control" as "the deprivation of rights and resources that are critical to personhood and citizenship" (p. 15). He states that "[I]t is the lost connection between women's status, domesticity, and dependence on men that coercive control is designed to reinstate … Each household governed by coercive control, each relationship, becomes a patriarchy in miniature." This political interpretation, however, does not explain why so many men (and women) engage in this personal micromanagement of their spouses' lives, without having it reinforced by present-day society. In my opinion, a developmental explanation makes more sense: A child deprived of control of his own life in childhood only feels safe as an adult when he is in complete control. The existence of another self whose decisions might impact on him is experienced as a threat, as such decisions, when they disagreed with him, might make him experience the shame he lived with when told he was "bad" as a child.

Disrupting the children's bond with the spouse

The spousal abuser frequently triangulates his children into the marital conflict. Jane's experience suggests that it may play an important role in passing on the dysfunction to the next generation.

If one of the children was accidentally hurt, John panicked and rushed in to soothe him, sometimes even physically pushing Jane out of the way so he could be the one to make things better for that child, and comfort himself in the process. He constantly interfered with her ability to provide motherly nurturing and soothing, presumably in the belief that she was a bad and dangerous person. He also regularly overturned Jane's parenting decisions, to convey the message that there was only one authority in the home—him.

When John abused Jane at night, the children could hear the sounds of him shouting and Jane weeping. They knew better than to come out, as it was not safe for them to approach either parent. If Jane asked John to keep his voice down so the children wouldn't hear, he raised his volume to defy her. If John and Jane were fighting, no one was available to comfort a frightened child, though sometimes John would pick the child up and hold him in his arms while loudly berating or even hitting Jane.

Jane wrote: "After the blowout, he would gather the huddled children into his arms and explain to them kindly what a mean and thoughtless person I was—how I'd deserved it—what a terrible parent I was. The children could evade his abuse by listening supportively to him bitch about me. The only safe place for a child in a spouse-abusing household is in the arms of the abuser. This happened literally when they were babies and infants, he would strike me holding a child in his arms. It happened psychologically all the time; if they took his side, they could be protected from harm. Often he would make them take sides, call them in as witnesses in some dispute, point out to them how bad I was."

I note that John genuinely believed that he was the mistreated person. In my view, the abusive spouse, defending himself against shame, needs desperately to see himself as the "good guy" and justified in his behavior. So he has to convince the only witnesses, the children, of his view of the situation. They know that their safety is contingent in their accepting this view and rejecting their other parent (Miller, 2006, 1998) Keeping safe from the frightening father involves accepting his verbal explanation that Mommy is the bad guy, even though the child's own eyes and ears tell him otherwise. Miller (2006) noted that Baker and O'Neil (1996) explain that such children may use dissociation to develop a secure ego state for the protecting father, a traumatized ego state for the threatening father, and an avoidant or resistant ego state for the unavailable mother. The contrast between the frightening father the child experiences intermittently at home, and the other father who appears at other times, especially in public, is difficult for a young child to grasp.

The abused partner

The early phase of the relationship

Jane's experience with John illustrates a more general pattern in intimate partner violence. The couple have not lived together for long before the victim partner becomes aware that there is a discrepancy between the wonderful man she fell in love with, and the terrorizing controller who appears only behind closed doors. Her previous reality continues outside the home, while an entirely new and terrifying reality presents itself within the home. Since no one else sees the violent and controlling behavior, she may begin to doubt her perceptions. Initially she sees the violence as an aberration which will not happen again. She may accept a major portion of the blame because she has been taught that "it takes two to fight." When the violence recurs, she changes her belief from "the violence will not happen again" to "if I alter my behavior, the violence will not recur." She still sees the violence as inconsistent with her partner's character and, therefore, avoidable. She has accepted her partner's core belief that future outbreaks of violence depend upon her, not him. The psychological contract which develops between the batterer and his spouse maintains that his emotional state depends on her (Miller, 2006). The spouse may reason that since he becomes violent only when he is home with her, she must be causing the violence, and his partner reinforces this belief by trying to change her behavior to improve his.

When John hit her for the first time, Jane was shocked. She also took responsibility for it: "I was so bad at being married that my marriage had degenerated into physical violence." After one fight, when John had gone out, she stood in the shower looking at the spiders and screamed repeatedly at the top of her lungs, while another part of her which appeared to be outside her body observed unemotionally, ***"This must be what it's like to go crazy."*** She had never before been conscious of such a distance between an observer part of her and an emotional part. If Jane had a prior abuse history, she might have developed a separate ego state or even alter personality to handle the abuse; as it was, she felt overwhelmed as she had never been before.

The middle phase

About 5 years into the marriage, after they had their first child, Jane had come to realize that expecting any nurturing or support from her husband was useless; she had to be emotionally independent of him. She reduced her expectations of John, but held herself to the commitment she had made in her marriage vows, and tried to treat him with kindness and consideration. She relied primarily on her spiritual faith and her journaling for personal support. John felt her withdrawal and when he pointed it out, Jane explained that it was because of his violence. He agreed to give her a time-limited period in which she could warm up to him without him hitting her. He continued to have cyclic emotional states and to attempt to control everything in the household, even though he had stopped hitting. Jane attempted to warm up, but found it difficult. When the period came to an end, John was dissatisfied and resumed his previous behavior. Jane put up with this and focused on her work and her children.

In the early stage of the marriage, Jane had become angry when John mistreated her, but after years she noticed that she was losing her ability to feel this anger, as it could not be expressed. John's criticisms were for a long time taken by Jane as expressions of conditional love—he would love and accept her "if only." She made lists of behaviors of her own which she needed to change to avoid conflict with John. Satir's (1988) well-known model of coping styles describes how the threat posed by a blamer such as John turns the partner into a placator, who takes responsibility for the situation in the hope of keeping the peace and avoiding the blamer's anger. Jane's initial attempts at placating, in the first few months of marriage, involved explaining herself. When she realized that such explanations only infuriated John, she attempted to placate by changing each behavior which John criticized.

Jane began to develop learned helplessness and chronic guilt, as none of her attempts to appease John or explain herself to him had worked:

"I've become nonassertive, dominated by others' demands, not taking initiative, 'put-upon' by kids and John, not saying (and often not knowing) what I want. Not feeling I have a right to be me. Alternating between guilt for not being what others want and guilt for not being what I want."

This bind made her unable to think, and she developed severe headaches. Tears would pour down her face, and the headaches would last for days after each fight.

Jane's journal entries show she adapted to each phase of the abuse cycle with an ego state of her own, as the following illustration shows.

In the buildup phase, as John increased his petty criticisms and accusations, Jane was an anxious caregiver, trying to placate him and avoid triggering a violent episode.

On occasion, when John was near the danger point, Jane would calculate when was the best time to trigger him. If she had an important work event coming up, she might antagonize John in order to get his violent episode over with before she was called on to be high-functioning.

During interrogations, she "blanked out" and became incapable of answering.

In the violent discharge phase, she was afraid and just in coping mode, trying to survive and to protect her children to the best of her ability, which sometimes meant staying away from them so they would not get hurt.

In the beginning of the safe phase of John's cycle, Jane kept her distance, did not look to John for any support, and tried not to antagonize him, hoping to postpone the re-emergence of the buildup.

If John's "good" phase lasted longer than a couple of weeks, she began to hope again that he might be changing, and would warm up to him, but would then notice that this closeness might be threatening to him, as he once again commenced the criticisms which signaled the start of the buildup phase.

In public, in the presence of John's warm and friendly public personality, Jane was much like her original assertive self, though she was careful not to criticize John. However, as the severity of John's behavior at home escalated, Jane became more consciously aware that "Mr. Hyde" was always watching even when "Dr. Jekyll" was being his charming self, so she became more subdued in public, knowing she would have to account and pay for any assertive behavior later.

She became adept at enjoying herself even in John's presence in places where she knew John wouldn't hurt her. She allowed herself to enjoy his holding her hand, smiling at her, and appearing solicitous, in order to impress others. At such moments, she was not thinking about the "other man" she had to deal with at home.

On the way to work, Jane imagined herself to be like a car turning on the windshield wipers, wiping away all the tears and stress and inadequacies and heartbreak of home, and starting afresh as her competent self in the workplace. On her way home, her meek, anxious, deferential, and supportive abused wife self would emerge, ready to anticipate John's next moves.

Within the marriage, Jane separated the "good time" and the "bad time" memories. In the bad times, she remembered only bad times, and felt extremely unhappy. In the good times, her memories of the bad times would become blurry. Jane knew they had happened, but it was easy to convince herself that John was changing and the bad times would soon be over. This state-dependent memory had important functions: it enabled Jane to enjoy herself and her marriage at the times when it was possible to do so, to have good times which weren't spoiled by the bad times, and to make other people believe that the couple were happy, which was what John wanted.

The late phase

It took Jane many years to recognize fully that her attempts to change behavior that John objected to made no difference to John's perception of her. When she had changed everything that she could think of, John responded that it was "too late," the damage had already been done, and she had ruined their relationship to a point where it could never recover. Jane finally realized that deliberate love and giving to her oppressor weren't transforming him: Instead, he felt increasingly entitled, aggrieved, and aggressive toward her.

Because of his pleasant personality, John was promoted at work to a position for which he was not really trained, and received criticism for mistakes. His emotions from the workplace entered the home, where he would rant to Jane about people at work mistreating him, then say "You're just like them," a phrase which signaled he was about to be violent. John became almost constantly abusive toward Jane, and started to be abusive toward their oldest child as well. Jane found herself more and more in survival mode, afraid to grieve or comfort herself. She promised herself that if she were ever to make the decision to leave John, she would never return. But leaving was a difficult thing to do after so many years with a social identity as part of an apparently happy married couple. She divided her hidden journal into a positive section to write in when things were good with John, and a negative section for when things were bad. She made herself read from the bad section in the good times, and vice versa. Then she deliberately read to herself statements from both sections, alternating so she could see the picture as a whole. This created anguish, but it helped her put the whole picture together and make the decision to leave. She was aware that John's attempts at coercive control would not end with her leaving, and that she would have to share the children with him, but she could have a home in which he was not present and she could again be a parent to her own children.

Discussion

This paper proposes that a spousal abuser who engages in domestic terrorism or coercive control alternates between preoccupied and fearful/rejecting attachment to his partner. There is evidence (Dutton, 2007, p. 13) that what Dutton calls the impulsive/undercontrolled batterer, typified by John, has cyclical phases, ambivalence toward his partner, fearful/angry attachment, and a borderline profile on the MCMI (Millon Clinical Multiaxial

Inventory-III). John is an example of someone who had never learned to soothe himself, and could not trust his wife to provide soothing when he was upset. He genuinely believed she was out to harm him, projecting malice onto her and misinterpreting her behavior and words. This suggests that his model of a significant other was of someone who would reject him and seek to harm or shame him. Given this model of an attachment figure, it makes sense that he would seek to neutralize the threat somehow: At the beginning of the marriage, it was through withdrawal, but when Jane pursued him to find out what was wrong, he increasingly turned to coercive control and violent outbursts.

Although the victimized partner is aware that her abuser has different ways of being, and a cycle of buildup and discharge, she finds herself in a completely different situation depending on which state he is in at the time. In public, she finds it difficult if not impossible to believe that this person turns into the monster she sees at home. As the violent spouse goes through the phases of his cycle, his partner adapts by developing parallel states which link together in separate chains of memory. Thus, she is able to enjoy the relief periods without contamination from memories of violence, continue to love her spouse, and maintain the marriage (Miller, 2006.) Jane found herself developing a different ego state to deal with each version of John. Stark (2007) insightfully points out that the theory of "battered woman's syndrome" attributes PTSD to victims of domestic violence, whereas their reactions to ongoing coercion and control could better be seen as adaptive or *intra*-traumatic. Dissociation is a very effective intra-traumatic response: it enables a person to live within a traumatizing situation without being overwhelmed.

The children, too, have to live with the different versions of their father (or mother, if the violent parent is a woman.) When he is being kind, he is playful and entertaining. However, there is always the implied threat that if the children don't behave and perhaps even think exactly as he wants, the abuse, shaming, and rejection will be focused on them. In our case example, it was evident that pleasing their father involved rejecting their mother. John reinforced that message by overturning Jane's parenting decisions, and preventing them from receiving comfort from her when they were distressed. Even after abusing his wife, John was in an apparently kind mood when he explained to the children that their mother was punished because she was bad. The children of the spouse abuser may feel safest when being comforted by him—but the price of this safety is rejecting the evidence of their own eyes and ears. Furthermore, when the children are distressed by the parental conflict, rather than having a secure, attuned mother to receive their distressed emotions and bring them calm, they have a volatile father whose distressed and distressing emotions add to their own turmoil. Even when mother has the capacity for attunement, she is only intermittently available.

This kind of homelife breeds dissociation in children through creating disorganized attachment. Siegel (1999) suggests that "the parents of children with disorganized attachments have provided frightened, frightening, or disorienting shifts in their own behavior, which create conflictual experiences leading to incoherent mental models. Such a child may develop an internal mental model for each aspect of the parent's behavior. Abrupt shifts in parental state force the child to adapt with suddenly shifting states of his own.... When such shifts are early, severe, and repeated, these states can become engrained in the child as self-states" (p. 317). Freyd's Betrayal Trauma theory (Freyd & Birrell, 2013) states that "unawareness and forgetting of abuse will be higher when the relationship between perpetrator and victim involves closeness, trust, and/or caregiving" (p. 101). This forgetting in my opinion indicates dissociation, a helpful defense which is necessary for living in such a situation.

With intimate partner violence, just as with child abuse, there is also a demand from the abuser that the reality of homelife be kept hidden from the outside world, and when the children are with their parents in the presence of others, the abusive parent appears to all to be a loving and sensible person. The fact that the victims (both spouse and children) in intimate partner violence cannot talk about their home experience influences their ability to articulate this experience for themselves. Freyd's (1983) Shareability theory proposes that "through the sharing of information—that is, through communication—internal knowledge is reorganized into more consciously available, categorical, and discrete forms of knowing. This means that information we have never shared with others is organized differently than information we have shared. So disclosure affects the *way* we know our own experiences internally" (Freyd & Birrell, 2013). Siegel (1999) makes a very similar suggestion: "Psychological trauma involving the blockage of explicit processing also impairs the victim's ability to cortically consolidate the experience. With dissociation or the prohibition of discussing with others what was experienced, as is so often the case in familial child abuse, there may be a profound blockage to the pathway toward consolidating memory" (p. 52). Words need to be found to breakthrough the blockages and link the disconnected experiences. We as therapists must attune to these disparate pieces to provide the bridge that Jane began to build for herself.

Note

1. I shall refer to the abuser as "he" or "him" and the spouse as "she" or "her," since evidence suggests that those violent spouses who engage in coercive control are primarily male (Dutton, 2007, p. 32; Stark, 2007, p. 15).

References

Ainsworth, M., Blehar, M., Waters, E., & Wall, S. (1978). *Patterns of attachment*. Hillsdale, NJ: Erlbaum.

Allison, C. J., Bartholomew, K., Mayseless, O., & Dutton, D. G. (2008). Love as a battlefield: Attachment and relationship dynamics in couples identified for male partner violence. *Journal of Family Issues, 29*, 125–150.

Baker, S., & O'Neil, J. (1996). *Transference & countertransference revisited: The interplay of trauma and attachment in the process of therapy with dissociative disorders*. Workshop presented at the 13th International Fall Conference of the International Society for the Study of Dissociation.

Dutton, D. G. (2007). *The abusive personality: Violence and control in intimate relationships* (2nd ed.). New York, NY: Guilford.

Freyd, J. (1983). Shareability: The social psychology of epistemology. *Cognitive Science, 7*, 191–210.

Freyd, J., & Birrell, P. (2013). *Blind to betrayal*. Hoboken, NJ: Wiley.

Holtzworth-Munroe, A. (2000). A typology of men who are violent toward their female partners: Making sense of the heterogeneity in husband violence. *Current Directions in Psychological Science 9*(4), 140–143.

Holtzworth-Munroe, A., & Stuart, G. L. (1994). Typologies of male batterers: Three subtypes and the differences among them. *Psychological Bulletin, 116*(3), 476–497. doi:10.1037/0033-2909.116.3.476

Jacobson, N.S. & Gottman, J.M. (1998). *When men batter women: New insights into ending abusive relationships*. New York, NY: Simon & Schuster.

Johnson, M. (2008). *Domestic violence: Intimate terrorism, violent resistance, and situational couple violence*. Boston, MA: Northeastern University Press.

Liotti, G. (2006). A model of dissociation based on attachment theory and research. *Journal of Trauma & Dissociation, 7*, 55–73. doi:10.1300/J229v07n04_04

Miller, A. (1998). The dissociative dance of spouse abuse. *Treating Abuse Today, 8*(3), 9–18.

Miller, A. (2006). The role of dissociation in spouse abuse. In N. A. Jackson (Ed.), *Encyclopedia of domestic violence* (pp. 241–246). New York, NY: Routledge. Retrieved from http://criminal-justice.iresearchnet.com/crime/domestic-violence/dissociation/

Perlman, D., & Bartholomew, K. (1994). Preface. In K. Bartholomew, & D. Perlman (Eds.), *Advances in personal relationships Volume 5: Attachment processes in adulthood*. London, UK: Jessica Kingsley Publishers.

Satir, V. (1988). *The new peoplemaking*. Mountain View, CA: Science and Behavior Books.

Shaw, D. (2014). *Traumatic narcissism: Relational systems of subjugation*. New York, NY: Routledge.

Siegel, D. J. (1999). *The developing mind: How relationships and the brain interact to shape who we are*. New York, NY: Guilford.

Stark, E. (2007). *Coercive control: The entrapment of women in personal life*. New York, NY: Oxford University Press.

Walker, L. (1979). *The battered woman*. New York, NY: Harper & Row.

Organized abuse in adulthood: Survivor and professional perspectives

Michael Salter, PhD

ABSTRACT
This paper reports on the preliminary findings of a qualitative study of Australian women disclosing organized abuse in adulthood and the mental health professionals who treat them. Drawing on interviews with survivors and mental health professionals, the paper analyses the fraught relationship between mental health and physical safety for adults subject to organized abuse. The therapeutic progress of adult organized abuse victims can be disrupted by ongoing threats, stalking, and group violence, which in turn reinforces the dissociative responses and pathological attachments that render them vulnerable to revictimization. The paper argues that breaking this cycle requires intervention from multiple agencies, and describes the responses of police, medical services, and child protection services to adult organized abuse from the perspective of survivors and mental health practitioners. Highlighting systemic failures but also opportunities, the paper calls for a coordinated response to organized abuse in adulthood, including inter-agency partnerships to support safety and bolster the efficacy of therapeutic interventions.

Introduction

This paper reports on the preliminary findings of an Australian interview study with women disclosing organized abuse in adulthood and the mental health professionals who support them. The term organized abuse refers to the sexual abuse of multiple children by multiple perpetrators acting in a coordinated way (Salter & Richters, 2012) and is reported by up to 11% of clients in dissociative disorder clinics (Middleton & Butler, 1998). The International Society for the Study of Trauma and Dissociation Chu (2011, p. 168) recognizes that, in the course of treatment, it is "not unusual" for adult organized abuse victims to indicate that "they are still being exploited by one or more primary perpetrators". The veracity of reports of adult organized abuse is contested. Mental health practitioners are often unable to definitively verify reports of adult organized abuse (Fraser, 1997). Accurate disclosures of adult organized abuse can be difficult to distinguish from "contagion, unconscious defensive elaborations, pseudomemories, delusion, or deliberate confabulation" (ISSTD, 2011, p. 168). Indeed, organized abuse survivors regularly question their own memories, recognizing the blurring of dreams, flashbacks, and hallucinations into their lived experience (Salter, 2013a). The "reality testing" of unusual disclosures or strange recollections of abuse is therefore important both clinically and forensically (Dalenberg, Hyland, Cuevas, Eisen, & Quas, 2002). However, where clinicians conclude that a client is experiencing ongoing organized victimization, it is unclear how they should respond. While reports of the ongoing victimization of organized abuse clients dates back to at least the early 1990s (Young, 1992), the clinical literature on the treatment of dissociative disorders is largely silent on how to enhance the safety of organized abuse victims.

While disclosures of organized abuse have been the subject of considerable skepticism, supporting evidence has accumulated to a "tipping point" (Middleton, 2015) albeit to varying degrees. Internationally, there are criminal prosecutions in cases of multi-generational incest (Middleton, 2013), technologically-facilitated organized abuse (Wolak, 2015) and the ritual abuse of children and adults (Salter, 2012). However, other features of organized abuse disclosures are less easily confirmed. "Mind control" or "programming", in which dissociation is deliberately inculcated and manipulated in organized abuse victims, has been described by a number of clinicians (e.g. Chu, 2011; Miller, 2012; Schwartz, 2013) although verification by other means, such as criminal prosecutions, is difficult to find. Claims of international conspiracies of ritual abuse, sometimes advanced under the rubric of "satanic ritual abuse", are entirely speculative, and perhaps illustrative of the challenges of coping with very traumatic experiences and disclosures of abuse (Fraser, 1997). Nonetheless, recent inquiries into child exploitation networks in England demonstrated that organized abuse can be geographically extensive, involve sophisticated grooming behaviors, and persist over many years without intervention by the authorities (Coffey, 2014; Jaye, 2014). While recognizing the limitations of the available evidence, it is important to avoid the premature foreclosure of knowledge in relation to organized abuse. Our understanding of organized and complex forms of victimization is still unfolding.

Given that adult organized abuse victims continue to present in a range of contexts, there is a need for empirical research that documents the experiences of this group of clients in their efforts to find care, and the "practice wisdom" of mental health professionals who are currently providing it. Drawing on interviews with survivors and mental health practitioners, this paper emphasizes the links between psychological wellbeing and physical safety for dissociative women with organized abuse histories. Eschewing simple dichotomies of "real" and "imagined" abuse, the paper acknowledges that the victim's[1] experiential world of dissociative symptoms and traumatic attachments can be manipulated by perpetrators to coerce them into organized abuse, which further exacerbates dissociative and traumatic symptoms and increases their vulnerability to revictimization. The efforts of mental health practitioners to break this "vicious cycle" is complicated by uncertainties over the factual accuracy of disclosures of ongoing abuse and their limited capacity to provide for the safety of the client. The reflections of survivors and professionals suggest that the cooperation of multiple agencies can support the physical safety of the survivor (and their children), enhancing the efficacy of therapeutic work. However, a lack of shared understanding and training amongst responding professionals and services can result in the premature dismissal of reports of adult organized abuse, the stigmatization of victims, and retraumatizing or potentially harmful interventions. The paper concludes with some thoughts on the implications of adult organized abuse for practice and policy.

Methodology

The paper is based on interviews with 16 survivors and 18 mental health professionals (with more interviews forthcoming).[2] Recruitment took place in partnership with key stakeholders and agencies in the field of dissociation, child abuse, sexual assault and domestic violence. The recruitment and interviewing strategy of the project has been approved by the Human Research Ethics Committee at Western Sydney University (H11234). The study has received funding from Western Sydney University and the Cannan Institute.

Survivor participants ranged in age from their early twenties to their late sixties, with most in their thirties and forties. The survivor cohort described organized abuse beginning in early childhood, typically facilitated by a father or both parents, and continuing into their twenties or beyond. All survivor participants disclosed sadistic forms of sexual violence (that is, abuse that is intended to cause extreme pain and fear, see Goodwin, 1994), and two thirds of survivor participants disclosed ritualistic experiences of abuse, often although not always with "satanic" overtones. About half of the survivor participants described the apparently deliberate inculcation of dissociation in childhood (ie "mind control") although this could be difficult to distinguish from the highly coercive dynamics within their families of origin. The professional cohort included psychiatrists, clinical psychologists, social

[1]The terminology of "victim", "survivor", and "perpetrator" is fraught in relation to organized abuse, since an adult may have survived organized abuse in childhood but continue to be victimized, and part of their victimization may include coerced perpetration (Salter, 2013b). This paper will use the term "victim" to refer to adults presently being victimized in organized abuse, recognizing that they are also "survivors" in the sense that they continue to survive extreme trauma and other obstacles. "Survivor" is used to refer to interview participants, the majority of whom have experienced a cessation of organized abuse. The term "perpetrator" is used to refer to those adults actively engaged in organized abuse, but the term is used provisionally, since they may be acting under coercion and have their own significant trauma history.

[2]The survivor interviews include seven interviews that have been incorporated from a prior study in which participants disclosed organized abuse in adulthood (Salter, 2013b).

workers, sexual assault workers, therapists, and counselors. The majority had been practicing for between 10 and 20 years with postgraduate clinical and therapeutic qualifications. Two thirds were in private practice with one third in community-based services such as rape crisis centers. The project did not aim to recruit a representative sample of survivors and the professionals in contact with them, but rather to analyze diverse accounts of organized abuse in adulthood in order to identify the range of circumstances in which it occurs and responses to it.

Interviews were conducted face to face or over Skype. Interviews with the professional cohort were between one to two hours in length, while interviews with the survivor cohort were generally between three or four hours. Multiple interviews were necessary for some survivor participants. Interviews were digitally recorded and provided to a professional transcription service. The researcher then removed identifying information from the transcripts and imported them into Nvivo, a software program that facilitates qualitative data analysis and enables users to assign a code to specific lines or segments of text. The interviews were analyzed according to a thematic methodology (Braun & Clarke 2006) in which data is coded to identify common themes in participant accounts. A critical psychosocial framework drawing on criminological frameworks of gendered violence, and theories of trauma, dissociation and attachment, structured the analysis of the interview data. An analysis of the preliminary findings of the study is presented below. Pseudonyms are used for all participants and details may have been changed where necessary to protect their identity.

Findings

In interview, survivors and professionals detailed the obstacles to recovery and safety at the intersection of the dissociative disorders and adult organized abuse. These obstacles are illustrated by the following case study, based on the account provided by Leona, an art therapist. Leona had been working for five years with Rosie, who was a woman in her forties disclosing ongoing organized abuse. Rosie's psychiatrist had diagnosed her with dissociative identity disorder and attributed her complaints of the current victimization to "flashbacks". However, he was troubled by her lack of therapeutic progress, and referred her to art therapy in the hope that another modality might assist her recovery. After a few months of treatment, Rosie began to speak to Leona about a group of men who sometimes waited for her in car parks, or forced her to the side of the road, triggering a dissociative response that left her vulnerable to group sexual sadism. Leona said:

> They would come up to her in the car park, when she was getting back into her car to leave from the shops. And as soon as she saw them, there would be a part that would get out of the car and go.

> And the other thing was that they would sometimes stop her on the road, because she has to travel quite a distance from work to home, and she said they worked with two cars. One car would go in front of her and slow down. The car would come up behind her and force her to the side.

Rosie recounted being taken to a property where she was sexually assaulted and subject to electroshock amongst other sadistic abuses. The electroshock was, according to Rosie, punishment for not going to the property of her own volition. After these events, Rosie presented in therapy in a profoundly traumatized state, in apparent physical pain and with unusual injuries. Leona said "I know the mind is an incredible thing, and theoretically she could be recreating all these symptoms". However, the consistency and coherence of Rosie's reports of stalking and abduction led Leona to conclude she was reporting actual events. Some external verification was available via Rosie's friends who confirmed that they had interrupted coordinated attempts to stalk and abduct Rosie.

Leona worked with Rosie to develop strategies so that she didn't dissociate and comply with these men when confronted by them. For instance, Rosie could call Leona when she saw the men, and Leona would talk with Rosie to ground her until the threat had passed. However, Leona said that Rosie would sometimes "lose consciousness and find herself at their property", after another part had "taken her there, from herself, in her own car". Feeling that the abuse was inevitable, Rosie began making arrangements with the men: her compliance with sexual assault if they stopped the electroshock. Leona said: "Sometimes they'd meet her in a car park and she'd go in their car and be returned to her car".

Leona attributed Rosie's lack of therapeutic progress, which had so puzzled her psychiatrist, to her lack of safety and the ongoing impact of severe traumatization. According to Leona, therapy could only offer Rosie brief respite from ongoing violence and hyper-arousal:

> Rosie in many ways is so receptive to the therapeutic process, and I see her make improvements, I see her make strides, I see her being able to work on something, and then it all just gets torn down. No matter what we do, it gets undone.
>
> … A lot of the time the session is just keeping her alive. Is just comforting her, helping her nervous system to have at least two hours where she's not in a state of terror, where she feels safe, and held, and cared about. A lot of the therapy is just spent doing that. It's just band aids, survival therapy.

In effect, a lack of safety kept Rosie within the initial or "first phase" of trauma therapy (Herman, 1992), but Leona found it difficult to connect Rosie with other potential supports or agencies that might improve her safety. Rosie refused to speak to police after a negative experience a number of years ago, in which a child part called a children's help line:

> The police came round to the house and discovered she was a woman in her thirties, just dismissed the whole thing. After that, she never trusted them again. That was it. She must have been just so wounded by that experience.

Leona's efforts to find medical care for Rosie fared poorly, after the general practitioner insisted that she was bound by mandatory reporting laws to report Rosie to the police.[3]

> I got her to agree to come to a GP [general practitioner] with me, because she was talking about stuff that was being done internally. And wounding her, and there ought to be evidence there. And I said, 'Well, if I came with you, would you allow a GP to look at you?'
>
> And she said, yes, she would, because she trusted me. We got to this GP in the clinic that I go to, who I thought I could trust, and as soon as we started telling the story, she said, 'Well you know I have to report this'. And I said, 'No you don't, she's an adult'. She said, 'Yes, I do. I have to report this, you know that. I'm sorry, I have to report this'. I was furious. So Rosie of course walked out and said, 'That's it, I'll never go do that again'.

While committed to Rosie as a client, Leona expressed despair at the prospect of improving Rosie's treatment trajectory while she was being targeted by a dedicated group of perpetrators, and while other agencies and services responded inappropriately to Rosie's complex presentation and needs. A number of professionals interviewed for this study described the paradoxical situation in which the efforts of adults to escape from the trauma of organized abuse were met with retraumatizing responses in mental health, law enforcement, and other settings. Social worker Charlotte said:

> It's my experience generally, the worse the abuse, the worse the system's response. But the more severe the abuse, the more likely the system isn't going to be able to manage it. And the response will be then turn on the client.

Mental health professionals working with this client group were not immune to such backlash, either from skeptical colleagues or from other agencies as they advocated on their client's behalf. A sexual assault manager interviewed for the study described this as "system abuse" and positioned it as amongst the most significant of the multiple traumatizations facing adult organized abuse victims. Addressing the impact of system abuse, it would seem, is crucial to securing the wellbeing and safety of adult organized abuse victims overall. The following discussion provides an overview of the responses of a range of agencies when

---

[3]All Australian states have mandatory reporting laws that require doctors to report child abuse where they have "reasonable grounds" to suspect or believe that a specific child has been, or is at risk of, abuse. The doctor in this instance is not required to report the sexual assault of an adult to the police, but may have felt obliged to report due to the likelihood that children were being victimized by the abusive group.

contacted by survivors or mental health professionals about adult organized abuse.

System responses to adult organized abuse

This section focuses on survivor encounters with (a) the police, (b) medical services, and (c) child protection services, drawing together some broad themes across survivor and practitioner interviews. Participants are of varying ages, and describing system responses from the early 1990s to the present day. These differences will be noted where appropriate.

Police and criminal justice system

It was fairly common for survivors to have had some contact with the police in relation to organized abuse. This may happen without the knowledge or consent of the survivor, generally with poor outcomes. For instance, one survivor was admitted to the emergency department of a public hospital after being abducted, assaulted and left semi-conscious on the side of the road, and the attending physician contacted police who then attempted to interview her in hospital. Traumatized and bedridden, she was unwilling to speak to them about the assault and they left exasperated.

Other victims actively sought out police assistance in maintaining their safety. However, a lack of training and understanding of complex trauma and dissociation amongst law enforcement was a major barrier to investigating and prosecuting adult organized abuse complaints. For instance, Claudia described how her complaint of organized abuse was quickly derailed when the investigating officer specializing in sexual offences was replaced with a non-specialist detective:

> I've got this strong sense of justice. I was sort of like, 'I need to tell the police, and get these twenty-plus people arrested, or at least one of them to send the message'. You know, like 'Let's tell the neighbours so their kids are safe' and all this sort of stuff.
>
> So I went to the police. Had initially had a really good experience with a woman in the sexual offenses unit. But she got moved. And then instead of being with the sexual offenses unit, my case went straight to general criminal investigation. And I got a real cowboy.

Following the appointment of a new detective, there were a number of changes in the investigation that made Claudia highly anxious. For instance, Claudia was obliged to attend a police station close to the suburb where much of her abuse took place, raising the prospect that perpetrators might see her as she entered the station. She was no longer permitted to provide her statement in writing, as the detective insisted that she continue her statement on video, which she found triggering. On at least two occasions, the detective visited Claudia at home without warning and against her explicit instructions. With the support of a pro bono lawyer and her psychiatrist, Claudia extricated herself from the investigation entirely, and it closed as a result.

Another significant barrier to making contact and establishing trust with police was alleged police involvement in organized abuse. Julia, a rape crisis worker, had been working for five years with a former police officer who refused to contact police about her own ongoing organized abuse because, when she was serving in the police force, she had been forced to participate in the abusive group and cover up their activities. Julia said:

> The woman described to me how she'd been in the police, and that she, being forced to do things to other people, and that's what made her feel unable to tell anybody [about her own abuse]. As a young woman she was recruited, she was a rookie. She was a young police officer and in uniform- she helped the men to do things.

This account dovetailed with the recollections of other survivors, who described adult organized abuse by men they were certain were serving police officers. Survivor participant Zoe made a formal complaint regarding the involvement of police officers in her organized abuse as an adult. The police investigation concluded that the sexual activity had taken place but was consensual. Trained from childhood to obey these men under threat of violence, Zoe did not resist when they came to her door. As she said, 'What are you supposed to do? These are, these are uniformed police officers that you're not supposed to say no to, and they have weapons, and they've got everything'. In the course of a police investigation into her complaint, her fear of the perpetrators and her dissociative patterns of compliance were misconstrued as consent.

B. Medical services

Survivors frequently required medical attention following abusive incidents, however, their atypical injuries and presentations could raise questions about their credibility in medical contexts. Health workers and doctors frequently assumed that their injuries were self-inflicted despite their complaints of victimization. Self-harm is indeed common amongst people with dissociative disorders (Middleton & Butler, 1998) who may be, in some instances, amnestic for the infliction of the injury. However, in this study, mental health workers were that concerned that the uncritical presumption of self-harm by health workers could obscure criminal victimization and legitimate safety concerns.

For instance, Maya was a psychiatrist working with a young woman who is presently extricating herself from organized abuse. This has triggered retaliation from the abusive group, including assaults that left burns and cuts to the client that Maya concluded could not have been self-inflicted. However, when the client presented at the emergency department after an assault, physical evidence was misdiagnosed as self-harm:

> Just before I started looking after her, the, the abuser came to the house and tortured her. He said, 'You're nothing but a filthy root' [Australian slang for sexual intercourse]. And took twigs, roots and leaves—like he had put—and inserted I think 12 or 15 large sticks into her vagina. All the way up, and she has gone to ED [emergency department] and she had them removed. Of course, they think she stuck them up there.

The correct assessment of such injuries is vital to ensure the appropriate treatment of the survivor. For instance, a client of Julia's had significant gynecological complications and Julia was worried about her impending surgery since the client was disclosing the current organized abuse. Julia's supervisor questioned whether the client's was disclosing actual events (rather than flashbacks or memories) so, with the client's permission, Julia contacted the woman's general practitioner. The doctor had over a decade of medical documentation of injuries consistent with the women's complaint of sadistic sexual violence. Julia recalled:

> [The client] had been seeing a doctor since she was a young woman. She gave me the name of the doctor, she said 'The doctor is ready to talk to you'. I rang the doctor, I confirmed. The doctor said that she is all prepared for if we got to court. She's got documentation of all the medical records, and she confirmed for me that this is real.

Medical confirmation of the client's disclosures of ongoing abuse had a number of important impacts. It changed how Julia supported the client to address her gynecological needs, so that surgery did not exacerbate her injuries or leave her vulnerable to further harm. It also gave Julia certainty that the client was presently unsafe rather than experiencing intensive flashbacks and memories. Finally, medical documentation provided another source of confirmation and evidence if the client wanted to press charges against her abusers. In this circumstance, the failure of either the mental health practitioner or the general practitioner to take the client's disclosures of ongoing organized abuse seriously could have had adverse implications, including the scheduling of major surgery during a period in which the client was at risk of sexual violence. This illustrates the importance of remaining open to the possibility of ongoing victimization, while nonetheless recognizing the frequency and complexity of self-harm in this population.

Child protection

Adult organized abuse raises important, and largely unaddressed, questions about the safety and protection of the children of victims. The specific patterns of victimization evident in adult organized abuse can be misunderstood by child protection agencies with serious implications for women and children. Richard, a psychiatrist, described a client married to a man, who was part of an organized group that abused her since childhood. He had sadistically assaulted her, resulting in her hospitalization on a number of occasions. The child protection officer accused the woman of injuring herself in front of her daughter, and permanently placed her daughter with the husband, despite advice from Richard and attending physicians that her injuries were not self-inflicted.

> [Child protection] have formed the belief that, oh, that the husband is wonderful, and that she's got a mental illness, and that she's self-harming, and that she needs to apologize to her daughter for self-harming. And, this is someone who's been actively, sadistically assaulted by someone who's trying to kill her.
>
> As of last week, child protection took the daughter away from her and put her in the hands of the husband. ... The hospital has now said that the nature of the injuries is that they're impossible to be self-inflicted, 'please do your job and find out who's doing it'.

The child protection officer, I have had a conversation with him, and then he tries to—Honestly, he tries then to completely misquote me to the patient. You know, "Your doctor agrees with us".

Other professionals described circumstances in which women experiencing organized abuse were either accused of self-harming or blamed for not leaving an abusive situation by child protection workers. Sexual assault worker Tamsin described this as a form of 'mother blaming' that denied adult organized abuse victims the support they needed to keep themselves or their children safe:

> Suddenly these clients, who've had really, really complex trauma histories, who've landed in DV [domestic violence], which isn't so unusual, and some of them with organized perpetrator group histories and some of them current—they suddenly come to the attention of child protection, who have taken their children. So we've gone, all of a sudden, it's back- flipped into mother blaming. And again, the perpetrators are invisible over here.

Nonetheless, child protection services can play a vital role in supporting women to escape from organized abuse and protecting their children. In the mid-1990s, Rhea was extracting herself from the abusive group that had abused her since childhood and was abusing her son. During this period, she endured a period of heightened threats and sexual assaults that included break-ins at her home. Her therapist was able to broker a placement for her son through a child protection manager who had experience in the area and was supportive of Rhea's aspirations to escape organized abuse.

> In the year that it was really bad, it got so bad that they took, they took my son into care. Child protection took my son into care. My therapist had to disclose to social services what was going on in terms of the threats that were being made against me and the things that were happening. And so they took him into care.

> There was one person that knew, she only, my therapist contacted the one person that understood what was going on in this area, who was a child protection manager called Vicki. Vickie had been involved in the removal of kids from a famous cult, and she'd done quite a lot of training.

In this instance, Rhea's victimization was acknowledged (rather than dismissed or misconstrued), and she was not blamed for her own ongoing abuse or indeed for the abuse of her child. Nonetheless, child protection recognized the danger to her son and took appropriate action. This enabled Rhea to focus on establishing her own safety, which included working intensely with her therapist, and cooperating with a larger police operation that she credits with bringing organized abuse to an end. Her son was returned to her care and she was able to raise him safely and continue her life free from victimization.

Discussion

Clinical treatment for the dissociative disorders has developed considerably over the last thirty years with outcome studies demonstrating significant gains across multiple clinical domains (Brand, Classen, McNary, & Zaveri, 2009). However, the preliminary findings of this study suggest that the responsiveness of multiple systems to dissociative adults has not kept pace with treatment improvements, although they are a high-needs group who often come to the attention of a range of agencies. In this study, the professional and survivor cohorts described a lack of consistency in service responses to adult organized abuse across mental health, law enforcement, medical and child protection agencies. A supportive response to a complaint or disclosure of adult organized abuse was largely a matter of luck. It was more common for the professional and survivor cohorts to describe trying to manage ongoing victimization and mental illness against the broader backdrop of systems and services that did not recognize either dissociation or organized abuse. Both cohorts described the difficulties in maintaining therapeutic boundaries and a sense of perspective during periods of crisis in the absence of a broader network of support and protection.

The balance between enhancing the survivor's wellbeing and autonomy while managing and reducing their risk of victimization was a difficult one for both survivors and professionals to strike. The dominant presumption that, upon reaching the age of majority, adults are independent and largely autonomous beings making choices of their own free will provides a poor lens through which to understand the actions of adult organized abuse victims. What may appear, to an external observer, to be an adult's "decision" to participate in sexual activity (however unusual or sadistic) or to engage in some other risky behavior is in fact better understood as a coerced response underpinned by a history of abuse, fear and manipulation. Some agencies treated the adult organized abuse victim as hyper-responsible when, for instance, they faulted her for her injuries, the risks to her children, or her apparent "non-compliance" with police instructions. Other agencies characterized the victim as incapable of responsibility by labeling her as "crazy", delusional or entirely passive in response to victimization. Such polarized responses could intensify dynamics of humiliation and self-blame, and further compromise the recovery and safety of the adult organized abuse victim. Survivors and practitioners alike remarked upon the irony that adults might escape the abusive system of organized abuse only to become enmeshed in another series of abusive systems.

Conclusion

The preliminary findings of the study suggest that there is a need for increased training and capacity building for a range of systems and agencies in contact with adult organized abuse victims. Positive outcomes for victims and their children can be secured when cooperation between relevant agencies created a context of relative safety. However, there were a number of fracture points evident in service and system responses. A lack of recognition of dissociation or organized abuse, and the stereotyping of women with mental illness as liars and fantasists, resulted in unconstructive skepticism, and sometimes outright hostility, to women reporting adult organized abuse. Where evidence of organized abuse was available, it was often used to impugn the victim's credibility e.g. injuries after assaults were misdiagnosed as self-harm, and dissociative compliance was misconstrued as consent to sexual activity. This maintained women and their children in a state of ongoing vulnerability to organized abuse, and could lead to misinformed child protection and medical interventions with potentially deleterious impacts. Training and knowledge of organized abuse was the critical factor that distinguished a supportive and effective intervention from an ineffectual or harmful one. This has implications not only for clinical practice and treatment but also for policy and service frameworks, as adult organized abuse is a specific pattern of victimization that is poorly addressed within existing responses to violence against women and children.

References

Brand, B. L., Classen, C. C., McNary, S. W., & Zaveri, P. (2009). A review of dissociative disorders treatment studies. *The Journal of Nervous and Mental Disease, 197* (9), 646–654. doi:10.1097/NMD.0b013e3181b3afaa

Braun, V., & Clarke, V. (2006). Using thematic analysis in psychology. *Qualitative Research in Psychology, 3* (2), 77–101. doi:10.1191/1478088706qp063oa

Chu, J. A. (2011). *Rebuilding shattered lives: Treating complex PTSD and dissociative disorders.* Hoboken, NJ: John Wiley & Sons.

Coffey, A. (2014). *Real voices: CSE in Greater Manchester, an independent inquiry.* http://www.gmpcc.org.uk/down-to-business/coffey-inquiry/.

Dalenberg, C. J., Hyland, K. Z., Cuevas, C. A., Eisen, M., & Quas, J. (2002). Sources of fantastic elements in allegations of abuse by adults and children. In M. L. Eisen, J. A. Quas, & G. S. Goodman (Eds.), *Memory and suggestibility in the forensic interview* (pp. 185–204). Mahwah, NJ & London: Lawrence Erlbaum Associates.

Fraser, G. (1997). Ritual abuse: Lessons learnt as a therapist. In G. Fraser (Ed.), *The dilemma of ritual abuse: Cautions and guides for therapists* (pp. 119–136). Washington, DC: American Psychiatric Press.

Goodwin JM. (1994). Sadistic abuse: Definition, recognition and treatment. In: Sinason, V. (Ed.) *Treating survivors of satanist abuse* (pp. 33–44). London & New York: Routledge.

Herman, J. (1992). *Trauma and recovery*. New York, NY: Basic Books.

ISSTD. (2011). Guidelines for treating dissociative identity disorder in adults, third revision. *Journal of Trauma & Dissociation, 12* (2), 115–187. doi:10.1080/15299732.2011.537247

Jaye, A. (2014). Independent inquiry into child sexual exploitation in Rotherham 1997-2013, http://www.rotherham.gov.uk/downloads/file/1407/independent_inquiry_cse_in_rotherham

Middleton, W. (2013). Ongoing incestuous abuse during adulthood. *Journal of Trauma & Dissociation, 14* (3), 251–272. doi:10.1080/15299732.2012.736932

Middleton, W. (2015). Tipping points and the accommodation of the abuser: The case of ongoing incestuous abuse during adulthood. *International Journal of Crime, Justice and Social Democracy, 4* (2), 4–17. doi:10.5204/ijcjsd.v4i2.210

Middleton, W., & Butler, J. (1998). Dissociative identity disorder: An Australian series. *Australian and New Zealand Journal of Psychiatry, 2* (6), 794–804. doi:10.3109/00048679809073868

Miller, A. (2012). *Healing the unimaginable: Treating ritual abuse and mind control*. London, UK: Karnac.

Salter, M. (2012). The role of ritual in the organised abuse of children. *Child Abuse Review, 21* (6), 440–451. doi:10.1002/car.2215

Salter, M. (2013a). *Organised sexual abuse*. London, UK: Glasshouse/Routledge.

Salter, M. (2013b). Through a glass, darkly: Representation and power in research on organised abuse. *Qualitative Sociology Review, 9* (3), 152–166.

Salter, M., & Richters, J. (2012). Organised abuse: A neglected category of sexual abuse with significant lifetime mental healthcare sequelae. *Journal of Mental Health, 21* (5), 499–508. doi:10.3109/09638237.2012.682264

Schwartz, H. L. (2013). *The alchemy of wolves and sheep: A relational approach to internalized perpetration in complex trauma survivors*. London & New York: Routledge.

Wolak, J. (2015). Technology-facilitated organized abuse: An examination of law enforcement arrest cases. *International Journal for Crime, Justice & Social Democracy, 4* (2), 18–33. doi:10.5204/ijcjsd.v4i2.227

Young, W. C. (1992). Recognition and treatment of survivors reporting ritual abuse. In D. K. Sakheim, & S. E. Devine (Eds.), *Out of darkness: Exploring Satanism and ritual abuse* (pp. 249–278). New York, NY: Lexington Books.

Treatment strategies for programming and ritual abuse

Colin Ross, MD

ABSTRACT
Individuals in treatment for dissociative identity disorder not uncommonly describe childhood involvement in organized, multi-perpetrator ritual abuse. They described being "programmed" by the perpetrators and feel that the programming is out of their control. The author has developed a set of treatment strategies and interventions for such cases. These are based on the principle of therapeutic neutrality and can be used no matter what assumptions the therapist makes about the historical accuracy of the memories and beliefs. In ritual abuse cases, there are commonly "cult alters" who express allegiance to and identification with the perpetrators, and who state the ideology of the cult as personal beliefs. Often, the host personality holds and expresses the opposite half of the ambivalent attachment to the perpetrators: the host takes the position of helpless, powerless victim of the cult alters and programming, and wants to be rescued and "deprogrammed" by the therapist. This is a victim–rescuer–perpetrator triangle re-enactment. The perpetrator introjects involved in the re-enactment can be engaged in the therapy, and can become allies in recovery and the process of integration. Techniques for accomplishing this are described.

Ross (1994, 1995, 1997, 2007a, 2007b, 2008) and Ross and Halpern (2009) describe principles for the treatment of complex dissociative disorders including individuals who report childhood involvement in ritual abuse (RA), and who believe they have been programmed by cult members, or by the CIA or military (Ross, 2006). The purpose of the present paper is to summarize these principles and the author's clinical experience working with RA and CIA/military mind control cases since 1992. Most of the cases have involved Satanic ritual abuse (SRA), although some patients describe RA occurring in Masonic, Mormon, Christian, New Age, and other cults.

Prior to moving to the United States in 1991, I had not encountered a RA case, or a case of CIA/military mind control. I had heard about such cases from colleagues while attending conferences in the United States. All I had heard about in Canada, in my clinical practice, was what sounded like teenage dabbling in the occult. I had not been told about involvement in multigenerational Satanic cults that sacrificed babies in ceremonies used teenage girls as breeders, and were run by well-organized adults. I had not been told about SRA ceremonies involving altars, goblets, robes, ritual chanting, invocations of Satan, ritual sex with children, and torture and sacrifice of children. These components define SRA in my vocabulary.

Upon my arrival in the United States in 1991, I began working on a Dissociative Disorders Unit specializing in multiple personality disorder (MPD). From early 1992 until 1994–1995, many patients with MPD described involvement in multigenerational SRA cults. By 1995, the percentage of patients describing such backgrounds had declined from a high of ~75% of the cases to under 10%. In the ensuing 20 years, the inpatient treatment program has been renamed, the Trauma Program, due to a focus on a wider range of DSM disorders than just the dissociative disorders, and MPD has been renamed as dissociative identity disorder (DID). The percentage of patients describing SRA in the Trauma Program is now under 5%, but has not declined to zero.

In the early 1990s, we spent a great deal of time at staff meetings talking about and debating individual cases and SRA in general. The staff included believers and nonbelievers in SRA, and we had to figure out how to proceed clinically in the absence of any peer-reviewed literature, professional guidelines, or professional books on how to treat such cases. At present, in 2016, all staff members take the principle of therapeutic neutrality for granted, we do not have debates between believers and nonbelievers, and the basic treatment approach is agreed upon. The same applies for patients reporting CIA and military mind control, and RA in other types of cults, who are fewer in number than the SRA cases in 2016, but with whom we still work.

There are still no peer-reviewed guidelines for treatment of RA cases available in the English-language literature; a PubMed search located only two papers on the topics of RA and Satanism published in the twenty-first century (Matthew & Barron, 2015; Precin, 2011). One of these is a single case report and the other describes the results of interviews with a series of self-reported RA survivors. Several academic books discuss RA (Fraser, 1997; Chu, 1998; Mollon, 1999; Salter, 1999; Sinason, 2011), but none of these books provide operationalized, manualized, or detailed guidelines on methods and techniques of treatment. None of these books were available during the height of concern about Satanism in the first half of the 1990s. Up until the present time, there is no discussion of, or accepted definition of "programming" in the peer-reviewed literature.

Although the majority of RA patients I have encountered describe growing up in multigenerational SRA cults, I have also treated cases of Masonic, Mormon, Christian, and New Age RA. In addition, I have seen several cases of RA in psychotherapy/recovery cults. I will refer to RA in general most of the time, and SRA in particular when talking specifically about SRA.

The therapeutic principles I describe are the ones I would use for any form of RA.

My definition of RA, for therapeutic purposes, is that it takes place in a destructive cult as defined by Singer (1995). Features of the cult may include a charismatic leader, a hierarchy of initiates with an inner circle at the top, extensive control of the individual's life space, deceptive recruitment into the organization in cases not born into the cult, questioning the doctrine of the cult is defined as lack of faith and commitment, and specific techniques of control and influence are employed. These may include sensory isolation and deprivation, good cop–bad cop techniques, hypnosis, drugs, forced memorization of cult materials, threat of death, sexual abuse, ceremonies to enforce submission and compliance, and defining outsiders as evil, ignorant or unenlightened.

I will discuss the meaning of the word "programming" below. Many RA survivors believe that they are "programmed" and use that word to describe implanted commands and codes put in place by their perpetrators. Although "programming" is not a defined or accepted word in the peer-reviewed literature, it is a term commonly used by survivors, which is why I use it in therapy.

Most of the RA controversy has been focused on SRA; I decline to estimate what percentage of SRA cases is "real." The reasons for this are: I do not objectively know what percentage of cases is real; it is not my job as a clinician to make this determination; I do not have the resources or expertise to investigate such cases; there is no point in interviewing alleged perpetrators because they would deny the SRA whether it was real or not real; a determination of whether a case was "real" or not would not affect the goals, principles, or techniques of treatment; and, I maintain therapeutic neutrality. In my experience, people who press for an estimate usually hold polarized all-or-nothing, black-and-white positions on whether SRA is "real" or not, and either want to congratulate you for agreeing with them, or vilify you for disagreeing. Debates about whether SRA is "real" or not are irrelevant to planning and conducting treatment within my approach.

I have placed "real" in brackets because "real versus not real" is itself a set of unreal dichotomized options. It is doubtful that any psychiatric patient's story is 100% real or 100% unreal because, on the one hand, memory is error-prone, and on the other hand, even the most paranoid delusional person still has a grasp of quite a bit of reality, and remembers where he was born, his parents' names, and so on.

The polarization of preconceived opinions about SRA is illustrated by two reader reviews of *Satanic Ritual Abuse. Principles of Treatment* (Ross, 1995) that were posted on www.amazon.com in the 1990s, one after the other. One reviewer attacked the author for not believing the survivors, while the other reviewer attacked the author for believing in SRA and fomenting an epidemic of false memories. Each reviewer had failed to read the book, and each was using the author as a kind of Rorschach inkblot test, projecting personal content onto him.

I will now describe my approach to RA and CIA/military mind control cases. I will refer to the client as female throughout because almost all DID RA clients I have seen are female. I will use *client* and *patient* interchangeably, since the same person is a patient when hospitalized, but a client when seen in an outpatient practice with a Master's or PhD-level therapist.

Principles of treatment in ritual abuse cases

The principle of therapeutic neutrality

The motto that sums up my approach to therapeutic neutrality is, "A strange game. The only winning move is not to play." This is a statement made by the computer, Joshua, in the 1983 movie, *War Games*. Joshua was a NORAD computer who was playing a game of thermonuclear war in the real world. He had taken control of the NORAD computer system and was about to launch nuclear missiles at Russia. The hero of the movie engaged him in a game of tic-tac-toe. In his efforts to solve the game, Joshua diverted all of his resources to figuring out how a person could win if the opponent's first move was to put an X or an O in a corner box. He shut down the thermonuclear war game in his efforts, disaster was averted, and Joshua made his pronouncement about nonengagement in the game.

In therapy, therapeutic neutrality means neither believing nor disbelieving. In the United States in general, people often take extreme polarized positions and assume that everyone who doesn't agree with them must be taking the opposite extreme position. As members of that culture, trauma survivors often assume there are only two possibilities concerning their therapist: (1) you actively believe me or (2) you actively disbelieve me. If the therapist does not directly say, "I believe you," then the therapist must be secretly disbelieving the person's trauma story.

In fact, in this approach, the therapist takes a meta-position and neither believes nor disbelieves. There are several reasons for adopting this position: the therapist doesn't actually know for an objective fact that the RA did or did not happen; there is no possibility of proving or disproving the reality of the RA with the therapist's time and resources, nor is this the therapist's job; adopting either the believer or disbeliever position aligns the therapist with some alters in the system against other alters; believing the client creates a trauma-driven transference conflict, namely that there is a perpetrator lurking behind the pleasant façade, who will sooner or later come out and disbelieve and betray the client; and "validating" the RA memories places the therapist in the superior adult position, and the client in the dependent child's position—the dependent child requires validation from the powerful adult, and cannot provide it for herself.

Taking the disbeliever position results in a different set of transference–countertransference distortions. The authority figure—therapist—now agrees with the perpetrator on the necessity of the client saying that nothing happened; the client is bad and does not deserve to be understood; the believer alters hide in the internal world; and the child client has to obey and comply with the worldview of the authoritative adult.

All these problems generated by the therapist either believing or disbelieving distort the transference–countertransference dyad no matter what the historical reality of the RA. Additionally, in my experience, therapists who take the believer position are much more prone to burnout, paranoia, and vicarious traumatization. It feels good to have a therapist who "believes" you in the short term, and it is natural to want "validation" after a childhood of betrayal, abuse, and neglect. The error is for the therapist to believe that aligning with the client, supporting her, and validating her feelings requires validating the memories.

The fact is that the therapist does not know whether the RA did or did not happen. Sooner or later, the believer therapist will validate "memories" that are not historically real. Reciprocally, sooner or later, the disbeliever therapist will invalidate memories that are historically real. For instance, a therapist who does not believe in RA could invalidate memories of involvement in child pornography with strange costumes, pentagrams, and ritual sex. I have no objective proof that such pornography exists, but it is hard to imagine that it would not, given the barbarity and depravity of all child pornography. Why would organized sex offenders decline to stimulate themselves with "Satanic" settings for their pornography?

The job of the therapist is to hold on to both possibilities: the RA memories are real, and they are not real. Aligning with one option or the other causes the problems outlined above.

Memories are not the primary focus in therapy

In my approach, trauma memories are not the primary focus of therapy. Certainly, a trauma narrative is constructed and the abuse is talked about, but the main targets of therapy include: the self-blame and self-hatred, called *the locus of control shift* in Trauma Model Therapy (Ross, 2007a; Ross & Halpern, 2009); the conflicted, ambivalent attachment to the perpetrators; self-defeating and addictive coping strategies; making a serious commitment to the work of recovery; mourning the loss of the childhood one never actually had; setting healthy boundaries; and victim–perpetrator triangle re-enactments.

The fact that the trauma memories are not the primary focus reduces the need for the therapist to take either the believer or disbeliever position. It reduces the risk of traumatic abreactions and exacerbation of posttraumatic stress disorder symptoms, and reduces the resulting need to act out to dampen down the hyperarousal.

Using black-and-white thinking, both therapists and clients might misinterpret this principle as an absolute injunction against talking about childhood trauma. That is a cognitive error. What is actually involved is a shift in emphasis, not a complete abandonment of talking about the trauma.

The problem of attachment to the perpetrator

A core principle of Trauma Model Therapy is *the problem of attachment to the perpetrator*. The abused and neglected child automatically bonded and attached to her parents because of the physiology of mammalian attachment. This was a biological necessity, not an option. However, when the primary attachment figures were also the primary perpetrators, a second biologically encoded reaction was set in motion; the child feared and hated the perpetrators and withdrew from them. This approach–avoidance conflict was the normal, unavoidable consequence of the problem of attachment to the perpetrator. The solution to the problem was dissociation: the child could not afford to see the whole picture. In order to maintain attachment, and protect the child's attachment system, the child had to split her psyche in two, figuratively, not literally. She had to create the illusion, from the perspective of her attachment systems, that mom and dad were OK. To create this illusion, the perpetrator mom and dad had to be dissociated and packaged in another subsystem of the psyche, as stated in *Betrayal Trauma Theory* (Freyd, 1999).

In the client with DID and a RA history (irrespective of the historical reality of that history), the system includes a host personality, and various subsystems of personalities. There may be one clearly defined host personality, a set of alters who act as host, or a more chaotic and less clearly defined host function. I will use a one-clear-host system to illustrate the treatment approach.

In SRA cases, there will almost always be "dark side" alters who want to return to the cult and participate in human sacrifices. They have pledged allegiance to Satan and the cult leader, who is usually their father. The host personality believes that these alters have been programmed by the cult. She, the host, wants these alters deprogrammed by the therapist. The host takes the victim position, sees the cult alters as perpetrator-persecutors, and wants to be rescued by the deprogrammer therapist. If the therapist agrees to "deprogram" the client, he or she is acting as the good deprogrammer who is undoing the programming put in place by the bad cult leader. The client remains in the position of dependent child who is controlled and manipulated by the powerful adult.

It took me quite a while, in the 1990s, to reframe this dilemma for myself, and then for the DID patients. The cult alters, I realized, were actually holding and expressing the positive attachment to the father, but in distorted language. The cult alters said that they wanted to go kill babies with their father. Often, they planned to do so next week or month, but thought they would do so in 1973, not realizing that over 20 years had passed and their father had died in the meantime.

What were the evil, programmed cult alters saying, translated into normal English?

> "I want to spend time with dad, hang out with him, do stuff he likes to do, and have him be proud of me."

Translated, this doesn't sound very evil or Satanic.

The cult alters were holding the biologically normal mammalian attachment to their father. The Christian host personality was defending against the pain and grief of this unfulfilled positive attachment with a triple defensive system: the alters were not her, they were separate people; the alters were Satanists while she was a Christian; and, the alters were programmed and she was not. The host failed to appreciate that the alters were part of her, and part of her survival strategy, and were holding her feelings for her. When the cult alters said that they wanted to kill babies, this made it easy for the host personality to disavow any positive attachment to her father.

The painful truth of the traumatic childhood remained, however: I loved the people who hurt me, and, I was hurt by the people I loved. This attachment conflict could not be solved by a trapped, dependent child. It could only be parceled out into separate modules or compartments. The treatment interventions include explaining all of this to the host personality and orienting the cult alters to the body and the present. Gradually, the cult alters begin to consider the possibility that, in the present, they could decide to do something different. Given that there has been no cult involvement for 20 years, and the father—cult leader— is dead, it might now be feasible to consider "changing jobs"—taking on new roles and tasks, being more flexible, having fun, and participating in normal life in the present. In 2015, the cult alters, who are usually children or teenagers, can easily be sold on the benefits of smart phones, computers, and video games. All these provide evidence that it is not the 1970s or 1980s now.

If the therapist did not maintain therapeutic neutrality, concerning both the memories and the attachment conflicts, it would not be possible to form a treatment alliance with the cult alters, orient them to the present, and resolve their trauma. They would remain hidden enemies in the back of the system. My goal is to make friends with everyone in the system. When doing so, I am modeling for the host personality a new way that she could relate to her system. I am working with the host personality to help her develop empathy with her parts, meaning with her self. The host has to become the nurturing mother for herself and her parts that her mother failed to be.

I might ask the host, who believes in the reality of the SRA and the power of the programming, what would have happened if, in the middle of a Satanic ceremony, she had suddenly stopped what she was doing, and said, "You guys suck. I'm not doing this anymore."

The answer is that she would have been killed.

> "So," I say, "in order to survive, you had to play the role of cooperative, programmed child perfectly, so perfectly that you fooled both them and yourself."
>
> "I guess so. I never looked at it that way," responds the host personality.
>
> "Right, and who played the role of programmed cult alter perfectly? You?"
>
> "Not me. It was them."
>
> "So they did what was necessary to help you survive. They were part of your survival strategy. But now they're stuck in the past and need help getting to the present."
>
> "OK, I'm starting to get it."

Meantime, in the background, the cult alters are overwhelmed with happiness and relief that the host personality might finally start to care for them. They likely won't admit it at first, but they will sooner rather than later. Rather than defining their hesitancy as *resistance*, I define it as *street smarts.* They have been betrayed many, many times by older people, so it would be dumb to trust the host too much too fast. The fact that they don't trust the host proves that they are smart, not that they are uncooperative.

There may be alters in the system who do not believe that the RA is real, which it may not be. No professional skeptic, in my experience, can match the intensity and tenacity of skeptical alters inside RA systems. The overarching principle is that the answers are inside the client. The therapist doesn't have the answers as to what happened in outside reality and what is an inside nightmare.

Let's consider two scenarios: (1) the RA really happened and (2) it is all made up. If it really happened, it is not hard to understand why the client has ambivalent attachment to her father: he killed babies. Highly conflicted, ambivalent attachment to such a father is unavoidable. On the other hand, if the RA is entirely made up, it's safe to say that it symbolizes a highly ambivalent attachment to the father. Why would a woman who grew up in a healthy, normal family imagine that her father killed babies and sexually abused her in Satanic ceremonies, and then believe that these imaginings are historical facts?

It doesn't matter which scenario is true. The targets of therapy are the conflicted, ambivalent attachment, and the guilt, grief, anger, and self-blame that go along with it. This set of feelings and cognitive errors is in place in the present, no matter what actually happened a long time ago.

I have worked with RA survivors who have become integrated and no longer have DID. Some have decided that the RA was real, some have decided that it was all symbolic and never happened in the outside world, and some are uncertain but at peace with the uncertainty: all the more reason to maintain therapeutic neutrality throughout the therapy.

Deprogramming without deprogramming

As stated above, there is no accepted definition of the term "programming" in the peer-reviewed literature, nor is there any peer-reviewed literature on how to treat it. When patients say that they have been "programmed," they generally mean that their perpetrators have deliberately implanted hypnotic codes that can be triggered externally through hand gestures, tones on the telephone, written messages, or other means. The "programs" are orders to report back to the cult, commit suicide, attend rituals, or carry out other instructions. Along with the programming, according to the patients, alter personalities loyal to the cult have been deliberately created by the perpetrators through torture, abuse, trickery, drugs, hypnosis, and other means. Not all patients reporting RA believe they have been "programmed;" however, the majority hold that belief. In the absence of any accepted definition of the term, I use this patient-generated definition of "programming" in my therapeutic work because that is what most patients mean by the term.

I advocate what I call *deprogramming without deprogramming* (Ross, 1995). I receive emails from people looking for a deprogrammer. I always advise them to try to find a skilled trauma therapist with good boundaries. In my experience, people who claim to be deprogrammers by and large do not publish, do not present their work at conferences, do not talk to mainstream therapists, and have no public treatment outcome data of any kind, even at the single case report level. They use techniques that are not described anywhere in the peer-reviewed literature. They create regression, paranoia, dependency, and increased dissociation. No doubt there are exceptions, but this is my experience, based on working clinically with DID patients who have previously been treated by deprogrammers.

Survivors who have been to deprogrammers are usually highly symptomatic. They usually take the stance of being helpless victims of their programming, and take a passive position, awaiting the prestidigitations of the deprogrammer, who unearths an endless series of internal keys, ciphers, codes, subsystems, and programmed alters. If the countertransference is healthy, it is possible that considerable healing can take place due to non-specific features of the countertransference, such as accurate empathy, congruence, and unconditional positive regard. In my experience, such outcomes are the exception rather than the rule, although I have encountered them.

When somebody tells me that they "have programming," I ask them what they mean by that, since different people mean different things. The survivor usually explains that she is helpless because the programming was put into her by the cult leader (or CIA doctor) and it controls her brain autonomously. She doesn't know how it works and can't control it.

I point out that if the cult leader and the programming were really in control, she wouldn't be sitting here talking to me about it. I tell her that I assume they didn't put in any *talk to Dr. Ross about us programs*. So, she is one step ahead of the programming simply because we are talking about it. I then demystify and de-catastrophize the programming by pointing out that we are all programmed. When I stub my toe, I don't say "ouch" in Swahili. I say it in English because I am programmed to speak English. Similarly, we are all programmed to like different clothes and hairstyles (thankfully) from what we liked in the 1970s. So programming at that level is just part of life.

The next level of programming is the non-cult incest father who said, "This is our special secret, Princess."

The child now has "special princess programming" that instructs her to keep the secret, but there is nothing mysterious about this. Keeping the secret follows from attachment and loyalty to the perpetrator, even if there were no threats involved. The RA survivor's programmer-perpetrators were more organized and systematic, but basically did the same thing. The RA survivor is not in a separate category of programmed person compared to everyone else: it's just a matter of degree. All of this is an effort to de-catatrophize the "programming," demystify it, and make it seem like something that can be worked on in therapy using conventional methods of treatment.

Then I will ask what the programming is made out of: wood, steel, plastic? The survivor is using magical child thinking and believes that a foreign machine was inserted into her brain. I point out that the programming was created by her own mind in response to what the programmers were telling her. It is part of her survival strategy. Nothing was literally inserted through her skull (this strategy fails if the person believes she has an implanted microchip). The person believes she is a victim of her own mind.

The target of the therapy is not the historical reality or nonreality of the RA. It is the helpless victim position adopted by the survivor.

Conclusions

For the reasons outlined above, I always recommend that the treatment of people DID and RA or CIA/military mind control memories should receive regular DID therapy. The therapist should maintain good boundaries, keep good records, seek consultation when necessary, and have a life outside therapy in order to prevent burnout and vicarious traumatization.

References

Chu, J. A. (1998). *Rebuilding shattered lives. The responsible treatment of post-traumatic and dissociative disorders*. New York, NY: John Wiley & Sons.

Fraser, G. A. (1997). *The dilemma of ritual abuse: Cautions and guides for therapists*. Washington, DC: American Psychiatric Press.

Freyd, J. J. (1999). *Betrayal trauma. The forgetting of childhood abuse*. Cambridge, MA: Harvard University Press.

Matthew, L., & Barron, I. G. (2015). Participatory action research on hel-seeking behaviors of self-defined ritual abuse survivors: A brief report. *Journal of Child Sexual Abuse*, *24*, 429–443. doi:10.1080/10538712.2015.1029104

Mollon, P. (1999). *Multiple selves, multiple voices: Working with trauma, violation and dissociation*. New York, NY: John Wiley.

Precin, P. (2011). Return to work: A case of PTSD, dissociative identity disorder, and satanic ritual abuse. *Work*, *38*, 57–66.

Ross, C. A. (1994). *The Osiris complex. Case studies of multiple personality disorder*. Toronto, ON: University of Toronto Press.

Ross, C. A. (1995). *Satanic ritual abuse. Principles of treatment*. Toronto, ON: University of Toronto Press.

Ross, C. A. (1997). *Dissociative identity disorder. Diagnosis, clinical features, and treatment of multiple personalities* (2nd ed.). New York, NY: John Wiley & Sons.

Ross, C. A. (2006). *The C.I.A. doctors. Human rights violations by American psychiatrists*. Richardson, TX: Manitou Communications.

Ross, C. A. (2007a). *The trauma model. A solution to the problem of comorbidity in psychiatry*. Richardson, TX: Manitou Communications.

Ross, C. A. (2007b). *Moon shadows. Stories of trauma and recovery*. Richardson, TX: Manitou Communications.

Ross, C. A. (2008). *Military mind control. A story of trauma and recovery*. Richardson, TX: Manitou Communications.

Ross, C. A., & Halpern, N. (2009). *Trauma model therapy. A treatment approach for trauma, dissociation, and complex comorbidity*. Richardson, TX: Manitou Communications.

Salter, A. (1999). *Transforming trauma: A guide to understanding and treating adult survivors of child sexual abuse*. New York, NY: Sage.

Sinason, V. (2011). *Attachment, trauma and multiplicity: Working with dissociative identity disorder*. New York, NY: Routledge.

Singer, M. (1995). *Cults in our midst. The hidden menace in our everyday lives*. San Francisco, CA: Jossey-Bass.

Issues in consultation for treatments with distressed activated abuser/protector self-states in dissociative identity disorder

Richard A. Chefetz

ABSTRACT

The identified "problem self-state" in a dissociative disorder consultation is like the identified patient in a family therapy; the one who is identified may have an assigned role to be blamed which serves the function of deflecting the activities of painful self-states in other family members. In consultation, the "family" includes the therapist in addition to the patient. When the state identified as a problem self-state is an abuser/protector self-state, complications often involve the profound nature of transference–countertransference enactments between patient and therapist, the delusion of separateness, chronic and acute threats of suicide, negative therapeutic reactions, and the evocation of intense negativity. They also involve affect phobia in both patient and therapist, and the emergence of intense shame in the clinical dyad amongst additional potential burdens in these complicated treatments. The task of the consultant is to protect both patient and therapist from an untoward outcome while relieving the painful burdens entailed by the treatment. The typical core dynamic of the abuser/protector state is as a repository for shame/humiliation welded to anger/rage. This dynamic, and others, must be understood in order to resolve these impasses and create useful movement toward growth in both patient and therapist.

Many years ago I tried to read Alice Miller's book, then named Prisoners of Childhood. It was not a great seller until it was renamed The Drama of the Gifted Child (Miller, 1981). That was a title much more congenial to people who were looking for an emotional lift. But why prisoners? Who was Miller really writing about? The first chapter was 32 pages and it took me 6 months and several starts to get through it. It was the story of a child who tried and tried to help his distressed mother to avoid collapse; it was his job to prop her up. He became parentified (Gelinas, 1983). Miller was writing about the psychological prototype of a future psychotherapist; frustrated child turned adult clinician. That's why it took me so long to get through it the first time. Who would want to appreciate their adult career was a repetition of a childhood failure?

Now as a psychiatrist I repeat the past in 50-minute aliquots. Doing consultation work is like including Dad in the picture too. Dyads are easy compared to triadic relationships. If the task is to fix the couple, then failure is inevitable. The only solution is to set in motion a new capacity for Mom and Dad to see how they interact and for them to leave the consultation with some hope for being able to figure out how to live with each other after all. The rest is up to them.

Consultation work in the dissociative disorders may be no different with a clinical couple, and even the wisest clinicians get into snafus that can boggle the imagination. Respecting both the patient's and clinician's abilities and willingness to engage in the consultation process is of the essence, and it speaks to a degree of openness that is required to do this work in a psychodynamic frame. Actually, I'm not sure there is another frame that can as effectively address the real needs of our dissociative disorder patients. I think that will become visible as I next spell out the elements of the consultation perspective.

The several specific areas of inquiry addressed below are some of the thorniest and most common problems clinicians encounter in practice. It's not that there aren't numerous others, it's just that these are particularly prone to disabling a treatment. The following potentially deadly issues are explored: *enactment between patient and therapist, the delusion of separateness, chronic and acute threats of suicide, negative therapeutic reactions, and intense negativity, affect phobia in both patient and clinician*, and *the problem of shame welded to rage*.

Enactment

There is an early literature on enactment that is informative. There was a one person model where the clinician and patient were less than equals in contributing to the fray (Chused, 1991; McLaughlin, 1991) but the compelling nature of the call to action in those treatments was clearly spelled out. Those actions could be understood from an additional perspective as consisting of scripts (Tomkins, 1995) as well as being role responsive (Ryle, 1999). In other words, in this early model both patient and clinician had their core conflictual scripts (Luborsky & Crits-Christoph, 1998) activated by the unconscious material in the patient.

In the psychoanalytic realm, processes like projective identification were called into play as representing the patient putting something into the analyst akin to a foreign body which the analyst would then struggle with to metabolize and then successfully and gently present back to the patient in a more coherent form (Ogden, 1989). Elsewhere (Chefetz, 2015) I've proposed that nothing is put into the therapist by the patient, it is *already* roughly present in the therapist in a related form. This is consistent with a more recent two-person psychology of enactment that has been highly developed and then extended (Bromberg, 2006, 2009, 2011; Stern, 1997, 2004, 2009, 2013).

Dissociative process in the analyst occludes painful emotion. Two people in the consultation room are each intolerant of a specific feeling, state, or script. Often the feeling is the same, but from a different origin. There is a knowledge in the treatment that something isn't working, and it is likely that both clinician and patient believe the other is at the center of what's stuck. In three chapters that include a fully verbatim session, this kind of process is illustrated (Chefetz, 2015). It can be very messy and there are times when either the patient or therapist may take the lead in identifying the sources of the difficulties. A significant level of trust must first be established before this kind of exchange can be tolerated. What is required is maintaining curiosity (the opposite of dissociation) in the face of emotional discomfort or pain, and attempting to understand what is being played out in the action between patient and therapist.

Shame, contempt, humiliation, anger, rage, helplessness, and hopelessness are typical of the feeling states conjured in both patient and therapist as enactment opens to view. In a well-established and respectful psychotherapy, it may still be very difficult to tolerate the emergence of these kinds of feelings. The therapist's honesty and potential willingness to disclose their feelings and thoughts may be more than sometimes useful; some authors have argued disclosure may be required to resolve these kinds of impasses (Bromberg, 2006; Levenkron, 2006). I agree with that clinical perspective.

For example, in a relatively minor enactment early in my work with Alice,[1] she was especially provocative and I met that with kindness and tolerance over several months. As I did that, she became more incensed. She declared we were at an impasse. I was sure it was because she was deflecting my inquiries about self-states and dissociative processes. At some point, I finally became openly angry with her about her behavior, and she thanked me for finally being honest with her. She had felt invisible when she knew she was detached from her own anger, behaved poorly, and couldn't control how she was behaving. I effectively denied her real behavior because of my own intolerance for feeling openly angry. When I noted that it would be nearly impossible for her to bring her anger into the session if I couldn't do that myself, she quipped that was the smartest thing I'd said in years. Each of us were intolerant of our anger in unique ways, and this created an enactment as we avoided anger that fueled each of us "taking a position" as we each knew we were right!

Delusion of separateness

Denial and disavowal of dissociative self-states can be desperately entrenched and become ensconced in a "not-me" position (Chefetz & Bromberg, 2004) where an aspect of self is subjectively experienced as a wholly separate person, creating a delusion of separateness (Kluft, 1991). A person may refer to this self-state in the language typical of dissociative identity disorder (DID) and casually say: "that's not me, that's Mary," for example. The delusion of separateness

[1]Chapters 10, 11, and 12 of Chefetz, R. A. (2015). *Intensive psychotherapy for persistent dissociative processes: The fear of feeling real*. New York: W.W. Norton.

establishes the locus of initiative of the "separate" self-state as outside the patient and outside their control (or of any conscious effort to know what that self-state is about). It can also ramp up fear reactions and internal hallucinations of being harmed by such a state in revivified beatings, rape, etc.

For example, one of my patients described being prostituted by their father during childhood and was engaging in adult compulsive sexual behavior via massage and other related business entities. In session, it became clear they were speaking with a voice of authority as if they were the patient's father. As is apparent from the following extract of our exchange, my verbalization of this provoked an angry retort from my patient, who begins the exchange:

> "I'll tell him [the patient] to do what I want to tell him and he'll do it!"
>
> "If that's the case, then how do you explain why you are saying this to me?"
>
> "Leave me alone."
>
> "I'd leave you alone if it were possible, but you seem to have the view that you are separate from Jack, as if you control him and he has a separate body."
>
> "I am and he is. What are you talking about?"
>
> "I figure that you're talking to me because you've pushed yourself ahead of Jack and that he's in the background of the mind you share with him and listening to you assert yourself. Can you feel him back there?"
>
> "I ignore that. It's just annoying. He's annoying. In fact, you're annoying. What the hell do you want, anyhow?"
>
> "I don't want anything in particular. I just find it curious that you are part of Jack but seem to think you're separate and have taken on the behavior and mannerisms that might be similar to his father."
>
> "I am his father!"
>
> "Then how did you get to this office and end up talking with me? I think you're confused about who you are. You are another way of being Jack; didn't you know that?"

Looking rather horrified, this father-like self-state of Jack's continued to talk with me about why he felt compelled to get Jack to enact what became obvious to him were old scenes of abuse. By the time we were done, the client was working internally with the part of him that was Jack. "Jack" was then back in the session and openly relieved not to feel as much pressure and anxiety in his mind and body.

Delusion of separateness often scuttles a therapy when the therapist doesn't appreciate the extent to which an abuser/protector state is taking a not-me position and the therapist approaches the patient as if that self-state has the same interests as the patient overall. The whole point of the abuser/protector position involves the patient's desperate effort to protect themselves from being overwhelmed or flooded by toxic emotion or forbidden knowledge by using techniques against their own mind (other self-states) that are a match for those a perpetrator in their life has used to control them.

Threats of suicide

Nothing cools enthusiasm for doing work with traumatized individuals like the ongoing threat of suicide, both acute and chronic. These threats of suicide deserve an entire book for discussion. In the context of consultation there is the need to remain cognizant of these kinds of threats, as well as to relieve them where possible —or at least make them more amenable to exploration—when the patient returns to meet with their therapist. Treatments often walk a fine line between threat of suicide and action toward suicide. Living with the threat creates tension in patient and therapist, but so long as it does not produce action, the role of suicidal thinking in the patient may actually and paradoxically be lifesaving. Many people stay suicidal for the duration of their treatment and only in the last stages find their suicidal thoughts abate. Those thoughts provide the fantasy of ending the pain of living in the service of self-regulation of thoughts and feelings; knowing there is a possible "out" may decrease feelings of torment that reside in the realm of chronic flashbacks, body memories, and internal threats from abuser/protector self-states. From this perspective, an intent to eliminate suicidal thoughts and feelings may be foolish and itself dangerous. An intent to understand which self-states harbor these particular thoughts and feelings—and how this helps the person modulate their pain—is both more realistic and manageable as a clinical goal.

Leaving control of suicidal thoughts and feelings with the patient is paramount. What does that mean? To try to stop the patient from feeling suicidal, or early in the treatment to believe these feelings can be resolved with any ease, is counter to many years of clinical experience. My patients benefit from being able to describe their suicide fantasies in some detail, and I respond in obsessive detail and open curiosity about what they believe they'd experience in all aspects of the potential scene. Once my detailed inquiry is part of the discussion, it's also part of the patient's fantasy. In that way I enter the fantasy space and stay there, but I don't try and stop the use of the fantasy. I often talk about the paradox of the lifesaving nature of keeping in mind a kind of escape hatch. If I denigrate the value of the fantasy, the patient might feel deprived of the only way they can imagine gaining relief from their pain or asserting their authority (an untenable position to be in when engaging in psychotherapy).

Imagination doesn't kill, action does, and I regularly say this out loud. That said, the use of imagination in relation to self-torture goes beyond mere provision of a sense of relief. Undermining that kind of activity may be critical to survival of the patient and the treatment. One size does not fit all, and the need to stabilize the patient is critical in a phase-oriented model or any other model (Steele, van der Hart, & Nijenhuis, 2005). Either way, heavy-handed threats in this context are nontherapeutic whether internally within the patient, from therapist to patient, or from consultant to the clinical couple. It may be essential to ask a patient "Do you believe you have adequate resources inside you to manage this apparent threat to your safety and keep yourself 'safe?'" Clinical judgment must err on the side of safety, even if a patient might be angry in the process. Angry live people are preferable to unchallenged dead people.

Negative therapeutic reaction, negativity, and affect phobia

The sudden increase in the level of risk of self-harm, suicide, or loss of function for a patient after both therapist and patient agree that good work has been done and the treatment has been advanced constitutes a classic negative therapeutic reaction (Horney, 1936; Novick, 1980; Olinick, 1964; Orgel, 2013; Ornstein, 2013; Seinfeld, 2002). *The carefully balanced internal world of the person with a complex dissociative disorder means that healing in one area might be experienced as threat in another.* A multiple self-state psychology is a parsimonious way to think of the nearly simultaneous gains and losses as a result of, and also within, a treatment when a negative therapeutic reaction occurs.

For example, in the case of Rachel, a middle-aged woman with dissociative identity disorder,[2] child-sized self-states who lived in fear of being controlled by mother were terrified of healing because that meant they would become more of an adult (be "bigger" in the parlance of her self-state system); something she knew was opposed by mother. Rachel was clear that it was important to her mother to completely dominate Rachel so as not to threaten her [mother's] self-esteem and the careful balance of what Rachel saw as the constellation of mother's dissociative self-state organization. Thus, each therapeutic gain was accompanied by increased efforts to maintain old systems of being. Progress in one area often provoked a decrement of function in another. These kinds of oscillations were especially painful to Rachel. Paradoxically, they also constituted a way for her to become conscious that while she struggled with the notion that she had been abused, there was no internal disagreement that she had been tortured. This tendency toward concreteness and insisting on the use of language that fit her beliefs exactly ("abused" was not horrific enough for her and she insisted that what happened was torture) was repeated elsewhere in her work with me and is not atypical amongst persons with dissociative disorders.

Intense negativity may be the only opportunity for the patient to effectively wield power and dominate the therapeutic scene. Though the cost may be continued "self-bashing", these are moments that are more than flickers of power as a distressed person demonstrates their ability to destroy, both in fantasy and in the reality of the treatment relationship. This may serve as a strategy and may actually be intended to keep the therapist at a distance. If the therapist does in fact emotionally dissolve, then the patient can be reassured they can't be helped and that the secrets inside their mind might not be discoverable.

[2]The story of Rachel is spelled out in chapters 8 and 9 of Chefetz, R. A. (2015). *Intensive psychotherapy for persistent dissociative processes: The fear of feeling real.* New York: W.W. Norton.

Thus, negativity might have a role internally to shore up self-esteem in some self-states while robbing it from others. The clinical dyad might also be powerfully controlled by negativity wielded like a hammer, bashing the reasonable intentions of a therapist and leaving the treatment at an impasse. *Negativity must be welcomed into the treatment and observed as a strategy of self-regulation that is toxic and self-defeating while simultaneously offering the benefit of a temporary surge of personal power.* The therapist's sustained curiosity about this will eventually be contagious and serve the clinical dyad well.

For example, a clinician sought consultation for a patient who was overwhelming them with evening phone calls of a highly provocative nature regarding ongoing flashbacks in the patient. The patient was highly suicidal and also overwhelmed by their flashbacks. The patient also had a blistering negativity that was usually aimed squarely at herself and impenetrable to the therapist seeking consultation. The intensity of the negativity and the emotional load caused the treating clinician to retreat, which was felt as a fatal blow to the patient who already considered themselves toxic. Neither the clinician nor the patient could tolerate the intense feelings generated and both were fearful of collapse (affect phobia) if the treatment continued. The treatment foundered since the patient's worst fears were enacted and referral was necessary.

Shame

Shame is recognized as perhaps the most toxic of emotions. It is often the feeling at the center of traumatic experience, with a global failure of self-efficacy and self-protection (Bromberg, 2001; Dorahy, 2010; Kessler & Bieschke, 1999; Talbot, Talbot, & Tu, 2004) that may provoke the activation of dissociative processes. It is not generally appreciated, however, that with in-session enactments shame in the therapist may play a significant role in the development of impasse. Shame may arise *in the therapist* as a result of their own childhood history of traumatic experience, developmental or gross sexual/physical abuse, threats of the suicide and loss of a patient, threat of loss of self-esteem in the event a case fails, or threat of feeling exposed as incompetent if overwhelmed by the extraordinary emotional pressures the treatment of trauma may generate. This may constitute a trauma in and of itself, and may take the form of a vicarious traumatization (Pearlman & Saakvitne, 1995) or a countertrauma transference (Gartner, 2014). It is also a most unwieldy experience.

In the small community of clinicians who regularly do trauma treatment, it may be essential to have a group of similarly experienced colleagues with whom this kind of material can be safely discussed and worked through. For those unable to access such expertise, a peer supervision is still advisable when engaging in trauma treatment. It is also the case that some patients may have a particularly strong expectation of incompetence in the "so-called authorities" with whom they consult. New clinicians (or clinicians new to the treatment of trauma, even if relatively experienced) can be swamped with feelings of countertransference incompetence (Chefetz, 1997) that may be difficult to discern from the normal learning curve present in difficult treatments. The patient experienced adults in their childhood as incompetent and they expect their therapist to be no different. Lest they become frightened, the patient may also prefer to externalize their own loss of competence in knowing their mind.

Importantly, attacks on the competence of the therapist might mimic attacks on the very existence of the patient as a child by a parent who was grandiosely narcissistic. The constellation of the traumatizing narcissist (Shaw, 2013) as abusive parent to a dissociative child is common. Daniel Shaw brilliantly explores this phenomenon and spells out the dynamics in these families and cults. In my experience, the reality is high that a patient might have an abuser/protector state with these characteristics.

An illustrative vignette

A 45-year-old professional man was in treatment with a male clinician in a distant city. The patient had a history of childhood sexual abuse, a hypercritical mother and an abusive father, multiple suicide attempts, multiple adult traumas, and the family lore was that he was crazy and defective. He lived at home with his elderly parents. There were multiple therapists and multiple treatment failures prior to this treatment of 2 years. He was in a panic because of a need to take advanced-level examinations that were required to guarantee his information technology position. He was aware of having self-states, some of the time, and during those times in therapy would talk about how he attempted, unsuccessfully, to bargain with his states so he could take time to study. He did not succeed. His narcissistic rage at his failures were washing over into his treatment and he'd become verbally abusive of his therapist. Self-states that went to work were pleading with the therapist for help, and other self-states were lambasting the therapist for not helping. The patient and therapist had come to the conclusion that *there were several self-states who were sitting in the middle of the self-state system and "directing traffic,"* stopping him from studying for his exams, sabotaging the treatment relationship, and undermining yet another treatment.

Asked to consult, I expected a highly provocative and off-putting interaction. What I was met with was a system of self-states that was quite willing to reveal the architecture of the system as well as the frustration that existed because there were several adult self-states who, while on the surface cooperative, had regularly and secretly undermined the wish of other self-states to come to therapy and talk about their hurts. In reaction to this long frustration of many years, there was much suicidality and a sense of hopelessness that anything would ever change. The so-called abuser/protector states felt like the situation was out of their control and were miserably frustrated. The picture that developed was that of a misalliance of adult parts who blamed their troubles on an abusive internal system of self-states while not acknowledging that they were themselves impeding the ability of the system to come to treatment.

This situation was complicated by the reality that the patient lived with elderly parents who it seemed were significantly involved in the patient's abuse. Loyalty in the transference aside, the trauma bonds and the need to protect the parents were well within the potential agenda of this patient in ways that were not expressed during the consultation. Was the patient treatable given this constellation? Was the effort to work with abuser/protector states going to bear fruit when the need to be honest about the reality of childhood abuse might not be tolerable for the patient? (While it might seem rather unbelievable, incestuous relationships can continue many years into adulthood (Middleton, 2013). At age 55, a patient of mine in treatment for many years startled and saddened us both by the spontaneous realization that her father had been sexually abusing her from her early childhood until his 89th year and the time of a recent disabling stroke. Who would have thought it possible?)

The therapist for whom I consulted was grateful to appreciate the sabotage that was going on with the misalliance of self-states, who on the one hand were desperate to study, but on the other hand had no intention of letting the system of self-states really ever come to treatment. The therapist had aligned with the distress of the patient in wanting to study, and was blinded by that heartfelt sentiment and the obfuscation it created in the service of shutting down communication from the system of self-states. This was blamed on the threats of abuser/protector states, but that was all they could do to get anybody's attention that there was a problem. Yes, there were abuser/protector self-states involved in the internal action. But they were "fall guys" for the activities that deflected attention from the main impediment to the treatment; namely self-states who presented themselves as wanting help but were intent on not getting what the therapy had to offer.

This consultation failed when the patient returned to treatment and excoriated the consultation as totally worthless. In retrospect, it is likely that a silent traumatizing narcissistic self-state was running the show and not acknowledging their role. The therapist's tolerance for the kind of emotional battering meted out by the patient was understandably limited (as would be the case for any clinician). The ability of the clinician to appreciate the traumatizing narcissistic self-state's concerns, while also challenging them without the clinician's anxiety rising beyond the manageable, requires exceptional emotional strength.

Summary

Consultation for abuser/protector self-state issues can be fraught with many interesting difficulties. One size does not fit all. Both clinicians who consult and those who seek consultation must remain aware of a plethora of potential themes and maintain active curiosity, rather than foreclose discovery of a nuanced scene of important dimensions to both the patient and the therapist. Perhaps the most problematic areas remain the intractability of shame, negativity, and traumatizing narcissistic phenotypy in abuser/protector states. An ongoing relationship with the consultant may be of some use to shore up the therapist in the wake of attacks by the patient.

References

Bromberg, P. M. (2001). Treating patients with symptoms—And symptoms with patience: Reflections on shame, dissociation, and eating disorders. *Psychoanalytic Dialogues, 11* (6), 891–912. doi:10.1080/10481881109348650

Bromberg, P. M. (2006). *Awakening the dreamer: Clinical journeys.* Mahwah, NJ: Analytic Press.

Bromberg, P. M. (2009). Truth, human relatedness, and the analytic process: An interpersonal/realational perspective. *International Journal of Psychoanalysis, 90* (2), 347–361. doi:10.1111/j.1745-8315.2009.00137.x

Bromberg, P. M. (2011). *The shadow of the tsunami and the growth of the relational mind.* New York, NY: Routledge.

Chefetz, R. A. (1997). Special case transference and countertransference in the treatment of dissociative identity disorder. *Dissociation, 10* (4), 255–265.

Chefetz, R. A. (2015). *Intensive psychotherapy for persistent dissociative processes: The fear of feeling real.* New York, NY: W.W. Norton.

Chefetz, R. A., & Bromberg, P. M. (2004). Talking with "Me" and "Not-Me": A dialogue. *Contemporary Psychoanalysis, 40* (3), 409–464. doi:10.1080/00107530.2004.10745840

Chused, J. F. (1991). The evocative power of enactments. *Journal of the American Psychoanalytic Association, 39,* 615–639. doi:10.1177/000306519103900302

Dorahy, M. J. (2010). The impact of dissociation, shame, and guilt on interpersonal relationships in chronically traumatized individuals: A pilot study*. *Journal of Traumatic Stress, 23* (5), 653–656. doi:10.1002/jts.20564

Gartner, R. B. (2014). Trauma and countertrauma, resilience and counterresilience. *Contemporary Psychoanalysis, 50* (4), 609–626. doi:10.1080/00107530.2014.945069

Gelinas, D. J. (1983). The persisting negative effects of incest. *Psychiatry, 46,* 312–332. doi:10.1080/00332747.1983.11024207

Horney, K. (1936). The problem of the negative therapeutic reaction. *The Psychoanalytic Quarterly, 5,* 29–44.

Kessler, B. L., & Bieschke, K. J. (1999). A retrospective analysis of shame, dissociation, and adult victimization in survivors of childhood sexual abuse. *Journal of Counseling Psychology, 46* (3), 335. doi:10.1037/0022-0167.46.3.335

Kluft, R. P. (1991). Multiple personality disorder. *American Psychiatric Press Review of Psychiatry, 10,* 161–188.

Levenkron, H. (2006). Love (and hate) with the proper stranger: Affective honesty and enactment. *Psychoanalytic Inquiry, 26* (2), 157–181.

Luborsky, L., & Crits-Christoph, P. (1998). *Understanding transference: The core conflictual relationship theme method.* Washington, DC: American Psychological Association.

McLaughlin, J. (1991). Clinical and theoretical aspects of enactment. *Journal of the American Psychoanalytic Association, 39,* 595–614. doi:10.1177/000306519103900301

Middleton, W. (2013). Parent–child incest that extends into adulthood: A survey of international press reports, 2007–2011. *Journal of Trauma & Dissociation, 14* (2), 184–197. doi:10.1080/15299732.2013.724341

Miller, A. (1981). *The drama of the gifted child.* New York, NY: Basic Books.

Novick, J. (1980). Negative therapeutic motivation and negative therapeutic alliance. *Psychoanalytic Study of the Child, 35*, 299–320.

Ogden, T. H. (1989). *The primitive edge of experience.* Northvale, NJ: Jason Aronson.

Olinick, S. L. (1964). The negative therapeutic reaction. *International Journal of Psychoanalysis, 45*, 540–548.

Orgel, S. (2013). On negative therapeutic reaction. In L. Wurmser, & H. Jarass (Ed.), *Nothing good is allowed to stand: An integrative view of the negative therapeutic reaction* (pp. 57–66). New York, NY: Routledge.

Ornstein, A. (2013). The negative therapeutic reaction revisited. In L. Wurmser, & H. Jarass (Eds.), *Nothing good is allowed to stand: An integrative view of the negative therapeutic reaction* (pp. 160–169). New York, NY: Routledge.

Pearlman, L. A., & Saakvitne, K. W. (1995). *The countertransference-vicarious traumatization cycle trauma and the therapist: Countertransference and vicarious traumatization in psychotherapy with incest survivors* (pp. 317-335). New York, NY: W.W. Norton & Co.

Ryle, A. (Ed.). (1999). *Cognitive analytic therapy: Developments in theory and practice.* New York, NY: John Wiley & Sons.

Seinfeld, J. (2002). *A primer of handling the negative therapeutic reaction.* New York, NY: Jason Aronson.

Shaw, D. (2013). *Traumatic narcissism: Relational systems of subjugation.* New York, NY: Routledge.

Steele, K., van der Hart, O., & Nijenhuis, E. R. S. (2005). Phase-oriented treatment of structural dissociation in complex traumatization: Overcoming trauma-related phobias. *Journal of Trauma & Dissociation, 6* (3), 11–53. doi:10.1300/J229v06n03_02

Stern, D. B. (1997). *Unformulated experience: From dissociation to imagination in psychoanalysis.* Hillsdale, NJ: The Analytic Press.

Stern, D. B. (2004). The eye sees itself: Dissociation, enactment, and the achievement of conflict. *Contemporary Psychoanalysis, 40*, 197–237. doi:10.1080/00107530.2004.10745828

Stern, D. B. (2009). Partners in thought: A clinical process theory of narrative. *The Psychoanalytic Quarterly, 78*, 701–731. doi:10.1002/j.2167-4086.2009.tb00410.x

Stern, D. B. (2013). Relational freedom and therapeutic action. *Journal of the American Psychoanalytic Association, 61* (2), 227–256. doi:10.1177/0003065113484060

Talbot, J. A., Talbot, N. L., & Tu, X. (2004). Shame-proneness as a diathesis for dissociation in women with histories of childhood sexual abuse. *Journal of Traumatic Stress, 17* (5), 445–448. doi:10.1023/B:JOTS.0000048959.29766.ae

Tomkins, S. S. (1995). Script theory. In E. V. Demos (Ed.), *Exploring affect: The selected writings of Silvan S. Tomkins* (pp. 312–388). New York, NY: Cambridge University Press.

Robert Fliess, Wilhelm Fliess, Sándor Ferenczi, Ernest Jones, and Sigmund Freud

Warwick Middleton, MD

ABSTRACT
In the 1970s, a band of intelligent and inquiring professionals acquired a critical mass as they rediscovered the sort of patient that Josef Breuer had grappled to understand when he first encountered Bertha Pappenheim in 1880. Just over a century after Breuer ceased treating Bertha Pappenheim, a society dedicated to the study of dissociation was founded in 1984 and named the International Society for the Study of Multiple Personality and Dissociation. In 2016, as President of this Society, which is now the International Society for the Study of Trauma and Dissociation (ISSTD), I took the opportunity to share some reflections on a previous journey undertaken by the early analysts and what contemporary lessons we might take from it. This paper expands on the content of that 2016 Presidential Editorial.

Although it is rarely quoted, a young Freud on his return to Vienna in April 1886 reflecting on his time with Charcot at the Salpêtrére and a subsequent shorter visit to Berlin, made some daring observations:

> Up to now, hysteria can scarcely be regarded as a name with any well-defined meaning. The state of illness to which it is applied is only characterized scientifically by *negative* signs; it has been studied little and unwillingly; and it labours under the odium of some very wide-spread prejudices … During the last few decades a hysterical woman would have been almost as certain to be treated as a malingerer, as in earlier centuries she would have been certain to be judged and condemned as a witch or as possessed by the devil… In the outpatient department in Berlin, however, I found that … when a diagnosis of "hysteria" had been made, all inclination to take any further notice of the patient seemed to be suppressed. (Freud, 1886–1899/2001a, pp. 11–12, italics in the original)

The sort of individual that Freud described and the sort of unhelpful societal reactions to understanding why such individuals exist are very familiar to those who seek a modern understanding of those with dissociative conditions. As we reflect on the reasons for the highs and lows that have ensued in the years since our Society formed, it is instructive to reflect on the intermingling of trauma in the lives of those that gathered around Freud. It is important to contemplate that a field that had its starting point in the reality of severe incestuous abuse and which engaged individuals with the intellectual ability of Sigmund Freud and his associates, should have been closely associated with individuals who it is very likely were themselves abusers, should have encompassed so many troubling boundary violations on the part of its practitioners, and should have attracted many who were themselves victims of abuse. The irony is that this grouping, with a few notable exceptions, managed to institutionalize a belief system that deemphasized the very sorts of trauma many had themselves experienced.

In their preliminary communications (1893), Breuer and Freud (1893–1895/2001) observed that

> The splitting of consciousness which is so striking in the well-known classical cases under the form of "double conscience" is present to a rudimentary degree in every hysteria, and that a tendency to such a dissociation, and with it the emergence of abnormal states of consciousness (which we shall bring together under the term "hypnoid") is the basic phenomenon of this neurosis. (p. 12)

In 1896, Freud (1893–1899/2001b) postulated that the cause of hysteria was sexual abuse beginning before age 8, perpetrated frequently by close relatives or other long-term household members: "Some adult looking after the child—a nursery maid or governess or tutor, or, unhappily all too often, a close relative—has initiated the child into sexual intercourse and has maintained a regular love relationship with it—a love relationship, moreover, with its mental side developed—which has often lasted for years" (p. 208). The actual naming of fathers as abusers was only mentioned in letters to Freud's closest confidant, Wilhelm Fliess (Masson, 1984).

Having been the first person to publicly proclaim a child sexual abuse theory for hysteria and by extension draw attention to the high frequency with which incest occurs in contemporary society, Freud, in the absence of any new data to justify his change of stance, and 17 months since publicly giving his paper "The Aetiology of Hysteria," announced in a letter to Wilhelm Fliess in September 1897 that he no longer believed in his "*neurotica* (theory of neuroses)" (Masson, 1985, p. 264, italics in the original). He reasoned that the prevalence of incestuous abuse by fathers would have to be "widespread" and "immeasurably" more frequent than the prevalence of hysteria, given that hysteria would only arise in susceptible individuals when there had been "an accumulation of events" (Masson, 1985, p. 264).

Writing in 1925, Freud (1925/2001c) reflected that "neurotic symptoms were not related directly to actual events but to wishful phantasies, and that as far as the neurosis was concerned psychical reality was of more importance than material reality" (p. 34). Freud lamely concluded his discussion on how he was led to the theory of Oedipal fantasy with the observation that "seduction during childhood retained a certain share, though a humbler one, in the etiology of neurosis. But the seducers turned out as a rule to have been older children" (pp. 34–35). He stated that when the "mistake" (i.e., his seduction theory) "had been cleared up, the path to the study of the sexual life of children lay open" (p. 35). There was an important consequence of the central role Freud gave to Oedipal fantasy—it really left little place for dissociation.

Predating Freud's self-analysis, Wilhelm Fliess had informed Freud how his son Robert, then in his second year of life, had become sexually aroused by the sight of his mother's naked body. Sulloway (1992) quoted Robert's wife Elenore describing Wilhelm as a man who however outwardly charming, was "a tyrant at home" (p. 191). In 1982, Elenore described Robert as having a "forbidding father, a subservient mother and meals with the servants" (p. 196).

Many have commented on the psychological blindness Freud displayed toward his slightly younger, charismatic, Berlin-based ear, nose, and throat (ENT) surgeon friend. The extent of Freud's idealization of Fliess, given Freud's enormous intellectual powers and his own perception of himself as a hard-headed man of science, is striking. Such idealization rarely lasts. The animosity between them became so bad that Fliess later accused Freud of physically attacking him. Decades on, members of Fliess' family recalled that Wilhelm believed Freud wanted to kill him (Makari, 2008).

In reply to a letter from Fliess in 1904 regarding the circumstances of how via a patient of Freud's (Herman Swoboda), a gifted but very disturbed young man, Otto Weininger, had appropriated Fliess's theory on bisexuality and published it in a book, *Sex and Character*, Freud obfuscated, covered up, and lied (Roazen, 1975). Of course Freud was never quite as honest as those who idealize him would wish to believe. We now know through a simple investigation carried out over a century after the event that Freud, while on holiday in Switzerland, and accompanied by his sister-in-law Minna Bernays, had spent the night with her, having checked into the second fanciest hotel in Maloja as man and wife on August 13, 1898, while at the same time corresponding with his wife Martha that they were staying in "humble" lodgings (Blumenthal, 2006). Roazen (1975) draws attention to Freud's sexual dissatisfaction, noting that in respect to one trip to Italy, Freud had recorded finding himself involuntarily walking again and again to the prostitutes' area.

Wilhelm Fliess's death in 1928 and his son's subsequent training as an analyst seemed to precipitate for Robert a considerable reevaluation of his father and his father's theories (Sulloway, 1992). Robert in 1933 moved to the United States, where in time he established himself as a New York psychoanalyst, meeting his wife Elenore in 1936 (Fliess, 1982). Seemingly sexually abused, likely by his own father, a man who was Freud's closest professional confidant during the years in which he developed his theory of Oedipal fantasy, he worked extensively with abused patients who had suffered childhood physical and sexual abuse and over time he became combatively direct in confronting the theories of his father's erstwhile closest friend. In 1956, he stated that he had "clarified the picture of my father in two expert and thorough analyses, the last in middle age with Ruth Mack Brunswick; and I have had an extended conversation with Freud himself about his onetime friend" (p. xviii).

The origins of what in 1908 was renamed the Vienna Psychoanalytic Society date from invitations Freud extended to four colleagues in 1902—Rudolf Reitler, Wilhelm Stekel, Max Kahane, and then Alfred Adler, to meet at his house to discuss issues of common interest. Over time, others joined the growing band (Roazen, 1975). Otto Rank met Freud in 1905, and for years was a prominent loyal supporter. The years 1924–1926 marked his painful disentanglement with Freud. Sándor Ferenczi met Freud for the first time on February 2, 1908. Their last meeting on August 24, 1932 was strained.

Ernest Jones first met Freud in April 1908 (Maddox, 2006) and became over time the chief exponent of Freudian orthodoxy. When Edoardo Weiss was asked what one could not doubt, and still stay on as an analyst, he "listed four central concepts of Freud's that were beyond discussion: dreams as wish-fulfillment, the instinct theory, the Oedipus complex, and the castration complex" (Roazen, 2005, p. 59). Freud's daughter Anna stated her father's position clearly: "Keeping up the seduction theory would mean to abandon the Oedipus Complex—and with it the whole importance of fantasy life—conscious and unconscious fantasy. In fact, I think there would have been no psychoanalysis afterwards" (quoted in Malcolm, 1984, p. 63).

The sexualized underpinnings of the idealized relationship Freud had with Wilhelm Fliess surfaced again, when Freud, in November 1912, fainted for the second time in Jung's presence. In a letter to Ernest Jones he attributed this fainting spell to an "unruly homosexual feeling," which involved a transference from his earlier intense friendship with Fliess (Donn, 1988, pp. 154–156).

Ernest Jones, Freud's official biographer, had a checkered history in matters of judgment, having been dismissed from his first hospital residency following a complaint regarding unsettling sexual questioning of a young female patient (Gillespie, 1974) but more particularly because he had been absent without leave from his duties on no less than three occasions (Maddox, 2006). In 1906, Jones was credibly accused by four children (three girls and a boy) of sexual abuse. The youngest child was 12, the rest teenagers. Jones was employed to conduct speech examinations at the St Edward's School in southeast London. The headmistress, Mrs. Hall, scolded the first two children who complained about Jones's conduct. The second complainant, Dorothy Freeman, told her headmistress that Jones had acted in a grossly indecent manner and that if she complied with his request her mother would beat her and put her to bed (Maddox, 2006). When a second girl made a complaint, Mrs. Hall told the girls to go home, as there must be some mistake, but when a third girl made a similar complaint, she resolved to act. An internal hearing into the matter was arranged involving the medical officer for the

London County Council's Education Department, Jones, the headmistress, and each of the four children appearing individually. Dorothy's father made a formal complaint at Blackheath police station on March 12, 1906. Police took as evidence a green baize tablecloth that had been on the table in the room where Jones examined the children and where his alleged indecent acts took place.

There were four court hearings. In the Edwardian society of 1906, the word *semen* was not spoken in public. However, in reference to the tablecloth under suspicion, Dr. Dudley Burney, the divisional surgeon, related how in examining it he had formed the opinion that the three or four stains identified "were of such a character that they should not have been there" (Maddox, 2006, p. 44). Charges against Jones were dropped, as the magistrate knew that no jury would convict on the evidence of mentally ineligible children. In "Free Associations," published in 1959, Jones claimed that the accusations involving him had been made up by "two small children." There were in fact four pupils who accused him on the same day, and they were not small (Maddox, 2006, p. 46).

In 1908, Jones moved to Canada, with Loë Kann joining him there. He subsequently was rumored to be recommending masturbation, distributing pornographic pictures to patients, or advising the use of prostitutes as part of therapy, and he paid $500 hush money to a female patient who threatened to allege that Jones had had sexual relations with her. Jones described his patient as a "hysterical homosexual woman" who aside from blackmailing him also attempted to shoot him (Gabbard & Lester, 1996, p. 79).

Freud became involved in what Gabbard and Lester (1996) characterized as a "boundary-less ménage à trois" (p. 78) when he took into analysis Loë Kann, Ernest Jones's de facto wife and former patient. Freud made regular reports to Jones on his treatment of Kann. As Jones became increasingly excluded from the process, he started a sexual relationship with Loë's maid, Lina, while Freud steered Kann toward a new lover (Gabbard & Lester, 1996).

Adding a new twist to Jones' exceedingly complicated sexual life, Lina moved in with him in 1914 in the London flat that Loë had furnished and decorated. Loè had alerted her analyst (Freud) that, alarmingly, Jones was interested in Freud's 18-year-old daughter, Anna. Freud wrote to Ferenczi that Loë Kann, who was by then living back in London and who was close to Anna, "will keep watch like a dragon" (Maddox, 2006, p. 114).

In 1907, Joan Riviere had a breakdown following the death of her father and in 1916 and 1917 she spent time in a sanatorium. In 1916, Joan Riviere began an analysis with Jones that spanned five years. Jones's boundary transgressions were multiple. He did not provide her with regular appointment times. He confided to her problems from both his marriages, and he regularly loaned her his summer cottage in Elsted. In addition, he worked closely with her in the translation of German psychoanalytic articles.

By January 1922, Jones wrote to Freud that Riviere represented "the worst failure I have ever had" as he referred her on to Freud (Maddox, 2006, p. 170). Freud interpreted Jones's earlier discourses as communicating subtly that he was sexually involved with her. On March 23, 1922, Freud wrote to Jones that Riviere's analysis was proceeding well, stating, "Mrs Riviere does not appear to me half as black as you have painted her," adding with some relief, "I am very glad you had no sexual relations with her." Jones reassured Freud, "It is over twelve years since I experienced any temptation in such ways, and then in special circumstances" (p. 170). Riviere was regarded by many as the most accomplished of Freud's translators and in time she was the analyst of John Bowlby and Donald Winnicott, among others (Maddox, 2006).

Jones's organizational talents meant that by remaining within the fold, he arguably played a greater practical role in the spread and influence of psychoanalysis than did Freud himself. Jones introduced psychoanalysis to Canada, founded the British Psycho-Analytic Society, and was cofounder with James Jackson Putnam of the American Psychoanalytic Association. The dust jacket of *The Life and Work of Sigmund Freud* (no doubt written by Jones) described him as "acknowledged to be one of the great scientists and writers in the field of psychoanalysis" (Jones, 1953). Jones, who was both a publicist and censor for the psychoanalytic movement was described by Roazen (1975) as "a fiery little man, with a staccato, military manner," and who "at his worst, could be spiteful, jealous and querulous … He did not make friends easily and was much hated" (p. 354). Psychoanalysis became particularly influential in the United States, reaching its zenith in the 1950s such that by 1952, 64% of the members of the International Psychoanalytic Association were in America (Roazen, 1975).

Both Sándor Ferenczi and Robert Fliess in their late careers became more emboldened in outlining what they saw as the true place incestuous and other sexual abuse played in society. Ferenczi (1932/1984) gave a very cogent description of dissociative identity disorder when he stated,

> If traumatic events accumulate during the life of the growing person, the number and variety of personality splits increase, and soon it will be rather difficult to maintain contact without confusion with all the fragments, which all act as separate personalities but mostly do not know each other. (p. 293)

A description of the cases Ferenczi treated in the later 1920s and early 1930s demonstrates that his patients were invariably suffering from childhood sexual trauma. Fortune (1993) argued that the case of Elizabeth Severn (born Leota Brown in the U.S. Midwest in 1879 and described by Freud as "Ferenczi's evil genius") was a critical factor precipitating Ferenczi's return to Freud's original trauma theory as well as furthering his recognition of the clinical significance of countertransference (Rachman, 2014).

Severn was the first recipient of Ferenczi's most controversial therapeutic experiment—that of mutual analysis. Fortune (1993) observed, "Elizabeth Severn not only convinced Ferenczi of her trauma but, as his analyst, helped uncover and persuade him of the significance of his own childhood traumas" (p. 111). The boundaries blurred to the point where Ferenczi observed that it was as though two halves had combined to form a whole soul. He spoke of "two equally terrified children who compare their experiences, and because of their common fate understood each other completely and instinctively try to comfort each other" (Ferenczi, 1932/1988, p. 56). Belatedly Ferenczi identified that there was significant risk in him placing himself "into the hands of a not undangerous patient" (Ferenczi, 1932/1988, p. 100). The analysis came to an end when Ferenczi was dying of pernicious anemia and Severn was broke.

In the last of his three-volume analytic series, published after his death in 1970, Robert Fliess (1973) reflected that his methods had "brought me face to face with material which was undoubtedly authentic, but which, on the face of it, was 'unbelievable'" (p. 204). He reflected,

> The average analyst … remains ignorant of his own psychotic parent, should he have one, and hence is not equipped for patients who confront him with fragments that are replicas of his own history—fragments that should, were he properly "trained" no longer be traumatic but actually still are. (p. 204)

In a late-life contradiction of Freudian psychoanalytic orthodoxy, Fliess (1973) took off the gloves, contradicting Freud head on:

> *No one is ever made sick by his fantasies.* Only traumatic memories in repression can cause the neurosis. This fact alone is sufficient reason for discounting Freud's later "denial." Fantasies, in particular compulsive ones, *are a symptom of the disease*, never its cause. (p. 212, italics in the original)

Fliess, more than half a century ago, found strong corroboration of his analytic findings in Leontine Young's unpublished doctoral thesis *Parents Who Neglect and Abuse Children* (for a published version, see Young, 1964):

> There were no exceptions to this pattern. The range of parental emotion in this group was from hatred to indifference. There is no evidence that the children at any time were seen as persons by the parents. On the contrary, they were treated as objects to be used or discarded. (quoted in Fliess, 1961, pp. 13–14)

Freud, despite his enormous intellect, was no Messiah. Psychoanalysis as a profession, and despite its many insights, found the means to explain away the uncomfortable accounts of traumatized, shamed, and dissociative individuals grappling with the fragmented reality of their own incest. Yet this façade, as represented by the later writings of Ferenczi and Robert Fliess, has been cracked multiple times. John Bowlby was critical of psychoanalysis's concentration on fantasy, stating,

> Ever since Freud made his famous, and in my view disastrous, volte-face in 1897, when he decided that the childhood seductions he had believed to be etiologically important were nothing more than the products of his patients' imagination, it has been extremely unfashionable to attribute psychopathology to real-life experiences. (Southgate, 2002, p. 86)

In his 1989 book, Shengold cites Ferenczi and Robert Fliess (1956, 1961, 1973) as the "most notable" of "many analysts" who had written about "the not infrequent occurrence of actual incest involving preadolescent children" (p. 160). He cites six other publications by presumably less notable analytic writers. Using Ferenczi and Robert Fliess to so prominently bolster the case of psychoanalysis' interest in the reality of childhood sexual abuse is a tad disingenuous given the response that both Ferenczi and Fliess endured at the hands of their contemporary psychoanalytic critics.

Freyd (2013), the originator of betrayal trauma theory, pointedly reminded us that "one of the many ways we can betray is by pathologizing victims and survivors of trauma and mistreatment" (p. 498).

The early history of psychoanalysis contains the names of many associated with the movement who it is known suffered substantial childhood trauma. Included in this number are Carl Jung, who early in his relationship with Freud had confessed that as a youth he had been homosexually assaulted by a man he trusted—and who, when he asked Freud for his photograph, admitted that he had "a religious crush" on Freud that he was aware had "clear erotic undertones" (see McGuire, 1974, p. 95).

Jung reflected on how the sexual abuse at the hands of a man whom he had once worshipped had hampered his relationships with all men who tried to become close or platonically intimate friends. He noted that invariably in his eyes, all such men became downright disgusting. The identity of the man who sexually assaulted Jung has never been fully confirmed. Throughout his life, Jung manifested a distinct discomfort toward Catholicism and Catholic priests, particularly Jesuits. One of several dreams dating from early childhood that Jung obsessed about for the rest of his life concerned a large tree trunk on the top of which was "an eye," but not "one that gazed." In time, Jung identified the image as a "ritual phallus" (Blair, 2004; Jung 1977). Jung indulged what he called his "polygamous nature" (see Breger 2000) and there are two documented love affairs with women who were his patients, the first of whom was with Sabina Spielrein who was literally his first psychoanalytic patient (Kerr, 1994).

Otto Rank came from an impoverished background and was estranged from his self-centered alcoholic father and living an isolated existence when he met Freud at age 21 (Taft, 1958). He wrote of his

> introduction to erotic experience in my seventh year through one of my friends, for which I still curse him even today, vividly remembering … the foundation stone of my later sufferings was laid at that time; it was at the same time the gravestone of my joy. (quoted in Breger, 2000, p. 311)

Sándor Ferenczi was also sexually abused as a child—by his mother and his nursemaid (Goldwert, 1986; Rudnytsky, 1996).

Sigmund Freud wrote to Wilhelm Fliess (October 3 and 4, 1897) referring to his old childhood nurse, whom he termed "my teacher in sexual matters," who "complained because I was clumsy and unable to do anything" (Masson, 1985, p. 269). He added,

> A severe critic might say that all this was phantasy projected into the past instead of being determined by the past. The experimenta crucis would decide the matter against him. The reddish water seems a point of this kind. Where do all patients derive the horrible perverse details which are often as alien to their experience as to their knowledge? (Masson, 1985, p. 269)

Like so many reflecting on the fragmentary memory of early childhood memory, Freud was simultaneously struggling with the possibility that it was a fantasy and the difficulty of otherwise explaining unique and poignant detail. Freud's childhood contained many other traumatic events including the deaths of an uncle and a brother, poverty, crowded living conditions, anti-Semitism, and his nanny's arrest and jailing for theft when he was aged two and a half (Roazen, 1975).

Hinting at much that was unresolved, a substantial number of the early analysts were to die by suicide. Included in this group are two of the brightest of the early analysts, Victor Tausk (who in 1919 shot himself) and William Stekel (who in 1940 poisoned himself with aspirin). Others who suicided include Johann Honegger, Tatiana Rosenthal, Max Kahane, Herbert Silberer, Klauss Schrötter, Karin Stephen (Virginia Woolf's sister-in-law), Eugenia Sokolnicka, Monroe Meyer, Martin Peck, and Paul Federn. Of these, Stekel, Sokolnicka, and Meyer had been personally analyzed by Freud. Although there is no evidence that Federn underwent formal analysis with Freud, he considered himself to have been trained by Freud and to have analyzed himself under Freud's guidance (Weiss, 1966). Hermine Hug-Hellmuth was murdered by her nephew/patient, whereas others died from substance-related misadventures (Otto Gross, Ruth Mack Brunswick). Elenore Fliess (1982) describes how her husband Robert, years after his training at the Berlin Psychoanalytic Institute, confronted Karen Horney with the fact that the Institute had assigned him to analyst who suffered from schizophrenia. She records Horney admitting, "We should not have done that" (p. 198). Robert Fliess' experiences with his father and with his "psychotic" first analyst underpinned his challenges to Freud's recanting of his original seduction hypothesis (Fishman, 1986).

The examples of Victor Tausk, Wilhelm Reich, Anna Freud, and Massud Khan in particular illustrate how problematic the boundaries were in the early, and not-so-early, decades of psychoanalysis. Victor Tausk, whose relationship with his own father was strained and antagonistic, was one of the most gifted of Freud's earlier followers. He had a romantic relationship in 1912–1913 with

Lou Andreas-Salomé (an older female follower of Freud who described Tausk as the most prominently outstanding of Freud's pupils). After the end of World War I, Tausk came to Vienna. He wanted, as did many of the early adherents, to be personally analyzed by Freud, and he also wanted recognition from Freud for the originality of his psychoanalytic contributions.

Freud was discomforted and threatened by his younger rival and advised Tausk to be analyzed by Helene Deutsch, a more junior and less experienced analyst than Tausk. Deutsch, at the time was being herself analyzed by Freud. Despite being to some degree humiliated by the arrangement, Tausk submitted. Given that psychoanalysis is based around the use of free association, it was totally predictable that Tausk, as he lay on Deutsch's couch, free-associated about Freud, and that Deutsch in turn, when she lay on Freud's couch, free-associated about her gifted and intriguing patient who had so much to say about Freud. Freud called a halt to the unworkable arrangement he had put in place and gave Deutsch an ultimatum—either she cease analyzing Tausk or she cease her analysis with him. Deutsch, not wanting to lose her analysis with Freud ceased the analysis with Tausk, something she deeply regretted over time. With his link to Freud severed, Tausk, about to be married to a pregnant former patient, wrote a letter to Freud and to his fiancé, stood on a chair, looped curtain braid attached to a ceiling rafter around his neck, and shot himself through the head with his service revolver. At the time Freud communicated to Salomé that he did not miss Tausk, someone he judged as being a threat to the future. The circumstances of Tausk's very disturbing death were covered for years by a blanket of silence on the part of mainstream psychoanalysis, a silence that was penetrated when Roazen (1969), nearly half a century later, investigated the circumstances.

Helene Deutsch was distraught when Freud abruptly terminated her analysis after a year, giving her hour to the Wolf Man, who clearly Freud found a far more interesting case. Freud had even fallen asleep during Helene's analysis when she talked about her nursing problems (Appignanesi & Forrester, 1993).

Sexually precocious, Wilhelm Reich (1897–1957) developed an attitude toward his mother that was deeply sexual and coloured all of his subsequent almost frenetic relationships with women (Corrington, 2003, p. 3).

Corrington noted that Reich's mother had encouraged fairly serious erotic play with Willy, especially with her breasts, and that he came to regard such boundary transgressions as within the bounds of normal behavior, perhaps as part of a legitimate means of testing his male prowess against the abusive father (p. 22).

Reich became sexually involved with one of the first female patients he analyzed, a 19-year-old kindergarten teacher, Lore Kahn. Not long after their sexual involvement commenced Lore became unwell, feverish and died eight days later. Lore's mother accused Reich of organizing an illegal botched abortion. Shortly after Lore's death, her mother committed suicide by gassing herself in December 1920. Reich continued to have sexual contact with various patients and to conduct simultaneous ongoing sexual relationships with more than one partner at a time. Around this time he reflected that a young man in his twenties should not be treating female patients (Corrington, 2003).

The enmeshed, boundary-less psychological hothouse environment that surfaced repeatedly in the earlier history of psychoanalysis was never more apparent than with Dorothy Burlingham (daughter of Louis Comfort Tiffany, the interior and glass designer) and her interactions with, her long-term psychoanalyst (Sigmund Freud), her closest friend/life partner (Anna Freud), and Dorothy's four children, Bob, Mabbie, Tinky, and Mikey, all of whom went into analysis with Anna Freud. Reflecting on the dual role Anna enjoyed as stepmother and analyst, Bob Burlingham's son Michael reflected, "That method, which today would subject Anna Freud to disciplinary action, hurt my father and his siblings" (Tylim, 2011).

Anna Freud's first book, *Introduction to the Technique of Child Analysis* appeared in 1927 (with the English translation appearing in 1928). Ten child analyses were featured in the book including Bob and Mabbie Burlingham. Anna considered Mabbie the most successful of these ten cases (Roazen, 2001). In May 1938, Dorothy's husband suicided, jumping from the fourteenth floor of his New York apartment, shortly after his daughter Mabbie's wedding. In 1947, Mabbie returned to Anna Freud for more analysis, and she continued to see her for analysis every summer. Mabbie became psychologically more unsettled, writing about her mental problems to her mother. In a desperate state, Mabbie did what she had been doing for the previous quarter century: she went to England to be with her mother and to have further analysis with "Mother Anna Freud" (Young-Bruehl, 1988). She again went to England in August 1974 so that Anna could see her during the summer holiday period. Before this could commence, Mabbie took an overdose of sleeping pills, dying seven days later. Roazen (2002) reflected on Anna's lack of reconsideration of the role she had played as a mother figure and long-term analyst of the daughter of her closest friend:

> Even when one of the Burlingham children killed herself in Anna's house in London, after years of analysis since early childhood, it would seem that Anna never allowed herself sufficient doubts about the efficiency of analysis as either therapy or prophylaxis. (p. 98)

Appignanesi and Forrester (1993) comment:

> Certainly the children, especially the two eldest, though they loved Anna, felt trapped by her double role and by the constant glare of analysis on their feelings and actions—much as Anna, as she had confessed to Lou, had felt "pulled apart … mishandled and mistreated" in her analysis by her own father. (p. 293)

While living together for the best part of their lives, it had remained unclear whether Anna Freud had a sexual relationship with Dorothy Burlingham (or with anyone else) (Appignanesi & Forester, 1993; Young-Bruehl, 1988). Michael

Burlingham, whose father was Bob Burlingham, learned about notes his father had made on his deathbed regarding the love between Anna and Dorothy. They shared a "very intimate relationship," something confirmed by Paula Fichtl who was Dorothy's cook (Tylim, 2011).

Masud Khan, a protégé of Anna Freud who had been analyzed by Donald Winnicott (with whom he collaborated), was a senior and prolific contributor to the psychoanalytic literature. Masson describes being cut adrift as Project Director for the Sigmund Freud Archives by Kurt Eissler and his fellow Archives board members, following the publication of a two-part article in the "Science" section of the Times on August 14 and August 21, 1981, which was based on Masson's research concerning the origins of Freud's seduction theory (Masson, 1992). He described how Eissler's rage knew no bounds, with Eissler telling him, "Just today Masud Khan called me from London and asked me to dismiss you from the Archives. The board members, all of them, or at least most of them, are asking for the same" (p. 194). This was the same Masud Khan who had boasted quite openly to Masson and others of sleeping with a patient. "He was seeing both her and her husband, and was now living with the woman, but continued to see her husband in analysis" (p. 194). Masson quoted Khan as telling him, "Nobody wants to say anything publicly because I know too much about all of them. If we were all to be honest with each other, that would be the end of British psychoanalysis" (pp. 194–195).

Hopkins (2006) records one of the analyst members of the British Psycho-Analytic Society Ethics Committee describing the meeting of July 30, 1988, when Khan was removed from membership of the Society:

> The letter was signed and given to the lawyer. As soon as the lawyer left, we started to talk openly, for the first time, about our own experiences with Masud. There were probably fifteen of us there and about a dozen of us had patients who had had a sexual involvement with him. (p. 371)

Many analysts attempted to analyze their own children, and this list includes A. A. Brill, Melanie Klein (who analyzed her son Hans and her daughter Melitta), Karl Abraham (who analyzed his daughter Hilda), Carl Jung (who analyzed his daughter Agathli), Edoardo Weiss (who attempted to analyze his son Emelio), and Ernst Kris (who analyzed both his children Anna and Anton). Erich Fromm analyzed the daughter of his lover, Karen Horney, and in one of the more problematic arrangements imaginable, Freud himself analyzed Sándor Ferenczi as well as Ferenczi's stepdaughter, with whom Ferenczi was in love (Roazen, 2001). In fact, Anna Freud's first patients were her nephews (Schwartz, 1999). Roazan, writing in 2003, posed the question as to how Anna Freud's analysis by her father went publicly unmentioned for more than four decades, "yet that analysis constituted such a striking ethical transgression that I am even today left bewildered about its implications" (p. 42). Edoardo Weiss maintained that Anna Freud had "never overcome her father complex" and that she had been "married spiritually to her father" (Roazen, 2005, p. 24). Weiss had written to Freud in 1935 to ask if he should carry out an analysis of his own eldest son. It was in this exchange of correspondence that Freud revealed to Weiss that he had analyzed his own daughter, Anna, claiming that it went "successfully." Emelio discontinued the analysis with his father because he accurately saw it as an intrusion into his privacy (Roazen, 2005). [Karl Menninger was so enthusiastic about psychoanalysis that he proposed that political leaders be subjected to psychiatric profiling before being allowed to govern (Roazen, 2001)].

Not only were many early analysts (despite at times demonstrating prodigious feats of intellect and productivity) psychologically troubled individuals, most, as Gabbard and Lester (1995/1996) pointed out, "were sucked into the vortex of a host of major boundary transgressions" (p. 69). Roazen (2001) commented, "Outsiders at the time could not be expected to share in the spiritual gratifications that Freud and his followers experienced. *They thought of themselves as in possession of deep 'truths' that the world had not yet acknowledged*" (p. 130, italics in the original). The early analysts represented an avant-garde movement, who not only attempted to analyze themselves, their children, or their spouses, but were eager to find new adherents to the "cause."

Regarding the epoch, Harold Blum (2007) observed,

> Analytic practice could be an exciting adventure with a daring, experimental character. Intra-psychic boundaries, infra-familial boundaries, clinical boundaries, and the psychoanalytic framework were in statu nascendi, unformulated or barely delineated. Many patients identified with their analysts and psychoanalysis and became analytic therapists. Some analytic couples were formerly, or even simultaneously analyst and patient without formal recognition at the time of analytic or ethical contra-indication. (p. 55)

Within the early decades, one sees the same sorts of dynamics in psychoanalysis that characterize many movements associated with a belief about having special knowledge. One suspects that, as individuals, early analysts had at least as many character flaws as any comparable group of intelligent, ambitious individuals bent on bringing to prominence their beliefs and discoveries. Though impossible to prove by an easily performed analysis, one reflects that early analysts may in their prior lives have been particularly traumatized, as borne out by their marked difficulty with boundaries (in situations in which it did not need analytic training to deduce that certain relationships or interpersonal arrangements could only end badly), the degree of evident personal psychopathology of a substantial number, and the associated high rate of suicide. Certainly, many had childhoods associated with marked traumas (e.g., Wilhelm Reich, Alfred Adler, Melanie Klein, Dorothy Burlingham) or sexual abuse (e.g., Clara

Thompson, Elizabeth Severn, Sabrina Spielrein, Robert Fleiss). It is perhaps hard to identify many early analysts who had unproblematic childhoods, for example, Karen Horney's seaman father is described as a cruel disciplinary figure and her mother as depressed, irritable, and dominating while Karen suffered bouts of depression herself and considered suicide. On July 9, 1911, she wrote a diary entry addressed to her analyst, Dr Karl Abraham,

> It is not going well at all. Won't I ever be getting well, completely well? I am beginning to despair of it. (p. 270)

Helene Deutsch feared and hated almost everything about her overbearing autocratic mother (Roazen, 1985). Marie Bonaparte grew up seeing little of her emotionally unavailable father who she vainly tried to please and she did not have a mother capable of giving her a minimum of love and attention (Bertin, 1982). Donald Winnicott had what he described as "a disturbed adolescence" (Roazen, 2001). Sándor Ferenczi, who analyzed a number of the early analysts, was described by one of them, Clara Thompson (1964), as departing from what was then Freudian orthodoxy.

Ferenczi … believed that love is as essential to a child's healthy growth as food. With it, the child feels secure and has confidence in himself. Without it, he becomes neurotically ill. Ferenczi even thought that children are actually more prone to disease and often die because of lack of love—in short, that lack of being loved is at the root of all neurotic disturbance. (p. 75)

It is cause for reflection that the closest collegial relationship that Freud had with anyone in his entire life was with Wilhelm Fliess, the man Freud was corresponding with so closely during the development of his original seduction theory and its renunciation. That same Wilhelm Fliess in the opinions of his son Robert and Robert's wife Elenore was an ambulatory psychotic and a tyrant who, it is strongly inferred, sexually abused that son, who as an analyst is most notably remembered for a lonely quest to confront psychoanalysis with the reality that incestuous abuse is widespread, frequently perverse and sadistic, and perpetrated by individuals who outwardly appear respectably normal (see Fliess, 1961/1970, 1973). Elenore Fliess stated in 1982, "My husband's conviction on this issue of parental abuse, sexual or aggressive, and its crucial position in the neurosis of the severely damaged adult had only deepened with time since he first voiced it in 1956" (p. 205).

It is an enduring but understandable irony that so many flagrantly abused individuals found themselves drawn to a profession that made a key tenet of belief, a strict dogmatic adherence to a notion of Oedipal fantasy, while any evidence of anyone being successfully cured of such a fantasy remained nonexistent (Simon, 1992). If it was integral to the manifestations of neurotic illness seen in those treated by psychoanalysis, then Freud's writings should have revealed how in the course of a successful psychoanalysis an Oedipal fantasy should have been able to be dealt with and with insights imparted and integrated, it no longer remained evident. The difficulty for the psychoanalyst Bennett Simon was that he assiduously reviewed the psychoanalytic literature but he could not find such an example.

> Neither Freud, nor, to my knowledge, any other analyst, published a case wherein a woman, not psychotic, told of an incestuous relationship with the father and then in the course of the treatment it turned out to be a fantasy! (Simon, 1992, pp. 968–969).

It is equally ironic that the very survival of psychoanalysis as an international movement and its flourishing by the mid-20th century owes so much to Ernest Jones, who in all probability did sexually abuse the four children for which he went to court in 1906 and whose early career was plagued by boundary violations.

The entry point for those who began to group together in what has become the modern dissociative disorders field is essentially the same group of traumatized and fragmented patients that so stimulated the interest of a young Freud. The history of psychoanalysis is punctuated by important insights, internal divisions, and the predictable mix of heroism and examples of human frailty that characterize many human endeavors. The challenge now, as it was in the late 19th century, is to peel back the defensive silence that is inevitably erected by society in its family structures and institutions, to not shirk researching any subset of trauma victims (or as Smith and Freyd put it in 2014, having "the courage to study what we wish did not exist"), and to not let expediency or the combative defensiveness of abusers and their protectors dilute or redirect our focus, at the same time being very mindful of boundaries in all domains and of the necessity of not making public pronouncements about assumed facts that go beyond the verifiable data. We are wise to reflect deeply on how closely the abused and abuser intermingled in the formative years of psychoanalysis, how traumatized so many theorists were (though they came together around a theory that deemphasized trauma), and how easy it is for individuals to rationalize boundary violations or other exceptions for themselves when they believe their circumstances or insights are special.

References

Appignanesi, L., & Forrester, J. (1993). *Freud's women*. London: Virago Press.
Bertin, C. (1982). *Marie Bonaparte: A life*. New York, NY: Harcourt.
Blair, D. (2004). *Jung: A biography*. London: Little, Brown and Company.
Blum, H. P. (2007). Little Hans: A contemporary overview. In R. A. King, P. B. Neubaur, S. Abrams, & A. S. Dowling (Eds.), *The Psychoanalytic Study of the Child* 62: 44–60.
Blumenthal, R. (2006). *Hotel log hints at illicit desire that Freud didn't repress*. Retrieved from http://tinyurl.com/kl8pc6z
Breger, L. (2000). *Freud: Darkness in the midst of vision*. New York, NY: Wiley.

Breuer, J., & Freud, S. (2001). *The standard edition of the complete psychological works of Sigmund Freud: Vol. 2. Studies on hysteria* (J. Stachey, Trans.). London, UK: Vintage, Hogarth Press. (Original work published 1893–1895)

Corrington, R. S. (2003). *Wilhelm Reich: Psychoanalyst and radical naturalist.* New York: Farrar, Straus and Giroux.

Donn, L. (1988). *Freud and Jung: Years of friendship, years of love.* New York, NY: Collier.

Ferenczi, S. (1984). Confusion of tongues between adults and the child (J. M. Masson, & M. Coring, Trans.). In J. M. Masson (Ed.), *The assault on truth: Freud's suppression of the seduction theory* (pp. 283–295). London, England: Faber and Faber. (Original work published 1932)

Ferenczi, S. (1988). *The clinical diary of Sándor Ferenczi* (J. Dupont, Trans.; M. Balint, & N. Z. Jackson, Eds.). Cambridge, MA: Harvard University Press. (Original work published 1932)

Fishman, G. G. (1986). American Imago. XXXIX, 1982. *Psychoanalytic Quarterly 55*: 554.

Fliess, E. (1982). Robert Fliess: A personality profile. *American Imago, 39*: 195–218.

Fliess, R. (1956). *Erogeneity and libido: Addenda to the theory of the psychosexual development of the human: Vol 1. Psychoanalytic series.* New York, NY: International Universities Press.

Fliess, R. (1961). *Ego and Body Ego: Contributions to Their Psychoanalytic Psychology.* New York, NY: Schulte Pub. Co.

Fliess, R. (1970). *Psychoanalytic series: Vol. 2. Ego and body ego: Contributions to their psychoanalytic psychology.* New York, NY: International Universities Press. (Original work published 1961)

Fliess, R. (1973). *Psychoanalytic series: Vol. 3. Symbol, dream, and psychosis with notes on technique.* New York, NY: International Universities Press.

Fortune, C. (1993). The case of "RN": Sándor Ferenczi's radical experiment in psychoanalysis. In L. Aron, & A. Harris (Eds.), *The legacy of Sándor Ferenczi* (pp. 101–120). Hillsdale, NJ: Analytic Press.

Freud, A. (1928). *Introduction to the technique of child analysis.* (L. P. Clark, Trans.). New York, NY: Nervous and Mental Diseases Publishing.

Freud, S. (2001a). *The standard edition of the complete psychological works of Sigmund Freud: Vol. 1. Pre-psycho-analytic publications and unpublished drafts* (J. Stachey, Trans.). London, UK: Vintage, Hogarth Press. (Original work published 1886–1899)

Freud, S. (2001b). *The standard edition of the complete psychological works of Sigmund Freud: Vol. 3. Early psycho-analytic publications (1893–1899)* (J. Stachey, Trans.). London, UK: Vintage, Hogarth Press. (Original work published 1893–1899)

Freud, S. (2001c). *The standard edition of the complete psychological works of Sigmund Freud: Vol. 20. An autobiographical study* (J. Stachey, Trans.). London, UK: Vintage, Hogarth Press. (Original work published 1925)

Freyd, J. (2013). Editorial: Preventing betrayal. *Journal of Trauma & Dissociation, 14* (5): 495–500. doi:10.1080/15299732.2013.824945.

Gabbard, G. O., & Lester, E. P. (1995/1996). *Boundaries and boundary Violations in psychoanalysis.* New York, NY: Basic Books.

Gillespie, W. (1974). Ernest Jones: The bonny fighter. *International Journal of Psycho-Analysis, 6*: 273–279.

Goldwert, M. (1986). Childhood seduction and the spiritualization of psychology: The case of Jung and Rank. *Child Abuse & Neglect, 10*: 555–557. doi:10.1016/0145-2134(86)90062-1.

Hopkins, L. (2006). False self: The life of Masud Khan. New York, NY: Other Press.

Horney, K. (1980). The adolescent diaries of Karen Horney. New York, NY: Basic Books.

Jones, E. (1953). *The life and work of Sigmund Freud: 1856–1900 the formative years and the great discoveries.* New York, NY: Basic Books.

Jung C. G. (1977). *Memories, dreams, reflections.* Glasgow, Scotland: Fount.

Kerr, J. (1994). *A most dangerous method.* London, UK: Sinclair – Stevenson.

Maddox, B. (2006). *Freud's wizard: The enigma of Ernest Jones.* Cambridge, MA: Da Capo Press.

Makari, G. (2008). *Revolution in mind: The creation of psychoanalysis.* Carlton, Victoria: Melbourne University Press.

Malcolm, J. (1984). *In the Freud archives.* London, England: Jonathan Cape.

Masson, J. M. (1984). *The assault on truth: Freud's suppression of the seduction theory.* London, England: Faber and Faber.

Masson, J. M. (Trans. & Ed.). (1985). *The complete letters of Sigmund Freud to Wilhelm Fliess 1887–1904*. Cambridge, MA: Belknap.
Masson, J. M. (1992). *Final analysis: The making and unmaking of a psychoanalyst*. London, UK: Fontana.
McGuire, W. (1974). *The Freud/Jung letters: The correspondence between Sigmund Freud and C.G. Jung*. Cambridge, MA: Harvard University Press.
Rachman, A. (2014). *The evil genius of psychoanalysis*. Library of Congress. Retrieved from www.youtube.com/watch?v=as1_7df7ReE
Roazen, P. (1969). *Brother animal: The story of Freud and Tausk*. New York, NY: Knopf.
Roazen, P. (1975). *Freud and his followers*. New York, NY: Knopf.
Roazen, P. (1985). Helene Deutsch: A psychoanalyst's life. New York: Anchor Press/Doubleday.
Roazen, P. (2001). *The historiography of psychoanalysis*. New Brunswick, NJ: Transaction.
Roazen, P. (2002). *The trauma of Freud: Controversies in psychoanalysis*. New Brunswick NJ: Transaction.
Roazen, P. (2003). *On the Freud watch: Public memoirs*. England: Free Association Books.
Roazen, P. (2005). *Edoardo Weiss: The house that Freud built*. New Brunswick, NJ: Transaction.
Rudnytsky, P. L. (1996). Introduction: Ferenczi's turn in psychoanalysis. In P. L. Rudnytsky, A. Bükay, & P. Giampieri-Deutsch (Eds.), *Ferenczi's turn in psychoanalysis* (pp. 1–22). New York, NY: New York University Press.
Schwartz, J. (1999). *Cassandra's daughter: A history of psychoanalysis*. New York, NY: Viking.
Shengold L. (1989). *Soul murder*. New Haven: Yale University Press.
Simon, B. (1992). Incest—See under Oedipus complex: The history of an error in psychoanalysis. *Journal of the American Psychoanalytic Association, 40*: 955–988.
Smith, C. P., & Freyd, J. (2014). Editorial: The courage to study what we wish did not exist. *Journal of Trauma & Dissociation, 15*: 521–526. doi:10.1080/15299732.2014.947910
Southgate, J. (2002). A theoretical framework for understanding multiplicity and dissociation. In V. Sinason (Ed.), *Attachment, trauma and multiplicity: Working with dissociative identity disorder* (pp. 86–106). East Sussex, England: Brunner-Routledge.
Sulloway, F. J. (1992). *Biologist of the mind*. Cambridge, MA: Basic Books.
Taft, J. (1958). Otto rank. New York, NY: Julian Press.
Thompson, C. M. (1964). *Interpersonal psychoanalysis: The selected papers of Clara M. Thompson*. (M. R. Green, Ed.). New York: Basic Books.
Tylim, I. (2011, October 26). *Dining with Anna Freud. Buenos Aires Herald*. Retrieved from www.youtube.com/watch?v=as1_7df7ReE
Weiss, E. P. F. (1966). Paul Federn: The theory of the psychoses. In F. Alexander, S. Eisenstein, & M. Grotjahn (Eds.), *Psychoanalytic pioneers* (pp. 142–159). New York, NY: Basic Books.
Young, L. (1964). *Wednesday's children: A study of child neglect and abuse*. New York, NY: McGraw-Hill.
Young-Bruehl, E. (1988). *Anna Freud: A biography*. New York, NY: Summit.

END NOTE

A personal perspective: The response to child abuse then and now

Jeffrey Masson, PhD

For a short while, early in my career, it appeared I had a bright future in psychoanalysis. Thanks to my friendship with the formidable Kurt Eissler, then the doyen of American psychoanalysis, I was offered a position with the Freud Archives. In fact, I was to take over from Eissler in a year or two. Meanwhile, he wanted me to work with Anna Freud so that eventually her home could become a research center for Freud studies.

Apart from my work for the Freud Archives, I was particularly interested in researching the reasons why Freud seemed to have changed his mind about child abuse: At first, he believed his patients remembered real abuse; later he changed his mind and decided that almost all reports of sexual abuse, especially if the father was accused, were likely to be a fantasy, or a screen memory that is a memory that screened an early desire for the parent of the opposite sex.

This always struck me as improbable. But I was interested in Freud's reasons, not my own views. I was hoping that if I was able to see the Freud–Fliess letters, those that remained unpublished, for the years when Freud was devising his views, say between 1895 and 1898, I would learn more. Well, I did learn more, far more than I had bargained for, and what I learned was to have consequences for my personal and professional life.

By 1980, now as Projects Director of the Freud Archives, I had developed a good working relation with Anna Freud and a sort of friendship. When we first discussed the question of child sexual abuse, I had not yet read the unpublished Freud/Fliess correspondence. So when she told me I was simply wrong to believe in its importance for psyche development, I was inclined to yield to her greater authority, both as Freud's daughter, and as somebody with many years of clinical experience. It was not as if I was somebody who could claim that I knew, for a fact, that there was a great deal of sexual violence in analytic patients, since my own experience was so limited.

When I returned to see Anna Freud some years after our earlier discussion, this time armed with the unpublished Freud/Fliess letters which I had in the meantime read, I could be more certain that my interpretation was at least worthy of serious attention. But Anna Freud told me: "My father was simply wrong the first time round." I disagreed, and said so. But I insisted that whatever she and I thought, the general public was entitled to see the evidence for themselves, and therefore, the entire Freud/Fliess letters should be published with *nothing* left out. To her credit and to her honor, she agreed, even though she insisted that people would be disappointed. She had her beliefs, and I had mine, but she did not impede the publication even though she could not understand why I, and others were so keen to see these early letters published. I would have been, I should add, just as keen, even if they did not contain precious ideas of Freud, that whether right or wrong, they deserved to see the light of day.

When it became clear to Anna and to me that my views about sexual abuse differed substantially from the views of orthodox psychoanalysis (I believed that most memories were of real abuse and were not based on fantasy), I assumed that this would be taken as a simple disagreement with no further implications. I was wrong. Kurt Eissler, who until then had been a close personal friend and a benefactor, was incensed, not so much because I held these views, but that I made them public (via an interview I gave to the *New York Times*). Eissler saw this as betrayal, and I was fired from my position at the Freud Archives. I did not speak to Anna Freud personally after I was fired, so I do not know where her sympathies lay. But we liked each other (one reason is that we both adored dogs!), and I think that she would not have so quickly agreed to my being dismissed for a difference of view. Not only was I fired from the Archives, but also I was told that I could no longer be a member of the International Psycho-Analytical Association which until then I belonged to. I was also let go as a director of the Freud Copyright. In short, I quickly became persona non-grata in the psychoanalytic world.

But to Anna Freud's credit, even after this happened, and all analysts who went on the record, without exception, took the same view as Kurt Eissler, Anna Freud allowed me to publish the complete Freud–Fliess letters with Harvard University Press (and several foreign editions over the following years). Despite our disagreements she honored her promise that I could publish these letters, even though she could easily have withdrawn permission. Why she did this, and even more important, why she permitted me to do the research I was doing in her house once I made clear to her the direction of my concerns and are matters of speculation. But I think it speaks well of her integrity. I made no secret of the fact that I believed her father had made a mistake of historic proportions in retracting his belief in the reality of childhood sexual abuse, one that was to have real-life consequences for the lives of untold individuals. She thought I was mistaken, but did not urge me to stop my historical research, nor did she put impediments in my way. I believe she had a more democratic approach to what was a very deeply divisive and contentious historical matter.

I liked Anna Freud very much, and I am sorry that this dispute caused her emotional turmoil (which I only learned about second-hand—nor am I certain it is entirely reliable as it came from a biography of Anna Freud and the sections about me were based on rumor rather than fact). I think she was a remarkably honest person and with a real sense of honor. No doubt it hurt her deeply to see anyone criticize her father. But I was concerned with an idea, and not a person. I really don't know why Freud gave up his theory of seduction and could only speculate. I do not believe he was a liar, or a dishonorable man. I think that the sexual abuse of children was a conceptual position whose time had not yet come. Freud had the amazing courage to recognize it in 1896, and then, when that courage was sorely tested, he gave in, I believe, to societal pressure. Call that moral cowardice if you like, but I wonder how many people, in 1896, would have had the personal resources to go against the entire society of Vienna?

I would have admired Freud all the more had he stood by women and men whose accounts he believed and published when nobody else would. But perhaps, had he continued, we would not have had psychoanalysis. And for all my criticism, I do believe that Freud was a genius, a great writer, and a man with many wonderful ideas. I just think he, and all his followers for years to come (with the notable exceptions of Sandor Ferenczi and Robert Fliess) were simply incapable of taking on the deeper truth of sexual trauma. That lay in the future.

The future, however, has taken the idea of sexual abuse and trauma in general very seriously. One could say that, at last, it has taken its place at the very heart of psychotherapy (at least I like to think so). We now have a very good idea of the actual statistics of child sexual abuse. To her credit again, right at the very end of her life, in 1982, Anna Freud recognized the significance of sexual abuse. She wrote about it a single time, but realized something of its prevalence and importance. It is a great pity that she had not done so from the very beginning (but imagine the conflict with her analyst who just happened to be her father!), because with her ability to think and write with great clarity, perhaps she would have been able to understand aspects of abuse that we still struggle with today.

As I reflect upon that unusual journey that took me from Sanskrit scholarship, though psychoanalytic training, to being appointed via Kurt Eissler as the custodian of the Freudian Archives, I would also like to share four very strange experiences related to child abuse to add additional context to the reality that incest is unfortunately commonplace, but that recognition of this, is less so.

The first experience took place in Munich: I was invited by a friend, who was the head of the adolescent psychiatry department at the University Medical School, to give a presentation about Freud's repudiation of Ferenczi's views on child abuse. This was something I was immersed in at the time and began, while I was working in Anna

Freud's London house. Sitting at her father's desk, I opened the top right drawer and found a series of letters concerning Sandor Ferenczi and his views about the reality of child abuse. Why Freud preserved these letters is anyone's guess. (My guess is that he knew this was of enormous significance). But there they were. I read through them with mounting excitement: here, in one bundle, was the whole history of child abuse within psychoanalysis, and the very existence of these letters was proof, to me at least, that Freud remained preoccupied with this issue to the last days of his life. Indeed, how could he not?

After much digging into archives in Vienna, Paris, London, and elsewhere, I had a story that made sense of these letters. It was that story I was eager to share with colleagues, and the first time was in that talk at Munich. The weekend before my friend and I, along with companions, had all gone skiing in Austria.

When I finished the talk, my "friend" stood up, shaking and said something like, "We in Germany have a law that allows two doctors to send a paranoid man to an institution for mentally ill. All that is required is the word of two psychiatrists. I, for one, proclaim Jeffrey Masson a mentally ill paranoid. I ask you here present to give me a second vote and we will send him to the asylum today." This was no joke. People were embarrassed and said nothing. I never saw him or spoke with him again.

The second experience took place in Berkeley, California: I was at a party where Erik Erikson was present. I was in the middle of my research that resulted in my book, "The Assault on Truth' (Masson, 1984), and he asked me to tell him what I had found. In a nutshell, I did. He was silent for a moment and then began a bitter speech about how could I hurt his dear friend Anna Freud in this way. Surely nothing I found could justify this? I wanted to redeem myself a bit in his eyes. So I told him about the letter that Anna Freud had omitted from her published edition of the Freud–Fliess letters where Freud recounts a very long detailed case history (one of the most important case histories of the early Freud) about a young girl who is raped by her father and nearly dies from the loss of blood. He ends this chilling account with a quotation from a poem by Goethe, "Mignon," one of the great and most mysterious poems of the German language. I knew that Erikson was a great fan of German literature, and I thought he would be fascinated by this poem, coming as it did, in a letter of Freud, and a letter that Anna Freud omitted from her collection, even though it could be fairly considered one of her father's most important letters: "Poor Child, what have they done to you?" Freud even told Fliess that this line should be the motto of psychoanalysis. Erikson was silent for a moment, digesting what I told him. Then, he nearly spat the words at me: "No doubt you will call your book by this very line, thereby hurting poor Anna even more!"

A few months later I was walking in the hills of Palo Alto with an old German friend, an elderly woman who had barely escaped Germany in time with her politically engaged father. We got lost and asked an old man we met how to find our way back. He spoke with a heavy German accent, and both my friend and I realized we were speaking with Bruno Bettelheim. We began chatting, and after a few moments he, like Erikson, asked me to tell him the single most interesting thing I had found in the Freud–Fliess letters. I guess I never learn my lesson, for I told him what I told Erikson. And when I finished I said: 'Isn't that interesting?' "No," was all he said, and he turned and walked away!

Finally, the fourth strange experience I had was seeing just about ALL my friends from my days as a candidate, and then as a psychoanalyst, turn away from me even at a personal level, once my book was published, as if even to be associated with such an apostate was dangerous. The most hurtful departure was Kurt Eissler, for we had been close.

Even in retrospect, some 35 years after the event, I remain puzzled about what I had done to bring down such rage. What had I done but attempt to understand a central puzzle in Freud's early life, his turning away from the reality of abuse to the theory of fantasy—from real trauma, to his Oedipus Complex? True, I believe he made a serious error in doing so, but all the evidence I had uncovered suggested that the story was not nearly as simple as we had been led to believe in our training seminars. The mere fact (which nobody, as far as I know, has ever commented on), that Freud kept the correspondence with Ferenczi in the top drawer of his personal desk, shows that the issue was hardly a trivial one for Freud.

We need to remember that when Robert Fliess took the reality of child abuse seriously in the 1960s, he was, even though a prominent analyst in New York City at the most prestigious of the training institutes (The New York Psychoanalytic Society), more or less banished from the city, and had to move to upstate New York, as I learned from his still indignant widow, Elenore Fliess. Even though he analyzed many modern prominent analysts, for example, Leonard Shengold (the author of "*Soul Murder*" 1989 and other psychoanalytic classics), even these analysts found it difficult to take up the full implications for trauma theory of real child sexual abuse. The tragedy is that while this was impossible to do during Freud's lifetime, it was not exactly easy in the ensuing decades. I believe, too, that there must have been analysts who (as had Robert Fleiss) were aware, from their own experience, or from their clinical experience that child abuse was real and pervasive. Some of them were no doubt supportive of my position, but I must say that I rarely heard from them.

In reflecting back on the reasons for my exit from psychoanalysis, I think my then colleagues were upset at having their analytic world-view challenged not by an outsider but by a functionary of the hallowed Freud archives and even more by the heretofore unknown letters written by Freud himself. It would mean taking trauma of all kinds far more seriously than had been the custom. Some analysts might have believed this would spell the end of classical analysis rather than a renewed and recharged commitment to patients and their real world suffering.

On my side I should have recognized that the anger directed toward me was not really personal. I knew the same thing had happened to Freud himself in 1896, to Sandor Ferenczi in 1933, and to Robert Fliess in the years that directly preceded my entry in psychoanalytic training.

The anger I felt at being suddenly and permanently excluded from what I had thought of as my community and my life's work would have been self-destructive had I not been able to see it in historical perspective. Even more important for my "healing" was the recognition that the true victims of real abuse and trauma suffered far more. They had the original suffering to contend with and then the refusal by professionals to validate their suffering.

In trying to understand what analysts believed during the 1970s, the time of my training, I remember the beautiful phrase of Freud that we should listen to our patients with even hovering attention. I took that to mean we should not be a jury or a judge. But given our years of training into a belief system where external trauma was secondary to internal fantasy dramas, it was almost impossible to listen without prejudices and with a truly open mind especially to experiences beyond our own direct knowledge. Truly Freud spoke of the "impossible profession."

Times have changed. Psychology has moved on and many are the voices deeply concerned with trauma and its aftermath on the lives of patients and even on the lives of nations. Let us be grateful that once again, we are listening and helping to heal the suffering of others.

When I read about the abuses in the Catholic Church and other major societal institutions, I do not read any outcry of disbelief. Times have definitely changed. Even the current Pope is prepared to listen to victims

Freud played a unique if imperfect role in this recognition. It is not clear where we would be today without his early courage to see and say what others could not.

It is perfectly true that my own direct experience in this highly charged debate about child abuse is confined to the 70s and 80s. I might add a small footnote that I found particularly telling: After my book, "The Assault on Truth" came out in 1984, I was invited to the University Colorado at Denver medical school for a lecture. The students there asked me about the discovery of the physical abuse of children, in the 1960s, and I told them this was a seminal moment. They then said that one of the original three authors was a psychoanalyst, and his office was just down the hall, would I like to meet him? Indeed I did. In front of the students I told him how much I admired his work, and the courage to publish it at the time. I wondered, then, how he would respond to my own work, so similar, about another form of child abuse, namely sexual. He took me aback by telling me that my book was nothing but "yellow journalism." I thanked him for being so honest, and then said since he was so honest and straightforward, could I ask him a question to which I hope to have an equally honest answer. Of course, he said. "Have you read it?" I asked. "No."

I was very friendly, briefly, with some of the psychiatrists, who were pioneers of trauma during the Second World War, especially William Niederland, who did so much to influence German courts over the issues of compensation for Jewish survivors of concentration camps (Wiedergutmachung). Kurt Eissler himself had written a very influential article on this very topic and certainly never denied the reality of trauma during the war. But I think that when it came specifically to child sexual abuse, the feminists really were the first to write about it in any sustained way. Florence Rush, as early as 1971, had some very strong comments.

I do realize that much changed in the 90s and progress continues now, from men and women alike. I am delighted to see this. But it is important to stress that the study of trauma was held back because of the reluctance to recognize the reality of child sexual abuse.

So what do we know today, as psychiatrists, psychoanalysts, psychologists and therapists who engage with people who speak about abuse during their therapy?

What still frightens me is that society is fickle. There was a time when nobody believed in the reality of abuse, and now it seems that just about everyone does, and yet, I realize we could still move backwards. It is important to stay firm: It took many years for the truth about sexual abuse to come to the fore. It is still fragile, and must be constantly nourished by research, reflection and above all, listening with empathy and an open heart to the stories of people who have been the victims of child abuse in its many forms and are now survivors. They have much to teach.

References

Masson, J. M. (1984). *The assault on truth: Freud's suppression of the seduction theory*. London, UK: Faber and Faber.

Rush, F. (1971, April). *The sexual abuse of children: A feminist point of view*. Paper, New York, NY: Radical Feminists (NYRF) Rape Conference.

Shengold, L. (1989). *Soul murder*. New Haven, CT: Yale University Press.

Index

Note: *Italic* and **boldface** page numbers refer to figures & tables, pagenumbers followed by "n" denote endnotes